COURAGE TASTES OF BLOOD

A BOOK IN THE SERIES

Radical Perspectives: A *Radical History Review* book series

Series editors: Daniel J. Walkowitz, New York University

Barbara Weinstein, University of Maryland at College Park

FLORENCIA E. MALLON

COURAGE TASTES OF BLOOD

The Mapuche Community of Nicolás Ailío

and the Chilean State, 1906–2001

Duke University Press *Durham and London* 2005

© 2005 DUKE UNIVERSITY PRESS

All rights reserved

Printed in the United States of America on acid-free paper ∞

Designed by Amy Ruth Buchanan

Typeset in Scala by Tseng Information Systems, Inc.

Library of Congress Cataloging-in-Publication Data appear

on the last printed page of this book.

Combined dedication

by the community

and the author:

To the communities

Nicolás Ailío I

and Nicolás Ailío II;

to all their generations,

past, present, and future

Fear tastes like a rusty knife . . .

Courage tastes of blood.

JOHN CHEEVER,

The Wapshot Chronicle

CONTENTS

ILLUSTRATIONS

ABOUT THE SERIES

History, as radical historians have long observed, cannot be severed from authorial subjectivity—indeed, from politics. Political concerns animate the questions we ask, the subjects on which we write. For over thirty years, the *Radical History Review* has led in nurturing and advancing politically engaged historical research. Radical Perspectives seeks to further the journal's mission: Any author wishing to be in the series makes a self-conscious decision to associate her or his work with a radical perspective. To be sure, many of us are currently struggling with the issue of what it means to be a radical historian in the early-twenty-first century, and this series is intended to provide some signposts for what we would judge to be radical history. It offers innovative ways of telling stories from multiple perspectives; comparative, transnational, and global histories that transcend conventional boundaries of region and nation; works that elaborate on the implications of the postcolonial move to "provincialize Europe"; studies of the public in and of the past, including those that consider the commodification of the past; and histories that explore the intersection of identities such as gender, race, class, and sexuality with an eye to their political implications and complications. Above all, this book series seeks to create an important intellectual space and discursive community to explore the very issue of what constitutes radical history. Within this context, some of the books published in the series may privilege alternative and oppositional political cultures, but all will be concerned with the way power is constituted, contested, used, and abused.

Florencia Mallon's pathbreaking contributions to the field of postcolonial Latin American history have consistently placed the question of community at the heart of her narrative and analysis. Writing from an explicitly radical perspective, she has sympathetically reconstructed the remarkable efforts of communities to survive or reconstitute themselves in the face of state repression and shrinking resources, while subjecting the tensions and conflicts within communities to an unblinking scrutiny that makes it impossible to lapse into a romanticized vision of community life or communal politics. These perceptions and concerns are particularly evident in her newest work, *Courage Tastes of Blood*, which reconstructs, in all its complexity, the contested history of the Mapuche communities of Nicolás Ailío I and II in southern Chile.

The memories of these communities illuminate some of the most dramatic moments of modern Chilean history, including the Mapuche resettlement at the dawn of the twentieth century, the loss of land to private investors promoted by state-backed developmentalism, the emergence of class-based rural activism and agrarian reform in the 1960s and '70s, the brutal repression of the Pinochet dictatorship, and the resurgence of ethnic-based strategies with the return to civilian rule in the 1990s. Mallon's reconstruction of this moving, and often sobering, history of community struggle, dispersal, and survival is constituted from the many different voices and perspectives within and outside Nicolás Ailío I and II. Indeed, a central point of her study is that a community's history cannot be meaningfully understood from a single perspective. At the same time, she acknowledges that she, as a historian, must still make sense of the distinct and frequently contradictory oral accounts that she has compiled—not so much by identifying which ones are "truer" than others, but by exploring how these different narratives allow the members of the communities and other actors in the communities' drama to make sense of their past and present actions. Finally, as a radical historian, Mallon also raises the thorny issue of her own relationship with the communities of Nicolás Ailío I and II, and how the writing of this book "intervenes" in the construction of their historical narratives.

In *Courage Tastes of Blood*, Florencia Mallon has given us a beautifully rendered account of the struggles of these Mapuche communities while raising some of the most fundamental questions confronting the politically engaged historian. We are delighted to welcome her to the Radical Perspectives series.

ACKNOWLEDGMENTS

Many are the people and organizations that have helped me get to know and understand the history of the community of Ailío, and that opened the door to the limited comprehension I presently have of Mapuche history in general. My research in Chile during 1996 and 1997 was funded through a sabbatical year from the University of Wisconsin, with additional funds from a John Simon Guggenheim Fellowship and a Landes Senior Fellowship from the Research Institute for the Study of Man. Subsequent visits in 1998, 1999, 2000, 2001, and 2003 were funded by a WARF Mid-Career Award from the University of Wisconsin. Between 2000 and 2005, the Institute for Research in the Humanities, University of Wisconsin, Madison, provided me with half-time teaching release as part of a Senior Residency, which immensely facilitated the completion of the book and its translation from Spanish to English.

In Temuco, the Instituto de Estudios Indígenas of the Universidad de la Frontera and the Centro de Estudios Socioculturales at the Catholic University in Temuco have always welcomed me and offered intellectual support. My colleagues at both institutions, especially José Aylwin, Teresa Durán, Alejandro Herrera, Jaime Flores, Roberto Morales, Jorge Pinto, and José Quidel, have generously provided help and intellectual conversation. Gustavo and Luis Peralta and María Angelica Celis, who through the Centro de Educación y Tecnología (today known as CET-Sur) have worked with the community of Ailío since the 1980s, have been exceedingly generous with their time and material resources. Although our work together has taken a different direction, Isolde Reuque Paillalef and Juan Sánchez Curihuentro were always there for me on my visits to Temuco. Isolde's family, especially her parents don Ernesto Reuque and doña Martina Paillalef, her daughter Liliana, her sister Elvira, and her brother Lionel, have always welcomed me as a part of their *lof.* My friends and colleagues Roberta Bacic, Mario Castro, Gonzalo Leiva, Víctor Maturana, Enrique Pérez, and Aldo Vidal were especially generous with their time and experience, helping me understand the history of the years after 1964. David Tecklin assisted me by researching the records of the Conservador de Bienes Raíces in Nueva Imperial; without his help I could not have traced the business dealings of the Duhalde family. With Mirians García I have explored the bibliography of the region and some archives originally housed in the Museo Regional de la Araucanía; as a result we have become good friends. Elisabeth Brevis secured access to the court records on Rucalán in the archive of the Temuco Court of Appeals, and thanks to her I was able to work in the intendant's archive of the IX Region. At different stages of the writing process, Christian Martínez and Rolf Foerster, both experienced researchers regarding Mapuche issues, provided much-needed support and feedback on the ideas developed here. Edith Meyer Durán, for many years in charge of the Asuntos Indígenas Archive, received me generously and patiently between 1996 and 1997, sharing with me the files belonging to many Mapuche communities. The archivists working in the national collections in Santiago, especially at the Archivo Nacional Miraflores and the Archivo Siglo XX, were always willing to help me in a friendly and interested way, even when my bulky requests taxed their patience on a daily basis. Erika Schilling helped me make contact with the Landarretche family, especially with Violeta Maffei de Landarretche and her children Luciano and Arlin. Magaly Ortiz transcribed the majority of the tapes from my interviews, for which she deserves an especially warm thank-you.

My editors at Duke, Valerie Millholland, Miriam Angress, and Mark Mastromarino, have been incredibly helpful and patient with me, and deserve a special word of thanks. So does Nyna B. Polumbaum, who has generously granted me permission to use the photographs her late husband Ted Polumbaum took of people from Ailío, on Rucalán in 1971, and in the community in 1991, and furnished copies of them. I take great pleasure in the fact that, in the process of sharing this common interest in the people from Ailío, Nyna and I have become friends. I also wish to thank my two reviewers, Greg Grandin and Heidi Tinsman, who not only provided crucial feedback for the revisions, but were gracious enough to share their identities with me. It is a special honor for me that the book is the first Latin American title to appear in the Radical Perspectives Series, and I thank Daniel Walkowitz and Barbara Weinstein for their willingness to include it.

Finally, my family — both north and south — has supported, inspired, and nurtured me during the nine years I have spent working with the community of Ailío. In Chile and the United States, my husband, Steve J. Stern, has been my intellectual and emotional anchor, always willing to talk about and to support my work. As a "single father" during my research trips, he has taken care of and supported our sons, giving me the gift, where humanly possible, of worry-free spaces in which to work. My sons, Ramón and Ralph, have traveled with me to the IX Region and have met the families of Ailío. Every time I return to the communities the first question I am asked is, How are your boys? My parents, Ignacia Bernales and Richard, are the origin of my multicultural interests and identity, and they have always nourished my commitment to Chile and to Latin America. The rest of my Chilean family—uncles and aunts Alfredo, Celina, and Nieves Bernales; Gastón Gómez and Smirna Romero; Eugenia Rodríguez and the late Roberto Prat; cousins Florencio and Gabriela, Gastón and Tita, Pablo and Soledad, Chimina and Gonzalo, Ignacio and Alejandra, and Diego; and all my nieces and nephews—have always welcomed me with affection and good cheer. At various points they have also given me a place to stay. Truly my extended family is an example of how love and hospitality cross borders, and I thank them all for their generosity.

CHAPTER 1

IN THE FOG BEFORE DAWN: DECEMBER 1970

On 20 December 1970, before first light, a small boat moved slowly against the current, up the Imperial River. Sitting in the fog that always seemed at its densest before dawn, with baskets full of food and a few young children, a small group of women, and the men who were rowing, silently pondered what they were about to do. Since September, when in the Mapuche community of Nicolás Ailío they had formed a committee to seek restitution of their lands, they had been preparing for what was about to happen. The majority of their group, men from the Mapuche communities of Ailío and Pichingual, with a few allies from the fishing town of Nehuentúe and some workers from the nearby *fundo* (large estate) of the same name, had left earlier and were walking along the road that ran from west to east along the bank of the river, from Nehuentúe toward the city of Carahue. The two groups planned to rendezvous about five and a half miles outside of Carahue and then proceed to occupy Rucalán, a landed estate belonging to Juan Bautista Landarretche Mendoza and his wife, Violeta Maffei Herrera. Doña Marta Antinao, wife of Heriberto Ailío, vice president of the Ailío Committee, was in the boat along with her small son Martín. She remembered that an aunt of her husband, doña Rosa Ailío, and her mother, doña Juana Ríos, were in the boat with her. "We got there," doña Marta explained, "and we walked onto the property; there was a big barn, and that's where we stopped and we formed a group right there."[1]

The majority of the occupiers clustered together a short distance from the door of the landowner's residence, while a smaller group made up of don Ricardo Mora Carrillo, president of the Ailío Committee, don Heriberto, and a comrade (*compañero*) from the Movimiento de Izquierda Revolucio-

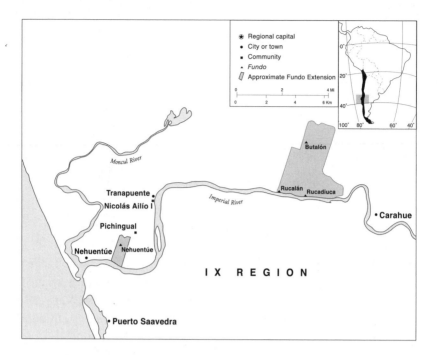

Map 1. The coastal section of the IX Region, between Carahue and Puerto Saavedra. Inset map shows location of region within Chile as a whole. Cartographic Laboratory, University of Wisconsin, Madison.

naria (Movement of the revolutionary left, or MIR) known only as Aquiles or Miguel approached the door and knocked. A few moments later they heard a woman's voice, probably that of a servant, asking who was at the door and what they wanted. Don Ricardo told her to inform the landowner that he and his companions had just taken over the property. The group waited in silence while the servant took the message to her boss.[2]

A quarter century later, the participants in the takeover still remembered that dark and foggy moment, steeped in fear and expectation, as a symbol of both the promise and the danger of that time. Chile had just experienced an election—one that proved to be historic—in which a left-dominated coalition of political parties, after garnering little more than a third of the popular vote, had managed to install a Socialist president. People were expecting a radicalization of the agrarian reform instituted by the previous Christian Democratic government, and indeed on the very morning Rucalán was being occupied, the newly installed president, Salvador Allende

Gossens, was en route to Temuco to preside over the closing ceremonies at a national Mapuche congress. Other land occupations had already taken place in the region, and the daily news was filled with the burst of mobilizations, almost the fever of agitation, that gripped the countryside. For the Mapuche and non-Mapuche peasants standing at the gates of Rucalán on that humid December morning, the pervading political climate had been a source of inspiration. One of the occupiers would comment a few weeks later that news about other land occupations had convinced them to move forward with their own plans.[3]

At the same time, of course, the furor of mobilization had alerted and alarmed the landowning class. In the last months of Eduardo Frei Montalva's Christian Democratic government it was clear there was already a problem with land takeovers: by the time of the presidential election on 1 September thirteen landed estates in the province of Cautín had been at least partially occupied by peasants. The landowners, for their part, reacted by organizing to defend their properties; when the Popular Unity government took power there was already talk of hidden weapons on the area's landed estates.[4]

This moment was also the culmination of a long process of social change and conflict in twentieth-century Chile. Beginning with the formation of the first workers' movement at the turn of the century and its alliance with emerging reformist and leftist political parties, the country had witnessed a series of attempts at social inclusion. Starting with the populist presidency of Arturo Alessandri in the 1920s, these attempts at social change, reform, and political opening toward the popular classes had generated moments of confrontation and repression. This first period of political effervescence ended in what has been called the "compromise state," a political compact that allowed for the legal electoral participation of reformist and leftist parties in the popular-front coalitions that, starting in 1938, would elect candidates to the presidency and the legislature. Although such a compact allowed for the partial incorporation of popular demands, the rural areas were in effect left out of the political agreements which privileged workers and popular urban sectors.[5]

If the countryside had been left out of the compromise state, the Mapuche people had been even more marginalized. Starting in the 1920s, Mapuche organizations formed by the urban-educated sons of the Mapuche leaders who had negotiated "peace" with the Chilean state had begun to support an integrationist agenda. With regard to the land, many of these leaders were

in favor of the division and privatization of Mapuche land-grant communities because they saw this arrangement as an attempt to keep the Mapuche
separate from Chilean society and economy and thus to discriminate against
them and prevent them from progressing. Thus Manuel Manquilef, the first
Mapuche congressman, when elected in 1925, introduced a bill to divide indigenous lands. His efforts bore fruit in Law No. 4,169, known as the first
Indigenous Lands Division Law, approved by Congress on 29 August 1927,
and signed into law on 4 July 1928. The legislation's most important provi-
sions were that any single member of a Mapuche community could request
the division of its lands, and that before such division could take place the
legal boundaries of the land grant needed to be confirmed according to the
original land title (*título de merced*) issued by the Chilean government. As
we shall see, the need to confirm the original boundaries of the land grant
as part of the process of subdivision was what inspired the community of
Ailío to present a division request in 1930, when what they really sought
was the restitution of the lands usurped after the original members of the
community had already received their *título de merced*.[6]

At the same time, however, neither the legal division of Mapuche communities nor the revindication of Mapuche territory within the limits established by the Chilean state during the process of resettlement at the end of
the nineteenth century, presented a viable solution to the increasing rural
poverty the Mapuche people faced in the twentieth century. For this reason, some leaders began to consider the possibility of an alliance with the
left that could confront the Mapuche land problem as part of the larger
agrarian problem in Chilean society as a whole. The class alliance option,
however, even as it opened the possibility of a coalition among "all the rural
poor," closed the more specific option of ethnic restitution, that is, restitution to the Mapuche as a people. Not only during the earlier Popular Front
period and the emergence of the trade union left (1920s to 1950s), but also
in the more radical new left mobilizations of the 1960s, the emphasis on
class exploitation and class alliance predominated. Even during the Popular Unity government, when for the first time the parties of the left dominated the coalition, agrarian policy reached out to peasants first and fore-
most as members of an exploited social class. This policy did not change
even within the more radical left, that is, in the MIR and its peasant front,
the Movimiento Campesino Revolucionario (Revolutionary peasant movement, or MCR), where the Mapuche were especially active and militant. The
MIR's regional program of struggle recognized that the Mapuche peasantry

had a distinctive history of exploitation because of their experience as a colonized people, but the regional committee concluded nevertheless that the class struggle unifying the so-called "Chilean" and Mapuche peasantries was a more "advanced" stage of struggle and thus a more desirable goal. The radical left of the 1960s, therefore, continued to subscribe to a "civilizing project" whose ultimate goal was to educate the Mapuche in the politics of class.[7]

With all its limitations, the agrarian reform project initiated by the Christian Democrats and radicalized by the Popular Unity government was nevertheless the first instance in the twentieth century in which the poor Mapuche peasantry could envision a real possibility of getting access to land. Together with other poor peasants, they initiated a wave of revindication, mobilization, and land invasions that, in conjunction with the other popular mobilizations of the time, brought the Chilean state's model of gradualist change into crisis. In September 1970, when the presidential elections yielded a slim plurality for Allende, the dominant classes were already living in a state of constant tension, fearing that the stability of the society they had always known was about to fall apart. The events of the next two years would progressively deepen and intensify these fears.

In addition to the tensions in Chilean society as a whole, there was at that moment a significant difference of opinion within the Mapuche community of Nicolás Ailío, one of the most important moving forces behind the takeover of Rucalán. A few days after the presidential election in 1970 a land committee had been formed in the community that included participants from several surrounding communities as well as laborers from nearby landed estates. Meeting at the house of don Martín Ailío Porma and his son Heriberto Ailío Pilquinao, they had first discussed recuperating Ailío's lost lands, 45 hectares out of their original grant of 130, that had been usurped by a local landowner. One of the first actions the group agreed on was running the fence on two medium-sized landowners who, over time, had ended up in possession of the community's original lands. But it quickly became apparent that such an action would not solve the problems of all the committee's members, since not all were part of Ailío and in any case the poverty of so many could not be relieved through the recuperation of only 45 hectares. Thus they began to consider a broader alternative, which almost by definition had to involve the takeover of a local estate.[8]

Not all members of the community, however, agreed that a takeover was necessary. Although the majority was in agreement, several considered the strategy foreign to local practice, which had always involved struggle through the courts and staying within the law. These same individuals thought that a takeover would not turn out well because it was not an action taken "in a good way."[9] Among those favoring direct action, on the other hand, there were strong criticisms of the legalistic strategies used up until then. People talked of the poverty suffered by the younger generations, of the half century of legalism that had yielded no results, of the need to find another strategy. The founders of the Ailío Committee also felt they derived support from the radicalization of class-based politics and from the MIR, the political party that best represented this radicalization. Several members of the committee had joined the MCR. The takeover of Rucalán was supported by the MIR and was carried out with the help of a *mirista*.[10]

Even more important than a debate over legalism, therefore, was the conflict being lived in Nicolás Ailío at the end of 1970 over the proper strategy for Mapuche restitution. Since the end of the nineteenth century, when the Chilean army finally managed to defeat the Mapuche people, the Chilean state had handed over reduced quantities of land to Mapuche communities between the Bío-Bío and Toltén rivers. Under the highly appropriate name *reducciones*, these land-grant communities, registered under the name of their *cacique* (*logko*, or head, in the Mapuche language), had received legal title to these land grants that were called, as noted above, *títulos de merced*. Supposedly these documents gave legal protection to the indigenous individuals originally settling there and to their direct descendants, and even though the land was held in common it was distributed in individual usufruct to heads of household. In practice, however, local state institutions tended first of all to protect the rights of non-Mapuche property owners, and little was done to preserve the interests of indigenous communities. In such a context it is not surprising that, according to the historian José Bengoa, the largest usurpations from within the *títulos de merced* took place between 1900 and 1930. As happened in Ailío, these usurpations frequently occurred during the first decade after a community received its original title, and the first generation of indigenous settlers also was forced to fight for the restitution of lands within their grants that had been taken illegally by national and foreign colonists.[11]

This first generation of Mapuche settlers in land-grant communities was forced to reorganize their internal system of authority and leadership. Before their military defeat, the Mapuche people were structured politically in a decentralized way, through a combination of lineage-based marriage alliances and a fairly complex and flexible relationship among territory, kinship, and identity. The *reducciones* fragmented and restructured the broader lineage and kin systems known as *aillarewe* and, in many cases, actually invented smaller and more isolated units. These communities, organized around a so-called original cacique who was supposed to have clear relations of kinship with all those who settled with him, were often partially created by bureaucrats during the very process of settlement. Whether composed of relatives or wandering war refugees or some combination of the two, these Mapuche communities managed to become new spaces of solidarity and cultural preservation. The original caciques listed on the *títulos de merced* became the *logkos* of their communities, and their sons and grandsons inherited the obligation to resolve internal conflicts while mediating between their communities and the state or larger society. Other original settlers and kin also had important roles to play, since all members of the community had more or less the same obligation. In addition, people labored to re-create the broader lineage and territorial linkages, the *aillarewe* that had existed before military defeat, by establishing connections with surrounding *reducciones*. The exchange of women through marriage between neighboring land-grant communities helped strengthen cultural, socioeconomic, and kinship ties.[12]

In the community of Nicolás Ailío, the original settlers and their children and grandchildren took very seriously their obligation to look after the interests of their community. Don Domingo Millamán Ailío, head of one of the original families, presented the first usurpation complaint in Temuco in 1908, only five years after the *título de merced* had been granted. Twenty-two years later his son Andrés Ailío began the legal process of division of community lands in order to receive restitution of the same forty-five hectares previously usurped. Another Domingo Ailío, son of another settler family, attempted to reopen the same legal file in 1939. And don Martín Ailío Porma, son of the "late Nicolás" registered in the *título de merced*, inherited the mantle of leadership from his father, maintaining Mapuche rituals, seeking the restitution of community lands, and attempting to rescue his community from the grip of poverty. As part of this broader effort he joined his son Heriberto Ailío in the agricultural committees of the 1960s, seeking a new solution through political organization and agrarian reform. His children Eduardina, Heriberto, and Robustiano Ailío Pilquinao, grandchildren of the original cacique, became leaders of the third generation, while don Antonio Ailío Currín, son of don Andrés Ailío, kept alive the memories of the original struggles against usurpation, following in the footsteps of his father by insisting on the restitution of the original hectares.

On that foggy December morning, then, when a part of the community of Ailío stood at the front door of Landarretche's house, they also stood at an important crossroads in the history of the community as a whole. If legal struggles for restitution had not been successful, they still had support among the descendants of don Andrés Ailío, an important leader and mediator of previous struggles. But don Martín Ailío and his son Heriberto, direct descendants of the original *logko*, had started down a different path that led to class-based political organization and state-sponsored agrarian reform. Standing at the beginning of this new road, the participants in the takeover of Rucalán could not discern where the road would ultimately take them. Like the fog that surrounded them, preventing them from seeing more than their own shadows, a thick mist of hope enveloped the beginnings of Salvador Allende's popular government, obscuring from view all but its first tentative outline.

When I arrived in Ailío twenty-six years later, the community had reached another important crossroads. Much had changed in the quarter century separating these two critical moments in local history. As we shall see, the land takeover resulted in the formation of an agrarian cooperative, and in a new, though fleeting, prosperity. With the military coup in 1973 and the subsequent dictatorship came fierce repression, followed by intense fear and profound poverty. The preexisting divisions in the community over restitution and struggles for land intensified and deepened. The dictatorship's Decree-Law No. 2568, promulgated in March 1979, abolished Mapuche communities and established conditions for the division and privatization of all indigenous land; it was put into effect in Ailío in 1984. Despite having been battered by repression, don Heriberto and don Robustiano Ailío persisted in the organizational efforts they had initiated decades before, helping to create in the second half of the 1980s a trade association with other communities and groups in the coastal region. With the transition to democratic rule, Ailío reconstituted itself as an indigenous community under new legislation passed in 1993, applying for a land subsidy under the conditions for restitution formulated by the first postauthoritarian government. In 1996, when I first made contact with the community's leaders, they had just secured a subsidy and closed on the purchase of a local landed estate. They were ready to become settlers once again.

I visited the community of Nicolás Ailío for the first time on 30 November 1996. I arrived at the community building with Enrique Pérez, an ex-*mirista* from the region who had returned from exile in 1989 and founded a grassroots organization called the Centro de Estudios Simón Bolívar. On my first visit to Temuco the month before I had met with a local anthropologist and mentioned my desire to get to know the history of a Mapuche community that had collaborated with the MCR during the Popular Unity government. He had suggested I talk with Enrique, who as a MIR activist had worked with various Mapuche communities between 1971 and 1973. After I first met with him at the Simón Bolívar center, Enrique expressed interest in cooperating with me and gave me a list of the Mapuche communities he was working with at that moment. He emphasized that in the majority of cases he had worked with the same communities during the Popular Unity years. We agreed that I would research the list at the Asuntos Indígenas archive, looking through the files and land-grant titles for each one to see if there was a particular case in which the documentation was especially interesting. When I called him back in November, I told him I had become intrigued by the files on the community of Nicolás Ailío. Coincidentally the leaders of this community were meeting with him that very week, and Enrique invited me to come by the center to meet them.

That is how I met don Heriberto Ailío and don José Garrido, at that point president and secretary, respectively, of the community. Although don Heriberto was a short man, especially when compared to Garrido, or don "Chami" as he was known, he was a large political and intellectual presence. After the introductions, I shared with them copies of the documents about their community I had found in the archive. Immediately don Heriberto began commenting on them, incident by incident, adding new information to what was on the page. Our discussion of the Popular Unity years was especially intense, and we all agreed that a dialogue between the archive, starting with the documents in hand, and human memory might be valuable for the community and help recover some forgotten dimensions of local history. I was invited to accompany Enrique on his next visit to Ailío, scheduled for the following day. For me this was an extremely valuable opportunity, since hearing the voices and perspectives of the main actors in this dramatic story would breathe life into the dusty documents I had been uncovering. "What a story of struggle and survival," I wrote in Spanish in my field notebook that night. "I want to accompany them, become a sort of secretary of memory,

sharing my notes, my discoveries, offering them the material I am finding
in order to facilitate their process of re-membering. They, too, can be my
teachers. I hope our common process of re-membering works out."

I spent a good part of the next day waiting, first for Enrique to pick me
up at my *pensión*. As the months went by I would learn that, given the overwhelming number of commitments Enrique took on, he was always late.
Next, I waited near the community building while Ailío's meeting was in
progress. Later I would learn that at that meeting the sale document for the
fundo Las Vertientes was being read, the property just purchased with a land
subsidy from the government and to which the applicants would soon move.
They were also designating a group of representatives to visit the new property the following week to inspect it and find the closest appropriate school
for the children, and they were organizing the formal ceremony by which
they would take possession of the land. This was obviously a full agenda and
took a long time. I was convinced they had forgotten about me, but then they
called me in.

Don Heriberto Ailío introduced me to the twenty or so members present
at the community assembly. He said I was a historian and that I had found
some interesting documents about the community in the Temuco archives
and had donated copies to the communal archive. He asked me to explain
to those present what I would be doing and what kind of help I needed. Not
entirely prepared for the situation, I fumbled a bit as I tried to explain the
process of collecting oral history: how I wanted to get people's stories and
visions of community life, then put them together into a larger story that
would teach all of us something new, simply by combining different perspectives. I explained that no individual could know the complete history
of the community, but that together we could approach the whole. People
seemed interested in this idea, though concerned about how much time
they might need to spend with me. Later on, having a fuller grasp of the
situation, I saw that this was an especially complicated moment, coming
as it did between the approaching harvest and the upcoming move to the
new land. Then one of the men in the room expressed a doubt. It seems for-
eigners have come into Mapuche communities a lot, he said; and after we
talk with them, take time off from our work for them, they take the results
home and we never hear from them again. I think you should leave us a report of your findings before you go away, that way we get something back
immediately. The assembly agreed, and I said I thought it was an excellent
idea. We set a date for my next visit, 4 January; don Heriberto designated

René Ailío, son of don Antonio Ailío Currín and a younger leader in the community, as my host for that visit. I promised to arrive at René's house on the appointed day.

René Ailío was part of the group in the community that had not applied for the land subsidy from the Fondo de Tierras y Aguas (Land and water fund), one of the programs of the new Corporación Nacional de Desarrollo Indígena (National indigenous development corporation), or CONADI, created by the government of President Patricio Aylwin. Don Heriberto was the leader of the group that had applied to CONADI and was expecting to move soon to Huellanto Alto, an area near the Andes mountains to the south of Temuco, immediately on the other side of the town of Gorbea. Only little by little did I begin to realize that I had arrived in the community at an especially complicated and emotionally intense moment in its history. The upcoming move, the inevitable division into two communities, access to new land for some and not for others—all these changes threatened to cause a profound rupture in what had been a single entity. The meeting at which I had been introduced was composed mainly of people who were moving, although the presence of René meant that some people from the other group were also there. At least at that moment people continued to nurture the hope that the community could remain unified and that people at both locations could cooperate and work together. The following Thursday, 5 December, when I accompanied don Heriberto, don Robustiano, doña Eduardina, Enrique, don Chami, and others to Huellanto Alto to see the new land, there was still a great deal of optimism about future unity. But as the months passed and people's hopes began to decline, the potential fissure between the two groups began to deepen.

In retrospect, I think don Heriberto and many of the other people present at the original assembly saw me as a potential healer of the rift, in the sense that I could help people remember their common history of struggle and privation, the history that made them a community and, at least in terms of the original land grant, an extended family or lineage. As a *logko*, consummate politician, and experienced organizer, don Heriberto wanted my presence to keep people's deeper motivations in the struggle for land alive, so that the process of moving and of negotiating with those who were staying could be easier. For me, certainly, the fact that Ailío was about to receive, from the Chilean government, a subsidized land grant in recognition of the previous century of exploitation made for a particularly compelling finale to the story I wanted to tell. The fact that the community had collaborated with the MCR and occupied a fundo during the Allende years, and that as a result several people had been imprisoned and tortured by the military, also made it an ideal case to explore in depth. For different reasons, then, we all participated enthusiastically in the common project of reconstituting community memory.

My pathway into the community opened some doors and closed others. Because I arrived with Enrique Pérez and had been invited by the leaders who had pushed for the land subsidy, several of whom had also been the main force during the agrarian reform years, most people in the community interpreted my interests in terms of social class and of their relation with the Chilean state. In the following months the majority of my conversations focused on the history of usurpation, the struggle for land restitution, the Popular Unity mobilizations and ensuing repression, and the land subsidy. While this was clearly an important part of the community's history as well as crucial to the narrative I wished to construct, it was not the whole story and tended to minimize Mapuche culture and religion. Only in June 1997, for example, in a conversation with the Ailío brothers and others in Temuco at the end of my research year, did I learn that Ailío had celebrated the main Mapuche religious ceremony, or *gillatun*, until the 1960s and that there had been a *machi*, or healer-shaman, at the agrarian reform center created on the ex-fundo Rucalán during the Popular Unity years.

Another reason for minimizing the importance of Mapuche cultural and religious practices could be found in the strong local presence of an Evangelical Protestant church. The Iglesia del Señor (Church of God), a charismatic congregation that did not tolerate indigenous spiritual practices, had arrived in the area in the 1960s and established a vigorous presence among some of Ailío's families. When I arrived at René Ailío's house in January 1997, I realized that his brother Antonio was in charge of supervising and maintaining the local church building on the family property. Other members of the community, on the other hand, especially doña Eduardina, don Robustiano, and don Heriberto Ailío, worshiped at the Anglican church, a denomination that had established its first local mission in Nehuentúe several decades before. Although the Anglicans were usually more tolerant of indigenous culture, Protestant conversion in conjunction with other factors had generally contributed to the marginalization of Mapuche practices in the community.

As a result of my experiences during that first research year and those of my shorter subsequent visits in 1998 and 1999, I began to discern distinctive characteristics in local history. When I compared the community of Nicolás Ailío to other communities I was getting to know, I saw that the extreme poverty the community experienced owing to usurpation and the subsequent degradation of the remaining lands had forced an early process of temporary migration as well as the participation of the men in the day labor force on surrounding fundos. This trend also led to cultural transformation, since relations of sociability between Mapuche and non-Mapuche, or *wigka*, laborers, on the coastal estates as well as in the cities, facilitated the development of a shared popular culture and intermarriage between *wigka* and Mapuche. My collaborators' lack of emphasis on their indigenous identity, therefore, was not only a result of my being an outsider, or of my having arrived in the community with a leftist ex-*compañero*. A whole history of social and cultural change also helped explain how and why it was this community, and not another, that played such a central role in the class mobilizations convulsing the coastal region during the agrarian reform decade of 1964–73.

It is especially important to emphasize, nonetheless, that the relationship I have developed with my collaborators in the community of Ailío, even if intially it took a very precise path, has expanded and taken sometimes unpredictable turns. A crucial point in this journey came when don Heriberto suggested that I first talk in depth with the family of don Antonio and his son René. The differences of perspective and experience that were opened up to me by this interview were absolutely central to my entire education about the community. They helped me understand how and why, at the local level, it was possible to develop and preserve such diverse and even conflictual opinions about a single experience with oppression and exploitation. As we shall see, don Antonio was opposed to the takeover of Rucalán, while his son Hugo—at the time a sixteen-year-old—got involved in mobilizations on the left. Don Antonio's younger son René would emerge as a leader only toward the end of the dictatorship and during the transition to democratic rule. All of them, however, for reasons I treat more fully below, took positions that differed from, and in some ways opposed, those of don Heriberto. By first opening a path for me to people with whom he disagreed, don Heriberto helped me understand that he had a broader interest in the history of his community, one that did not necessarily lie in his own preferences and opinions. A good part of what is complex and true in this book, I owe to him and his closest relatives.

I must also note the important influence of other colleagues and friends, both within and outside the community of Ailío, on how the research method for this work has developed. From the beginning Enrique Pérez demanded copies of the materials I was finding in the Asuntos Indígenas archive, and the leaders in Ailío also liked the idea of developing a communal archive made up of copies of the documents I was finding. Throughout my deepening relationship with the community, therefore, and in most of the interviews I have had with its members and families, we have combined conversation and questions with a sharing of documents, newspapers, and other materials that I have found in regional and national archives. As part of this process of dialogue, I have given copies of the most important documents concerning communal history to the community archive. Sometimes a conversation began in reaction to a document or to a fact gleaned in another interview, thus establishing a give-and-take among different versions or interpretations of the same event. And the suggestion made by one of the community's members in the meeting at which I was introduced, namely, that it would be good if I left them a report before I departed from the country, also contributed to a deepening dialogue around the facts and interpretations I was able to gather. Indeed, in August 2001 I returned to Temuco and Ailío to present a new report, no longer the original eighty-page version but an entire book manuscript. Later on in this chapter I discuss in more detail the results of our collaborative work on that occasion, and how my interlocutors' comments have modified this text.

Another part of the dialogue we established was the individual interview. Beyond the more informal conversations, during which I generally took fewer systematic notes in my field notebook, every formal conversation or interview began with a preliminary discussion in which I offered two alternatives. One was to record the interview on a cassette, which would preserve the person's exact words relatively intact. If we chose this alternative, I promised a copy of the transcript so that the individual could read, revise, and correct the written version. If the interviewee chose not to be recorded, then my notes were less exact, and there was no way to produce a verbatim copy of the conversation. We also discussed, before beginning the formal part of the interview, the option of anonymity: should I use the person's real name? In general all my interviewees in the community opted to use their real names.[13]

In the process of writing this book I have come to understand ever more clearly both the benefits and the difficulties inherent in the dialogical method. On one side, it has allowed me to preserve, up to a certain point, the narrative forms and expressions of the protagonists themselves. Many times I am able to describe an event or process using the words of the person or persons who explained it to me. At other times I have been able to take a local perspective on a document and thus interpret it differently or use the memory of an event as it was preserved in the community in order to search the written record. A particularly dramatic example of the fruitfulness of this dialogue can be found in chapter 2, when during our conversation don Antonio Ailío told me for the first time about the death of the landowner Duhalde. As I searched the archives to find evidence supporting his narrative, I was able to explore new dimensions of the community's relationship to Duhalde. I discovered a divergent perspective on the process of land accumulation in the coastal region and could analyze the subsequent agrarian reform through a lens that focused on a Mapuche concept of territoriality. If I had not learned through a dialogue with my interviewees, it would never have occurred to me either to consider the local landowning class or to map the coastal region from such a vantage point.

But the dialogical method also has pitfalls, in large part because the two sides of the dialogue do not have equal power over the final form taken by the narrative. As I explained to those present at the first community assembly I attended, as researcher and historian I had final authority over the book's form and content. Sometimes, such as in the discussion of the Mapuche question and the disparities among researchers that I develop in chapter 3, it is possible that I stray too far from the specific history of the community. Despite the dialogical method, in this case I made the decision unilaterally. In other places, such as in the last section of chapter 5 and in a good part of chapter 6, I have built a narrative about the community that depends more on external sources than on conversations with people in Ailío, perhaps because these are subjects that still hurt too much to remember or discuss in depth or because they have yet to be fully reflected upon and analyzed. As a result it was easier to have access through other means; but in doing this, have I strayed too far from the original collaborative purpose?

This last concern also raises another issue that seems inherent to the method used: the dialogue between oral and written sources did not work in the same way throughout the project and the resulting narrative. In chapters 2 and 3, which deal with the period before the agrarian reform, there are fewer oral sources simply because I relied, inevitably, on the older generation, and my access to their memories was of necessity mediated through a thicker temporal filter. Fewer outsiders visited the community in this earlier period, moreover, and thus I did not have access to interviews with others who had passed through and had a different vision. This changed during the years of the agrarian reform process, and I was able to talk with some of the *miristas* who worked in the region. The same was true of the years of military dictatorship, when individuals and organizations collaborating with the Catholic Church established a presence in the community. And yet despite their relative paucity, the memories and oral histories I was able to collect for the earlier period have given this narrative an invaluable personal and human dimension. Sometimes, therefore, qualitative criteria must win out over quantitative. But it is nevertheless inevitable that the comparative richness of oral and written sources for the period after 1964, when the community more actively established political and class relations with the broader society, makes the information gaps in the earlier period stand out in starker relief.

Even as the dynamics of the dialogical method help reveal its imperfections and contradictions, however, the method itself made possible a much deeper understanding of the community's history than would have been possible solely through oral or archival sources. As I returned several times to talk with some of the people, I was able to deepen conversations and friendships in the very process of conducting my research. This allowed me access to different layers of interpretation by the same person. In my first conversation with René Ailío in January 1997, for example, he emphasized the positive aspects of the land subsidy and the unity between the two parts of the community. In March, when the families who were part of the subsidy had moved to the new land and misunderstandings had arisen, René was more critical about the subsidy project as a whole and the way it had been carried out. Don Heriberto also emphasized various aspects of his experience or distinct assessments of the community's historical process, depending on the moment or on the degree of trust we had built in our relationship.

In the end this dialogue has no finite end but is instead a continuous process that will conclude, somewhat arbitrarily, with publication. The friendships and personal connections, as well as the very history of the community, are also ongoing even if they reach a certain textual culmination when the book goes to press. At the same time, however, the dialogical method has yielded concrete results, most notably in its contribution to my understanding of the two large transitions in the community's history: first, the intense connection with the larger society that developed during the agrarian reform and subsequent repression; and second, the land subsidy and new settlement that resulted in the creation of two communities, Nicolás Ailío I and Nicolás Ailío II. My conversations with people in the communities, moreover, helped me see how the explanations offered for these two transitions were themselves interconnected.

Using the differences of opinion between the families of don Antonio and don Heriberto as an entry point, I was able to understand how the manner in which the decade of agrarian reform was lived by people could be articulated with very distinct narratives about local history, which then culminated in contrasting moral lessons. Don Antonio's and René's family organized their narrative around the original usurpation of the forty-five hectares, followed by the group's ability to withstand and survive the failure of attempts at restitution. "That happened many years ago," explained don Antonio during my first visit, initiating a narration whose rhythmic flow and imagery suggested many repetitions over the years. It began with a man by the name of Duhalde, who used the wood of native trees he had cut down to build a fence around part of the community. It continued with the expulsion of don Antonio's newlywed parents and the burning of their small *ruka*, or dwelling. And it ended with the death of Duhalde at the hands of a businessman to whom he owed money because, as don Antonio made clear, Duhalde was an arrogant man dedicated to "bad works." René's brother Antonio, who was in charge of the Church of God and who had clearly heard the story many times, added another layer of moral explanation. "He thought he was king of these lands," he said, "but he didn't know that there's another King upstairs, another King Who's on top of him, Who got to order him around."[14] Now this particular tale did not end with the restitution of the land because it was not about victory, but rather a fable about the ability to survive and endure. It did, however, end with a certain kind of moral restitution, for the murder of Duhalde was a classic morality tale that cut to the very heart of local relations with an easy, quick, and satisfying thrust: the exploitative landowner, rotten and corrupt to his very core, will sooner or later be hoisted on his own petard.

For don Heriberto, and in general for those who participated in the agrarian reform, the takeover of Rucalán in December 1970 was the centerpiece of a story about overcoming exploitation through direct action. This version of the community's history was the same through 1965, since it also began with Duhalde's original usurpation. Eduardo Frei's agrarian reform, however, opened a new chapter in the relationship between peasants and the state, and the community once again requested the restitution of the original hectares. Unfortunately, the state's earlier purchase and subdivision of the fundo Tranapuente had so complicated local land tenure relations that the trial simply dragged on. People began to lose hope, and some sought other solutions. This resulted in the formation of a land committee and finally the takeover of Rucalán, which was justified by the failure of the legal strategy. "Taking the fundo at the time was totally illegal," don Heriberto admitted, "but we said it wasn't illegal. Why? Whose permission had they asked earlier when they'd taken over our lands in the first place? Nobody's. They just arrived and they said, OK, move over that way, this land is ours now. So afterward we also said to them, clear as day: this land is ours."[15]

In contrast to the earlier narrative of usurpation, in this story restitution is direct, dramatic, and very satisfying: if previously the landowner had thrown people out without asking anyone's permission, now the peasants returned the favor. If don Antonio's moral lesson was perseverance and moral superiority, the agrarian reform narrative emphasized the need to respond to the failure of the more traditional restitution strategy with political militancy and innovation. As further support for their position, the participants in the agrarian reform noted that, despite the fact that the court ultimately found in the community's favor in the case of the forty-five hectares, it was able to obtain possession of part of the land only by running the fence: in other words, through direct action. Besides, they pointed out that the three years they lived on the agrarian reform center was the only period of real prosperity their generation has known. Don Antonio responded, on the other hand, in disagreement with the takeover, that the coup of 1973 and subsequent military repression demonstrated that illegal occupations do not work. The rupture that 1973 produced in local and national history proved to don Antonio that one must always do things "in a good way."[16]

To a certain extent these two narratives are classic perspectives on how to confront oppression and exploitation. One way is simply to endure, to demonstrate a Christian moral superiority by suffering with dignity and not lowering oneself to the level of the oppressor. The other possibility is to emphasize the morality of action in a context of retribution: confrontation is justified because of previous injustice. Both positions have a religious basis: the first in a suffering Christianity, when rewards will be forthcoming in the afterlife for those who act morally; the second in a liberationist discourse that dialogues more directly with the Old Testament, especially with the story of the Exodus from Egypt and the liberation of the Jewish people from slavery. By the 1960s, the liberationist tendency had found new expression through a Christianity based on social action, Christian base communities, and, finally, in liberation theology. As we shall see, don Heriberto and his family participated directly in this second tradition.

At the same time these two concrete narratives were being constructed in conversations with me, the community was living through a second dramatic transition in which a successful application for a state subsidy had led to the purchase of new land and the resettlement on it of part of the community's population. Perhaps my presence at this specific conjuncture helped differentiate more dramatically between the two perspectives, but it is not too surprising that those who emphasized human endurance and survival and criticized illegal action did not take part in the subsidy process. For those who did participate, especially don Heriberto, this new action was a link in the same chain of all previous actions and would ultimately lead, as he explained, to a phoenix organization, "reborn from amongst the ashes." In this sense, resettlement on new land could be seen as a much more satisfactory ending to the narrative about action in the face of exploitation, to a certain extent an answer to the criticism that direct action had led only to suffering and repression.

This second major transition in the history of the post-*reducción* community, which I witnessed and learned to write about with the help of the participants, has resulted in the creation of two communities Nicolás Ailío. The original one, Nicolás Ailío I Tranapuente, today represents continuity and survival, whereas the new one, Nicolás Ailío II Huellanto Alto, stands for having dared to confront the unknown, where everything—climate, surroundings, the neighbors, the agricultural system, labor relations, the future—is new. If in Tranapuente, every now and then, people think that those in Huellanto Alto have all the luck and a new future in front of them, sometimes in Huellanto Alto there is nostalgia for the good old days, the old neighbors, the well-known and softly worn landscape of the coast. In the following pages, I try to explain how the community's history reached this point.

But I also want to point out that the history of the two communities I present here is neither complete nor entirely objective. In both meanings of the word, this is a *partial* history.[17] I do not apologize for this. Quite the contrary, I openly admit it and take responsibility for it. This is a partial history in the sense that it is only a part of the possible history of the community, since I did not talk to everyone and was not able to locate all relevant documents in the overwhelmingly huge, though already quite clearly "selective," collections housed in regional and national archives.[18] In that I am a non-Mapuche outsider, moreover, it would be impossible for me to see the whole picture from a local perspective. My attempts to understand Mapuche territoriality, culture, and religion; poverty; the experience of usurpation; the pain, fear, and anguish of repression; the hunger of winter are extremely partial. I do not think there is a way to avoid these partialities, but this does not mean I must abandon my attempt to get close to this history and carry on a dialogue about it. Besides, I am convinced that I am not the only one with a partial vision of things. People in the community have their own partialities, which luckily are different from mine. Together, through conversation, discussion, and debate, we have perhaps helped each other see a more complete whole.

This history is also partial because the historian writing it is partial. My narrative springs from my support for the community and its people. The subjectivity of Ailío's families is what I most want to understand and reflect. Now this does not mean that I represent their perspectives or opinions in an uncritical way. During my research I learned that sometimes it is important to disagree or to question the versions of events being offered. When presented with conflicting evidence, I learned it was necessary to discuss and confront it, not only in the interviews, but also in my reports to the community and in the final text. The result is the kind of complex human history the community deserves, rather than a flattened or heroic version that is prettier perhaps but hard to square with real life. To disagree is not always easy or comfortable, but in the long run I think it takes one toward a more honest and valuable history, not only for the reader, but also for those who have participated in the writing of it.

This history is thus a collective ethnography in which many people from the community have collaborated. Although the part of the community that invited me to write it was the same sector that participated in the agrarian reform and applied for the land subsidy, with the help of don Heriberto and others I have been able to bring in other perspectives as well. Nonetheless, don Heriberto and doña Marta, don Robustiano and doña Eduardina, have continued to be my most active critics. To them I have recently added their younger sister doña Cecilia Ailío. They are the ones who read my reports with the greatest care and offered me the most important comments and pointed criticisms. Through our conversations I have learned that getting to know a reality or collective life does not necessarily lead to a definitive or complete understanding. In many ways it means noticing the impossibility of complete or polished knowledge and gaining a deeper respect for complexity itself.

At the same time, however, it is perhaps useful to make clear at the outset that I have organized this complexity around several central themes. One is the dramatic extent to which the historical lens provided by Mapuche history modifies our understanding of Chilean history more generally. As will become clear in the material that follows, many of the well-known narratives of twentieth-century Chilean history—the gradual incorporation of workers and popular sectors into a national-level practice of coalition politics; the unique characteristics of the Chilean compromise state; the unique experiment with social inclusion represented by the agrarian reform decade of 1964–73; the military coup of 1973 as a bloody rupture in an otherwise effective consolidation of Chilean democracy–become more complicated when viewed from a Mapuche perspective. Indeed, the very nature of Mapuche history and memory forces us to rethink notions of continuity and change and to disturb many of our more closely guarded chronologies and periodizations.

A second broader theme is, to some extent, the mirror image of the first. Since the moment of military defeat and resettlement, the history of the Mapuche people in southern Chile has been completely intermingled with the policies and actions of the Chilean state. This has meant that efforts at preservation and reconstitution of Mapuche culture, as well as restitution of Mapuche lands, have occurred within the confines and parameters established by state policy. The ultimate result of these struggles is not the transparent autonomy or access to "tradition" that many contemporary indigenous activists might desire. But as the experiences of the community of Ailío demonstrate, a more nuanced and realistic history of the conflicts and creativity of the Mapuche as a people actually yields a more humanly believable story, not only of survival against overwhelming odds, but also of creative if unequal intervention in the politics and process of the Chilean nation as a whole. Neither Mapuche history nor Chilean national history can be completely understood in isolation from the other.

Finally, a crucial third theme that emerges from the first two is the importance of listening to and recovering the versions of Mapuche history that exist at the local level, among the common folk in the communities, often somewhat distant from the more educated and often more urban leadership of the Mapuche organizations. People's interpretive frames at the local level often mix aspects that from the outside may be seen as contradictory: ethnicity and class; Mapuche worldview and evangelical religion; radical grassroots mobilization and loyalty to the political parties; a profound and sometimes humiliating experience of exploitation and subordination with a stubborn will to survive and a complex individual subjectivity. From the conversations that gave shape to this text has emerged the notion that this give-and-take between apparently contradictory relationships and identities is a central part of people's lived experience and should, as such, be contextualized historically.

In this context, my experience of returning the book to the community in August 2001 takes on greater relevance. I arrived in Temuco at the end of July of that year with multiple copies of a complete first draft in Spanish that I aimed to distribute to my closest collaborators in the communities of Nicolás Ailío I and II as well as to a few additional people. With the help both of my colleagues at the Centro de Educación y Tecnología (CET) who had been working in the communities and of the leaders from Tranapuente and Huellanto Alto, we had prepared a first meeting and manuscript presentation at the Temuco offices of the CET, a location chosen by the community leaders themselves. At this first meeting, attended by people from both communities, including the elected presidents of both, I presented a short summary of how the book came to be and invited comments from all those present. I promised that all royalties from the book would be reinvested in the communities. Don Heriberto and don Robustiano took the opportunity to make a connection between the struggles of their community and the historical and contemporary struggles of the Mapuche people in general, a connection that is noted where appropriate in this last version of the book. For me, an especially satisfying and productive moment at this meeting came when several of those present read parts of the book out loud. This allowed more people to join in the conversation, and several of them expressed their sense of identification with parts of the text. Overall, the resulting conversation was so positive that we decided to follow the model of reading aloud at the meetings scheduled in Tranapuente and Huellanto Alto.

The reaction at the two additional meetings was also positive, although additional questions and doubts were raised. In Tranapuente I was asked how the community would benefit from the book, which prompted an additional discussion about the royalties. In Huellanto Alto we discussed how best to represent differences of opinion about the criteria that defined community membership. We found a way to respect differing sensibilities without silencing anyone.

The most unexpected result of my visit in August 2001 was the amount of new information I collected for the revision. In part, this was due to the fact that people were reacting, for the first time, to a completed narrative, and this prompted additional memories and facts both to supplement and correct the version I presented. But a good part of the new information came from my deepening friendship with Angélica Celis, who had been working for a long time on the life histories of three of the women in Huellanto Alto—doña Marta Antinao and doña Cecilia and doña Marcelina Ailío—and whose interviews she made available to me. Along with the new permanent settlement of Cecilia Ailío in Huellanto Alto, my exchanges and conversations with Angélica facilitated a fresh and deeper understanding of women's perspectives on the history and daily life of the community. All of this has enriched the text but also modified it in surprising ways. The result is an even more collective effort containing many voices and interweaving many stories and variant narratives.

Because this history is a collective effort, it is especially important that it reach diverse publics. Of course I want historians and students of Mapuche, Chilean, Latin American, and indigenous history to be interested in this story and find something of value in it. I would also be very happy if students in survey courses on Latin America found in these pages an accessible version of a much larger history about the exploitation and resistance that have marked the lives of indigenous and rural peoples in the Western Hemisphere. But it is also important that the people in Ailío, not only my collaborators and colleagues but also the new generations, find something of value in this book. Although it is neither a complete nor a definitive history, I hope that Martín Ailío Antinao, son of don Heriberto and doña Marta, as well as other young people who grew up under dictatorship, find in the Spanish version of this text an answer to their question, And why was it that you took over Rucalán?

The history of my relationship with the community is also reflected in my use in the text of "don" and "doña," Spanish terms of respect. I use them in general when referring to people in the community who form a part of the mature generation, those who were already adults during the agrarian reform. While researching and writing this history, I have come to feel such deep respect for them that I cannot help but refer to them in this way. I see the younger members of the community from a more horizontal vantage point. In general, although I make occasional exceptions when referring to the more outstanding leaders of the 1990s, I do not use "don" or "doña" when referring to them. I also do not use these terms when referring to my interviewees or to other actors who are not a part of the community. There is thus no objective consistency to my use of "don" and "doña," but rather an emotional consistency that rests on friendship and respect.

Another inconsistency, inevitably, is my use of Mapuche words. It is always difficult to spell consistently in a language that, given its history, did not have its own alphabet. I have learned to spell in *Mapunzugun* with the help of a recent dictionary (*grafemario*) published by CONADI.[19] Explanations for most of my specific usages can be found there. I also do not use the plural when referring to the Mapuche because such usage became customary in the contemporary Mapuche movement in order to respect the lack of a plural form in Mapunzugun.

I could not finish this introductory chapter without expressing my deep gratitude to all the people in the two communities of Ailío who have collaborated with me. They welcomed me into their homes no matter when I arrived at their door, and always with caring and generosity. They killed too many chickens, and offered me too many eggs and *mate* brews, too, and much freshly baked bread, even when they did not have enough. Through several rainy winters they were generous with their time, lives, memories, joys, and sorrows. In Tranapuente, I am especially grateful to the late don Antonio Ailío Currín, his widow, doña Felicia Concha de Ailío, and their sons Antonio and René. When I arrived in Tranapuente the second time in January 1997, in the middle of harvest, a week later than I had promised and accompanied by my son Ramón, they fed us and gave us a place to sleep while they shared with us their recollections of the past. It took me until August 1999 to dial the telephone number René had written down for me on a piece of paper during that first visit, the number of his brother Hugo in Concepción. When I finally did call, it was almost as if Hugo had been waiting for me to get in touch. When I visited him and his wife, Mercedes Zambrano, in addition to serving me a delicious lunch they talked openly and at length with me. I also learned a great deal from my conversations with don Luis Ernesto Quijón, master mechanic, and enjoyed sharing the tasty chicken and *sopaipillas* (fried bread) his wife prepared for me. In Huellanto Alto, don José Garrido and doña Juana Pincheira; doña Carmen Huentemilla and don Armando Ailío; doña Marcelina Ailío; don José Queipul, Juan Ailío, Lidia del Pilar Llancao, and Magaly Riquelme all generously helped me understand local reality and told me about the ups and downs of their resettlement. Don Chami and doña Juana also talked at length with me about their lives and the challenges of the new community experience they had taken on.

Finally, both in Huellanto Alto and in Tranapuente, I have gotten to know and love doña Eduardina, don Robustiano, and don Heriberto Ailío as well as doña Marta Antinao. These four have taken care of me and guided me along my journey through the history of their community. They have been my hosts, sharing with me and helping me to understand. They have welcomed my sons and my student. Their generosity has known no limits. I also include here the two younger sisters, Elisa and Cecilia Ailío Pilquinao, whom I got to know later on because of their history of migration to Santiago. When I returned in 2001, doña Cecilia had settled permanently in Huellanto Alto, and she became an especially sharp and dedicated interlocutor, filling a copy of the manuscript with bits of yarn to mark her comments and reactions. Together with doña Marcelina, doña Cecilia helped me grasp the distinct experience of women who were heads of household. I spent a pleasurable afternoon in Santiago with doña Elisa in August of that year, walking with her as she dropped her daughter off at school, talking at length about her family and the experience of the agrarian reform, sharing a delicious lunch she prepared.

I hope these pages can contribute, certainly not to pay off the debt I have incurred with all my interlocutors and most especially with the Ailío Pilquinao and Ailío Antinao families, something which I consider impossible, but rather toward expressing a small part of my gratitude and admiration. As part of a friendship that continues even after the book is complete, it now extends my connection toward the next generations: Sandra, Yanet, and Martín Ailío Antinao, the children of don Heriberto and doña Marta; and Andrea and Samuel Ailío Ailío, the children of doña Cecilia who were raised in Tranapuente by doña Eduardina. I remember especially a cold, rainy afternoon in August, one among many I spent sitting at doña Marta Antinao's table in Huellanto Alto, warming my feet on the brazier filled with hot coals she had lovingly pushed toward me. While I sipped on a sweet mate brew, don Heriberto returned from the fields, shaking the water off his hat, and sat with me. "So," he said after greeting me more formally, "how's that book we're writing coming along?" Here is the answer to your question, don Heri.

Two members of the *asentamiento* Arnoldo Ríos standing in the door of the barn
of the ex-*fundo* Rucalán, 1971. The poster on the door bears the Movimiento de
Izquierda Revolucionaria (MIR), slogan, "Bread, Land, and Socialism," and the
handmade portrait of Che Guevara above the door sports the slogan "Land or
Death" and MCR, the initials for the Movimiento Campesino Revolucionario, the
MIR's peasant arm. The man on the right is don Heriberto Ailío, the man on the
left is unidentified. © Ted Polumbaum/Newseum; used by permission.

The family of don Antonio Ailío outside their house in Nicolás Ailío I-Tranapuente in 1997. From left to right: René, Antonio Jr., don Antonio, doña Felicia Concha, and Juana with two of her children and their dog. Author photo.

Doña Marta Antinao and don Heriberto Ailío standing outside their house in Huellanto Alto, August 2001. Author photo.

Don Armando Ailío and his wife, doña
Carmen Huentemilla, with their children,
in front of their house in Tranapuente, 1991.
© Ted Polumbaum/Newseum; used by
permission.

A landscape view of the coastal zone, taken from the
community of Nicolás Ailío I, in 1999. The Imperial
River is in the background. Author photo.

Northern part of the *fundo* Nehuentúe taken in
1996. In the background, on the hill, stands the
landowner's house. Author photo.

Field on the *fundo* Nehuentúe, in the lowlands
near the Imperial River, in 1999. Author photo.

Fishing boats on the Imperial River, at
the port of Nehuentúe. Author photo.

Partial view of the living room of the new Landarretche family home, *fundo* Rucalán, in 1997. A portrait of the deceased patriarch, Juan Bautista Landarretche, hangs over the fireplace. Author photo.

Members of the community of Nicolás Ailío share a joke during their first visit to their new lands in Gorbea in December 1996. In the black jacket with her back to the camera is Cecilia Ailío. Don Heriberto is holding the white plastic bag. The tall man to the right is don José ("Chami") Garrido, and to the right of him in the foreground is don Robustiano. Ailío Author photo.

Part of the group that came to the reading and talk back on the completed book manuscript, August 2001, in Nicolás Ailío I-Tranapuente. The young woman on the right is holding a copy of the manuscript. Among the people pictured are Dionisio Ailío (*second from left*), then president of Nicolás Ailío I and brother of Juan Ailío, who lives in Huellanto Alto; René Ailío (*third from left*); and don Robustiano Ailío (*fourth from left*). Author photo.

Andrea Ailío (*left*), daughter of doña Cecilia, standing with doña Eduardina and don Robustiano near their greenhouse in Nicolás Ailío I-Tranapuente, March 2003. Author photo.

CHAPTER 2

AND THEN, SUDDENLY, THE LAND

DISAPPEARED, 1906–1940

They came from the north, fleeing the Arauco war. They may have migrated along the coast and, when they got to the place where two large rivers met at the sea, they decided to stay. When the "late Nicolás," original *logko*, or head, of the group, went down to Puerto Saavedra to request a land-grant title, or *título de merced*, for the lands they were occupying, the official who recorded the request gave him the last name Ailío. According to doña Eduardina, don Nicolás's granddaughter, the official simply did not understand her grandfather's real name and said, "Well, I guess we'll just call you Ailío." Or perhaps because there were conflicts and confrontations in the area, he said, "Hay lío," which means there's a ruckus, and it stuck as a last name.[1]

When we read and discussed this story with several members of the community in 2001, another version of these events surfaced, a version preserved by the grandsons of the late Nicolás, don Heriberto and don Robustiano Ailío. There were four brothers from Cañete—Nicolás, Domingo, Martín, and Manuel—who were taken prisoner during the war with the Spanish. That was when they received the last name Ailío, and it stuck after they escaped and migrated south. In this version, therefore, the last name was imposed by the enemy, and in the coastal region where they settled, it marked them as outsiders. When they formally settled down and asked for their *título de merced*, only three brothers were registered in the document; Manuel was no longer present, or else he gave his name as Millaman.[2]

Doña Eduardina also heard her aunt Rosa, the daughter of Millamán Ailío, say that when the late Nicolás traveled to Puerto Saavedra to request legal settlement (*radicación*), she had been a child. Still, because she was tall,

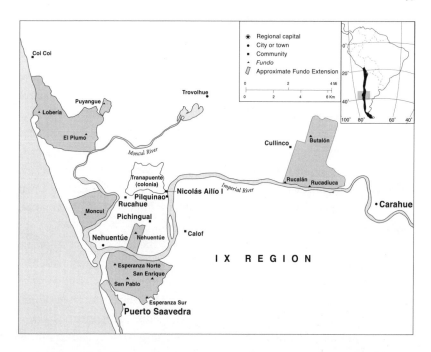

Map 2. Process of *fundo* expansion along the coastal sector of the IX Region, between Carahue and Puerto Saavedra. Inset map shows location of region within Chile as a whole. Cartographic Laboratory, University of Wisconsin, Madison.

they dressed her up as an adult, even giving her falsies, so that she could be counted as an original settler and thus increase the size of the community's land grant. If, however, we examine the written *título de merced* given to the *cacique* Nicolás Ailío and twenty-nine members of his family in December 1906, it seems the strategy doña Rosa remembered did not work. Her father is listed as a nephew—of whom, is somewhat unclear—married to Masall Licanqueo; the document does not record whether they had children at the time of settlement. Only in later documents does it become clear that doña Rosa had already been born and, if we are to believe the later record, she was three years old in 1906.[3]

It is not surprising that doña Rosa remembered such manipulations in the process of requesting legal settlement or land-grant title. When I attempted to draw the community's family tree, comparing several written sources produced at various times, it became clear that the original land title did not simply record, but selectively reorganized, the kinship relations within the group. To begin with, when Nicolás Ailío Quilaqueo was designated the "original *cacique*," this tended to elide the presence of doña Venancia Quilaqueo, his mother and principal matriarch of the family group. Doña Venancia is not only the mother of Miguel, Martín, and Nicolás, but, upon closer inspection, also the aunt of Millamán Ailío, who very well could have been the son of her deceased husband with another wife, which would have been in keeping with Mapuche practice of polygamy at the time. It is also unclear what relation two other brothers who appear in the original land title, Carmen and Domingo Ailío, have with the main branch of the family. Indeed, in the original document they appear separately from each other, and it is only by comparing the earlier documentation with a census taken in 1930 that we can derive an initial, albeit very imperfect, approximation to the whole.[4]

The lack of clarity concerning kinship lines, the lack of respect for the internal structure of the group, is in fact part and parcel of a whole resettlement process in which existing traditions were not respected, and even the spirit of the indigenous settlement law was systematically violated. When the Ley de Radicación de Indígenas (Law of indigenous settlement) was promulgated in 1866, five years after the Chilean government had begun its military campaign into previously autonomous Mapuche territory south of the Bío-Bío River, it was considered a victory by the forces advocating state protection of indigenous lands. It was an attempt at protecting native people from the abuses inherent in private contracts by prohibiting the purchase or sale of native lands. In theory, the mapping of indigenous territory being brought under Chilean state control would begin with the legal settlement, or *radicación*, of the native population on their ancestral lands, and only afterward would government officials have the right to define how much land was left for other uses. In practice, however, the reverse was true.[5]

Not only in Ailío but throughout Mapuche territory the definition of the lineage groups, the location of the lands composing the *títulos de merced*, and the amount of land assigned per person neither followed a predictable pattern, nor conformed to Mapuche usage or custom. In the case of Ailío this becomes evident in what doña Eduardina and her brothers remember, that even the last name assigned to their extended family was the result of a lack of understanding of the Mapuche language (*mapunzugun*) or of the conflicts taking place in the area, or else of the war that was shattering their people. When the people of Ailío recall that they came from the north as refugees of the Arauco war, they emphasize that their presence in the region between the Moncul and Imperial rivers, near Puerto Saavedra and the Pacific Ocean, was occasioned by violence and aggression. Once settled, the people of Ailío managed to become part of the *aillarewe*, or broader territorial unit, composed of the communities of Calof, Machaco, Collico, Pichingual, Pilquinao, Rucahue, and Lincay. "We were family," don Heriberto explained.[6]

Aggression against native territory continued as well in times of peace. Near cities that were being formed, such as Temuco or Carahue, there was an attempt to modify Mapuche territorial claims so that the lands granted to native lineages did not interfere too much with the projects of urban and commercial expansion through which political officials hoped to attract non-Mapuche settlers, both immigrants and Chileans. If a native leader refused to move his lineage to another location, oftentimes government officials tried to reduce the size of the land grant. Or, in a mocking reversal of the *radicación* law's original intent, they waited until all other groups had settled in first—national and foreign colonists as well as owners of recently auctioned fiscal properties—before legalizing indigenous community claims.

The case of Pedro Cayupi, *cacique* from Cullinco, near Ailío but closer to Carahue, is relevant in this context. On 26 September 1902, Cayupi sent a letter to the Ministry of Land and Colonization that read in part, "I am the owner of the lands located in the place named Cullinco, making up a total of two hundred and fifty hectares more or less. The most excellent Government has ordered that the property I own be registered to me and I have been settled on it. This operation was carried out following the findings of four engineers who had been named to investigate the case." However, Cayupi continued, he had been unable to remain in tranquil possession of his land: "It has been absolutely impossible for me to work my land in peace in order to secure my fortune. The cause is that I have no map that indicates clearly what are the boundaries of my property; and since I do not yet have definitive legal title, my peaceful possession, so necessary to my ability to progress, has been interrupted a multitude of times." Cayupi concluded his letter— ironically using the same language of progress that the state was using to justify reducing the territory occupied by the Mapuche—by requesting he be given definitive title to his property.

The *protector de indígenas* (protector of natives) agreed with Cayupi. A Chilean colonist by the name of Ricardo Herrera had encroached on the lands claimed by Cayupi and had even lodged a legal claim demanding settlement on them. "I think that if we order the prompt legal settlement of this

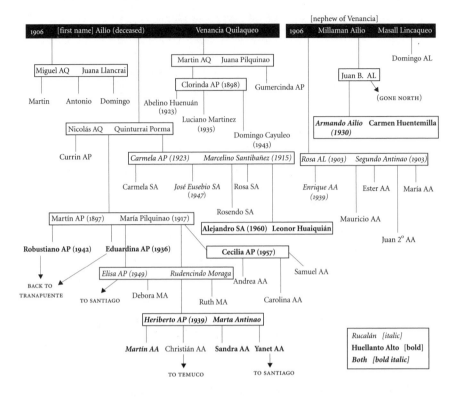

Partial Genealogy of the Community of Nicolás Ailío, 1906–2001. Based on the following sources: CONADI, Archivo de Asuntos Indígenas, T.M. 1112-Comunidad de Nicolás
Ailío: Título de Merced, Lugar Tranapuente, 29 December 1906; Carpeta Administrativa: Expediente de División, Juzgado de Indios de Imperial, iniciado 16 July 1930,
which includes a 1930 census of the community of Nicolás Ailío; and Ministerio de
Tierras y Colonización, Dirección de Asuntos Indígenas, Censo de la Comunidad de
Nicolás Ailío, 30 and 31 May 1963.

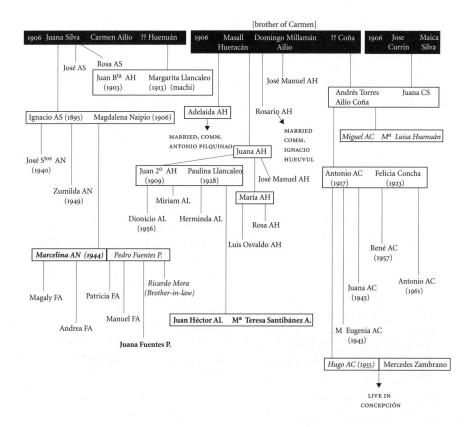

Indian, the abuses of which he is victim would end and any efforts to protect him would be successful because they would be based on the *título de merced*," the protector concluded.

But according to Leoncio Rivera, president of the *Comisión Radicadora* ([Indigenous] Settlement commission), the situation was a bit more complicated than it seemed. It was impossible to legally settle Cayupi and his people because the map of Nehuentúe was inaccurate, and it had been impossible to find a cartographer who could do the job well. Thus

> The Settlement Commission cannot work there on its own, setting the boundaries for the Indians, because there have already been government auctions and transfers of plots of land in that area. If we had done so we would have injured, perhaps unnecessarily, the interests of the successful auction bidders; whereas if we wait until the map is fixed, the Indians can be settled together with or immediately following the private owners, thus leaving in the best circumstances and without damage the interests of private citizens and of the State.

In other words, before the commission had permanently settled the native population of the region, the Chilean state had already defined the lands as state property and auctioned off a part of them. With newly created private interests in the way, it became difficult to settle Cayupi's claim. According to the final report presented to the minister of land and colonization, it was "preferable to finish this task in order to avoid future difficulties with the successful bidders at state auctions and be able to assign Cayupi a realistic parcel that will not put him in conflict with the interests or rights of his neighbors."[7]

Cayupi's was not the only case in the coastal region, near the community of Ailío, in which the priorities of Chilean indigenous legislation were absurdly reversed. Thanks to the work of the historian Christian Martínez, we also have access to the story of land conflict in the Coi Coi Valley and in the whole coastal Lafkenche[8] region south of Danguil. According to the oral tradition recorded by Martínez, conflicts over land began decades before the three surviving communities were granted *títulos de merced* between 1908 and 1913. Beginning in the 1890s there was much violence in the region, remembered in almost emblematic fashion as the abusive wanderings of a mythical bandit by the name of Patricio Rojas. Rojas may not be as mythical as he appears today, however: in the 1901 map of Moncul, on a plot of land at the edge of the Moncul River where it meets the Imperial, a settler by that very name appears.[9] The testimonies recorded by Martínez suggest that the intense pressure put on the Mapuche families in this region had a dual purpose: first, to remove them from the best lands before the auctions began in Santiago; and second, to force them to become rural workers for the new commercial enterprises that had begun to appear in the area. Between the Moncul River and the sierras of Quichihue only one Lafkenche community survived, allowing for the "legalization" of boundaries on the state plots auctioned off in 1893 that reached the beaches of Lobería and Coi Coi. Yet until the 1920s and 1930s Mapuche families remained in de facto control of the coastal region despite having lost de jure title. Only in the 1930s, when advances in drainage technology made the commercial exploitation of oceanside swampland profitable, did a new landowning class revindicate the actual boundary lines that had been drawn between 1903 and 1913 by the *títulos de merced*.[10]

In the coastal region, therefore, from Danguil and Hueñalihuén in the north to Puerto Saavedra and Lake Budi in the south, and due east to Carahue and Imperial, the years between 1900 and 1915 saw numerous conflicts over land and power. Local landowners, merchants, and foreign and national colonists all vied for the best lands, economic connections, and local political posts. The Mapuche, original owners of the land, were in many cases the losers in these unequal battles. It is no coincidence, after all, that the process of indigenous settlement is called by its Spanish colonial name, *reducción*, which also translates as "reduction" or "shrinkage." And as we have seen, in many cases Mapuche losses of territory and resources occurred, through violence, before the *títulos de merced* were granted. Still, despite the inequality of circumstances, the Mapuche tenaciously resisted the abuses perpetrated upon them, and they did not always lose. The case of *cacique* Lorenzo Paillao, from Carahue, is important, not only because he defended himself against the usurpations of a Chilean colonist, but also because the case directly touches upon the history of the community of Ailío.

On 8 October 1900, the Temuco office of the Ministry of Tierras y Colonización (Lands and colonization) sent a letter to the intendant of Cautín province, informing him that a retired sergeant major, Luis C. Ubeda, had been the victim of an abuse of power. According to law, Ubeda had the right, as a retired soldier, to a 150-hectare plot of fiscal land, 100 hectares of which was located south of the Imperial River, facing the town of Carahue. "After having peacefully taken possession of this plot of land and built houses and fences on it and having planted crops," the letter continued, "Mr. Ubeda has been recently thrown off his land due to an order issued by the Governor of Imperial [district]." This order had been carried out by Inspector Marín, "who in the company of one soldier and about fifteen private citizens destroyed Mr. Ubeda's houses, fences, and crops." Temuco's inspector of lands and colonization consequently ordered the intendant to remove from Ubeda's property an indigenous person by the name of Lorenzo Paillao, who had apparently already been settled elsewhere by the Indigenous Settlement Commission, "and also his patron Pedro Vergara."[11]

The facts of the case look very different from a local perspective. On 9 October, the governor of Imperial district answered a query from the intendant that had been prompted by the earlier letter. "On a visit I made to Carahue," he wrote, "I was able to confirm that Mr. Luis C. Ubeda had invaded the *reducción* (land-grant community) of the Indian Lorenzo Paillao, for he had plowed the land up to the very doors of the houses." He continued,

> This office was not aware that the *reducción* belonging to the aforementioned Indian had been registered at a different location. In repeated communications the Protector of Indians has asked this office to observe Article 1 of the law of 20 January 1883 . . . and not permit, under any circumstances, that private individuals molest indigenous people on their properties. For these reasons, I gave the order to the subdelegate of the 3rd subdistrict [to evict Ubeda], and the order was carried out as you can see from the report he submitted to this office, the original of which you will find attached.

The governor also counteracted the version of the colonization ministry's subinspector, saying that Ubeda had not been interrupted in the possession of his plot, since "what was done was only to reverse the invasion Ubeda himself had done into the land contiguous to his property, land which is today occupied by the Indian Paillao and that will become state property only if it is not formally granted to him." And finally, the governor also declared Ubeda's assertion about the destruction of houses, etc. to be false, since "he has never had houses in the part he invaded unfairly, but rather a kind of small lean-to, and the fences that were destroyed were only those with which this man had closed the public road from Carahue to Puerto Saavedra, which must remain open; and since, as I have been told, the plaintiff had the road planted with crops, undoubtedly those were the crops that suffered."[12]

When we explore this case in more detail, we uncover a very complex history. Already at the beginning of October, the governor of Imperial district had explained to the subinspector from the colonization ministry that Ubeda's assigned plot was actually a different one, also claimed by a third party and thus unavailable to him; it was for this reason that Ubeda had been "bothered in a multitude of ways by the Indians, because he was occupying a plot that, according to the facts at my disposal, the Inspector had only given him on a provisional basis."[13] In addition, the boundaries described in the plot given to Ubeda were so general that they could be interpreted in a variety of ways. José Duhalde, at that moment the subdelegate of Puerto Saavedra, the third subdistrict of Imperial, was clearly aware of the problem. When he received the file for the Ubeda case, along with the subinspector's order to return possession of the plot to Ubeda, he wrote the following to the governor of his district:

> I was present when the General Inspector of Colonization ordered the engineer Mr. Cabrera to give one hundred hectares of land to Mr. Ubeda and I remember that it was decided that he would receive one hundred meters of riverfront on the Imperial River but, I repeat, I am not cognizant of the real boundaries of said plot. The Indians allege that they are not within the boundaries of the plot given to the plaintiff.
>
> In order to resolve these difficulties, I believe it would be convenient, unless you esteem otherwise . . . , that you request from the relevant office an engineer who could travel here to measure the boundaries of the plot belonging to Mr. Ubeda so that it will be possible to enforce his rights within the boundaries that are pointed out to me.[14]

The colonization ministry's response was, perhaps, unexpectedly sharp and categorical. The same day that Duhalde's request reached the ministry's regional office, the subinspector decreed that the 4th Cavalry Regiment of Temuco restore Ubeda's possession by force. On 29 October, Ubeda himself and eleven soldiers under the command of cavalry lieutenant César Plaza arrived on the scene and confronted Lorenzo Paillao, Pedro Vergara, and others. According to Plaza's report, they encountered a total of twenty men "armed with axes, knives and clubs"; the men had been drinking and from the beginning they assumed "a menacing stance." Plaza reported that the Indians and the three Vergara brothers attacked them first, when Plaza was preparing to show them the official order he was carrying. The two groups traded blows and saber slashes, suffering injuries on both sides.[15] Local authorities, however, reported a somewhat different scenario. J. Alberto Marín, subdelegate for Carahue, wrote in a telegram sent shortly after having witnessed the battle,

> Yesterday five o'clock near Huedaquintue Luis Ubeda, lieutenant Plaza with ten soldiers Temuco Cavalry Regiment destroyed several houses, some belonging to Indians, all in land of *cacique* Paillao Lorenzo. Pedro Vergara and two brothers were there, as force neared they asked commander to show orders, lieutenant did not do so; Vergaras were wounded with sabers and tied up and Indians trampled. Indians stripped of their possessions were left in the fields in a lamentable state. Understand that my authority was trampled, soldiers proceeded without my knowledge; origin of orders unknown. Witnessed destruction of houses on Carahue's riverfront.[16]

How was the case of *cacique* Lorenzo Paillao resolved? Paillao and his family had been pressured to move from the land on which they had customarily been settled along the Imperial River's southern bank to land further east near the Andes mountains. Despite the best efforts of authorities in Temuco, however, including those of the subinspector of colonization, don Lorenzo Paillao refused to accept the new land. This is why the cavalry defended Ubeda, even though local authorities had repeated over and over that Ubeda was the usurper. This is why the cavalry detachment obeyed orders given in Temuco, without informing local officials of their plans. But the case did not end there. On 3 September 1903, almost three years after having been violently evicted, don Lorenzo Paillao filed a request for legal settlement in Huedaquintue, the place where the battle had occurred. Sadly, *cacique* Paillao died before his request could be processed; but it continued to wind its way through the bureaucracy and, in December 1907, Lorenzo Paillao's family received legal title to their lands in Huedaquintue, under the name of a new *cacique*, Paillao Curivil.[17]

Even more important for the community of Ailío than the small victory of the Paillao family in its confrontation with the government was the presence in the case of José Duhalde. As subdelegate of Puerto Saavedra, Duhalde had attempted to represent the interests of all the parties involved and to do so by accessing the correct information regarding the boundary between Ubeda's fiscal plot and indigenous lands. Temuco responded to his request for information by sending a cavalry detachment to support the interests of the Chilean colonist Luis C. Ubeda. What lesson did Duhalde learn from all this? Certainly it was not to emphasize the justice of a particular claim, or to respect on-the-ground knowledge of the boundaries between properties.

Instead, he learned that the most important thing was to have good connections in Temuco, especially with the authorities who would ultimately resolve local struggles over land and power. And Duhalde would use the lesson he learned in 1900 to excellent effect in 1908, when he managed to usurp forty-five hectares from the community of Ailío.

Indeed, on 12 October 1908, don Domingo Ailío, identified in the document as the *cacique* of the community, complained that Messrs. José Duhalde and Juan de Dios Lobos "have entered my community's reserve without any right to do so." After receiving official notice to that effect, the subdelegate of Bajo Imperial notified the landowners, who obviously denied any wrongdoing. Nothing further was done, and a mere two years after receiving legal title to their land, the members of the community of Ailío found that Duhalde's usurpation had dramatically reduced their holdings, from an average of 4.3 hectares per person, to approximately 2.8 hectares per capita.[18]

"That happened many years ago," explained don Antonio Ailío, son of Andrés Ailío, one of the community's original settlers. "We hadn't even thought about being born yet, the old folks weren't even married. That's when a gentleman came, by the name of Duhalde, from Puerto Saavedra, I don't know where he was from before, but that's when he began robbing our land." Don Antonio remembered that his father fought this usurpation, traveling to Temuco many times, "but he always came back empty-handed, because that gentleman got there first." When don Andrés arrived at the appropriate office, the secretary in charge would tell him things had already been taken care of and that "your opponent just left, Ailío." Despite many long, difficult trips, therefore, nothing was accomplished. Don Antonio explained,

> That gentleman marked the land, he closed it off, he made a fence. This whole part of the community was forest back then, native trees, *hualles*, *pellines*. They turned those over and cut them, and with that wood they made the fence. They began here at this river [Imperial] all the way to the other river, Puyangue, to there they made the fence, taking everyone's land, all the edges that belonged to the community. It included from Nehuentúe all the way to over here, this place is called Tranapuente. And that's how, when time passed, they said they had to get out of there.
>
> My parents, because they lived there and didn't want to leave, were told they had to get out because the land had been bought at auction by Duhalde. My father had just married my mother. What are we going to do now? You'll

just have to settle in somewhere else, the workers told them. We're just following orders, the workers said, we have to do what the boss says. But my
parents just sat down, they didn't want to leave.

After a couple of days they returned with violence. The workers tore down
the house, they left it in pieces, they threw all my parents' stuff out, and after
undoing the houses they burned them, they burned all the wood the houses
had contained. My old folks were left homeless, that's what my father used
to tell me.[19]

Don Antonio's memory can be traced vividly through the written record.
The usurpation, his father's many trips to Temuco, the violence committed
against his parents — all is clearly reflected in the legal case the community
brought against Duhalde. In 1928, don Currín Ailío, son of the original *cacique*, requested the legal division of the community of Nicolás Ailío. This
request seems to have been motivated by the fact that Duhalde and Co. still
possessed forty-five hectares of community land, and by filing a legal request
for subdivision the community hoped to achieve restitution. The two parties
were ordered to face each other in court on 25 May 1928, and the discussions began. Only in 1930, however, was an actual restitution suit begun in
local court, at the special indigenous claims court, or Juzgado de Indios, in
Imperial. Don Antonio's father, Andrés Ailío, presented the first complaint,
which said in part,

> I am a member of the indigenous reserve No. 39A, One hundred and thirty
> hectares of land granted to *cacique* Nicolás Ailío in the place already named.
> I am not, however, in possession of all the land that belongs to me as a titled
> settler, because about 18 or 20 years ago, the private citizen Mr. Jose Du-
> halde, living in Puerto Saavedra, violently took from me a good portion of
> the best land.
>
> Allow me to emphasize to Your Honor that Mr. Duhalde, not content with
> the usurpation alone, also ordered his administrator, the late Mr. Laurie, to
> burn my house. I have complained about this many times to the Protector
> of Indians in Temuco without ever having obtained satisfactory results.[20]

Although he never learned how to read or write, don Andrés Ailío had
been struggling for a long time, as he himself emphasized and his son would
remember many years later, to obtain restitution of the community's lands.
He had traveled repeatedly to Temuco, always with frustrating results; he
had watched as his house was destroyed at the hands of Duhalde's admin-

istrator. But only twenty-two years after the original usurpation did don Andrés Ailío manage, in the name of the community, to begin legal restitution proceedings.

José Duhalde defended himself before the judge by using all the tricks he had learned in the Ubeda case in 1900. He began his brief by saying there was an error in the map of the Moncul region that had been drawn in 1903 by the engineer Agustín Cabrera and that this was the map upon which the community of Ailío was basing its boundaries. In 1893, he argued, fifteen years before the community had received its legal land grant, Domingo Echeverría had bought a plot of fiscal lands at auction, a plot that included the forty-five hectares in dispute. Duhalde and Co. had later bought this plot from Echeverría and thus had rights previous to those established in the *título de merced*. This story of a previous auction, also remembered by don Antonio, was a common one in land disputes with Mapuche communities throughout the region, as was the tone of moral superiority with which the usurper justified his claim, basing himself on the principle of private property. "Your Honor surely understands," Duhalde wrote, "that the settlement of Indians on lands already auctioned off by the Government and adjudicated to third parties is simply not permitted."[21]

But the juez de indios hearing the case did not understand Duhalde's position. After comparing the various official maps, the local indigenous court found that the famous Moncul map of 1903 was in accordance with all the rest, and that the forty-five hectares really belonged to the community of Ailío. The most important proof of this, according to the court's own surveyor, was to be found in the measurement of the community's eastern boundary. While the rest of the boundaries matched up with the *título de merced*, "the difference between the 550 meters this boundary has today and the 900 meters defined in the *Título de Merced*, matches up exactly with the fact that Mr. Duhalde has occupied a piece of land that along its western boundary has a length of 350 meters and along its eastern side measures 390 meters."[22] Thus, ruled the judge, "even though it is true that the auction from which Duhalde and Co. traces its rights occurred before the legal land grant, the difference in dates cannot be taken into consideration because in reality we are talking about different pieces of land, not about a single plot that had been auctioned off first to a private citizen and then later granted as part of a *Título de Merced* to an indigenous reserve."[23]

At the local level, then, the case was resolved in favor of the community. José Duhalde and Co. were ordered to return to the community of Ailío the

45.69 hectares they had seized. But Duhalde continued to use the strategies he had learned in the Ubeda case and appealed the case to Temuco, where on 16 April 1931 the Appellate Court reversed the finding and ordered the case shelved. Maintaining the status quo ante favored Duhalde, of course, since he had de facto possession of the forty-five hectares. Eight years later, on 15 February 1939, don Martín Ailío legally requested the reopening of the case, and five months later don Domingo Ailío once again requested the legal division of the community's lands. He justified his petition as follows: "I am the son of Miguel Ailío and Juana Llancrai, who are married according to indigenous custom and civil law. They are both legally settled in the community. Along with all the members of the community, I am interested in proceeding to divide our lands, especially because the landowner Mr. Duhalde has taken over 45.69 hectares belonging to us and, consequently, we all wish that this land be returned to the community."[24]

In 1939, thirty-one years after receiving their legal land grant and twenty-nine years after the original usurpation, the community of Ailío continued demanding justice. The struggle would continue for a long time, forming the most important and constant thread in the community's history. But in 1939, there was also a very specific reason motivating don Martín and don Domingo Ailío to request the reopening of the case. Graciano Duhalde, don José's son, had offered to sell the *fundo* Tranapuente, which included the community's forty-five hectares, to the government, specifically to the government's Caja de Colonización Agrícola (Agricultural colonization office). In August the Caja had recommended to the colonization ministry, of which it was a part, that the expropriation of the fundo be approved; at the end of September that same year, the ministry had formally accepted, by decree, the Caja's recommendation.[25] As we shall see below, the sale of the fundo Tranapuente to the government was part of a broader commercial strategy that Graciano and his father had been carrying out since the beginning of the 1930s. But from the community's point of view, accepting the sale and subdivision of this fundo could very well mean losing forever the hope of restitution. And that was unacceptable.

José and Graciano Duhalde:
The Regional Accumulation of Wealth

Today, between Carahue and Puerto Saavedra, people around still remember Duhalde as a cruel, powerful man. At his office in Puerto Saavedra, people used to line up to see him. At a factory he owned he paid his workers next to nothing and was always late with the payroll. If a worker complained or demanded back pay, people say, Duhalde would meet him at the factory and throw him into the boiler that provided energy for the plant.[26]

Who was this abusive and powerful landowner, who in the most dramatic oral memory literally consumed the bodies of his workers by throwing them into the factory boiler? Duhalde was a French Basque immigrant who arrived in Chile in 1888, a few years after the military defeat of the Mapuche. According to the writer Aníbal Escobar, the French community in Chile, "most of them Basques," contributed the most, as a group, to the development of frontier cities in the south, because they were "hardworking, innovative, and persistent people who set up stores, agricultural properties and small industries that, bit by bit, became highly developed."[27] At first sight, Duhalde fit this model perfectly. His first investments in property, recorded in Nueva Imperial between 1896 and 1897, consisted of urban lots and small urban estates. His first commercial partnership was apparently with Duhart Hnos. (Bros.), a French Basque firm founded to the north in the coal mining region of Lota in 1858 and, by the beginning of the twentieth century, prominent at the national level. In 1899 Duhalde began to buy agricultural land, in his own name and in the name of Duhart Hnos. At the same time he must have established himself in Puerto Saavedra, since in 1900, as we saw in the case of Lorenzo Paillao and Luis Ubeda, Duhalde was already subdelegate in that town. Also during his first years in Chile, specifically in Nueva Imperial in 1892, Duhalde's wife, Rosa Silva, gave birth to a son whom they named Víctor Graciano.[28]

What Escobar does not mention in his description of French Basque entrepreneurship is its frequent reliance on violent expansion into indigenous lands. Between 1900 and 1930, precisely the years in which they seized Ailío's lands, José Duhalde and his son Graciano established one of the most important business firms in the coastal region. Beginning under the name of Duhart Hnos., José Duhalde accumulated lands throughout the region, oftentimes through the kinds of manipulations and abuse he used in the case of Ailío. The fundo Tranapuente is typical in this regard. Formally registered in 1909 as the property of Duhart Hnos., the fundo had, at that point, a total of 1,576 hectares in four separate lots, all of them patchworks of fiscal plots bought between 1907 and 1909 from individuals who had bid successfully for them at government auctions. The first of the four lots, totaling 310 hectares, contained Ailío's 45 hectares and combined two purchases made in 1907: fiscal plot no. 18, previously belonging to Enrique Gama; and fiscal plot no. 19, bought from Domingo Echeverría.[29]

Beyond Tranapuente, in 1909 Duhart Hnos. also formalized its ownership of two other important coastal fundos: Nehuentúe and Esperanza. In 1909, the fundo Nehuentúe had a total of 1,039 hectares, composed of three lots that also had their origins in auctions or adjudications of fiscal property. It is interesting to note in this case that, along Nehuentúe's northern boundary, there was a dispute with the Mapuche community of Andrés Curimán, located in Rucahue-Moncul. Not long before Nehuentúe's formalization, on 31 July 1908, and with the participation of Nicolás Ailío, among other witnesses, the *cacique* Andrés Curimán had received formal title to 485 hectares for himself and ninety-one persons in his family. According to testimony given many years later by two members of this community, they were approximately thirty hectares short of their legal holding along the southern boundary, "because the fence marker had been moved toward our Reserve many years ago, approximately in 1908."[30] And finally, the fundo Esperanza, although it did not seem to have an outstanding claim of usurpation brought by a specific Mapuche community, between 1900 and 1909 followed a familiar pattern of consolidation. Adjudicated or auctioned fiscal properties were sold to new owners, often partners in Duhart Hnos.; these sales were subsequently consolidated under the ownership of the firm. One difference in the case of Esperanza was that José Bunster, another entrepreneur famous for his early and speculative accumulation of frontier lands, seems to have consolidated most of this property before its 1,773 hectares passed to Duhart Hnos.[31]

In 1910, only a few months after registering the fundos Tranapuente and Nehuentúe, Duhart Hnos. was dissolved. In a formal adjudication on 29 April, José Duhalde was declared the legal owner of the fundos Esperanza, Tranapuente, and Nehuentúe; the *hijuela* (plot) Tondreau and Doña Inés Island, the first on the Imperial River's southern bank and the second in the middle of the river itself, facing the community of Ailío; and of various other small urban estates and properties in the towns of Carahue, Puerto Saavedra, and Nueva Imperial. The total value of the properties was estimated to be 2,658,151 pesos. Thus in twenty years José Duhalde had managed, through a series of accumulation and usurpation strategies, to consolidate a personal and family fortune whose core was made up of three rich fundos located around the mouth of the Imperial River on the Pacific Ocean. Made up of a total of 4,388 hectares, these three fundos would, in the first three decades of the twentieth century, constitute a single property divided only by the Imperial River and would be employed in commercial agriculture and livestock raising.[32]

Between 1910 and 1930, more or less, this accumulation that rested in part on the violent seizure of indigenous territory would also serve as the basis for one of the region's largest fortunes. But in 1910, when he became the owner of these three important coastal fundos, Duhalde was only beginning his career of speculation. Two years later he managed something even more dramatic: he became the owner of the fundo El Budi, 42,000 hectares originally granted by the government to the Spanish entrepreneur Eleuterio Domínguez. Though Duhalde remained the owner of this vast expanse for only two years, an analysis of the purchase and sale of this property helps us understand that the usurpations of indigenous lands committed by Duhalde were only the tip of an enormous iceberg of legal and financial manipulation on which he based his fortune.

The story of the El Budi colony began more or less at the same time as the tale of the Duhalde family. On 23 August 1902, the Chilean government signed a contract with the Spanish businessman Francisco Sánchez Ruiz in which Sánchez committed himself to bringing up to three hundred Spanish families from the Canary Islands and settling them, as colonists, between the Imperial and Toltén rivers. Soon afterward, on 27 March 1903, Sánchez received the first piece of land from the government, a total of 12,500 hectares calculated to settle the first twenty-five families. Interestingly, the state committed to providing 150 hectares per head of household and an additional 65 hectares per son older than ten years. Compared to the 130 hectares granted to the entire community of Nicolás Ailío, this transaction shows quite clearly how the state constructed differences in access to resources between Mapuche agriculturalists and foreign colonists. But in addition, the contract between Sánchez and the government stipulated that

> the Chilean Government will give the colonists medical care, medicines, seeds and in general the same advances that have been given to the colonists of Chiloé, to wit: thirty cents a day and fifteen more for each child older than ten years, from the day they reach Chile until they are given possession of their plot and twenty pesos per month per family to help them support themselves during the first year after they become established in the colony. The advances in kind will be the following: a team of oxen, a dairy cow and a mare to be shoed. A merino sheep, a pig, three poultry. A house already

built or one hundred and fifty boards and twenty-three kilos of nails; and a sawmill per group of families whose size will be determined by the General Inspector of *Tierras*. A yoke, a plow, saws, sticks, axes and chains.[33]

On 12 May 1903, the government extended the contract to include colonists from various Spanish mainland provinces and transferred it from Sánchez Ruiz to the Empresa Colonizadora del Budi, run by Eleuterio Domínguez and Co. Despite the extremely favorable terms of this colonization contract, however, between 1904 and 1907 Domínguez stumbled upon a series of roadblocks that made the creation of a peaceful and prosperous colony seem nearly impossible. The first problem was that the state kept reneging on its financial obligations as stipulated in the contract. Other colonization companies also began to compete for the colonists who were established in El Budi, attempting to attract them south toward Valdivia. But the worst problem, the one that marked the ultimate failure of the project, was that the government had not taken into account that most of the lands promised to Domínguez were already occupied by others, both national colonists and native people, and was unable to solve the conflicts before turning the lands over to the colonization company.[34]

Despite attempts to come to terms with the occupants, by 1905 Domínguez was already trying to find a way out of the contract. The final accord between Domínguez and the government was formalized by decree on 25 October 1907, whereby Domínguez promised to return to the state, out of a total of 56,025 hectares he had already received, 6,025 that could be used to settle national colonists and indigenous people. Subtracting an additional 7,932 hectares that corresponded to the foreign colonists already settled, the agreement left Domínguez with 42,068 hectares "over which he has full control, free of all debt or mortgage."[35]

This large expanse did not remain in the hands of the Domínguez family for long. Don Eleuterio and his wife both died within the next four years, and in September 1911 the heirs adjudicated the properties in the Domínguez estate to Samuel Larraín Bulnes, identified in the document as an investor and an employee of the Caja de Crédito Hipotecario (National Mortgage Bank). The heirs had no interest in resolving the problems left hanging in the Budi region, among which figured prominently the conflicts with "the colonists, occupants and authorities of Imperial who have frankly taken sides with and fomented the unfair demands of occupants and colonists." For example, "sixty to seventy court cases [were] still being heard in Nueva Imperial involving the colonists or occupants, whose total cost can be estimated at around four hundred and one thousand one hundred and thirty pesos and sixty-nine cents." Added to this were other problems, outstanding debts, and so forth, and the heirs simply decided to pass the estate to Larraín for a total of 1,945,332 pesos, with the understanding that he would take responsibility for resolving all the existing issues.[36]

In addition to these deeper, more enduring problems preventing the establishment of clear and secure rights over the property, there was also a more immediate issue that lent the adjudication process a particular urgency. As the executor representing the interests of the heirs, Arturo Alessandri made clear that, in a notarized transaction, José Duhalde "had paid the five overdue payments on the mortgage the [Domínguez] estate had with the Banco Garantizador de Valores." In addition, Alessandri explained, "Mr. Duhalde has presented a brief in one of Santiago's civil courts requesting a legal transfer of rights, which clearly shows that his purpose is to collect on this debt in court, which constitutes a grave danger to the estate, since it could be dragged by force into a case that might result in the auction of all assets, with severe consequences for the heirs. This situation further deepens the difficulties the estate now faces in the already pending court cases." It was in the context of this immediate threat that Samuel Larraín "dared to offer to confront the situation himself and thus requested that all the existing property rights in the estate be adjudicated to him."[37]

Larraín's dare did not yield him immediate profits, however. A few months later, on 31 July 1912, José Duhalde became the legal owner of the fundo El Budi, with a total of 42,000 hectares, as well as of a few other properties that were part of the Domínguez estate, "due to the legal adjudication decided by the Honorable Judge don Dagoberto Lagos in Santiago, in the case the said new owner had initiated against the estate of don Eleuterio Domínguez and others, over the payment of a debt. The case is settled for a total of three million one thousand five hundred pesos, to be paid in the way and under the conditions established in the aforesaid title."[38] But if the case is examined in broader perspective, it turns out that Larraín's dare yielded tremendous dividends in the slightly longer short term, for only two years later Duhalde sold the fundo El Budi to the Sociedad Agrícola El Budi in exchange for 150,000 pounds sterling in shares, 1,418,770 pesos, and the cancelation of a 500,000-peso debt he owed to none other than Samuel Larraín Bulnes. In the meantime Duhalde had sold a few small parcels of the fundo to individual property holders, possibly in an attempt to settle a few of the outstanding claims (the total price of these sales was 392,477 pesos), and he also kept the urban properties that had been a part of the original estate. The president of the Sociedad Agrícola El Budi, it turned out, was Arturo Alessandri, previously the executor of the Domínguez estate, and its chief executive officer was Larraín: between 1911 and 1914, in other words, the three partners had managed a brilliant bait and switch that left them as owners of the largest fundo in the region and, according to the analyst Colonel I. Anabalón y Urzúa, "one of the most important agricultural properties in the country."[39]

Between 1910 and 1930, José Duhalde and his son Graciano benefited from the wealth they were accumulating through Duhalde and Co., the firm they created in 1910 when Duhart Hnos. closed its doors. Duhalde and Co. bought El Budi and subsequently received shares in the Sociedad Agrícola. The firm also continued accumulating other agricultural properties, innovating in the livestock industry and participating in commerce around Puerto Saavedra. It owned two steamboats, *Cholchol* and *Cautín*, that plied the river routes on the Imperial between Carahue and Puerto Saavedra. Starting in 1908, Duhart Hnos. and subsequently Duhalde and Co. held the contract, on their fundo Esperanza, for supplying the navy. Overall, then, the decade of the 1920s was a golden age for the Duhalde family firm.

In 1922, when Col. Anabalón y Urzúa published his preliminary work on Chilean agriculture, his discussion of the Esperanza Livestock Breeding Farm, which he defined as an expanse that included the fundos Esperanza, Nehuentúe, and Tranapuente, was fifteen pages long. According to Anabalón, the fundo did not have resident workers but instead used "contract or day laborers, most of them from neighboring areas." The farm was known internationally for its livestock breeding and improvement of stock and had won national prizes since 1906. Other activities on the fundo included livestock fattening of up to five thousand head and potato cultivation. The owners, Duhalde and Co., reported Anabalón, had improved the property by building fences, planting groves of fruit trees and pine forest, installing drainage canals, and constructing modern storage facilities. Products not used to supply the Chilean navy were marketed in Santiago, Concepción, and Talcahuano. "As one can see," Anabalón concluded, "this is without a doubt one of the most important cattle breeding centers that exists today among us. It is enough to note the fact that one of its breeders, the bull named 'Eaglethorp Reformer,' was bought for the enormous sum of 200,000 pesos and that not a single one of its cows is worth less than 4,000 pesos. In reality, the breeding center belonging to Messrs. Duhalde and Co. represents a true fortune."[40]

The prosperity of Duhalde and Co. is also reflected in the additional purchases of land it made near Nehuentúe and Moncul, including some pieces of the fundos Puyangue and Trovolhue, and the plot known as Los Colihues located on the other side of the Imperial River. From about 1930, however, the firm's situation began to change. It is tempting to suppose that this change was due to the fact that the community of Ailío opened restitution proceedings in local court; but given the size of the Duhalde fortune, Ailío's suit could not have been more than one of many factors that began to affect the firm. Beginning in 1930, for example, the world depression hit hard in Chile. A firm like Duhalde and Co., dependent on the markets in Santiago, Concepción, and Talcahuano, could not help but feel the impact. Also in 1930, the status of the fundo Esperanza as one of the foci for hoof-and-mouth disease in the region was confirmed, perhaps in part because it was bringing livestock from Argentina through the mountain pass located at Pucón.[41] Furthermore, family conflicts began to affect the firm during this period.

On 8 August 1930, Duhalde's second wife, Lucrecia Pinto, died. Her two daughters, Edelmira and Lucila Duhalde, became involved in a court case over inheritance rights that debated the definition and division of what had been community property during this second marriage. The finding in the case went against the two sisters, for the judge decided that "no property had been acquired during the marriage, and therefore there was nothing to divide among the heirs." Lucila Duhalde Pinto was not satisfied with this result and began collecting the necessary evidence to open a new court case "annulling this division, and annulling all the sales Duhalde and Co. carried out after my mother's death." According to Lucila's calculations, she had been cheated out of "more than one and a half million pesos." She based this calculation on the legal judgment that any sale or transfer of property by Duhalde and Co. after her mother's death that did not take into account the prior need to divide up conjugal property could very well be considered illegal or temporary.[42]

This inheritance struggle boils down to a confrontation between Graciano Duhalde, the only son of José Duhalde's first marriage and designated heir to Duhalde and Co., and Lucila Duhalde, daughter of Duhalde's second marriage and the only offspring completely left out of the family fortune. It is in the context of this struggle that Duhalde and Co. began to sell off some of its assets. The first important sale was the fundo Nehuentúe, sold to Larroulet Hnos., another firm in Puerto Saavedra, sometime between 1930 and 1935. This was followed by Graciano Duhalde's offer of the fundo Tranapuente to the Caja de Colonización Agrícola, and, as noted, the colonization ministry accepted the sale and parcelization of this fundo in September 1938. It is interesting to note that in 1910 Tranapuente was calculated at 1,576 hectares, whereas by the time it was expropriated in 1938 it had grown to 2,160 hectares. The Duhalde family's process of expansion had continued, and as a result Graciano Duhalde received, according to the Caja de Colonización Agrícola's own calculations, a total of 2,769,945 pesos. Seen in this light, Graciano's resistance to sharing the wealth of Duhalde and Co. with his half sisters is perhaps not surprising.[43]

The plot thickens even further if we compare the fate of Graciano's various half sisters. Edelmira, Lucila's sister, had been married to Martín Biscar, José Duhalde's old business partner and one of the founding members of Duhalde and Co. As a result, she ended up in a much better financial position than her sister, for when Biscar died, she inherited half of the property remaining in Duhalde and Co. after 1938, which included some urban properties in Puerto Saavedra, the fundo Esperanza, the *hijuela* Tondreau, and the fundo Los Colihues. Shortly thereafter Edelmira sold her share to Pablo Lüer Metzger, a German investor established in Traiguén, who bought the property for his sons, thus positioning them, at the beginning of the 1940s, as important landowners in the coastal region. Also figuring in these transactions was a third half sister, Elena Duhalde de Lange, whose mother was never formally married to don José. In Graciano's will, Elena's two children were designated as heirs, together with his wife, doña Berta Fagalde de Duhalde. This fact took on a great deal of importance after 25 December 1940, when Graciano Duhalde Silva was murdered in his office on the fundo Esperanza.[44]

At eight in the morning on that Christmas day, Lorenzo Henríquez Escar, owner of a mill in Puerto Saavedra, arrived at the fundo Esperanza looking for Graciano. According to the medical examiner's report, the two men fought, and, after receiving more superficial bullet wounds in the hand and stomach, Duhalde was killed by two shots to the chest. When the police responded to the call they went in search of Henriquez and found him in his office about to expire because he had attempted suicide by firing his revolver into his right temple. "On the desk in his office we found an unfinished letter," wrote Puerto Saavedra's prefect of police, "in which he says he killed Mr. Duhalde, calling him a bandit and usurper of lands." Henríquez was taken to the hospital, where he died shortly after midday.[45]

"They killed him, too," don Antonio Ailío explained. "Duhalde borrowed money from a man who owned a mill in Puerto Saavedra, and when the man tried to get the money back, or get him to sign a check, Duhalde said he didn't have it. So the man finally got tired of this, and didn't try to collect anymore, and one day he arrived very early and saw Duhalde in his office and killed him. So that's how Duhalde ended up."[46] For don Antonio, Duhalde's end had several meanings. On one side, it had a moral meaning: Duhalde ended badly because he had lived badly, because he treated people badly. On another side, Duhalde's end marked the end of what he had represented: the voraciousness of the early landowners, who laid waste to everything that stood in their path, cutting down forests, moving fences, burning *rukas*, consuming people's lives and lands. In the end, Duhalde was consumed in the fire of his own boiler.

But Duhalde's end had a further meaning as well. Duhalde as a code word for Duhalde and Co., for José and Graciano Duhalde taken together, also came to an end that Christmas day in 1940. Graciano did not have children, and thus there would not be another generation of Duhaldes in the coastal region. His widow, Berta Fagalde, and his illegitimate sister Elena divided up the inheritance and moved to Santiago, living at first in the house that had served as the Santiago office for Duhalde and Co. in the 1930s. Edelmira Duhalde, widow of Martín Biscar, sold her part in the firm to the Lüer family, who were among the German immigrants just beginning to arrive in the region. Shortly thereafter Berta Fagalde bought up the portion of her late husband's inheritance that had belonged to his nephews, but she never returned to live in Puerto Saavedra. Until the 1960s she continued to rent out her half of the fundo Esperanza, known as Esperanza Norte; as late as 1951 she was still listed as one of the ten largest property holders in Puerto Saavedra by the national tax office. That same year Fernando Lüer, for whom his father, Pablo Lüer, had bought the southern half of Esperanza from Edelmira Duhalde, was mayor of Puerto Saavedra. He was also renting Esperanza Norte from doña Berta. And Miguel Larroulet, one of the brothers who had bought the fundo Nehuentúe from Duhalde and Co. more than fifteen years before, was on the city council.[47]

Duhalde as Prototype of an Abusive Landowner: A Local Geography and Genealogy of Power

It had all been native land at first. As we have seen in the cases of Ailío and its neighbors, the legal land-grant titles themselves, the *títulos de merced*, were the result of violent imposition, war, and confrontation. After the war the maps were drawn slowly; there was a shortage of personnel, and many errors occurred along the way. Often the delays favored non-Mapuches who claimed lands that supposedly belonged to the state. Along the coast, the auctions and allotment of fiscal plots began in 1893, while the *títulos de merced* were generally given out between 1903 and 1915. In such a context, the obvious conclusion is that the state favored private and entrepreneurial interests over its legal obligation first to settle indigenous groups on the land. In fact, the general inspector of the Tierras y Colonización ministry explained, in a report on a 1904 colonization proposal, that a previous project for Valdivia and Llanquihue had been rejected because the land requested "was not indigenous territory." The inescapable conclusion is that the state saw native territory as a region entirely suitable for colonization and usurpation, and that the very process of land titling was heavily slanted in favor of colonists and entrepreneurs.[48]

But even having the cards stacked in their favor was not enough. Investors like Duhalde not only bought the lands originally auctioned off or adjudicated to Chilean property holders, but also pushed the fence markers into lands that had actually been granted to indigenous communities as part of their already reduced holdings. Beginning in the last decades of the nineteenth century, the regional economy was built upon this double usurpation, which was condoned and supported by the government even though it was in contradiction to its own existing laws. Ironically, the myth of the enterprising immigrant who built a fortune bit by bit is constructed on this same foundation. What is left unsaid is that these fortunes rest on the illegal appropriation of native resources, an appropriation abetted by the state. This dramatic silence, in which Duhalde is typically complicit, is the mirror image of the moral discourse of the entrepreneur, which Duhalde also helped construct. In that narrative, the state cannot allow the trampling of private interests because it has been the individual investor who, by the sweat of his brow, has lifted the frontier out of its backwardness.

By encouraging a selective amnesia around the origins of regional fortunes, this same silence also facilitated the evolution, by the mid-1950s, of an opposite memory: that because they possessed the best lands of the region, the Mapuche were actually responsible for the lack of economic growth! This argument was advanced in 1955 by León Erbeta, prosecutor for Temuco's Appelate Court, in a report he wrote to the prosecutor at the Supreme Court. According to Erbeta, the state had "followed the mistaken policy of converting the Indians into the owners of all the land they inhabited, instead of assigning property rights only over the land they were capable of occupying and making productive." As a result, Erbeta continued, the region of Cautín, considered "the country's most productive agricultural, livestock, and lumber region," could not develop in a normal fashion. The state was to blame, he concluded, because it had "given over to the indigenous population around 500,000 hectares of superior agricultural land, located near the frontier's cities and population centers, forming thus what is now called 'steel rings' that impede or slow down their growth."[49]

The memories of don Antonio Ailío and others in his community, when combined with a consideration of the surviving archival documentation, prove the contrary. It was the entrepreneurs who, by monopolizing others' lands and abusing state power, placed a steel ring around the communities. And it was the same large landowners who, basing their fortunes on aggression and depredation, established relations with the people and the land that also limited their capacity to grow and develop. Duhalde came to a bad end because he abused everybody, "because he did bad works," emphasized don Antonio:

> He looked down on the poor, as if they were dogs. For example, I worked for him for a while. His resident workers would tell me, go ahead, come work for Duhalde, there's work for you. One day he called me. Ailío—he said—come here! I went running, of course. Put my spurs on!—he said. I put his spurs on, one upside down, the other right side up, because I was shivering with fright (laughs). There they are. Are they ready, Ailío? Yes, boss, I said. And he set off on horseback. That gentleman never stopped, even when his workers had to talk to him. No, his workers had to follow along behind his horse, like little dogs, if they wanted to talk to him.[50]

The lesson learned by one of don Antonio's sons was that this arrogance, this lack of respect for other human beings, finally did Duhalde in. "He thought he was king of these lands," he said, "but he didn't know that there's another King upstairs, another King Who's on top of him, Who got to order *him* around."[51] Arrogance can be seen as well in other aspects of the Du-

halde family enterprise, aspects about which the people of Ailío had no direct knowledge, such as Graciano's attempt to deny his father's daughters a
share of the inheritance. As we have seen, this greed is what led to the sale
of Nehuentúe and to the offering of Tranapuente to the Caja de Colonización Agrícola. The region's wealthy entrepreneurs, alleged pioneers on the
frontier, had feet made of clay that they themselves had dug.

Indeed, the figure of Duhalde, who in the eyes of the people of Ailío
and environs readily melds into a single abusive prototype combining José
and Graciano, can also be made to stand for an entire cohort of individual
landowners who engaged in these same practices, articulating a geography and genealogy of power that spread across the land from Carahue to
the coast. Four of the area's most important agricultural properties passed
through Duhalde's hands. The fundo El Budi, after becoming the property
of the Sociedad Agrícola, moved into the hands of the Alessandri family,
who were expropriated by the Agrarian Reform in February 1971. The pieces
of the fundo Esperanza were expropriated by the Corporación de Reforma
Agraria (Agrarian reform corporation) (CORA) between June and November 1972, and the southern portions belonging to the Lüer brothers became agrarian reform centers. During the presidency of Salvador Allende,
Esperanza Norte, which since 1966 had belonged to the same Landarretche
family that owned the fundo whose takeover is described above in chapter 1,
would become part of the same production center as Nehuentúe, sold first
to the Larroulet brothers and subsequently to Mario Alvarez.[52] Along the
coast, therefore, twentieth-century landowners were connected at most by
two degrees of separation. Substituting Duhalde for a Lüer, Landarretche,
or Larroulet involved at best elementary mental gymnastics on the part of
the region's Mapuche communities. In 2001, commenting on the abuses
that today's lumber companies are committing against Mapuche communities and their ecological destruction of the region, don Robustiano Ailío
found new meaning for the abusive landowner prototype: "They are today's
Duhalde," he suggested.[53]

But the reconstructing of this local geography of power, prompted as
it was by don Antonio Ailío's morally satisfying memories of Duhalde's
demise, does not change the fact that the subdivision of the fundo Tranapuente continued after the murder. In August 1938, José Maige, agronomist
for the Caja de Colonización Agrícola, reported that the property "had many
advantages" as the site for an agricultural colony, "given its large size, 2,160
hectares, and the good quality of its lands." He recommended the creation

of around 35 separate plots, with an average size of 62 hectares, but emphasized the need to invest in some improvements first, because "the fundo has only been modestly exploited."[54] Don Antonio recalled that Tranapuente had been subdivided among the resident laborers who worked for the former owner, some of whom then sold to other landowners from the area. According to the documentation of the Caja de Colonización Agrícola, confirmed by don Antonio's testimony, Ailío's hectares became part of plots 10 and 11, allocated to Florencio Riquelme and Dionisio Benavente, respectively, passing then to the Astorga brothers and to Sergio Benavente upon the death of Dionisio.[55] By the end of the 1940s and beginning of the 1950s, therefore, the forty-five hectares Duhalde had taken, land on which don Antonio's parents had originally lived and that don Antonio could still see from the door of his house, seemed further and further away.

CHAPTER 3

A GENERATION WITHOUT SHOES:

ENDURING IN POVERTY, 1940–1970

In the community of Nicolás Ailío, as in many other Mapuche communities, the second and third postsettlement generations found themselves submerged in an ever-deepening cycle of poverty. The original land grants, in many cases already reduced by illegal usurpations, would be reduced even further by inheritance and the need to maintain a new generation. According to information collected by the Dirección de Asuntos Indígenas (Bureau of Indian affairs) in 1966, the average amount of land per person in Mapuche communities had declined to 2.3 hectares. These averages hid large variations, both within and between communities. Using the same 1966 data, Alejandro Saavedra calculated that approximately 42 percent of Mapuche families controlled fewer than 5 hectares, while almost 15 percent of the families controlled 50 hectares or more.[1]

In this context, the situation in Ailío was particularly onerous. The land, already limited in size, had been cultivated beyond its capacity and no longer produced as before. Poverty ground people down; the census of 1963 recorded an average of 2.3 hectares per family in Ailío, the same as the average holding per person in the Mapuche population as a whole. The average holding per person in Ailío stood at approximately 0.7 hectares.[2] We can easily understand the reaction of two agronomy students who passed through the community in 1963 while conducting a survey as part of their doctoral research at the Universidad de Chile:

> The topography is very uneven, with the existence of sharp hilly areas, and small meadows in between used for cultivating potatoes. Given the poor

quality of the soil and its uneven topography it is difficult to determine which, among the various crops, is the principal one. Undoubtedly, those who possess lands in the meadows preferentially cultivate potatoes. Given the bad quality of the natural pastures, livestock raising in this *reducción* is given only secondary importance.

This *reducción* is one of the poorest among all those we have surveyed, since some families find they cannot even cover their food and clothing from what they produce on their land, and thus are forced to rely on other family members who have migrated to the cities, seeking better incomes.[3]

Indeed, if we compare the situation of the community of Ailío with that of other coastal communities, its level of poverty does stand out. In the community of Bartolo Queipán, for example, in Rucatraro-Budi, the average amount of land per family in 1962 was 10.4 hectares, almost five times that in Ailío. Interestingly, the differences between families were greater in Queipán, where several families possessed between 20 and 40 hectares and there was also one landless family. But even in communities closer to Ailío, those on the same side of the Imperial River, we find in the community of Andrés Curimán an average holding of 5.5 hectares per family, twice Ailío's average, and in the much smaller community of Juan de Dios Pilquinao also an average of 5.5 hectares.[4]

Another important element in this general picture is the percentage of land people were able to cultivate. In Ailío, about half the land was under cultivation at any one time. This proportion is similar to that in other communities of the region, in which cultivation percentages ran between 30 and 60 percent of the land people possessed, with the majority of cases hovering between 40 and 48 percent.[5] At first sight it is puzzling that, being in a situation of extreme scarcity, people did not cultivate their land more intensively. There are many and varied explanations for this, including the eroded, worn-out nature of the soil; the balance between agricultural and livestock activity; the lack of capital, fertilizer, tools, and draft animals; and even poverty itself, since the burden of economic want forced children to migrate to the city just when they became productive workers, causing a scarcity of labor power on the family farm.

To this more quantitative and external gaze, however, we must add the memories and experiences of the people living in Ailío at the time. In the last chapter don Antonio described how his parents had been the most direct target of the abusive landowner who originally usurped the community's forty-five hectares. One of the results of this experience was his early migration to Santiago in search of work, a move which fit the pattern of migration being followed by young people from many Mapuche communities in the 1930s and 1940s. By the end of May 1963, nonetheless, when two census takers from the Dirección de Asuntos Indígenas arrived in the community of Ailío to conduct a survey of the population, they established a record for the household of don Antonio Ailío. Don Antonio had returned from his migration to Santiago and was married to doña Felicia Concha, whom he had met in the city and with whom he had returned to his community. At the time of the survey don Antonio and doña Felicia were forty-six and forty years old, respectively, and had five children. María Eugenia, fourteen years old, was in third grade at school, and Juana, twelve, was in second. Their oldest son, eight-year-old Hugo, had not been able to go to school because "he lacked the necessary clothes." The family had only one hectare of land and managed to cultivate half of it in wheat, potatoes, and vegetables; they had one pig, four sheep, and eight hens. Under the category "most urgent needs" the census takers wrote down many items, including a team of oxen, a plow, wheat seed, fertilizer, and a new house or at least enough zinc for a new roof. At the end they wrote, "[They need] more land, since they do not have anyplace to work."[6]

Doña Felicia Concha Arias was from Coronel, one of the most important mining towns in the province of Concepción. Orphaned around the age of ten, she had begun to work as a domestic servant in the house of an Arab merchant by the name of Benedicto Awad, and, when the Awad family moved to Santiago, she had gone with them. "I continued working with them," she told me. "And there, well I didn't go out anywhere, I never liked going out, in other words I was afraid. I was always afraid of things when I was little, not like today's young people who aren't afraid of anything, because my late mother was a very simple lady, she was from the countryside. So I followed in her footsteps, I had her same ideas and I still do." Even the daughter of the house where doña Felicia worked would ask her why she did not go to the matinee, "so you get a little lost," which to doña Felicia meant that "I could breathe a little fresh air, since I was always working inside."[7]

Since she was always inside the house, she got to know don Antonio because he always walked by on the street right below her window:

> So it turned out that he passed by on the street, right? And that's how he got to know me, I'd be looking out on the street from my window, the street was

right in front of the house and the living quarters were on the second floor. He'd pass by and look at me, and I'd look at him, too. And later, when I'd go out to buy bread or meat, since the bakery and the butcher shop were close by, he'd say hello. He'd say, "good day, miss," and I'd say good day back, real serious.

[Question: So that he wouldn't take any liberties with you, I imagine?]

Yes. So I didn't give it too much importance. And that's how we began to know each other, I began to get to know him and he got to know me, and he told me he'd noticed that I never went out. Because there were lots of young girls around, and they'd be friendly with me and invite me out. Later, when he and I had begun to talk more, he invited me to the theater—that's what people used to call it when you went to the movies, to the matinee— but why not, he'd ask me, when all the other girls go out, why don't you want to go out?

Only when they got to know each other a bit more, when even the lady of the house noticed and commented on don Antonio to doña Felicia, did she consider accepting his invitation. Even then she demanded that he ask permission from her employer because "I couldn't just up and leave, go out without permission." Only with the lady's permission did they finally go out, and even then, as doña Felicia remembered, "to the matinee and nothing else, and come home early, and that's how it was."

When don Antonio met doña Felicia, he had been in Santiago for about three or four years. Bit by bit, their relationship deepened: "He would tell me his life, and I would also tell him my life." Doña Felicia remembered that the relationship was based on mutual respect—"I honored him and he honored me"—but she wondered why he had chosen her. "At first I rejected him because I'd tell him, look, your last name—immediately I recognized it—you have an Araucanian last name, I'd tell him; there are so many girls here from your own race. But he'd tell me, I've always wanted a 'Chilean,' that's what he'd say. And then one time I . . . well, afterwards, I don't know . . . maybe it was God who decided we should be together."[8]

Don Antonio and doña Felicia spent several years together in Santiago, where their two daughters, María and Juana, were born. Doña Felicia remembered that once she and don Antonio had their picture taken together: "We're arm in arm, on the Cerro Santa Lucía in Santiago."[9] But the time came to return to the community:

He told me he wanted me in an honorable way, that he wanted to marry me, but I can't get married here, he said. I'd love to get married here, right away, he said, but I don't have my documents, my elders back home have my documents. So we have to go back, he said, I'll take you to the countryside, to my father's house. He also talked to the lady where I worked so she'd give me permission and the lady cried because she said she was accustomed to me. "But if you want to get married, Felicia," she told me, "what can I say, only I'm sorry to see you go." "I'm sorry too, ma'am," I told her. And so the lady gave in and I came to the countryside with him.

Before they left Santiago don Antonio and doña Felicia had another picture taken, this time with their two daughters. And they traveled south on the train. Inexplicably, however,

when the train left the station I just wanted to cry. It was really a terrible thing, I don't know what happened to me, you know I just couldn't understand it, I just wanted to cry, cry, cry, cry, I don't know, I just couldn't calm down, I don't know why I got like that. And he told me, but why are you crying, he'd ask, back home it's very pretty, I have little animals, a lovely orchard, apples, cherries, pears, everything is lovely there, he'd say. I have cute little lambs, I have animals, he said. And then he brought me here.

Judging by the ages of their daughters, don Antonio and doña Felicia arrived back in Tranapuente at the beginning of the 1950s, about a decade before the census. Doña Felicia remembers that her father-in-law accepted her right away. Don Antonio had told his father that she was a serious girl who had never gone out with anyone and was always working. Because don Antonio's mother had already died, doña Felicia immediately began to care for her father-in-law as well as for a brother-in-law who was paralyzed. She served their meals and washed their clothes in addition to caring for her own children, not only her two girls but shortly thereafter a newborn son, Hugo Alberto. It took her awhile to get used to her new life, for she had never lived in the countryside before. She finally "adapted," as she put it; but, she admitted, "I've suffered a lot."[10]

In doña Felicia's story, her inexplicable tears on the train serve as foreshadowing for the many tribulations that awaited her in the countryside, amidst the poverty and domestic obligations that, for years, will tie her down between needy relatives and her small children. Her suffering stands in stark contrast to the romance she remembers in her early years with don Antonio, from the moment she noticed him as she sat in the window of the house where she worked, until the day he confirmed his honorable intentions. On one side, her journey south begins a family life about which she can reflect with me at the age of seventy-four, emphasizing that "now, thanks be to God, I'm happy because I have my sons and I have my daughters, also."[11] But on the other side, the tears on the train ride began a life of poverty in which she would struggle mightily just to survive. "They've always lived the best way they could," doña Felicia's oldest son Hugo told me, referring to his parents, "in other words, like the salmon swimming upstream, it's always been that way." Hugo, the eight-year-old boy who could not go to school "for lack of clothes," remembered poverty as a lack of opportunity for the children, who "grow up incomplete, underdeveloped in every way. That's the sad reality."[12]

Hugo experienced these frustrations in an especially intense way because he was an intellectually gifted young man with a thirst for knowledge. Though he was late entering school, he said, "I didn't have too many problems" because his older sister and a cousin had already taught him how to read. "One's born with that kind of ability," he explained, "it's like a way to dig yourself out, try to climb up, you understand, like a desperate attempt." He remembered having that thirst from the time he was very small, taking advantage of every opportunity he had to read: "In the country stores where they'd sell us peasants sugar, *yerba mate*, all those things, our parents would send us to pick up what we needed. And afterward they'd keep the newspapers that were used to wrap what we bought, and use them as toilet paper. But before wiping myself with them I'd read them, that's how I learned, you could say at a very personal level, ah? And I'd read about politics, about the world situation."[13]

When Hugo was finally able to take this curiosity, this hunger for learning, to school, he encountered structural problems caused by his poverty and Mapuche identity. During this period the government of Eduardo Frei Montalva increased aid to the schools, and shoes and uniforms arrived to distribute to the neediest students. Don Lisandro González, the principal of the Agricultural School in Tranapuente, kept these supplies in his office. Since Hugo always "arrived at school badly dressed, with the same clothes I wore at home, no shoes, my feet covered with muck," his teacher told him one day,

> "Hugo," she told me, "I'm going to give you this little piece of paper so you can go down to Mr. González's office so they can give you some shoes and a sweater." OK. I went down there half dirty, half shy, because when I was a

kid I was a bit shy. "What do you want, man?" the principal asked me. "Miss Cheli sent me," I answered, "with this note." "Let's see," he said, "pass it over. Let's see, go over there and look," he told me, "if any of the shoes fit you." Then, with this secretary, I guess, I don't know who she was, they began to look around. "What's your size?" he asked. I told him I didn't know. "That's a bitch of bad luck," he answered, "you don't have a shoe size. Well, then, that's all there is to it. You'll just have to leave, man." And right behind him was this huge pile of shoes. Years later I would ask myself, and what happened to those shoes? What happened to all those clothes?[14]

Hugo considered this deliberate humiliation—obviously, if Hugo had never worn a pair of shoes he could not know his shoe size—to be a form of "racial segregation." The only explanation he could come up with was that González was settling a score with don Antonio Ailío. "I think he had a grudge against my father," Hugo explained, "because my father had worked for him as a gardener. And my father began to ask him about his social security registration, but the old guy didn't want to open a record for my father. And one day my dad just lost his temper and argued with him, it seems they had a pretty sharp confrontation." Whatever the reason for González's humiliation of Hugo, however, the young boy soon found he could not stand to spend more time in an environment in which everyone looked down on him. Even though sometimes he could forget about his situation and have fun playing with the other children, most of the time in school, he said, "I felt humiliated, sometimes all I could do was hide." So he decided to leave school, "fed up with my whole situation, of poverty, of neglect you could say, I didn't want to keep studying under those conditions. My father even hit me when I told him, how can you leave school, he said, my mother cried. But I told them I wasn't going back, even though my soul was aching because I'd wanted to be different."

In the Ailío Concha family, people narrate poverty in a variety of tones, from doña Felicia's dignified suffering to Hugo's anger, frustration, and humiliation. Don Antonio is remembered by his son as confronting his boss when González refused to open a social security record for him. But don Antonio himself remembers having to work for the same landowner who had usurped land from his parents, at one point even having to put the man's spurs on for him, kneeling symbolically at his feet. Perhaps here lies a gendered difference of experience between women and men. Because Mapuche culture reserves for men the majority of the public sphere and political relations, they experience a higher degree of humiliation in their confrontations with the outside world, highlighting their subordination and powerlessness and intensifying their anger and frustration. For women, their control over the garden plots and the daily domestic tasks has a double effect on how they live their poverty. On the one hand, it emphasizes daily suffering and the struggle to keep their dignity even though they may lack the most basic elements for survival. On the other hand, it permits them a certain satisfaction in the reproduction of life, be it through plants, flowers, and crops, or through the children who will accompany them in old age. But at the same time we see here a generational dynamic. Don Antonio takes comfort in the fact he has lived a moral life, despite the suffering. Even if only through reading the newspapers he used as toilet paper, young Hugo, by contrast, has been exposed to the dramatic hunger for justice that came with the radicalization of the 1960s. As a result, the wrath and bitterness he feels in the face of discrimination is perhaps more intense and certainly is expressed more openly than is the case with his father.

Doña Felicia's dual experience of poverty—suffering it daily in scarcity and hard labor, while at the same time taking satisfaction in the growth of children and plants—is a general theme in the memories of other women in Ailío. Doña Marcelina Ailío remembers working with her mother, doña Magdalena, on the family plot, while also recalling the fishing expeditions that Lafkenche families went on to supplement their subsistence. In this sense, it is not just statistics on cultivated land available in public documents that are relevant to our understanding of people's survival strategies. Even when doña Marcelina was very small, she carried water to irrigate her mother's garden plot: "We suffered so much to get water for the garden." At the same time, she remembers that doña Magdalena had a deep, subtle understanding of the land, fertilizers, and plants. "She taught me that animal manure is not good for scallions, she told me it gave them a different flavor, too strong, don't you see that some onions have a very strong flavor when you chop them up?" Thus she used chicken or sheep droppings to fertilize scallions and left the manure from the larger animals for the chili peppers and the leeks. Doña Magdalena also paid close attention to the quality of the soil: "My mom would say that the red soil wasn't good, 'you always have to look for that black soil that collects under the trees,' she was always looking for that."[15]

Water and the act of fishing, on the other hand, elicit memories that are more mixed, combining danger and abundance. "I never saw the sea," doña Marcelina explained:

> My mom never took us to the ocean. She'd go with my father, the two of them would go. She went collecting clams, we were little and stayed at home. When she went we'd say "Mommy, don't drown" . . . I don't know why we'd cry. She'd tell us "don't cry, children, I'm coming back." We'd ask her not to go.
>
> Once she almost drowned, after that we were so afraid, we'd ask her not to go anymore. We'd hang onto her crying, me and my sister who now lives in Puerto [Saavedra] and my brother José, we all felt the same way, like we'd never see her again. When she went collecting clams we didn't eat anything until she got back. "But go ahead and eat," she'd say, and she'd leave us bread, flour. "No, Mommy," we'd tell her, "when you get back, that's when we'll eat." She'd come back by wagon, really late, when she went. . . .
>
> People brought back wagonfuls of clams, several people went collecting clams and seaweed. That's when we'd be happy, the three of us, when she returned.[16]

The children waited, crying and refusing to eat, almost as if their sacrifice was necessary for their mother to return unharmed. She would arrive late, with wagonfuls of clams, bringing abundance and happiness as a reward for facing danger.

And indeed, the sea and large rivers had a power that both nourished and endangered life. "My mom would tell us, don't go there because there's a *ngenco* over there! We'd ask her, what's that, Mommy? And she'd tell us, he's the owner of the water, you shouldn't pass through there late in the day . . . never jump over the water, always spit in the water first. She taught us we had to ask permission to cross the big streams." Asking permission was the way to show respect for the water spirits and animals because the place and its resources belonged to them. Doña Marcelina also remembered that, in order to fish, her father would follow the crows because they would gather at the places in the river where there were a lot of fish. This strategy worked well for him until one day he met up with a water animal, a dangerous being in the shape of a bird, who was carrying a strap in order to trap unsuspecting creatures. "Right then my mom told him: 'Don't go back, Ignacio, that bird can carry you away and take you down into the river with it.'"[17]

Especially in her younger years, doña Magdalena was the spiritual center of the family and the main provider of family subsistence. By 1963, when the census takers recorded that the family needed food and that their land was exhausted, she was fifty-seven years old. By then it was difficult for her to collect clams as energetically as before; but in her daughter's recollections, doña Magdalena kept mediating between her family and the dangerous abundance of the natural world, bringing home wagonfuls of clams and finding fertile, dark soil underneath the trees. Doña Magdalena also participated in the Mapuche rituals that were still celebrated at the time, making *muday* and *mushka*, toasting the cornmeal and then preparing it "in a huge pot and they'd put it in these little clay bowls, and boy did that *chicha* drink come out good!" With her family, including her cousins who lived in Tranapuente, doña Marcelina would dance in the *gillatun*: "They'd all dress in Mapuche clothes and buy things, ribbons and such, and put them on, they'd look so pretty." The person who organized them and kept them going was doña Margarita Llancaleo, the *machi*, or ritual specialist, who lived in Ailío. "The late *machi*, she'd make sure the young people danced," doña Marcelina commented. "Yes indeed, she was really serious about it, she'd be barefoot, no shoes allowed, everyone barefoot and we had to do it that way because she ordered us to." Near machi Margarita's house there was "a field where people played *chueca* [*palin*]," inviting teams from Cullinco and Rucahue, "and it was done with Mapuche dances, because it's prettier that way, that's what I remember."[18]

The place of the mother at the center of subsistence and spirituality is also a strong theme in the story of the Ailío Pilquinao family. Don Martín Ailío Porma, father of Heriberto, Robustiano, Eduardina, Elisa, and Cecilia, inherited from his father, Nicolás Ailío, the role of *logko*, or head, of the community. His wife, doña María Pilquinao Mariñan, was from the neighboring community of Pichingual and, Cecilia remembered, "married my dad and he had to pay for her, like they did in the old days."[19] When the Ailío Pilquinao siblings were still small, all the nearby communities that were part of the same *aillarewe*—Calof, Machaco, Collico, Pichingual, Pilquinao, Rucahue, Lincay, and, of course, Ailío—would have large get-togethers. Grandfather Nicolás and Aunt Rosa, with their strong voices, would call out from one side of the Imperial River to the other in order to gather everyone together. That is also how people did the *gillatun*, and people would arrive on horseback and in wagons. Halfway through the ceremony the horses would gallop around the field. These get-togethers would last one or two days, don Heriberto explained; that's where he learned to play *palin*. He thought that maybe his reputation as an excellent *palin* player was due to the fact he always made his stick out of wood from the native *boldo* tree because it does not cushion the impact.[20]

As they raised a family together, don Martín Ailío and doña María Pilquinao experienced directly the pain of poverty. In 1963, the Ailío Pilquinao family was able to cultivate only two of their four hectares in wheat, potatoes, and vegetables. They had a cow, a calf, two pigs, four sheep, and fifteen chickens. In addition to the five children living at home with them, don Martín and doña María declared to the census takers that they also had "5 children who had died between the ages of two and five."[21] It was because of these very painful losses, Cecilia remembered, that her mother "wished to receive the gift of being a healer. We had been fifteen [children]," she explained, "and she was left with five." The death of one of her children in her arms changed doña María's life. "She took her sick child in her arms," Cecilia recounted. "She went to a healer in Machaco, she spent time walking around over there. And she returned with her child dead in her arms and when she came back with her dead child, she asked, she prayed to know about healing, about natural remedies. With her child in her arms she kneeled down, asking God to give her this gift . . . but not for ill, but for good. She asked God directly."[22]

And so, even though like a machi she knew how to read a sick person's urine, clothes, or photograph and had a deep knowledge of medicinal plants, according to her children, doña María was never a machi, but rather a healer (*médica*), because she received her knowledge directly from God. The mother's gift, her power for healing and knowing how to treat people well, was one of the family's most important sources of strength. Doña María's spirituality also marked the family's religious path, taking them in the direction of accepting the Gospel. "She decided to become a Christian because of a daughter, because of Elisa," Cecilia explained. "Elisa was ill and couldn't get well, and my mother, even with what she knew of healing, couldn't heal her daughter. So she contacted God directly, and asked God what was the matter, why couldn't she heal her daughter, 'even knowing that You have given me this gift I can't heal her.' And God told her that having given her such an awesome gift, He now wanted her entirely for Him, her and her whole family." Despite her great strength of personality, however, doña María always consulted her husband about everything, and they made the decision to become Christians together. "They'd talk and she'd say, what do you think, Martín, about this idea of mine?"[23]

The Ailío Pilquinao family's internal harmony, however, was unable to keep out the suffering that poverty and the larger society imposed on the Mapuche. Rubbing up against the larger society brought into sharp relief the pain and frustration of lost opportunities, similar to what Hugo Ailío experienced when he dropped out of school, remembering that "I'd wanted to be different." Doña Eduardina Ailío, eldest daughter of don Martín and doña María, was twenty-seven years old in 1963. She had finished sixth grade, which was more than any of her younger siblings had done. She had a hunger for knowledge similar to Hugo's. When she went to school in the neighboring community of Pichingual,

> I was always following the teacher around, and when he taught us something I'd want to learn more and I'd ask him, "What else is there, sir?" And especially about mathematics, because he'd teach me, and I loved to add, subtract, divide, those kinds of things, it was like playing with the numbers, it was like a game to me, and I'd ask him, "What else can you do with numbers?" And he'd tell me, he'd teach me, I liked that. He said I was intelligent, he'd tell me that.

The teacher was so impressed with doña Eduardina's ability that he suggested she move on to a specialized high school where she could train to be a schoolteacher. Because of her late start, however, she had only made it through fourth grade by the time she turned fourteen, so her father took her out of school and sent her to work as a domestic in a convent in Concepción, where she had an aunt who was a nun. Things did not go well for her, since at fourteen she had a hard time working at the pace they set for her. She returned to the community with some clothes she had been given as a gift and hoped she would be able to return to school. "I brought back a black coat they'd bought me," she remembered; "they gave me shoes, a dress, and that's why I talked to my father again and told him I could go to the teacher's high school with those clothes, that I was qualified to study. But my father didn't want that, he told me he didn't have the resources, and where would I get them, he said, so it didn't work out." As a concession her father let her finish sixth grade, but then he sent her to work as a domestic in Temuco and later in Santiago.[24]

Doña Eduardina remembered that poverty affected all aspects of their lives, just as it had in Hugo's family: "With one set of clothes and one little sweater we'd spend the year in school, that's all we had. In order to go back on Monday we'd have to wash the clothes, take them off and wash them and then put them back on to go back to school." She also remembered the humiliation her parents suffered at the hands of the more powerful non-Mapuches of their region. Her mother, for example, was an accomplished weaver, and, knowing that "we had no clothes," she approached the wife of don Alejandro Méndez, one of the smallholders on the Colonia Tranapuente, "and told the lady that if she gave us clothes my mother would weave something for her on the loom." They made a deal, but in exchange for the beautiful weaving doña María made, the woman gave her "some clothes, but they were old, so old! I remember we cried over how old those clothes were, and my mother felt very sad."

Don Alejandro Méndez had land, oxen, and plenty of agricultural tools, and therefore the Mapuche were forced to work for him. Don Martín Ailío got paid an *almud* (seven kilograms) of wheat per *tarea* (task); in general, people were not paid more than "food for the winter." Don Martín always worked with another man named Manuel Fuentes, and one day don Manuel said to him, " 'Listen, Martín,' he said to my father, 'let's play a trick on old man Méndez, with all he's stolen from us, our work, our energy,' he said. 'Let's ask him for potatoes and then we won't ever pay him back. Let's go work for him and play this trick on him.' So they got together and they went and asked Méndez for a cart full of potatoes, and they were given a cart of potatoes each. Then they never worked for him again."[25]

Don Heriberto, one of doña Eduardina's two younger brothers, also recalled the exploitative relationships they had with non-Mapuche small-holders. When they were still small, their father sharecropped with a *wigka* partner who was able to get loans at the bank. This partner would charge their father for the use of his draft animals and agricultural tools, since their family had none, and even though their father did all the work during plant-ing, weeding, and harvesting, at the end of the year he was left with almost nothing. Only when the children got bigger and began to work was it pos-sible to bring some money into the household. Once, when don Heriberto and his brother got paid, they each brought home a one-hundred-pound sack of flour and several other items, and still they had money left over. Their mother made *tortillas*, a special kind of Mapuche leavened bread, and they all sat down to eat. Their father cried because he could not remember having had such a well-stocked table, and afterward, don Heriberto recalled, his father sang in *mapunzugun* while chopping firewood because the family had finally overcome the most extreme forms of poverty.

What don Heriberto learned from this experience was that his family needed to cultivate the land on their own because sharecropping partners "were like drones who stole honey from the bees." When doña María managed to cure an old man whose daughter had promised them a calf, the animal became the family pet because she could potentially give birth to the team of oxen that would help them work the land. They even slept with the calf, don Heriberto remembered; she was like a member of the family.[26] But even when they could count on the wages of several grown children, don Heriberto's family continued to confront a system of extreme exploitation, one that could make a grown man like don Martín Ailío cry for joy when sitting at a well-stocked table or enable him to avenge himself only by stealing a cartful of potatoes.

Don Robustiano Ailío, doña Eduardina's other brother, remembered that between the ages of five and eight, before he entered school, he was in charge of tending the family's sheep. He stayed in school only five years because he had to go to work. First he worked as a day laborer, like his father, on nearby large and medium-sized estates; but teenagers were not paid an adult's wages until they could carry a large sack of wheat or potatoes. "I really knew exploitation when I was young," he explained, because even his father, who was paid as an adult,

> would work for those bosses, and they gave him an *almud* of wheat which meant seven kilos of wheat per *tarea* of wheat or barley, whatever needed to be cut.

> *[Q: A* tarea *is what can be done in a day, or how is it you calculate it?]*

> No, a *tarea* is seventy meters, seventy *varas*, long, by fifty wide, it's two days of work. So that's what they gave him for a *tarea*, and I could see this was a tremendous exploitation, they'd say thank you and that's all there was to it, they wouldn't even throw him a *peso*, nothing, and we'd all move around on foot and all we got was our food.

> *[Q: So you were really badly off.]*

> Of course, it was really bad pay. When I became, when I became a man around seventeen years old, was the first time I put on a pair of shoes and learned how to walk on them, because before I didn't know how to walk with shoes.[27]

When we read aloud the accounts of the Ailío Concha and Ailío Pilquinao families from the earlier book manuscript at one of our meetings in August 2001, don Armando Ailío, the eldest man to have moved to Huellanto

Alto, began to cry. He remembered the abuses he too had suffered at the hands of non-Mapuche landowners who made sharecropping agreements with the men of the community. At that time, he added, it was true that people had no shoes and walked barefoot over rocks and everything. When people got home and washed their feet, he explained, they would realize they were bleeding.[28]

The Consequences of State Resettlement: Erosion, Subdivision, and Fragmentation

In Ailío, people's memories combine feelings of family unity and maternal spirituality with concrete experiences of what it meant to be submerged in poverty's vicious cycle. "Like salmon swimming upstream," Hugo Ailío said. Don Antonio remembered having worked for the same landowner who had usurped his parents' lands, once even putting on the man's spurs. The only explanation Hugo could muster for the torment inflicted on him by the principal at his school was that his father had worked as this man's gardener, and they had fought over social security and retirement benefits. In doña Eduardina's and don Robustiano's family, all the children began to work around the age of fourteen or fifteen, as day laborers and domestic workers; their father had also needed to work for other large to medium-sized landowners in the area because he lacked tools, seed, animals, and capital to make his own land productive. And once people began working outside the family, labor scarcity at crucial moments in the agricultural cycle—either because of migration to the city or with the crush of work at harvest or planting time on the surrounding properties—made it even more difficult to cultivate one's own land.

Here is where we can begin to see concretely, at the local level, what José Bengoa calls "the hacienda-community complex." Beginning with the reduced size of the original land grants, the Mapuche were forced to become peasants and small agricultural producers despite the fact they were most accustomed to a less intensive use of resources that combined agriculture with livestock raising. "This transition from extensive forms of agriculture to a system of small properties caused a brutal rupture in the communities," writes Bengoa:

> The Indian was forced to become a peasant without having the know-how
> for it; he or she did not have the technological or agrarian background to

be able to cultivate a small property appropriately. Livestock grazing, which used to occur in larger areas, degraded pastures and soils when transferred to a small space; the natural rotation system among cultivated and fallow fields was reduced to the point that the land became exhausted and eroded. If the land grants were already given out on the poorest quality lands, the use Mapuche peasants were forced to give them only degraded them further.[29]

As a result of this process that began with the original resettlement, Mapuche communities got caught in a subsistence economy that could not meet their needs. Because of economic want, the communities functioned partially as a reserve labor force for nearby enterprises and large estates, developing a dependent relationship with them. By the 1960s, poverty in the communities had increased to the point that, in many cases, migration to the cities became a permanent phenomenon. Because they could not reproduce themselves by cultivating their own lands, Mapuche peasants thus became a source of cheap labor for Chilean investors and companies, both urban and rural.

To this must be added, especially in regard to the coastal region, the disastrous effects of the earthquake of 1960. In May 1961, Armando Holzapfel, congressional representative for the province of Cautín, wrote to the economics minister that in the area around Puerto Saavedra

> there are still families in shelters, some even in government buildings. These families, owners of one-room houses and modest supplies of food, lost everything. These people were workers. At present, they have no work and not even a minimum of capital with which they could undertake some small commercial endeavor.
>
> For them, there is only one hope to renew their lives and set out in search of opportunities that might permit them the reasonable and dignified hope of bettering their sad state.
>
> For them, I request the aid approved by the Supreme government for those left homeless in this region. They are living in the hallways of Public School No. 59 in the place known as Pichingual, municipality of Puerto Saavedra, Nehuentúe district.

Representative Holzapfel then presented a list of four homeless families, one of which was the family of don Domingo Ailío Currín, which included his wife and four children.[30]

In addition to those who lost everything, many lost lands in the low areas and meadows near the water's edge, because the massive earthquake caused the land to sink for good, and flooding in these areas became permanent. According to the data gathered by CORA in conjunction with the Dirección de Asuntos Indígenas, in a total of 33 Mapuche land-grant communities between Imperial and Toltén departments, 379 families needed to be settled on new lands because they had lost a majority of their territory. The group as a whole had lost 2,370.8 hectares, or 49 percent of their pre-earthquake area. Considering that these losses were entirely in fertile lowland areas, almost without exception the best land for cultivation, the devastation clearly was even greater than the numbers suggest.[31]

According to some, those whose losses entitled them to be settled elsewhere might actually have been the lucky ones because they got to start over on new lands.[32] In the other cases people just had to absorb the loss and, since the land was permanently gone, simply continue working as best they could on the hilly portions they had left, which were of poorer quality and also more eroded. In the community of Andrés Curiman, for example, the individual family surveys in the 1963 census report again and again that people had lost five, eight, four, two hectares with the 1960 earthquake and tsunami. The census takers recorded that the land left to many families was hilly and of poor quality; much of it could simply not be put to any efficient use other than reforestation. Lorenzo Traipi Lincopi explained to the census takers that he had lost seven hectares in 1960, symbolizing a broader problem when he added that he therefore "was obligated to find a place to sow outside the community because he had lost his land." Ignacio Yaupe, widower and head of household with six children and one grandchild, also reported losing seven hectares and was forced to sharecrop on the *fundo* Nehuentúe.[33]

The situation seemed even more dramatic in some of the communities near Lake Budi, where the lake became larger as a result of the earthquake. The census taker who visited the community of Bartolo Queipan, in Rucatraro-Budi, commented in 1962, "The lands are generally eroded and used up, and the lowlands, invaded by Lake Budi and its inlets. Poverty is palpable and generalized. People would like to move forward, but they need economic aid. Winter makes it very difficult to reach the city, because people must go by boat and walk a good part of the way. There are absolutely no public services in the place."[34] And in the community of Pascual Painemilla, in Collileufo, by 1964 endemic flooding had caused such desperation that the families had begun to fight over the little land they had left. In a letter to the intendant of Cautín, the mother of one of the most severely affected families explained that

> we are suffering gravely since May of 1960 and the situation grows worse every year, as happened in 1963, when two different times we had to suffer the rising waters of Lake Budi, since our Community of Collileufo has been invaded almost entirely by the new inlets of the lake, and the floodwaters last for six months.
>
> This year of 1964, the water began to rise in the middle of April, to the point where the majority of the houses had their floors under as much as 70 cm. of water, practically every family has to struggle and we've built temporary shacks made of branches in the highest parts where the water doesn't reach.[35]

According to Angélica Celis, this climate of disaster and insecurity had important Mapuche mythological referents, especially when people climbed the hills to escape the rising waters; the Mapuche believed the floods were caused by the evil doings of the malevolent serpent Kai-Kai, deeds to which the good serpent Xeng-Xeng responded by causing the hills to rise.[36] Under such extreme conditions, it is not surprising that people sought out explanations and protection from a divine power. Throughout the province of Cautín the number of *gillatun* went up significantly in 1960. The same period witnessed the dramatic expansion of Protestant missionizing. Specifically in Ailío, interest in the Anglican church began to increase. According to doña Eduardina Ailío, "The year of the earthquake, there was a little *gringa* living in Nehuentúe, her name was Leonor, and when she saw that people were suffering she came here to the community and talked with them, she told them that what had happened was caused by nature, not by God, that people needed to calm down. And she began to visit constantly, she visited us again and again."[37]

To the intensification of religious feeling, whether Mapuche spirituality or the stronger presence of Protestant and Evangelical religions, was added a bevy of additional sociopolitical changes that began to affect many Mapuche communities during the 1960s, changes that were perhaps accelerated in the coastal region because of the earthquake's destructive effects. By the early to mid-1960s, as we have seen briefly through the eyes of Hugo Ailío and in the new systematic efforts by the government to survey the economic situation of Mapuche communities, a new era of state commitment to the poor, especially the rural poor, was in the making. Even though in

Chile there had been, across the 1930s and 1940s, a period of popular-front coalition governments during which social welfare went from being mainly about charity to being considered a set of social rights, these rights had a tendency to remain the province of urban and often industrial workers. For rural or informal workers such as don Antonio, employers resisted opening a social security record, and as a result few were covered by the benefits available to their unionized *compañeros*. Domestic servants, moreover, a sector that included large numbers of young Mapuche women, continued to be invisible as far as the welfare state was concerned. Thus, despite important electoral and policy gains by the left under the Popular Front governments, they were less noticeable precisely in those sectors of the economy and the labor force in which the Mapuche were concentrated. This would continue to be the case in the more conservative 1950s, when the Popular Front coalitions disintegrated after President Gabriel González Videla outlawed the Communist Party in 1948. It was only with the emergence of the Christian Democratic Party in the second half of the 1950s and the election of Eduardo Frei Montalva in 1964 as the first Christian Democratic president that state policy took a new progressive turn that, with its emphasis on rural unionization and agrarian reform, began potentially to provide new opportunities for the Mapuche as well. Not only did state agencies begin to take a more empathetic and active tone toward the rural poor, but the possibility of real social change energized the countryside.

As we shall see below, as of 1964 an intensifying social and popular mobilization began to create a climate of expectation and revindication that would also inspire Mapuche communities. In Nicolás Ailío, an especially poor community in which the second and third postresettlement generations struggled mightily to eke out a bare living on their ever more reduced lands, an early experience with migration and day labor on neighboring estates had helped generate a culture of shared hopes and dreams with their poor non-Mapuche neighbors. From early on the two groups had mutually negotiated their identities and expectations at the local level, combining Mapuche traditions with relations of sociability and kinship that formed a part of rural popular culture. Across the decade of change that was the 1960s, however, tensions between different lifeways and political strategies seemed to deepen throughout Chilean society. In Mapuche communities, some began to ask themselves if it was really worth it to hold on to specifically Mapuche ways of doing things, or if, in the long run, it made better sense to establish an alliance "among all the rural poor."

A Poor Peasantry or an Oppressed Indigenous Nation?
The 1960s "Mapuche Question" as Seen from Nicolás Ailío

Poverty, migration, an ever-deepening embeddedness in the larger society, even the arrival of Protestant religions—all these tendencies seemed to combine into an inexorable process of pauperization, exploitation, and social change that stripped many Mapuche communities of their capacity to resist the dominant culture. In the community of Nicolás Ailío the process of pauperization had begun especially early, with the original usurpation of forty-five hectares in 1908. By the 1960s, Ailío seemed to represent all the tendencies toward social change in an extreme, almost exaggerated way. The majority of young people and even many adults had already passed, in a seemingly routine way, through a migration experience. Those who did not migrate to Temuco, Concepción, or Santiago traveled around the coastal region, sharecropping or working for wages on the medium to large properties in the area. In all of these contexts they shared experiences of exploitation, and perhaps also of sociability or solidarity, with non-Mapuche peasants and workers. They met many of the non-Mapuche poor in the nearby towns, such as Nehuentúe, Trovolhue, Tranapuente. They learned that some of the *inquilinos* (resident laborers) on the neighboring *fundos* were attempting to get a plot on a subdivided estate; they heard talk about committees of "aspiring colonists" that were trying to convince the Caja de Colonización Agrícola (Agricultural Colonization Office), sometime in the 1940s and 1950s, that more of the district's *fundos* should be bought and parceled out by the state. And in some cases, they heard, these efforts were successful, as at the *fundos* Loncoyamo, San Juan de Trovolhue, Las Ñochas, Santa Celia.[38]

The community also began to witness a substantial amount of intermarriage with non-Mapuche, in some cases—like that of don Antonio Ailío and doña Felicia Concha—as a result of migration. In other instances, sharing life experiences with poor *wigka* peasants who lived nearby might facilitate meeting and falling in love with the daughter or sister of a fellow worker, and the young wife would be incorporated into the community. Sometimes a landless *wigka* man, like don Oscar Jara, might arrive in the region as a migrant worker and end up marrying and settling down in the community. To these new social and cultural practices would be added, starting with the earthquake in 1960 and the arrival of evangelical religions, diminishing observance of the Mapuche ritual calendar. *Palin* tournaments were set aside in favor of soccer. And with the beginning of Frei's presidency and his new commitment to the organization of the rural poor and the intensifying expectations of agrarian reform, didn't it seem logical that the greatest possibilities for progress lay in an alliance of all poor peasants, Mapuche and non-Mapuche, in the newly organized Comités de Pequeños Agricultores (Committees of small agricultural producers) or perhaps in the reformed sector itself?[39]

The changes already under way in many communities, when combined with the new political situation at the national level, encouraged many analysts and even some Mapuche leaders to regard the cultural and historical specificities of the Mapuche people as having at best secondary importance. In the context of an increasingly developmentalist and interventionist state, strategies for social change and economic improvement tended to emphasize forms of economic exploitation and class identity that were shared by Mapuche and non-Mapuche peasants alike. The principal goal was to recommend social policies that would involve all the rural poor in a single mobilization in order to transform the rural sector as a whole. What was important, in this context, was to identify the enemies the two groups had in common and to build the kind of political coalition that could successfully defeat them. Don Heriberto Ailío remembered that during those years people were searching for an alternative within the Agrarian Reform that would unify Mapuches and the *wigka* poor; the idea was not to expropriate the non-Mapuche peasantry, but to unify the two groups in search of mutually beneficial change.[40]

The more radical sectors of the left, those interested in structural change in the countryside to whom the Mapuche turned in large numbers as the 1960s progressed, were also convinced that the Mapuche had stopped being a separate culture, ethnic group, or race. Alejandro Saavedra, an influential Marxist sociologist at the University of Concepción who helped define the MIR's rural strategy, made the most systematic case for this position in a book he published in 1971. Continuing to divide the peasantry according to race, he argued, only benefited the dominant classes, because it divided the dominated among themselves and created a racial justification, based on stereotypes about Mapuche inferiority and "lack of civilization," for the entire system of domination. For this reason, Saavedra concluded, it was important not to fall into a false separation of the Mapuche and non-Mapuche poor, for "their [the Mapuche's] class position is the same as that of any non-Mapuche small producer. This means that a 'Mapuche problem' does not exist separately from the agrarian problem as a whole, and that the solution to their problems will only be found in the revolutionary transformation of the agrarian structure and not in some ingenious or brilliant solution for the development of 'indigenous groups.' " Saavedra called for a general accumulation of social forces to help institute radical change in the countryside, change within which Mapuche peasants would necessarily be an important force. "To the extent that the [desired] change will affect the interests of the dominant groups, the attempt will generate conflict," he wrote, "and this fact cannot be diminished or avoided by development programs. On the contrary, 'organization' among these groups should be focused on winning the coming conflict."[41]

This radicalization of the agrarian discourse, this promise of a class unity that would bring about dramatic change and, in the end, restitution of land through agrarian reform had a strong impact on Mapuche communities at the end of the 1960s. But focusing on the communities preferentially through a class lens left aside a whole other dimension of life and history that was also important at the local level. Don Antonio Ailío, for example, remembering his father's struggle, found it difficult to contemplate how the possibility of acquiring a different piece of land would somehow provide restitution for the loss suffered in 1908. "My father, an Indian born and bred, is a very intuitive man, and he held on tight to his land," Hugo Ailío told me. "My father loves the land very much, as an Indian, as an *Araucano* he loves the land, he cherishes the inheritance his parents left him."[42] Thus he and a few others in the community held on to the possibility of getting back the original forty-five hectares, for what might be called ethnic reasons, a desire for the restitution due them as part of the Mapuche people.

Beyond the specific problem of land, a lens that focused on social class overlooked an entire fabric of social relations, a particular view of the world and of the land, and a system of labor organization that differentiated the Mapuche from other groups within the rural poor. A history of kinship with neighboring communities based on the exchange of women between lineages and on preferentially patrilocal residence patterns had generated a strong connection with neighboring groups that facilitated the exchange of goods and labor. These intercommunity relations were strengthened and reproduced through the yearly ritual calendar and life cycle ceremonies, in which people from several nearby communities would participate. Doña Marcelina Ailío recalled these practices when she discussed the *gillatun* and the *palin* or *chueca* tournaments, to which people from neighboring communities were invited. She also remembered forms of cooperation or solidarity practiced during harvest time, especially at the wheat harvest, wanting to re-create that sense of unity in the present: "I don't know, because that's the idea, when people work for me I have to give them food, when they worked over there in the community also, when we used to harvest wheat, among all of us we'd set up a common pot to feed the workers, for the harvest. We'd all contribute, a chicken, potatoes, noodles, whatever." She also followed established custom when she married a man from Pichingual, a neighboring community, but poverty and a lack of resources caused great tensions between them, especially when they were unable to make ends meet in her husband's community.[43]

Another dimension ignored by the overreliance on class distinctions was the reproduction of traditional knowledge about sacred places, medicines, and cures for illness. Doña María Pilquinao, who as a *médica* could read a person's urine in order to diagnose illness and provide cures based on traditional herbal remedies, was not the only person who had access to these more traditional forms of knowledge. According to Mario Castro, a young student who lived in doña María's household at the beginning of the 1970s, don Robustiano also knew a great deal about medicinal plants and had a close relationship with his mother. "I'd go out walking with him all the time, in the early mornings when a deep fog came across the river," he recalled. "We'd look across the meadows and comment, for example, on the milk production of so and so's cow. We'd always have a very deep conversation there somewhere, about why things happened the way they did, and I'd always find something strange, almost something magical in what Robustiano told me; he seemed so strong, he had a special aura, his words and attitude somehow seemed magical to me."[44]

For Mario, a fourteen- or fifteen-year-old adolescent who had left his father's home looking to become part of the revolution of the time, don Robustiano—"I remember him still, wearing a gray baseball cap and a gray suit jacket"—took on the qualities of a romantic father figure. Mario himself remembered that he felt protected in the Ailío household, as if they were his family; he could still feel in his memory even the texture of the sheets they put on his bed. When he went back to the community in the 1990s, he noted once again how special and strong his connection with don Robustiano had been. He still called him by his nickname, "Reuche":

> The first time I went back to the community, I returned with Enrique about four, five years ago, the first thing I did was ask for Reuche, but I didn't recog-

nize him. So I asked, standing right in front of him, "And what has happened to Reuche?" And everybody laughed, and someone said, "No, he died," but I didn't know he was standing right there. But then Enrique said, "That's him, that's Reuche." And I just hugged him tight, I was ready to kiss him, I don't know, but for me it was like returning to that romantic time, that time of sacrifice and courage that has meant so much to me personally.[45]

Yet despite the romanticism that characterized his memories, Mario recalled a specific incident that helps us understand a bit better the many kinds of knowledge don Robustiano possessed:

There were sacred places in the community. Right in front of their house there was an *enoco*, a kind of swamp no one entered, and one day I wanted to enter it and I remember that Robustiano said, "Don't go in there." He said that place had gold, but the gold wouldn't come out, I remember that really clearly. Now I think it was probably a kind of sacred place, a sort of natural place of worship that had a special force, some kind of power, a power that should be used only by a *machi*.[46]

Even in the community of Nicolás Ailío, then, a community deeply affected by the forms of expropriation, pauperization, and cultural transformation that were slowly affecting the Mapuche as a whole, people still wove strands of traditional knowledge and practice into a complex web that also contained new experiences and identities. But cultural influences could go in both directions. In 1967, for example, don Heriberto recollected that there was a great drought, and people responded with several gillatun, including two held in Calof and Cullinco. The elders of Ailío also held a gillatun, and non-Mapuche smallholders arrived with wheat, peas, and potatoes to make muday as well as lamb and pork for the ceremony. The smallholders obeyed the orders they were given, even taking off their shoes, although at first no one believed the ceremony would have any effect. The second day there were two machis in attendance, and one of them ordered that the ceremony take place near a small waterfall. After the ceremony at the waterfall, the sky suddenly clouded up and the rain and wind picked up. The smallholders were very happy because the crops revived, and everyone had a good harvest. After that the smallholders would ask every year, "When are we going to do it again?"[47]

The influence of Mapuche customs on non-Mapuche practices within rural culture emerged with special force in the experience of a couple who made their home in Ailío. Doña Marta Antinao Ríos was born in Chomío, in the community of Rucahue; her family had no land. Her parents had met in Lebu, and her mother, doña Juana Ríos, was not Mapuche. "My dad was from Puerto Saavedra," doña Marta explained; "his parents had their land there but they never welcomed them in, they hated my mom because she was Chilean." Thus they had to live elsewhere, and her father ended up share-cropping with a non-Mapuche smallholder. At the same time her family went to an Evangelical church in Rucahue which people from a variety of communities attended; among them was the Ailío Pilquinao family. As it turned out, the two families met.[48]

Doña Marta recalled that one day when she went out with her mother, "an envious woman prepared a *mate* and a fried egg." The woman wanted to give these to doña Juana, but she did not accept them; when doña Marta consumed them instead, she said, "from that day on I began to decline and I wasn't capable of doing anything. At the church a gentleman told my mom she should go to the lady who was such a good healer. The healer checked my body fluids and my clothes, and she told me someone had put a curse on me, and then she prayed in her language."[49] The healer was doña María Pilquinao, and that is how doña Marta met don Heriberto Ailío. They fell in love, and despite initial opposition from her parents, doña Marta moved in with don Heriberto, and they were later married. Doña Marta joined her husband's household, following Mapuche custom, and established a close relationship with her mother-in-law, learning about the cultivation of a garden plot from her as well as starting to learn Mapunzugun. "I would help her, I'd follow her around hoping to gain her affection," doña Marta recalled. "She was happy that I'd moved in with Heri. Afterward my mother got over her doubts. Then I started seeing them again; my dad had missed me when I left, I was his favorite."[50]

When doña Marta and don Heriberto's first child was born, doña María oversaw the birth at her house. They named the boy Martín in honor of the grandfather who, according to doña Marta, "was a very calm man, very loving." There was much joy in the Ailío Pilquinao household with the birth of the first grandson; according to Elisa Ailío, don Martín took the baby in his arms and presented him to the rest of the family, saying, "Look, here's my *tocayo* (namesake)."[51]

In this case Mapuche cultural knowledge — language, healing, herbs, cultivation techniques — was passed along from mother-in-law to daughter-in-law. At first there seemed to be a certain opposition from doña Marta's parents, but slowly they accepted the situation. So much so that when the community of Ailío began the process of the agrarian reform in 1970, doña Juana Ríos was an enthusiastic participant, from the occupation itself through actually being arrested for a short time after the military coup.

The anthropologists working in Cautín in the 1960s, who generally tended to work in communities that had undergone fewer transformations, like those in Cholchol or Maquehue, emphasized the more traditional strands in this overall cultural pattern. They described the Mapuche as living in a separate cultural world that, despite the changes and impoverishment brought on by state resettlement, exhibited characteristics that could not be explained solely by poverty or class relations. In her work on Maquehue, for example, Ximena Bunster emphasized family relations, marriage customs, and the gender division of labor. Milan Stuchlik focused on networks of social recruitment and life cycle rituals, seeing discrete Mapuche patterns and characteristics in sharecropping and the other labor exchanges that went on between families and neighboring communities in Cholchol. Although neither author completely discounted the changing patterns of migration, family structure, marriage rituals, and other customs, both emphasized the survival of a distinct culture and worldview.[52]

In a sense, then, Saavedra's more sociological perspective—one might say, more political as well—was constituted in direct opposition to this anthropological perspective, partially in reaction to the debate that emerged in the second half of the 1960s between the more "developmentalist" vision of change espoused by Frei's Christian Democratic government and the more "revolutionary" vision that began to be formulated from the left. If Saavedra openly sought to support the more leftist perspective about the need for a revolutionary change in the countryside, Bunster and others were part of a pioneering experiment in applied anthropology whose purpose was to improve the quality and effectiveness of the aid being provided to the Mapuche by the state. In this context, and in contrast to Saavedra, Bunster's main concern was not the mobilization or political organization of the population in order to effect fundamental structural change.[53] Yet what is most fascinating about these intellectual and policy conflicts is precisely the fact that they were mirrored, at the local level, in the disagreements within Mapuche communities like Nicolás Ailío over the best way to take advantage of the new opportunities offered during the agrarian reform era.

From Indian to Peasant: State Policy, Mapuche Organizations,
and Land-Grant Communities, 1880–1972

At the end of the 1960s, political radicalization and the emergence of the
leftist Popular Unity coalition created particularly intense pressure on the
Mapuche to form part of a broad front of the rural poor, leaving aside cultural and historical specificities in order to receive land. Under existing conditions, this position was strategically quite reasonable. Jacques Chonchol,
minister of agriculture during the Popular Unity government and previously
executive vice president of the Instituto Nacional de Desarrollo Agropecuario (INDAP) (National Institute of Agricultural and Livestock Development),
a position in which he had closely followed the Mapuche situation, explained
the situation to me in the following way:

> It wasn't always easy to find a solution, because they [the Mapuche] some-
> times demanded land that had been usurped from them many years before,
> and much of this land could not be expropriated, it wasn't within the cate-
> gories defined by law; often it was in the hands of medium or small pro-
> ducers. And so the government was faced with a dilemma because, first, it
> was not possible to expropriate this land unless it were very badly worked
> or abandoned; and second, we didn't want to create a common front for the
> nonindigenous small producers. Because precisely what the Right was try-
> ing to do was to create the impression that the government wanted to ex-
> propriate all the lands and collectivize all the lands, starting with the large
> landowners, but then going on to the small producers.[54]

It almost seemed that Chonchol was talking precisely about the community
of Ailío, although in reality he was referring to a broader problem of which
Ailío was a particularly dramatic example. In a situation like this, the weight
of historical memory, the relationship to a concrete landscape or territory,
had to be put aside in order to negotiate new terms. As we shall see in greater
detail, the need to choose between the land the state could expropriate and
the land that had historically belonged to the community caused much dis-
sension within the community of Ailío, a division that would only deepen
in the 1970s. Yet despite the drama of the Agrarian Reform years, Mapuche
leaders and organizations throughout the twentieth century had faced this
same choice between a broad front based on class and the specific demands
of the Mapuche as a people.

To a certain extent this contradiction was etched into the very process of military defeat and land-grant resettlement that the Mapuche people suffered between 1880 and 1930. The sons of the *caciques* who had been defeated in war were generally urban men, José Bengoa has pointed out. Educated in the urban schools of the region, they began in the first decades of the twentieth century to form organizations dedicated to integrating the Mapuche into the dominant society. Sincerely believing that integration into Chilean society was the best way to protect the rights of all Mapuche, these leaders saw this strategy as a way of fulfilling their felt responsibilities to their people as a whole. On the issue of the land, these leaders often supported the privatization and subdivision of land-grant communities because they thought these communities only segregated the Mapuche from the broader society and economy, discriminating against them as a people and contributing to their backwardness. An outstanding example of this tendency from the 1920s was the career of the congressional representative don Manuel Manquilef, who drafted the first Law of Subdivision for Mapuche communities (1927) and defended it in Congress. At that time, Bengoa reminds us, supporting the subdivision of Mapuche communities was considered a progressive position, since "in general, it was the most authoritarian sectors of Chilean society that wished to maintain the Mapuche on their reservations [*sic*], for they aimed to condemn indigenous people to a separate marginality, not integrating them into the development process but instead dealing with them historically as a problem for the police."[55]

Even though most Mapuche leaders supported the subdivision of community lands between 1911 and 1930, another tendency began to take shape around the same time. Emerging more directly from rural communities and supported by a number of more traditional *logkos* or caciques, this "radical indigenist" tendency was led by Manuel Aburto Panguilef. From the moment he founded the Mapuche Mutual Protection Society of Loncoche, Aburto Panguilef fought to preserve Mapuche cultural traditions and practices, to denounce the abuse and usurpations suffered by indigenous people, and to criticize state policy when it threatened Mapuche lands. In addition to its concerted resistance to the subdivision of community lands, which reached the point of demanding a new resettlement, Aburto Panguilef's movement hosted a series of indigenous congresses at which, according to Bengoa, "people prayed, recounted their dreams, sang and danced according to ancient custom, but also discussed strategy vis-à-vis the Chilean state." Among his many campaigns Aburto sponsored legal reforms aimed at engendering respect for Mapuche custom, such as the creation of a Mapuche cemetery in every land-grant community, something the government did not accept. He also defended Mapuche marriage customs, suggesting they should be recognized as being at least on a par with Chilean civil law.[56]

Aburto's connection to the communities and logkos gave him access to a distinct perspective on the importance of the land-grant communities as spaces of cultural reconstruction and resistance, spaces from which the new generation was attempting to revindicate its territory and identity vis-à-vis the Chilean state. This perspective allowed Aburto to envision the problem of Mapuche lands from a distinct angle, not only as property or means of production, but also as a site for historical memory and cultural reproduction. Thus the land problem—which, more than any other single issue, unified Aburto's political activity across more than two decades of struggle—could never be considered separately from the problems of culture and ethnic identity.

This sense of unity between territorial and cultural revindications did not translate easily into existing political definitions. On one side, one could not deny the importance of the Mapuche's connections to the larger society through labor migration and unequal exchange in labor and product markets. On the other side, a whole host of characteristics—a language, historical memory, distinct religiosity and spirituality, specific relation with the landscape and territory, unique marriage customs, family organization, labor and product exchanges, communal solidarity networks—separated Mapuche and non-Mapuche peasantries, regardless of their common exploitation by the broader society. In the 1960s, nonetheless, and despite the fact that people in the communities still lived and remembered specifically Mapuche forms of rural poverty, the pressure to sacrifice culture and ethnic unity in a struggle for the land was even stronger. This was because, at least in part, the land really did begin to change hands. In many Mapuche communities, including Ailío, people lived in prosperity for a few years, a period that today is still remembered with a certain nostalgia.

In 1973, however, it became clear that a lasting transformation would not be possible this time either. Perhaps this was why, when the military government passed an authoritarian Law of Subdivision that aimed to obliterate the land-grant communities as such, the Mapuche people responded with a political revival of ethnic identity. Perhaps this was why, when I arrived in Ailío in 1996, it was possible once again to think about the importance of Mapuche identity within political struggle. Perhaps this was why we were able to start, albeit with difficulty, a discussion on the subject of Mapuche tradition and custom. Despite this new historical opening, when I began working in Ailío people did not speak readily about the Mapuche side of their culture and history. Beyond the fact that most people had converted to Protestantism, which in general tended to look down on Mapuche ritual practice, I had arrived in the community as the friend of a leftist *compañero* from the old days; so that was the side of local history they emphasized in their discussions with me. A year passed before I knew that in Ailío people had celebrated gillatun; it was nearly two years later that I found out that don Heriberto Ailío had been a really good palin player. And not until 2001 did don Heriberto share with me not only his opinion about the importance of boldo wood to the power of a palin stick, but also the fact that in 1967 wigka smallholders had participated in a Mapuche gillatun in the community of Ailío.[57]

CHAPTER 4

A FLEETING PROSPERITY, 1968–1973

It was about three in the morning, Camila Fierro remembered, when she heard the knock at her boss's door. She did not get out of bed immediately, but as the domestic servant in the Landarretche family, when she realized no one was going to the door to answer, she was forced to get up. As she approached the door she asked the men she could see through the window what they wanted. "At that point," she continued, "looking outside, I saw a group of men armed with revolvers and shotguns, and the leader told me he wanted to talk to the boss in order to tell him they'd taken over the *fundo*, that all the gates were closed and that he shouldn't worry." Fierro immediately went to the Landarretches' bedroom to let them know what was happening, and afterward, "since I heard my baby crying, I went back to my bedroom and got into bed." She heard her boss talking with the people, but she could not make out what they said.[1]

Doña Violeta Maffei de Landarretche woke up when her servant knocked on the bedroom door. A few days after the takeover, she declared that "immediately I shook my husband, who at that moment was also waking up and I said, 'Juanucho, they've taken over the fundo.' Juan got dressed and went to the bedroom window, and he could see, as could I, that there were at least 20 people in the patio in front of the window, in addition to two guards at the door, all of whom were armed with firearms, because I could see the barrels." She listened while her husband talked to the men, and when he returned she said to him, "Leave them alone, it's not worth it, let's just go."[2] More than twenty years later doña Violeta, now a widow, remembered additional details:

We turned on the light and Juan asks me, what do you think, he says. Yeah, I tell him, we can't do anything, look at all the people out there in the patio. The house was surrounded, completely surrounded. At one point I thought we might go sound the alarm at the neighboring fundo, but we couldn't get out through the window or any other way. So I said look, it's better that we just turn it over. I began packing a bag with clothes, packing certain little things I hoped I could take with me, like my jewelry, my clothes, and such. Look, I said, I think right now we can't do anything else.[3]

In their testimonies and memories, the men of the family put more emphasis on the threat of violence they felt hung over them. Don Juan Bautista Landarretche, for example, testified that before approaching the door he strapped on his Colt revolver, and when he opened the door he tried to shine his flashlight on the group. Don Ricardo Mora Carrillo, president of the Ailío Committee, "tried to take the flashlight away [from me], cursing me." According to Landarretche, he had to "fight off the attack" by Mora. Years later Luciano Landarretche, don Juan's son, recalled that "there was a tremendous scuffle and Father even threw a punch at him, and at that moment I thought they would shoot Father, but under the circumstances they forced Father to hand over the keys." The two men's testimonies agree that a man wearing a brown leather jacket who was not a peasant calmed everyone down and gave the owners a deadline by which they would have to leave for Carahue in the two cars they had on the property. "I saw this man point a Colt revolver at me," don Juan added, "and the rest had revolvers and, it seemed, Luger pistols." Given the situation, when Landarretche confirmed that "they refused to budge, and didn't accept that we pack the most necessary things to take with us," he decided they should leave the house as soon as possible, which they did around six in the morning.[4]

Doña Violeta and her servant remembered the situation a bit differently. Doña Violeta declared in December 1970 that she took the time she needed to shower and dress and that they did not leave until 7:30. Camila Fierro remembered, moreover, that the lady of the house came to tell her that they had to hand over the property at eight o'clock in the morning, and therefore she got up "and boiled water and served my bosses coffee." When they went out to the cars, Fierro added, "we were surrounded by about one hundred armed men, who were carrying revolvers, shotguns, rifles and sticks, and they checked all our clothes and suitcases, to such an extreme that they even checked my baby." And yet twenty years later, doña Violeta recollected that in the end they had let her take her overnight bag with her jewelry inside, without checking it because she had stubbornly refused to open it, even when they threatened not to let her leave; "Then the *mirista* arrived and said, 'OK, let her go.'"[5]

Don Heriberto Ailío had walked from Tranapuente with the rest of the men, and they met up with the women when they got to the estate. "We put the women in a place where they'd be safe, and then the men, we went ahead to talk to the rich guy." In addition to about forty families, between people from the community of Ailío and their neighbors, a few "buddies" (*compadres*) from outside "supported us." Already at that point, he remembered, the majority of the *compadres*—by which he meant local leaders from the MIR who supported the MCR—were working with people near Loncoche, closer to the mountains, "so we had only a couple of *compadres* over here, but they were a big help, that's for sure, because it turned out they had a much better idea about self-defense than we did, so they helped us a lot." Don Heriberto did not remember using any violence against "the rich guy" at the moment of the takeover, though he did say they managed to search the house. "We had two, maybe three people who were prepared," he recalled, "so those three approached him. They said 'Excuse us, but we've taken over the fundo, at this point it's taken,' so we said we needed to search the house, and they went inside and did the search, and they found revolvers, shotguns, too, old carbines, and we took them. And then we told them to stay calm, to go back to sleep peacefully, but in the morning they'd have to leave because the property was ours."[6]

Don Heriberto is the only participant from either side who remembered a house search before the Landarretches left; possibly this was carried out afterward.[7] The testimony presented by José Segundo Pilquinao Ailío, from the community of Pichingual, gives us another perspective from the group occupying the estate and summarizes effectively this first confrontation between the peasants and the Landarretche family:

> We entered through the front gate and approached the landowner's house armed only with sticks, and our leader Ricardo Mora knocked on the door of the Landarretche residence, receiving an answer from a women who did not open the door, and I think she was probably the servant. She asked what they wanted and Mora said "tell the boss we've taken over the fundo." A quarter of an hour later Juan Landarretche appeared with his two sons and asked what we were after at this hour, and President Mora answered that the Fundo was

taken and he should go back to bed peacefully and tomorrow they would talk, because the Fundo was taken because of the need for land. At that point we were in front of the house next to Mora, in a semicircle, each of us holding a stick and Mora also. Right after this me and ten comrades (*compañeros*) went to guard the gates, and the rest of the comrades stayed with Mora near the house.

About 8 in the morning Landarretche left his property together with his whole family in two cars.[8]

To a certain extent it is natural for each side in this dramatic confrontation to emphasize points that are in agreement with their own perspective and position. The peasants remember their reasonableness and peaceful attitude in relation to the landowner, to the point where many deny having had any weapons; we can confirm, however, that don Ricardo had a revolver, and surely the mirista had one too. The Landarretches, however, remember many weapons; their domestic servant also, at the moment she got in the car, said she saw one hundred men armed with rifles, shotguns, and revolvers. When I mentioned to doña Violeta, her son Luciano, and her daughter Arlin the point of view of the occupiers, we had the following conversation:

Florencia: Now I talked with one of the men who participated in the occupation and he told me that they'd come, almost the same words you've used, they only had the kinds of weapons you have in the countryside, a few sticks, that was all they had, that's what they said.

Arlin: The people who had sticks were the Indians who were accompanying them, but all the ones who were miristas had machine guns, all of them.

Da. Violeta: The man you talked to, was on our side, or . . .

Luciano: On their side.

V: Their side.

F: I talked with someone from the community.

V: Of Ailío.

F: Ailío, that's right.

A: Yes, there were weapons, but everyone who was a mirista, in other words, that young guy, because you could totally see the difference, they had machine guns.

F: I see. And do you remember, since in the group you could tell the difference between those who were indigenous and from the area and the others, how many were in each group?

L: During the occupation?

F: Yes.

A: During the occupation I daresay we couldn't say, because, in other words, the Mapuches had their faces uncovered and the miristas, the few that made their presence known, actually had their faces covered, with the exception of the one that talked with my father and the rest were all hiding in the orchard and since it was night, I'd be lying if I said there were 10 or 30 or 200, I'd be lying.

V: And they were even in the barn, the one with the machines, there were people hiding there and in the garage in the front, there were people in the cars.

F: I see. But then the people who approached the house were a small group compared to all the people who had arrived on the property.

V: No, no, no, no, they were all around the house, because everything is close to the house.

L: The road that's in front of the house, in other words where you can enter the barns, there's a tall mesh fence. They were all standing in front of that mesh fence and there were these miristas on the ends, and others here in the middle.

A: But we couldn't tell you how many.

F: OK, but the miristas had machine guns and their faces covered.

A: Yes.

F: And the indigenous people had their faces uncovered, and . . .

A: There was even a woman with her baby.

V: Almost all of them with their ponchos.

L: The Mapuches had sticks, pitchforks, a machete, that kind of thing, but not . . .

V: They were drunk, because we could tell they'd been given alcohol.[9]

In this exchange, the Mapuche peasants were transformed into little more than puppets for a group of armed miristas who, with covered faces, were hiding in the wings, making it impossible to know if there were ten, thirty, or two hundred. What was clear, however, was that they were there, concealed offstage, pulling the strings. They had gotten the poor peasants drunk and convinced them not to cover their faces and even to bring their babies. This version of a mirista conspiracy, constructed more than twenty years later and inflected by all the accusations against the left, the famous fabrication of a leftist conspiracy known as the "Plan Zeta," and the images of chaos elaborated ex post facto by the military dictatorship, is a living example of how memory and narrative are constructed and reconstructed over time, depending on the available images and beliefs.[10] Having access to the discourses of the military dictatorship about guerrillas, revolutionary marxists, and internal war, the Landarretches were able to weave an apocalyptic version of what they remembered facing that morning in December 1970.

Yet at the same time, as we shall see below, extravagant versions of leftist conspiracy would take shape relatively early in the coastal region of Cautín, as landowners and rightist politicians in the province as a whole began to discuss extreme scenarios even in the early months of the Allende administration. In this context the takeover of Rucalán, the first such action in the municipality of Carahue, would in many ways become emblematic of the situation in the countryside at large and help feed the elite's fears, since many landowners had already faced or were about to face the same situation: a knock at the door in the early hours of the morning that would suddenly sever a whole way of life, an entire view of the world. At the same time, the need to defend their violent reoccupation of Rucalán during the court case initiated against them by the government meant that the Landarretches and their allies had to construct an exaggerated script about the need to respond to the left's violent threat. Indeed, it is probably reasonable to suggest that this script, subsequently enacted and revised in numerous similar scenarios, was part of the raw material that fed into the Plan Zeta. And then, ironically, the images contained in the Plan Zeta themselves flowed back into the recollections of the occupation that were constructed almost a quarter century later.

But Juan Bautista Landarretche Mendoza did not need ex post facto constructions to know he must react quickly. On 24 December 1970, a mere five days after the occupation and in a torrential downpour, he led a violent reoccupation of Rucalán that wounded three of the fleeing peasants.

Two days later Cautín's intendant, Gastón Lobos Barrientos, opened criminal proceedings in the Temuco Court of Appeals against Landarretche and others, charging them with violating the Law of Internal State Security (Ley de Seguridad Interior del Estado). Despite the defendants' early and masterful scripting of the leftist threat, they were unable to defend their property. By the end of February 1971, even though the state failed to prove its charges in court, the Landarretche family had lost both Rucadiuca (as Rucalán was also known) and the neighboring fundo Butalón to the Agrarian Reform. Life for the Landarretches had apparently changed forever.

"Take the Measures Your Own Conscience Dictates":
Landowners, the Government, and the Retaking of Rucalán

Ricardo Mora Carrillo, identified by everyone as the leader of the takeover of Rucalán, was the most seriously wounded of the occupiers during the retaking of the property. Interviewed at Temuco's Regional Hospital while he was recuperating, Mora gave the following account: "On the twenty-fourth of this month, several of my *compañeros* had gone to their homes and only myself and 14 other men, as well as some women and children, were left on Rucalán. At 4:30 in the afternoon, more or less, when we were all together in the aforementioned barn, sheltering ourselves from the heavy rain falling at the time, I became aware of a green automobile that had stopped on the road in front of the entrance to the fundo."[11]

The passengers in the vehicle said they were having mechanical difficulties. A few moments later more cars arrived, and then a group of armed men appeared along the tops of the hills on the north side. According to Luciano Landarretche, this group, made up of himself, his father and brother, and numerous friends, had already divided in three and "marched out of the three gullies in an encircling motion."[12] The peasants became aware of the presence of the invaders, and at that point the recollections of the two sides once again diverge. "Faced with this situation," Mora recalled,

> I called out an invitation to parlay, but they immediately began shooting, forcing us to take cover in the barn behind the agricultural machinery that was stored there. While they were shooting they also got closer to where we were and when they were about 20 meters away I saw Chelo Riquelme aim his rifle at me and my *compañero* Francisco Pilquinao Mariñan and shoot, wounding us both. When I realized I was wounded, I fired my revolver, using up the three bullets it contained.[13]

Luciano, on the other hand, was sure that the invaders first yelled out to the peasants "to please leave the property because we were retaking the fundo." He explained that his family "is not a family of delinquents, quite to the contrary," and thus they made sure that "there wouldn't be problems with bullets, dead or wounded." It was only after their warning was answered by two shots and, Luciano insisted, several dynamite explosions that "the shootout began."[14]

Curiously, in contrast to the image he described of a heavily armed group of illegal occupants who had dynamite, Luciano also insisted that the confrontation lasted only ten to fifteen minutes: "They were preparing a big party, because they had already killed a steer."[15] Mora, even though he emphasized that he only had three bullets, calculated that the retreat began after twenty-five minutes, toward the west in the direction of the community of Ailío.[16] Adding to this the testimony of others who were present but did not take a leadership role accentuates the human side of the confrontation. José Segundo Pilquinao, a young peasant from the community of Pichingual, remembered that there were about twenty people on the property at the time of the attack because the rest had gone to get food and because of the heavy rainfall had not yet returned. Like Mora, he remembered that at first, while "we were killing a sick steer," a vehicle with apparent mechanical difficulties stopped suspiciously at the front gate. In his retelling,

> About ten minutes later we saw six groups, each composed of about eight or ten people, appear from the hills that separate this property from the fundo of the Leal family. A person from one of the groups yelled out that we should leave the fundo and that they gave us 10 minutes, otherwise they would kill us. When no one moved, since our president Mora ordered us not to retreat, they began shooting. I ran to the barn where we hid with the women under the machines. President Mora was the only one among us who had a gun, so he opened fire and remained outside confronting the groups until he was wounded, at which point he yelled to us to abandon the Fundo because they had beaten us. We ran through a field and these people kept shooting at us, both in the air and at our bodies.[17]

The shootout bred fear, even panic, among the unarmed occupants. Doña Marta Antinao remembered especially how she felt while running away with her small child:

> That was really hard for us. When I left the field up there, running straight down we had to cross a canal. Some of the older ladies, they ended up serving

as a human bridge, because the young folks just got there and crossed first right over them. I had a brother with me, he was pretty young too, and he caught my little boy. I got to the edge there, and in my hurry I just threw the little boy across the canal. The canal was really wide, and I just threw my little boy across to my brother. I had a basket with me, the kind we use for potatoes, I'd thrown what I could into it, I thought to myself, well, if they're throwing us out, then we won't be back, so I took what I could in my basket and took off running. And I told my brother to go ahead with the basket and I'd follow with the kid. I'd put him here in front of me so that they wouldn't . . . I was afraid they'd kill him. I thought, if they kill me, maybe the bullet will get him, too, and better that I put my little boy in front of me.

We were desperate, at one point we even had to retrace our steps, but thank God we got out all right. Many people got hurt, some folks around here still have the nicks from the bullets they shot at us. And we got out over there, and came down toward Collinco, on foot, and some very nice people gave us shelter, they lent us a barn where we could rest because the weather was so bad. A lady kept us there a couple of days until we could come back home.

My husband was in Temuco, it seems he was coming back and was going to get off the bus right there and another gentleman went up to him and held him along this part of his back and said, don't get off, he said, because they're throwing the people off over there, do you want to be killed. So that's how they stopped him and he just stayed on the bus until further along, where we were hiding, and that's where he got off.[18]

A desperate effort to protect the small children, combined with the experience of solidarity among the bus passengers, also permeates the memory of doña Carmela Huentemilla, who had originally disagreed with her husband, don Armando Ailío, about the land occupation:

Yes, yes, he went to the *toma* [invasion] and I stayed home, I didn't want to go. We went round and round about it, he'd say yes and I'd cut him off, and finally I said, go. And later we went with another lady who's a friend of mine. Let's go take them something to eat, she told me. I took the eight o'clock bus and the driver said to me, where are you going, my dear, he said. To Rucalán. To Rucalán, he said. Yes, I told him, I'm taking some vittles to my folks over there. Ma'am, he said, don't go to Rucalán. Something's going to happen there this afternoon around five. And I didn't believe him, I'd brought all my little ones, my three little children. Later I told my brother-in-law, the bus driver said that for sure they were coming to chase us off. Don't be afraid, sis, he told me. No, I said, better I leave right away, even if I'm on foot the bus will catch up with me soon. But they stopped me, don't go, stay till tomorrow, and while we were discussing it the group arrived with the dogs.

[Q: The ones who were retaking it]

Yes. So there wasn't anywhere to run and they began shooting, and my little girl just stayed under the machine, my little girl began wandering around, in and out she went, back and forth. And suddenly I realize she's not with me, and I have to go back to get her. And that's when they started scolding me! Don't shoot me, I answered, don't kill me with my little girl, I said, because I'm not guilty of anything, I haven't done anything wrong, I said. And there I also helped out a couple of old men, I said to Bastías, he's deceased now, I said take my little girl so they won't shoot you. And I took the two little boys, one on each side, and that's how that poor man didn't get shot. They began scolding him, too, you're going to get away because of that woman, they said, and they kept shooting, though into the air. And that's how I got to the road, I ended up on the road with my kids, who else was left up there, I don't know who got the bullets in the legs.[19]

Three days later a judicial inspection found evidence of the fracas and the panicked retreat. According to the inspectors, the barn where people had camped had, along its eastern edge, "a shed with wooden pillars and a zinc roof where the agricultural machines had been parked." They found five bullet holes in the wood of the pillars, four of which showed evidence of having been shot from north to south—that is, by members of the group retaking the property. Among the signs of occupation still visible in the barn, like "leftover food, ashes from campfires, animal blood and straw for sleeping," the inspectors also found indications of a hasty flight, including "diapers, underwear, men's clothes. . . . In addition we found cooking utensils, spoons, plates, large and small jars. Also we found an abundance of ponchos large and small, shoes for men, women, and children in every size, even little woolen baby booties."[20]

By dramatically publicizing a conflict that had been intensifying throughout the Chilean countryside in the last year of the Christian Democratic government, the retaking of Rucalán sent shock waves through Cautín province, the Chilean countryside in general, and the agrarian policy of the newly minted Popular Unity government. Before the Landarretches retook their estate, the provincial government had approached the occupation very cautiously. The governor of Nueva Imperial district and the local police office had kept the case under observation, while Intendant Lobos had publicly criticized the action, emphasizing that Rucalán was an efficient and well-managed property (*"bien explotada"*) and would therefore not be vulnerable to expropriation.[21] Lobos and, through him, the national government would change position as of 24 December. In the original charges brought before the Temuco Court of Appeals, Intendant Lobos emphasized that in the countryside at that moment "one finds a double activity. On one side the exhortation of the peasantry and indigenous population to engage in illegal activities in order to solve their problems, practicing what has received the name of land occupations; and on the other side, pressure to stockpile weapons in order to fight off, also illegitimately and without the intervention of the relevant authorities, these supposed land takeovers."[22]

Thus the retaking of Rucalán brought out into the open a larger problem affecting landowners, who increasingly seemed willing to take the law into their own hands. For this reason the government brought charges against the Landarretches, making an example of them. Though Lobos conceded the existence of a potentially violent attitude among the peasants taking over the estates, he placed more of the blame on the landowners because government officials had confirmed, during arms searches on the area's fundos, that the owners of the estates had been forewarned and had therefore hidden their weapons. This proved, according to Lobos, that "government functionaries, in open defiance of their duties, have cooperated with individuals who are guilty of crimes against the Law of State Security."[23] At the same time, however, the intendant's public position was contradictory, since the landowners had ample public evidence that the government was looking for illegal weapons. On 20 December, for example, the newspaper *El Mercurio* had quoted Interior Minister José Tohá as saying, "We have very concrete evidence that weapons are being kept on the fundos in that region and the President said as much to the leaders of the landowner's organizations who met with him this week." In this context, Lobos's later declaration to *La Tercera* is also somewhat confusing. He said on 29 December that "the searches of the fundos will continue until we find the machine guns and other weapons the landowners have," and yet he immediately added, "but now we will do the searches without letting anyone know and thus we hope to find the firearms in possession of the landowners." There was a certain disingenuousness to Lobos's declaration, since by announcing new searches he was in fact ensuring that the landowners would have time to hide their weapons. One is forced to conclude he was warning them on purpose, in case they had not yet realized that the government was on to their activities. It was an attempt to control or discipline the landowning class, but without actually finding the weapons in their possession, because such a finding would have led to an uncomfortable confrontation with the landowner group as a whole.[24]

At the Landarretches' trial a lot of energy was spent investigating a mysterious mirista, the man with the brown leather jacket known only as "Aquiles" or "Miguel," who apparently arrived in Ailío the day before the land occupation and supposedly served as an adviser in the operation. Aquiles allegedly was wounded during the reoccupation but escaped without a trace. The investigation took the police to Puerto Saavedra, where they searched the house of Dr. Arturo Hillerns, the director of the town's hospital, and interrogated him and the social worker Maritza Eltit, who lived in the same house. In Temuco the search was concentrated in the offices of a charitable organization known as the Traperos de Emaús (Ragpickers of Emmaus), which was a frequent participant in the community projects initiated by the hospital in Puerto Saavedra.[25] Ultimately, however, the government adhered to a policy similar to the one followed with the landowners: rather than repressing the MIR or the MCR, the idea was to affirm state authority in the countryside and to stress the already established, legal plan for agrarian reform.

A good example of this official position is found in the public declarations of the governor of Imperial District, who in the context of the Landarretche trial "energetically [condemned] the illegal land occupations that, at this time, lead nowhere, since the Popular Government's wish is to carry out a profound and effective Agrarian Reform, properly planned, that will permit the incorporation into the national economy of all those who work the land." At the same time, the governor emphasized, after the takeover of Rucalán, "I have been participating in the consciousness raising and prevention campaign throughout the area, but especially in Puerto Saavedra where many landowners can bear witness to my collaboration in the surveillance operations prompted by rumors of possible occupations." And he completed his statement by deploring the violent events of 24 December, especially since he had been convinced it would have been possible to reach an agreement "peacefully and harmoniously between the occupying peasants and the owner of the estate, with the presence of a mediator who had been requested from the Labor Ministry as soon as one of Mr. Landarretche's sons accompanied Carahue's subdelegate to my office to report the interruption of work on their estate."[26]

The landowners' perspective, however, was quite different. Juan Bautista Landarretche saw in the district governor's refusal simply to throw the invaders off the land a total lack of cooperation. The following day Landarretche joined other landowners from the area in conducting nocturnal missions of armed surveillance meant to prevent additional takeovers.[27] The belief that the government would do nothing to help them spread through the landowner class as a whole. The landowners' attitude was given perhaps its most dramatic expression by Víctor Carmine, owner of an estate in Cautín province, deputy in the National Assembly, and original defense counsel in the Landarretche case. "The province of Cautín has had the rare privilege of being the guinea pig in the Marxist government's Master Plan to squelch all opposition and take control of its enemies' property," he editorialized in the local newspaper. According to Carmine, the government was motivated by the fact that the Popular Unity coalition had received the "smallest percentage of votes" in the province of Cautín, and therefore the government needed to wreak its vengeance on that region's landowning class. Although Carmine did not mention Rucalán directly, his supposedly general description of what the government was planning to do relied heavily on the events in that particular case. "It is necessary to take notice of what is happening to us," he concluded after describing, step by step, the events of Rucalán while characterizing them as a general pattern:

> We must be aware that, on any given night, a gang of delinquents can make its way to our houses, throw us out and do what they want with our belongings, since they can do so with impunity. And if any one of us gets the idea that we can defend ourselves and repel the usurpers, we will be jailed for being "seditious," "reactionary" [momios], and "arrogant," simply for committing the crime of wishing to live in a democracy and defending the product of our own hard work.
>
> Let no one be deceived and may each of you take the measures your own conscience dictates![28]

Thanks to the Rucalán case, this vision of a vast government conspiracy against the landowning class received national publicity. Not only did Juan Bautista Landarretche's photograph appear on the front page of many national newspapers, but the Sociedad Nacional de Agricultura, or Land-owners' Association, made him their cause célèbre, the emblematic example of the injustices the new government was committing against the land-owners as a group.[29] On 30 December, Minister Tohá traveled to Temuco, in reaction to, according to *El Diario Austral,* "the national-level commotion prompted by events in Cautín." As evidence, the Temuco newspaper reproduced on its front page recent headlines from the national press, most of which had been accompanied by a photograph of Landarretche and son, under police escort, arriving to testify at the Court of Appeals. The same day the government announced that Agriculture Minister Jacques Chonchol would travel to Temuco at the beginning of January "to inaugurate an emergency plan for Cautín province, including policies for the lumber industry, the expansion of beet sugar cultivation, the improvement of education and new scholarship programs, and the completion of a general study of the region's large estates in preparation for their expropriation by the Agrarian Reform."[30]

Yet despite all the attention given to the Landarretche case at the beginning of 1971, it is important to remember that on that same morning of 20 December, when the Mapuche peasants of Ailío, Pichingual, and Nehuentúe were taking Rucalán, President Allende was on his way to Temuco, according to that morning's newspaper, "to personally be brought up to date on the tense situation that province is facing with more than 50 illegally occupied agricultural properties." The same article quoted Minister Tohá, who announced, "We have very concrete evidence that weapons are being stockpiled on that region's fundos."[31] Congressmen Víctor Carmine and Hardy Momberg, both from Cautín, had confirmed the ongoing nature of the situation by entering into the congressional record a series of documents concerning land takeovers in the province. Momberg, for example, pointed out that forty-four fundos had already been occupied in the province by 14 December 1970. Carmine added more statistics, pointing out that "the first takeover happened on 12 June 1970, that is, during the last months of the presidency of Mr. Frei. On 1 September 1970, that is, before the presidential election, there were already 13 fundos suffering from usurpation problems."[32] This was clearly a problem that had existed before Allende took power, a problem originating in deep discrepancies over the speed and efficiency of the Agrarian Reform. And no one understood the frustrations inherent in the process better than Chonchol, a high-level functionary in the Instituto Nacional de Desarrollo Agropecuario (National Institute of Agricultural and Livestock Development), or INDAP, during the Frei administration and agriculture minister under Allende.

When Chonchol arrived in Temuco on 4 January 1971, bringing his ministry with him, he was willing to work hard to solve existing problems as quickly as possible.[33] The danger he represented to the landowners was clearly summarized in a local editorial on the day of his arrival:

> Mr. Chonchol is to private property what the jungle tiger is to the frightened and fugitive gazelle. Since he was named Minister of Agriculture the landowners have lost all hope of working peacefully. Mr. Chonchol was a Christian Democrat, today he is *mapucista* (in the case of Cautín we might better say he is "*mapuchista*"), and his political philosophy is Marxist-Leninist. He was an advisor to Fidel Castro's agrarian reform in Cuba and Executive Vice President of INDAP during the government of President Frei.[34]

Chonchol lived up to the landowners' predictions rather quickly upon arriving in Temuco. Four days later he announced that the Agrarian Reform law would be applied to the broadest extent possible in the province. In his explanations to the press, he demonstrated a deep understanding of the distinctive agrarian problem in Cautín, where the history of land scarcity was especially acute and dramatic among the Mapuche peasantry. He attributed recent problems in the province to the inequality of land distribution which, while felt by both Mapuche and non-Mapuche peasants,

> is particularly important among Mapuche peasants who, when their land-grant communities were first constituted, had around 6 or 7 hectares per person, but with the passing of time have been reduced to less than 2 has. and in some cases less than 1 ha. of exhausted or eroded lands which is, without a doubt, quite serious from the standpoint of their life chances and possibilities for development. At the same time, economic problems [at a more general level] have led to an increase in unemployment.[35]

What to do under such conditions? Whenever possible, Chonchol continued, the best solution would be the expropriation of larger properties, especially in those cases where size, inefficient exploitation, or abandonment clearly made the fundo liable to such action under existing law. In those cases, his office would simply gather the pertinent information in order to initiate standard expropriation proceedings. Especially in the cases involving Mapuche communities, however, properties tended to be smaller than the minimum size the law established for expropriation. In those situations, which clearly included Rucalán, Chonchol insisted that expropriation was still legitimate, because "the same owner often has 4 or 5 properties and in such a case the Law establishes that we add up all the properties, no matter if they are in the same municipality or province, or if they are spread throughout the country."[36]

Between 9 and 12 January, the total number of properties to be expropriated by the government in Cautín kept rising, from 180 (of which a third were below the minimum size established by law) to somewhere between 200 and 300. Among the 36 expropriations confirmed for Cautín on 4 February 1971, was, in Carahue municipality, the fundo Rucalán and Butalón belonging to Juan Landarretche.[37] Chonchol had issued his warning the month before when he announced that the criterion of size would be based on the total land area owned by a single proprietor, whether or not it constituted a single fundo. But for Landarretche and the others who felt the sting of expropriation, Chonchol was a Marxist who, by attacking the principle of private property, was changing the rules of the game. Under such conditions, they felt the game, too, needed to change.

"Bread, Land and Socialism!": The Asentamiento Arnoldo Ríos, the Movimiento Campesino Revolucionario, and the Community of Nicolás Ailío

In September 1970, a few days after Salvador Allende won the presidential election, a committee was formed in the community of Ailío to study the land problem people had been enduring for more than sixty years. In addition to the new hope generated by the Popular Unity's electoral victory, people were inspired by the wave of social mobilization among the Mapuche peasants of Cautín province that was being supported by the Movimiento Campesino Revolucionario (MCR). According to the manifesto approved at its congress that same month, the MCR was "formed principally by indigenous peasants, by Mapuches, who are going forward with the fence runnings [corridas de cerco] in order to recuperate their usurped lands." Starting on 15 September, when the committee had its first meeting and elected Ricardo Mora Carrillo provisional president and Heriberto Ailío secretary, the group met every Sunday at the house of don Martín Ailío Porma and his son, don Heriberto. Among the resolutions reached by the group, Mora remembered a few months later, was "to move the fence on the plots of Florencio Riquelme and Sergio Benavente, because these people had, many years before, included indigenous lands when they marked their parcels."[38]

Little by little, as people kept talking, they began to think about a different kind of action that would not be only about recuperating Ailío's original lands. In part, this was because not all the members of the committee were from the community of Ailío. Pedro Fuentes Pilquinao, elected prosecretary (*prosecretario*) in the provisional election, was from the community of Pichingual, as was José Segundo Pilquinao Ailío. The president of the committee, Ricardo Mora, had been born in the town of Nehuentúe, lived in the community of Pichingual, and worked as a day laborer on the fundo Nehuentúe, property of Mario Alvarez. Humberto Venegas Riquelme, a landless peasant who had been given a bit of land in the community of Pichingual on which to build a house, worked alongside Mora on the same fundo. Under such circumstances, it was impossible to solve the land problems of all the participants simply by running the fence and getting back Ailío's original hectares.[39]

Another reason for changing strategies was the extreme poverty and shortage of land suffered by many members of the committee, a situation that could not be remedied with the few hectares of Ailío in the hands of Astorga and Benavente. "I live on indigenous land in the community of Pichingual, but I do not have land of my own," explained Humberto Venegas during his testimony in the Rucalán case. "Until the takeover of Rucalán I worked as a day laborer on the property of don Mario Alvarez," he added.[40] José Segundo Pilquinao testified that he was a farmer,

> and I possess a property collectively with my four brothers and sisters in Pichingual that totals three hectares. My family is made up of three married sisters and one married brother, in addition to my father who is 82 years old. We work this land together, between my sisters, my brothers-in-law and my brother, we sow mainly wheat and potatoes and divide the harvest up equally, which is not enough to live even modestly, since the family is already numerous, for I have eight nieces and nephews.[41]

Pedro Fuentes Pilquinao described his situation in almost identical terms: "I live on land inherited from my parents, which totals one and a half hectares, and there are five heirs, four women and I am the only man, and I work the land with my brother-in-law Ricardo Mora and what we get from it is not enough to live on, since I have two children and my sister who is married to Mora has three, and all of us live together in one house."[42]

A third reason to change strategies was the inspiration of the moment. "We began this action inspired by the news we heard on the radio and read in the newspapers, about other land takeovers," José Pilquinao explained.[43] Pedro Fuentes maintained that the committee had been formed "with the goal of obtaining land through takeovers, since we had become enthusiastic after hearing the news on the radio and in the press, and because almost all of us are landless."[44] To this was added the support of people associated with the hospital in Puerto Saavedra, where a group of students and recent graduates from the University of Concepción had formed a Christian base community. These doctors, nurses, and social workers were young idealists who formed part of the Christian base community movement that was beginning among Catholic youth. Inspired by the Brazilian educator Paulo Freire and his pedagogy of the oppressed, they had arrived in Puerto Saavedra hoping to nurture among local communities the development of grassroots solutions to local problems. Using health work as a starting point, they made contact with all the communities in the region, but one of the people working at the hospital remembered that Ailío was special. After one of the committee's members was treated at the hospital, this hospital worker was invited to several of the group's meetings between October and November. She remembered that, in contrast to the committees of smallholders being formed by INDAP, the Ailío committee sought out broader participation, including landless people of both Mapuche and non-Mapuche origin and single women as well as men.[45]

Thus, even though the Ailío committee did not forget the forty-five hectares originally usurped by José Duhalde and later parceled out in the *colonia* Tranapuente, conditions in 1970 ended up taking them in a different direction. The presence of a Christian base community in Puerto Saavedra, a connection as well with the Anglican church in Nehuentúe, to which several families from Ailío belonged, and the availability of advice and support from MIR activists through the MCR—all these factors helped give priority to a different strategy. Of all the members of the Ailío committee, it was perhaps don Heriberto who best represented the combination of all these ingredients.

Along with his brother Robustiano and sister Eduardina, among many others, don Heriberto had grown up as part of the "generation without shoes" that had known extreme poverty in the community. From this experience he learned to question and to search out new alternatives. In the 1960s, doña Eduardina remembered, don Heriberto had joined the Church of God, a charismatic Protestant congregation, and became an assistant preacher. As of 1970, partly in reaction to that congregation's criticisms of doña María Pilquinao's healing activities, the family joined the Anglican church.[46] Don Heriberto and his siblings found spiritual inspiration in the Protestant churches, which prompted don Heriberto in particular to adopt a spiritual and biblical vision in order to more deeply understand his people's situation and to contemplate their liberation. Once, when he had crossed the Imperial River by boat to bring several people from Puerto Saavedra back to a committee meeting, he compared the Mapuche people to the Jews during the Exodus from Egypt. While he rowed back across the river, he commented to his passengers that the situation of the two peoples was very similar; both were chosen people because "Jehovah offers the oppressed a land of milk and honey." The Mapuche, he concluded, must continue to wander in the desert until they find the promised land.[47]

Crossing the desert, however, was easier with guidance and instruction, and for this don Heriberto turned to the MIR and the MCR. That this guidance had a moral as well as strategic purpose is clear from a document called "The Peasant's Charter of Liberation," a copy of which was found, with don Heriberto's name written across the top, among the many items abandoned by the fleeing peasants during the retaking of Rucalán. Parts of this manifesto were read by Miguel Schweitzer, the lawyer for the Landarretches, during his appeal to the court, and his purpose in so doing was to paint the peasants as full of seditious ideologies; yet even Schweitzer himself ended up calling the document a "catechism," pointing precisely to its religious and moral underpinnings. Among the parts that must have strongly inspired the Mapuche peasants during those years, summarizing their situation in the countryside, were the following:

> B. Never forget that your best friend is your brother in suffering, the one who has no land or very little and doesn't know how tomorrow will look for him, his wife and his children.
>
> C. Prepare yourself with your brothers in order to invade unoccupied or usurped lands, because land exists in order to be cultivated;
>
> D. Don't expect too much from the courts, because they have a class character, there are few judges who stand with the poor and most stand next to the rich, eating the good and the best;

E. When your brother is attacked by the landowners, or by the police who obey their orders, and is thrown off the land, help him even if it means risking your life;

F. Keep your shotgun [*tralca*, the Mapuche word, is used] behind the door and always well oiled so that you can defend yourself against your aggressive enemies, who are: the landowners, the bourgeoisie and the police who serve them, so that someday you can square accounts with all those who starved your parents and grandparents.[48]

During the agrarian mobilizations of those years, don Heriberto remembered, the "class politics" of the MCR that is represented in this document reached the communities. "When that politics arrived we said, this is our politics, too. If the *peñi* [brothers] here are fighting for their ideas, in order to be able to work, then we can also fight to be able to work, and if we don't have land, we'll take it from the fundos." As a founding member of the MCR, don Heriberto was an important figure in the adaptation and implementation of class politics in the coastal region during those years. In addition to Rucalán, he remembered participating in the takeover of the Taladrí family property alongside Moisés Huentelaf, another Mapuche leader in the MCR who was later killed by landowners during the attempted takeover of the fundo Chesque. He took part as well in the occupations of the fundos Mon--cul, Lobería, and Esperanza Norte in Puerto Saavedra, and Mañío Manzanal south of Imperial, where they confronted the police.[49]

Some members of the community, however, did not agree with the class strategy. Don Antonio Ailío Currín, son of don Andrés Ailío, who had suffered the original usurpation most directly, and himself among those who most urgently needed additional land, did not want to consider the possibility of a land takeover. "They went to take lands in Rucalán, where Landarretche was called the owner," he remembered; "several [people] from here went, but I didn't at all, and my brothers didn't either, well I had one brother who went but I didn't go." This difference of opinion caused problems among members of the community of Ailío. "Later they called me a coward," don Antonio told me, "why didn't you go to Rucalán and are slinking around, they said; I just didn't want to, I answered, I didn't want to risk myself, I said, you can go if you want." But at the same time, the people who had not participated in the Rucalán takeover felt supported by their comrades when, in 1972, they decided to follow the original fence running strategy and take back part of the original forty-five hectares: "Here there were about five of us left, but we had support from those, from the ones who took over lands in Rucalán, like Heriberto, one of my brothers, and a few friends like that who had gone in to take lands in Rucalán, they all supported us so we could keep working Astorga's land." In addition to having the support of the others, according to don Antonio, it also helped to differentiate themselves from those who were on Rucalán, emphasizing that they had not done things illegally: "Astorga himself told me, go ahead and plant, and later he told me, since we were friends, he said don Antonio, he said, take advantage of the land another year, because you're not in with those others. No, I said, not me, I do things the right way, if I can get the land back in a good way, that's fine, and if not, well that's just bad luck then, I said. But I'm not mixed up with those who went to take land in Rucalán."[50]

And yet, starting in January 1971, those who were mixed up with the Rucalán takeover were given the opportunity, for the first time in their lives, to enjoy the bountiful fruits of their work and harvest. During the first days of the new year, the government intervened the fundo because of social conflict and began expropriation proceedings, which were completed by the beginning of February. Moritz Milies Wortzman, an agronomist with the Servicio Agrícola Ganadero (Agricultural and livestock service, or SAG) in Cautín, was put in charge and, under the authority given him by the Labor Ministry's decree, he contracted as personnel for the fundo the same peasants who had carried out the original takeover. From that moment on, in January 1971, the systematic occupation of the estate began, which, according to the expropriation agreement reached by the Council of the Corporación de Reforma Agraria (CORA) on 3 February of that year, included the two contiguous properties belonging to Juan Bautista Landarretche and his wife, Violeta Maffei, named Rucadiuca and Butalón. CORA's Council based the agreement on the cultivation report it received the same day, which judged both properties together as poorly exploited, not only in technical and economic terms, but also "for reasons of a social nature."[51]

On 30 March 1971, Juan Bautista Landarretche requested the reconsideration of the expropriation agreement, alleging that his fundo Rucalán, composed of Rucadiuca and Butalón, was well cultivated, and that organizing production on this property was his only activity. His summary of the cultivation plan is especially interesting because of its differences from the earlier reports done by CORA: supposedly, of a total of 738.6 hectares, 668.8 were being well utilized, and the remaining 70 hectares of degraded pasture were "to be ploughed up in the 1971–72 agricultural year." Attached to his request were a series of receipts for seed and other agricultural inputs for the years 1968 to 1970, a certificate recognizing charitable acts signed by the principal of a school in Carahue, another certificate from a Temuco veterinarian confirming that he had treated the animals on Rucalán, and finally a certificate confirming the existence of agricultural machinery that had been verified by a notary public in Carahue on 24 March 1971. Despite his efforts, however, CORA's National Council in Santiago confirmed the expropriation the following year, citing the lack of a formal plan of cultivation, the "inadequate rotation of crops," the "bad quality" and "lack of adequate use" of the natural pasturelands, the "bad state" of the workers' houses, and a lack of compliance with social welfare laws. The Council did accept, however, that compensation be paid in cash since the fundo was deemed to belong in the category of smaller and less developed properties.[52] But according to his son, Juan Bautista Landarretche never signed the expropriation agreement. "They had been insisting that Father had to sign the expropriation agreement for the property," Luciano explained,

> where they estimated the value of the animals, I'm not sure, but they estimated the value of a number of things. But the only answer Father gave was always look, you stole my land and the only thing I can tell you now is go ahead, take it, steal the whole thing, but I'll never sign anything, because the prices you're estimating here aren't real, they're not even close to reality. So if you want to steal it, go ahead, but I'll never accept it and I'll never sign anything.[53]

While Landarretche's request to reverse the expropriation was still winding its way through the bureaucracy, however, on the ex-fundos Rucadiuca and Butalón people were experiencing a period of prosperity during which, participants remembered, the government helped out and it was possible to work productively. The inhabitants of the new asentamiento Arnoldo Ríos, as the ex-fundos were now known, began to know the meaning of abundance. When the state intervened the fundo, don Heriberto recalled, poverty stopped knocking at people's doors. "Since we took nothing with us," he explained,

> the State sent us people from INDAP, they were our ambassadors. At that time it was CORA, CORA gave everything, they gave us technical aid, fertilizers, herbicides, all those things, machinery, CORA gave out all those things.

They gave us tractors to replace the oxen; cows, seeds, fertilizers; everything the fundo needed for the peasants to work it, CORA would give us. And then, well, we got to work. From there on we made agreements so nothing would go wrong, because of thoughtlessness, and to get support from several communities. At that point we brought in the community of Cullinco, which was the closest, right next to us, so we added about six members from Cullinco and, well, they worked with us.

[Q: But they arrived once you had gone back. They weren't with you during the takeover.]

No, they weren't. But that's how we talked things out. How to make things better, how to do things, what was our interest in having Cullinco get involved [in the asentamiento] and how they should participate with us. And we found some positive things that would help us out, that Cullinco could support us, too, and we found that the leaders from Cullinco made some declarations in our favor at the [local] trial, and that was why we won and were able to work peacefully.

[Q: How did you organize yourselves on the land?]

Look, we worked the whole fundo in common, because at that time the work was in common for the asentamiento and with that we were paying back what they had lent us, in addition to which we were paying off the fundo itself.

So what we did was we thought about it, and we said O.K., for example, let's each take two hectares of land, for each member of the asentamiento, but since the members didn't have time to work those two hectares, they'd find a partner from outside, from nearby, and he'd do the work, cultivating the land, sowing the crop, putting down herbicide, or if it was potatoes, weeding by hand, all that work was done by the partner, and we'd give the seed, fertilizers, and the land. They'd give the work, two crops, weeding, all those things.

[Q: And at the end, the harvest was split in half, one half for you and one half for your partner?]

Yes, that's right.[54]

The asentamiento Arnoldo Ríos, as don Heriberto recalled, received aid from the state to assure the economic security and prosperity of the *asen-*

tados, or members of the asentamiento. CORA, for example, built twenty-three new houses for *asentado* families, who in 1973 totaled thirty-six individuals in thirty-one family groups. Between 1971 and 1973, moreover, people also received fertilizer; seed for pasture; crop seeds for wheat, barley, corn, potato, peas, and garlic; and four tractors, two plows, one sowing machine, a thresher, and a weeding machine. Don Heriberto also recalled that, in the lowlands near the river that regularly flooded during rainy season, they constructed a system of drainage canals that allowed them to sow crops. The Corporación de Fomento a la Producción (CORFO; Corporation for the Advancement of Production), a government investment agency, took charge of the livestock plan, which included a dairy and had accumulated, by 1973, 112 cows, 36 heifers, 48 calves, 5 mature and 31 young bulls, and 29 oxen. Additional animals included 4 horses, 19 sows, and 103 piglets three months old. For a group of asentados who had grown up in poverty, who had lacked everything from a pair of shoes to the oxen and agricultural tools needed to cultivate the land, this was abundance indeed.[55]

The asentamiento Arnoldo Ríos mixed Christian Democratic agrarian reform policy, mirista politics, and Mapuche exchange relations. As an asentamiento created under the 1967 Agrarian Reform law passed by the government of Eduardo Frei, Arnoldo Ríos was a cooperative composed of individual families in which heads of household, in collaboration with state representatives sent by CORA, defined a production plan for the property. As don Heriberto explained, the asentados worked the land in common, and part of what they produced went to pay back the loans and the agrarian debt. While the majority of the property was farmed collectively, each household was also given about two hectares of private usufruct. In contrast to other experiences with the asentamiento model, however, on Arnoldo Ríos there was no effort among the asentados to differentiate themselves from the surrounding peasant population.

One reason for this was that on Rucalán there had not been a large or stable resident labor force (*inquilinos*),[56] which in other cases served as the base population for the cooperative. Thus most people came from outside to form the asentamiento Arnoldo Ríos, minimizing the kinds of divisions between asentados and outsiders (*afuerinos*) that were fairly common on other asentamientos. All the asentados, moreover, had lacked land to farm. Of the thirty-six individuals counted in the census at the end of 1973, seventeen were Mapuche and nineteen were not. Among the asentados who were not Mapuche, one had been an *inquilino* on Rucalán, one had sharecropped with Mapuche peasants, thirteen had worked as day laborers on the estates or smaller properties of the region, and of the remaining four two were workers, one was a student, and one a petty merchant. The seventeen Mapuche asentados were divided fairly evenly between those who were landless and those who had had inheritance rights, along with numerous brothers and sisters, to a single small plot in a land-grant community. Slightly less than half had also sharecropped with non-Mapuche on the fundos or medium-sized properties nearby, whereas the rest had worked as an *inquilino* (on Rucalán) or as day laborers on other estates.[57]

A second reason for the relatively good relations the asentados maintained with surrounding peasants and communities was the strong presence of the MIR and the MCR, both among the Mapuche leaders of the cooperative and in the region in general. Even the name of the cooperative made clear that this was not an average asentamiento: Arnoldo Ríos had been a mirista student at the University of Concepción who was killed in a confrontation between mirista and Communist student groups. As we have seen, moreover, don Heriberto remembered that there were relations of solidarity and reciprocity with people in the rest of the coastal zone, as he himself participated in the land invasions of several other nearby estates. From the very beginning, therefore, the presence of the MCR helped prevent the formation of a newly prosperous group of small proprietors eager to differentiate themselves from the surrounding peasant population, a problem generated in many other parts of the country by the mix of a cooperative with private family enterprises that was represented by the asentamiento model.[58]

An important aspect of the asentamiento's success that did not depend either on the MIR and the MCR or on the state was its reliance on the preexisting network of solidarity and exchange among the area's Mapuche communities. In many cases, since the asentados were busy working on the communal enterprise, the two hectares of private usufruct allocated to each household were cultivated in a sharecropping agreement with a partner from one of the surrounding communities. Though sharecropping with peasants outside the asentamientos seems to have been a common practice during those years, on the asentamiento Arnoldo Ríos the form of sharecropping was defined according to Mapuche norms of exchange and kinship. This was don Robustiano's experience, for he sharecropped his brother

Heriberto's two hectares on Rucalán while also working the family lands in the community of Ailío. The Popular Unity years were a time of plenty, don Robustiano remembered:

> That year we all became active, in our work, too, because at the time of the Popular Unity it was the first time we used fertilizer. The government at the time gave us broad technological support, there was a lot of help in the countryside, because at the time you could almost trade a sack of fertilizer for a sack of wheat, they cost about the same. Not like today when sometimes we have to pay for a sack of fertilizer with 10 sacks of wheat. So with all of that the youth began to make money, the young folk, boys 15, 16 years old, already went around with money.[59]

The combination of Mapuche customary relations with the abundance of state aid for agriculture yielded a prosperity no one had previously experienced. In addition to their agreements with sharecroppers from the communities, the asentados developed a system based on kinship that distributed food and other necessities from the asentamiento to the nearby communities. "We worked hard, we saw tremendous improvements," don Heriberto explained.

> In those days I was newly married. There was enough so my family could stock up, we never lacked for bread, for my house, for my family, and in addition back then we had an uncle living with us, and my mother and father who are since deceased. So I'd give to them, from what I made I'd give to them, and I could support two households.

> [Q: Your parents also lived on Rucalán?]

> No, they lived here [in Tranapuente].

> [Q: So you'd bring things back here.]

> Back here, exactly. CORA did a good job then, because they gave us the right to distribute some of what we planted to people. The entire community, all of it communal work, what we planted was tremendously productive. So what we did, we'd say, OK, we'll give people 600 kilos per load, so we'd give out, say, wheat or potatoes by the load. Each family would get, for example, six sacks of wheat per load. And that's how we maintained ourselves and bought the other things we needed. Because we also had a cooperative. We were able to keep the cooperative stocked, in fact we watched it grow, we were able to

do things right in those years, no one was left owing money, we all came out well. Things were well organized back then.[60]

Visitors from the outside were impressed by the amount of work and the degree of optimism they witnessed. Mario Castro, then a student in the mirista student organization, the Frente Estudiantil Revolucionario (Revolutionary student front, or FER), arrived at Rucalán at the end of August or beginning of September 1972, staying in the house of Heriberto Ailío and Marta Antinao. "I remember, for example, the image of this elderly couple," he told me,

> I thought the old man was the most beautiful old man I'd ever seen, bald with just a fringe of white hair, but he had such a special face . . . he'd been a miner, and he'd participated in the takeover . . . they were a couple, and I noticed they were very close, so for me they were, I tell you, like the prototype of the real family. I'd always go drink *mate* with them, and eat potatoes, and at a certain moment I also helped them plant potatoes, throwing down the potatoes while riding on a horse, so when I remember Arnoldo Ríos, I think of them.

Mario Castro felt great satisfaction when he participated in the social life of the place. In one case, a wedding celebration filled him with a sense of closeness and friendship toward the asentado families:

> They were from a group of houses that had been built in the lower part of the estate, near the old landowner's house, there was a group of houses down there that were built really close together, almost like an urban neighborhood; they were houses that looked almost like emergency dwellings, yet they were high quality. Well, I've been by there recently and they aren't there anymore. But that's where the couple was from who decided to get married. I know there was a Mapuche ceremony but I didn't participate in that, and the next day they had the official civil ceremony with all the people, and I was the only *wigka*, the only one from outside who was there and got invited.
>
> I felt really close to them. A few days before I'd received some money that the Party used to send me every month, what today would be worth 30 *lucas* (30,000 pesos), something like that, and I remember that I bought them a pot, I'd never given a gift to anyone and I gave them a pot. Then I shared in the party, the barbecue, the wine, and after nightfall they passed me a guitar. I don't know how to play the guitar, but people seemed to think I did know how, I don't know how long I played and sang, but people began to dance.[61]

Castro's memories, even though filtered through two decades of nostalgia, give us access to a climate of solidarity and cooperation, a sense of celebration, optimism, and joy that was part of people's lives during these years of plenty, when they were able to form, with the help of a friendly government, a cooperative that paid its debts and fed its members and could distribute the surplus to kin in neighboring communities. Castro also traveled the area and participated actively in agricultural work, getting to know the situation of people who lived in various parts of the asentamiento Arnoldo Ríos:

> I'd get together with them and go out to look around, I'd go on horseback to Butalón, which is behind Arnoldo Ríos, I'd visit the comrades up there and share their food, I'd participate in the potato harvest, I don't know, I'd hitch the carts to the tractors. I was involved in almost all the agricultural activities, like the *mingacos* (reciprocal labor exchanges) for planting potatoes, the *mingacos* organized by the community. I'd travel through all the zones, in the forests, too, I'd go up to the mining area, the Santa Celia mines, I'd go up to Butalón, I traveled around a lot.
>
> When the peasants were in charge there was a lot of work, a lot of movement. People were very reliable. I remember the potato campaign, when the community got organized to harvest all the potatoes, and to fix up the fields. I never saw, let me tell you, thinking about it now, I never saw unnecessary cutting in the forests, I never saw depredation of resources in the forest. What I did see was a lot of commitment, a lot of strength, people got up, the comrades got up at seven in the morning to start up the tractors, there were several tractors. I saw a huge accumulation of potatoes, everyone was involved in planting, I participated in December, I don't know how it had been before.
>
> But there was a lot of work, every family, in all the comrades' houses there were rooms full of potato seed. That's what I saw the most, potatoes; and also a lot of wheat. But all the fields, at that point when the peasants were in charge, the fields were clean, they were well cultivated, you saw a lot of animals.[62]

These remembered accomplishments should not close our eyes to the problems that also existed. Not everyone who lived on or visited the cooperative agreed that it was as well organized as possible. Doña Eduardina Ailío, for example, remembered that people fought and drank too much, "that they didn't work, that they went around drunk, all they did was drink, get drunk, and then go off drunk to work. What didn't they do, they crashed the tractor, broke it into pieces. Sure, those who worked, it must have given them a good return, but I didn't understand that part too well. But I saw they drank too much, there were too many binges, even the women fought, they acted like those women from the slums [*callampas*], what didn't they say to each other."[63] Her brother Robustiano agreed in part, saying there were "a lot of drunken binges and little responsibility for the work . . . in part they produced, and in part they didn't. But the part that was well worked turned out well, there was production, productivity, all of that. There was responsibility."[64]

Some people resented the lack of sensitivity MIR organizers showed concerning the issue of religion. According to Cecilia Ailío, when the MIR organizers who arrived "heard the word God their hair stood on end, they didn't want to have anything to do with God." This lack of religiosity was in part responsible, according to the Ailío sisters, for the fact that the work and the organization were not as good as they could have been and also alienated some people from the organization. As doña Eduardina put it, echoing in part the original biblical vision of her brother Heriberto about the liberation of oppressed peoples,

> I think that's another reason why I didn't give of myself that much, because I think all things come out better if you do them with God, they always turn out better than if you do them without God. We see this in the case of Moses, for example, who got his people out; Moses got them out with God, but there were people who really weren't with God. Moses wanted people to work together, to stay united. The people who didn't agree with him, they weren't with God, and they were always doing things backwards and it's always been the same. God wants us to work that way, it's always been God's will that we be together working. For some reason he said six days are for work, and the seventh is for God. That means that six days are for working, you need to be there working, doing everything that needs to be done, because we all depend on our work. If you're a peasant you work the land, everything that has to do with the land, and on the seventh day you rest. That's always been God's commandment. And if we acted that way, I think our government would also work out all right.[65]

Don Robustiano also remembered a lack of discipline. He attributed it to the political changes of the time, which he felt had confused people on the issue of work and on what was expected from them for the purposes of production. "In part it was good because there was work," he said, "but people behaved badly, in my opinion, because they took advantage of the licentiousness. People said there were no more bosses. So when one asked a comrade to work, they'd get angry because they said there were no more bosses. So that wasn't good."[66] His sister Elisa, married to the young student Rudecindo Moraga, remembered as well that her husband "worked in the asentamiento, but he was the one who got the least money out of it, because he was careless, they said he didn't work, he just stood around, or else he'd leave and go somewhere else."[67]

Mario Castro did not remember these problems. In addition to working well and in solidarity, he observed,

> People had good relations between them, I never saw a fight . . . or an injustice and that's even though I was involved in family life, I'd go into one house, then another, and I never saw anything strange, no argument, nothing. I saw a really good relationship among the workers, there was a kind of cooperative where people went to get sugar, *yerba mate*, noodles, lard, the kinds of things you need to maintain a family. People bought things, too. I remember that one time a shipment of onions arrived. So I never saw any kind of . . . meanness or jealousy [*envidia*].[68]

Finally, among the possible problems, the people I interviewed also mentioned issues of culture and gender. "It's just that there weren't that many things for women to do," doña Eduardina recalled; "just the housework." Her sister Elisa agreed: "The women only had meetings, but they didn't make any progress, they didn't have anything, not like now when women are more advanced."[69] Doña Marta, sister-in-law to both, remembered a more positive situation for women. "I liked it a lot," she explained. "I raised beautiful pigs, very good pigs." She was also lucky with her garden plot, which was near the water; she planted many flowers and taught the younger women how to "cultivate the garden [*huertear*]." "We had a Mothers' Center," she remembered, "and they knitted, spun, embroidered tablecloths."[70] On the issue of indigenous culture, Castro recalled that "in those days people didn't understand the cultural issues, the ethnic question, in other words, they didn't differentiate between the Mapuche peasant and the *wigka* peasant. And well, I'm still convinced that this was one of the biggest problems we had back then."[71]

To a certain extent, the problems on the asentamiento Arnoldo Ríos recounted by residents and visitors were typical of the model of agrarian mobilization people used at that time. Like other projects on the left, the Popular Unity government emphasized unity among all the rural poor in order to find a common solution in which they could all participate. "That was a class struggle," don Heriberto Ailío explained. "We marked the stages together, between *wigka* and Mapuche."[72] Class unity was a goal shared by all the political parties that made up the Popular Unity coalition and also by the MIR and the MCR. As Cautín's Regional Secretariat for the MIR declared in a policy statement published in the mirista publication *Punto Final*, "This struggle will be carried out by the Movimiento Campesino Revolucionario (MCR), defined as a class front that brings together all the exploited of the countryside."[73] As we saw in chapter 3, moreover, the need to form a class alliance in order to achieve the restitution of usurped land had been debated in the Mapuche movement since the 1920s. And indeed, such an alliance had its positive aspects, for it opened up the possibility of a broader solution to the agrarian problem than any smaller group of peasants could achieve on their own. At the same time, however, in cases like Arnoldo Ríos the language and practice of class tended to elide the importance of Mapuche traditions, whether in the exchange of goods or labor or in the ceremonies that marked spirituality and life cycle transitions. "I know there was a Mapuche ceremony but I didn't participate in that," Castro commented in describing the wedding at the asentamiento he had attended. In that period, indigenous cultural practices were relegated to a secondary, almost clandestine, plane.[74]

Some felt a similar clandestinity applied to Christian religious practices. In a conversation I had with don Robustiano, doña Eduardina, and Castro, don Robustiano insisted that religion had not been prohibited on the asentamiento, but he did recount how, because people had money, they tended to drink more, and this led to an abandonment of Christianity. In Arnoldo Ríos, Castro added, it was not possible to practice Mapuche religion openly, even though there had been a *machi* present; as a result, Mapuche religiosity was kept hidden. Though the participants in the conversation could not agree on the causes, all concurred that in 1972 the political climate did not encourage an open or consistent practice of religious traditions, whatever they might be.[75]

The problem of gender—especially the difficult inclusion of women in the broader agrarian reform project—was also something Arnoldo Ríos shared with other asentamientos. By encouraging the growth of peasant family enterprises, the Christian Democratic model tended to reinforce the authority of the male head of household in decisions about production and labor allocation. Thus women and youth tended to depend on the father, who was invariably defined as household head. As doña Marta remembered, within a more traditional definition of gender roles, in which women worked on the family garden plot, raised small animals, and did handicrafts at the mothers' centers, everyone could benefit from a greater prosperity. The situation was different for single women and for young people who sought independence. And despite the Popular Unity's attempt to break this pattern by declaring women and youth independent members of the Centros de Reforma Agraria (CERAS), the agrarian reform centers created during Allende's presidency, on the ground there were few differences between the two models.[76]

At a broader level, it seems quite possible that the limitations of the agrarian reform model and the almost exclusive emphasis on the class elements of mobilization closed off powerful sources of inspiration and political strength that formed part of Mapuche peasant identity. We have seen the importance of a religious vision of liberation to the leaders of the asentamiento, and how such an outlook proved to be a crucial point of connection with Puerto Saavedra's Christian base community. We have also noted how Mapuche networks of kinship and exchange helped nurture relationships of solidarity and reciprocity between people inside and outside the asentamiento. Finally, the traditional strength and power of Mapuche women, especially within their families and communities, was a motivating element that could not be entirely integrated into the mobilizations of the period. In the community of Ailío, for example, doña Rosa Ailío, daughter of an original settler and aunt to Heriberto, Robustiano, Eduardina, Cecilia, and Elisa, was remembered as a tall, strong woman. When she stood in the doorway of her house to call her family home, her voice echoed through the hills and could be heard on the other side of the Imperial River. She spent her whole life reminding the rest of the community that they had to fight to get back their lands and telling stories about the struggles of the previous generation. She would say, in *mapunzugun*, that the *wigkas* were responsible for the lack of land among the Mapuche, and that it was time to get rid of the power of the *wigkas*. She recollected with pride and happiness that President Allende had greeted her personally once when she traveled to Concepción and ended up in a demonstration.[77] Aunt Rosa's strength and power, as well as that of other women like doña María Pilquinao and doña Juana Ríos and, in the next generation, doña Eduardina, Cecilia, Elisa, and doña Marta, were not truly integrated into the work of the asentamiento because of the organizational model being used.[78]

And yet, when all was said and done, the restitution of land and reorganization of production brought prosperity and a certain moral satisfaction to the asentados on Arnoldo Ríos. They proved to themselves that they could run an agricultural enterprise, that they could make it work. They saw they could feed their families on and off the asentamiento. That is why there was also a great deal of support for the MIR and the MCR, including don Martín Ailío Porma and doña Juana Ríos. "They taught us a pretty good form of struggle," doña Eduardina commented. All this gave asentado families a sense of pride and optimism, a feeling of success that some still remembered almost thirty years later. When don Heriberto Ailío was arrested and tortured in September 1973, for example, he continued insisting he had been president of agriculture on the asentamiento. The military taunted him by calling him "President of the Defeat of the Revolution," but he simply repeated over and over that people had progressed and had what they had because they had worked together. "I don't know if you're aware," he explained in 1997, "that ours was the best asentamiento, because we know that ours was the best of all the asentamientos there were, even before the time of the late Allende, in the time of Frei, in every sense, pig breeding, livestock breeding, I don't know, in all the breeding, and in agriculture."[79] And a few minutes later, he continued, "Can you imagine, we left that fundo squeaky clean, clean and well cultivated. We sowed wheat, potatoes, everything we planted would grow. The bad thing is that the army arrived, and it all was returned to the landowners."[80] And truth be told, beyond the mortal offense inflicted on him with the confiscation of his land, for Juan Bautista Landarretche there could be no graver insult than the peasants claiming they were the ones who really knew how to make the fundo produce.

Land, Morality, and Restitution: Landowners, Mapuche Communities, and Agrarian Mobilization near the Coast

Productivity on the asentamiento Arnoldo Ríos became a very controversial subject. At the beginning of 1971, the sociopolitical conflict between Landarretche and the asentado population revolved largely around the efficiency of the fundo's system of cultivation. The peasants justified their takeover by referring to the landowner's inefficient use of the property. In a public declaration reproduced in *Punto Final*, they explained their action as follows:

> We occupied the fundo because it was abandoned, without cultivation, while we were dying of hunger on half a hectare of land for a whole family. We took

the property at night, armed with only a few sticks and a shotgun without ammunition. It's not strange that Mr. Landaretche [*sic*], with the fright he suffered, somehow confused our sticks with machine guns, but it is strange that he has such detailed knowledge of guns and their various makes and sizes. We live in poverty and don't have enough to eat. Where would we have gotten the money to buy the weapons Landaretche saw in his imagination?

And they emphasized, further on in the same document,

Landaretche says that his fundo was well cultivated. Here there were only 200 cows that he was feeding, from his other fundo "La Esperanza" that he has in Puerto Saavedra. Of these he milked barely three, which he had begun doing in December. This dairy that he talks so much about was barely six 30-liter containers we found discarded in a shed.

The total sown was 40 hectares of wheat and 25 of *raps*, plus three hectares of pasture. The rest of this 737-hectare farm was very well sown with weeds, brambles and hemlock.[81]

At the time of the takeover in December 1970, Luciano Landarretche remembered, his father had been in the middle of a complicated reorganization of his agricultural enterprise. For many years Landarretche had been at the forefront of regional agriculture, producing high-quality wheat and wheat seed for the State Bank, milling wheat on Rucalán that provided flour for a good part of the coastal zone. "One of the main banners of struggle my father held up," Luciano told me,

one of the things he personally treasured the most, I would say, was that he had been one of the pioneers in the implementation of new forms of cultivation and production. He had a mill here on the farm, a wheat mill with which he provisioned the whole coastal zone, in other words, part of Imperial, the entire zone of Carahue, Puerto Saavedra, Trovolhue, Nehuentúe. Afterward my father was also a wheat seed producer for the State Bank. He even won the Silver Wheat Spike Award given to the best producers. So my father always set high standards, a high production goal, within the farm.[82]

A few years before the Popular Unity government took power, however, Juan Landarretche decided to reorganize his family enterprise. Even though wheat had been, for many years, a principal regional crop, it seemed to have less of a future by the 1960s than livestock raising and dairy production.

Thus Landarretche decided to sell his wheat mill and invest in livestock. As Luciano told the story:

> The truth is that Father had seen the wheat mill he had here as a way to industrialize his agricultural production. But then he liquidated the mill around 1965, 1966. He did this, in fact, thinking he could move his business up a couple of notches. That was the motive for buying the fundo Esperanza Norte, which is in the Puerto Saavedra region, where the grazing capacity was much greater, and this meant he could increase his herd, lower costs and so on, because that is a fundo of much higher quality.[83]

As we saw in chapter 2, the fundo Esperanza Norte, which Landarretche bought in 1966 from Berta Fagalde, widow of Graciano Duhalde, was a piece of quality property. In order to pay for it Landarretche had to stretch his resources pretty thin and could manage it only after selling his mill. Even so, according to his son Luciano, it took him three or four years to finish paying it off. "In other words," Luciano explained,

> selling the mill was, I think, one of the things that allowed Father to consider buying another property, because it was really expensive, this property was very valuable in money terms, very valuable. So you had to produce a lot in order to pay for it, a property that it took Father three or four years to pay off. And keeping in mind that at the time, to put it in Chilean slang, he had his batteries really charged up, in the sense that he had a lot of livestock here on this farm, a lot of livestock. And this also forced Father to farm out some of his livestock to other agriculturalists in exchange for half the calves [*mediería*]. His goal was to manage a livestock enterprise in a rational and integrated fashion.[84]

Why did Landarretche stretch himself so thin, risk so much financially, at the precise moment when agrarian reform was creating insecurity? A simple mathematical calculation makes clear that, when Rucalán was occupied, Landarretche had barely finished paying off Esperanza Norte. Why did he do it this way? Once again according to his son Luciano, there were two reasons for taking such a risk. "I think Father would have never been able to buy the new property," Luciano explained,

> if it wasn't for the quote, unquote bogeyman of the agrarian reform, because it was already beginning, we're talking about the government of Eduardo Frei Montalva. And that lady felt pressured by this business of the agrarian

reform, because she didn't work her fundo directly but rented it out, and so she was worried that the government would expropriate her property. And it was under these conditions that she began talking with Father, and these conversations ultimately resulted in her selling him the land. But for no other reason than this fear of the agrarian reform.[85]

Don Juan Bautista Landarretche was a good capitalist who took advantage of the climate of insecurity—which always drives prices down—to buy something he could not have afforded under other circumstances. He did try to protect himself from potential problems by registering the fundo Esperanza Norte in the name of his six children, rather than in his own name. But at the same time, given his long, distinguished trajectory as a model agricultural entrepreneur, he sincerely seemed to think the agrarian reform would never arrive at his own doorstep. This is the second reason for Juan Bautista Landarretche's willingness to take a risk: he did not see it as a high risk in personal terms. Thus he took advantage of the situation to expand his investments and to diversify into livestock raising and dairy production, activities that in the long run would allow further capitalization of his business.[86]

In 1997, the Landarretche family insisted that the occupation and subsequent expropriation of their property came as a total surprise, since they considered themselves exceptions within the landowning class. In contrast to the average landowner, who, according to Luciano, "worried very little about the land, and lived elsewhere," during nearly thirty years of marriage his parents always lived on their property, "all 365 days of the year." If the reform, as Luciano explained it, was meant to expropriate lands that belonged to absentee landowners, in order to transfer resources to people who would actually work them, then it should not have affected the Landarretches. In addition, Luciano and his mother, Violeta Maffei viuda de Landarretche, recalled that they had excellent relations with the Mapuche community that bordered on their land: they would take people to the hospital at two or three in the morning, and they always gave them work. Thus their Mapuche neighbors did not participate in the toma.[87]

Given the conditions of social conflict that existed in the Chilean countryside at the end of the 1960s, however, the confidence and security the Landarretches felt, as agrarian entrepreneurs who maintained good, paternalistic relations with their Mapuche neighbors, would be violently and dramatically shattered on a humid, foggy December morning. "When they knocked on our door at three-thirty in the morning," insisted doña Violeta, "for us it was, well, maybe a logical thing given the government we had, but for us it was a total surprise."[88] Examined in a broader context, however, this claim of total surprise is perhaps a bit exaggerated, and don Juan Bautista Landarretche does not strike us as having been innocent or naive. After all, he had registered his new fundo in his children's names. A man taken entirely by surprise does not manage to organize, in only four days, a violent armed reoccupation of his property with the participation of several other known landowners from the region. And finally, though it seems that Cullinco, the neighboring Mapuche community, did not participate in the initial *toma*, we have seen that some of its members aided the occupants after the violent reoccupation, testified in their favor at the ensuing trial, and participated in the asentamiento created through the agrarian reform.

Perhaps the more convincing surprise was that, knowingly or not, the Mapuche peasants of Ailío and Pichingual confronted Landarretche at his most vulnerable moment. He had been a model landowner in the region, but at the time of the *toma* he was in transition toward a livestock enterprise. As early as 1951 he was listed as one of the ten highest taxpayers in the municipality of Carahue, but at the moment of the *toma* he had just finished paying off a land purchase that had indebted him over the short run.[89] It is particularly ironic, from Landarretche's point of view, that at precisely this moment the government placed his agricultural practices on Rucalán under a microscope. Beginning in January 1971, three separate evaluations were carried out on the estate: one by INDAP as evidence for the case against the Landarretches in Temuco's Court of Appeals; another by the SAG agronomist Moritz Milies Wortzman, who on 31 December 1970 had been named administrator of the fundo by the Labor Ministry; and finally the expropriation report already cited that was carried out in February. Although they all agreed that the peasant dwellings on the estate were not up to minimum legal code, the estimates of land in crops, and even of overall area, varied a great deal among the participants in this larger drama.[90]

A comparison of the three evaluations reveals that conditions at Rucalán in late 1970 and early 1971 seemed to vary a great deal depending on the identity and position of the observer. And Landarretche himself alleged in his request for reconsideration of the expropriation that 90 percent of his fundo was being used efficiently. Members of the Landarretche family presently claim that the property was cultivated in an exemplary fashion but was in transition toward livestock raising. And we should not forget the perspective of the occupying peasants, who reported 65 hectares in crops, 3 hectares in pasture, and the rest "very well sown with weeds, brambles and hemlock"; and, in their view, the size of Rucalán (presented by all the government officials as 439 hectares) actually amounted to 737 hectares. Despite these variations, however, all observers agreed on one point: the property was not generally apt for commercial agriculture, for only 25 hectares were considered arable (Class IV, according to agronomic criteria). Under the terms of the Agrarian Reform Law, therefore, the criteria for good or bad exploitation were established not according to the percentage sown in agricultural crops, but instead by assessing the condition of the grasslands and pastures. And here, with the exception of Landarretche's own estimate, no one thought that at Rucalán there were more than 100 hectares in pastureland that could be recognized as such. The rest—between 60 and 66 percent, depending on the calculation—was not being used. According to the criteria established by Frei's government in 1968, properties smaller than the 80 *hectáreas de riego básico* (basic irrigated hectares, or H.R.B.) limit defined by law (according to CORA officials, in March 1971 Rucalán had the equivalent of 21.3 H.R.B.) and with no irrigation capacity would be considered badly exploited and therefore subject to expropriation, "if less than 70% of its usable surface was dedicated to annual or permanent cultivation or plantings, artificial or improved natural pasture."[91]

In other words, it did not matter, in a legal sense, that Landarretche was in transition to livestock raising, or that he was integrating several properties into a more capital-intensive family enterprise, or that he had taken a risk in order to innovate in regional agriculture, or that he had lived his entire married life on Rucalán without maintaining even an apartment in Temuco. We can imagine how profoundly insulted Landarretche must have felt. Don't they understand, he must have asked himself, how long I have struggled, how much I have sacrificed, to get ahead? It was in this context that he formulated his request for reconsideration, whose allegations could not be accepted subsequently even by the CORA functionaries who continued working for the military government. What mattered in 1971, however, were the calculations done in accordance with the Regulations of 1968, and under these terms, Rucalán was badly exploited. And that was the end of that, at least from an Agrarian Reform point of view.

The peasants defined good or bad exploitation from an entirely opposite set of criteria. They saw a property of more than 700 hectares, the majority of which was not cultivated, "while we were dying of hunger on half a hectare of land for a whole family." Given the scarcity of land in Mapuche communities, entire families had been forced to cultivate hilly lands of poor quality in order to survive. Under such conditions, what possible relevance could a landowner's vision have? What difference could it possibly make that an overall assessment of three separate estates, with a grand total of more than 1,000 hectares, had confirmed that Rucalán had few lands that were suitable for commercial cultivation? On the asentamiento Arnoldo Ríos people obeyed a different rationale, one that depended on the cooperation of asentado families in order to plant, according to a postcoup assessment by the CORA official Héctor Jensen in 1973, "more than 270 hectares of spring and winter wheat, barley, potatoes, peas, pasture, etc."[92] Thought of in this way, a good or efficient exploitation of the land was based not on commercial or market criteria, but on how well it provided for human subsistence. Through this lens, the legitimacy and accomplishments of the asentamiento Arnoldo Ríos were impressive indeed.

The example of Arnoldo Ríos inspired peasants throughout Cautín's coastal region between January 1971 and May 1972. Already in February 1971, a few days after the formal Agrarian Reform decree on Rucalán and Butalón, Pablo Lüer Westermeyer, owner of Puerto Saavedra's fundo San Pablo, was informing the intendant that "agitators of unknown political stripe are instigating the Mapuches of the area to illegally occupy the fundos San Pablo, belonging to me, San Enrique, belonging to Enrique Lüer W., Esperanza Sur, belonging to Fernando Lüer W., and Esperanza Norte, belonging to Mr. Juan Bautista Landarretche." From the time of Rucalán's takeover in December, the landowners had been organizing night patrols throughout the region, precisely because they feared additional occupations. In February, however, as Lüer himself explained, it was necessary to request government aid because "we are in the middle of the grain harvest, in addition to doing the milking, and must work hard every day." The intendant's answer was to order additional surveillance from the Police Prefect, asking that particular attention be paid to the properties Lüer mentioned but adding to the list the fundos Nehuentúe, belonging to Mario Alvarez, and Tondreau, property of Antonio Alvarez.[93]

Despite the vigilance of property owners and police, on 2 March 1971, Mapuche peasants, with help from the MCR and students from the University of Concepción, successfully occupied the fundo Moncul, located near Nehuentúe and belonging to Domingo Durán Neumann. A week later temporary Intendant Renato Maturana informed the police that "it has come to our attention that some of the people who participated in the illegal takeover of the fundo Moncul, property of Mr. Domingo Durán N., . . . are lobbying the Mapuches from Pullanque, Jupehue and Lobería communities to take another of the same landowner's properties, known as Lobería and located in the same area." The rumors turned out to be false at that point, though a few days later it became known that a student from Concepción by the name of Jorge Fernández had been killed by a homemade bomb he was carrying while galloping on horseback on the fundo Moncul. The incident intensified rumors concerning the MIR's violent plans for the coastal region.[94]

The fundo Lobería was successfully taken over on 17 October 1971, by peasants from the Mapuche community of Pilolcura demanding restitution of more than three hundred hectares they claimed had been usurped by Domingo Durán. The same day, according to Imperial District Governor Audito Gavilán, the occupation was expanded to include the other three properties that had originally been part of the fundo El Plumo. The peasants had occupied a total of more than two thousand hectares. According to the governor, "the workers and other laborers on those properties, totaling 150 people," had participated in the action "entirely of their own accord." The occupants were unarmed, he added, and "willing to negotiate."[95] By the end of November, however, Juventino Velásquez, a Socialist member of Puerto Saavedra's municipal council, informed the Police Prefect that

> agriculturalists from the region are organizing the "retaking" of the fundo Lobería, and with this purpose they have frequent meetings in the house of Pablo Lüer in Puerto Saavedra, at which are present Mario and Sergio Alvarez, from Carahue, who were implicated in the retaking of Rucalán.
>
> In addition, he was informed by the present occupants of the fundo Lobería that recently, during the night, they have seen the vehicles of several landowners prowling about at the edges of the property, seemingly studying the lay of the land. This is how on Saturday the 20th of the month, around 8 in the evening, five unknown white trucks parked in front of the Puyangue ferry, along with a blue one belonging to Juan Bautista Landarretche, with the clear purpose of crossing the river, which they were unable to do because the ferry captain refused to take them. These activities, which the occupants of Lobería define as espionage, have worried them greatly, for they fear a confrontation whose consequences are easy to imagine.
>
> The same city official suggested that existing evidence points to the organization, in the region of Puerto Saavedra, of "white guards," for which a so-called "Chelo" Riquelme, who lives between Carahue and Puerto Saave-

dra and was also mixed up in the events of Rucalán, would be primarily responsible.

These "white guards" would have as their primary purpose the elimination of some of the indigenous leaders from the area who have been organizing land takeovers.

Three days later, police in Temuco stopped Juan Kind Morstand, son of the owner of the fundo El Plumo and its ex-administrator, and confiscated "a Remington 8-A large game hunting rifle, year 1907," with sixty cartridges of "Dum Dum" bullets.[96] The battle continued.

This coastal battle between a peasantry hungry for land and prosperity and an innovative landowning class that did not consider itself, according to its interpretation of the Agrarian Reform law, legally liable to expropriation, continued through 1971 and 1972. A second wave of takeovers between March and June 1972 affected the remaining fundos between Puerto Saavedra and Nehuentúe. Near the end of March 1972 a group of occupiers camped out on the fundos Nehuentúe and San Antonio, belonging to the brothers Mario and Sergio Alvarez, because, they said, the ex-owners were decapitalizing and sabotaging the properties, which lay unoccupied between the expropriation decree of 24 March and CORA's formal takeover on 31 March. This campground, made up of resident workers from both properties in collaboration with Mapuche and non-Mapuche peasants from the surrounding area, elected a "land struggle committee" and a "production surveillance committee" and took the name Jorge Fernández in honor of the student who had died the previous year on the fundo Moncul.[97] By the middle of June of the same year, a government decree had ordered the intervention of the fundo San Pablo, belonging to Pablo Lüer Westermeyer, in Puerto Saavedra. Despite the night patrols, San Pablo, San Enrique, Esperanza Norte, and Esperanza Sur would all pass into the agrarian reform sector. "One morning," Luciano Landarretche recalled, "we'd gone that day to patrol the countryside and very early in the morning we'd returned to Carahue, and we were just getting into bed when they came to tell us that the fundo Esperanza had been taken." With the occupation of the fundo El Budi, belonging to the Alessandri family, the area's peasants completed their recuperation of the entire large property sector. Not surprisingly under such circumstances, the opposition to the Popular Unity government began to consider Cautín's coastal region to be under the control of the enemy, whom they defined as commandos from the MIR.[98]

From the perspective of the region's Mapuche peasantry, however, the coastal mobilization had managed to recuperate a territory that, not too long before, had been indigenous. The commercial properties created between 1900 and 1930, which in most cases contained land usurped from the communities, were the same properties subject to agrarian reform at the beginning of the 1970s. José and Graciano Duhalde, prototypes of the abusive landowner, had a hand in the formation of almost all these estates, helping to articulate a geography of power that extended from Carahue to Puerto Saavedra. The next generation, intimately linked through relations of property, kinship, and friendship, participated in the same geography and genealogy. To recall some of the most dramatic connections, the fundo Esperanza, the flagship property within the Duhalde fortune, was divided in two upon the death of Graciano and the southernmost half sold to the Lüer family. The three Lüer brothers then divided it up among themselves, forming the fundos San Pablo, San Enrique, and Esperanza Sur. Graciano's widow, Berta Fagalde, kept control of the northern half and rented it out to the Lüer brothers until the "bogeyman" of Agrarian Reform—as Luciano Landarretche called it—convinced her to sell Esperanza Norte to Luciano's father, Juan Bautista Landarretche. The fundo Nehuentúe, another centerpiece of the Duhalde family firm, was sold first to Miguel Larroulet and later to Mario Alvarez, whose brother Sergio bought Tondreau, another property originally belonging to the Duhalde family. As we have seen, the fundo Tranapuente was sold to the state and divided up, Florencio Riquelme, Sergio Benavente, and Mario Astorga receiving the hectares that had been usurped from the community of Ailío. Emilio Fagalde Maldonado, Berta Fagalde's brother, also owned a plot on the *colonia* Tranapuente and was implicated—along with the Riquelmes, Mario Alvarez, and others—in the retaking of Rucalán. Similar networks of ownership and power could be established in the cases of the fundos El Plumo and Moncul, on the northern bank of the Imperial river, and El Budi, southwest of Puerto Saavedra.

By the middle of 1972, territorial restitution had been combined, within the agrarian reform sector, with a new style of agricultural administration and a different exercising of local power. On the ex-fundo Nehuentúe, for example, now known as Jorge Fernández, a Centro de Producción (Production center, or CEPRO) was created in order to increase production with government financial and technical help. The Popular Unity government attempted to use this model to reestablish the earlier prosperity of coastal agriculture as pioneered by the Duhaldes, but now with an eye toward a social redistribution of the profits. Further proof of this strategy can be found in the fact that the fundo Esperanza Norte, on the other side of the Imperial River, was added to the same CEPRO, replicating Duhalde's initial strategy of forming a single agricultural property on both sides of the river.[99] Meanwhile the Consejos Comunales Campesinos (Communal peasant councils) in Carahue and Puerto Saavedra, elected from the grassroots, became a new venue through which popular power could become a reality. The Popular Unity government had initially created these councils as tools to mobilize in rural areas, but they worked differently in distinct parts of the country. In Carahue and Puerto Saavedra the very intensity of grassroots organization turned them into more autonomous tools of popular mobilization.[100] And finally, combining help from the MIR and the MCR with more local traditions of Mapuche kinship and sociability, a coalition of asentamientos, CERAS, and CEPROS extended from Arnoldo Ríos to Lobería and Jorge Fernández, making connections on the other side of the Imperial river, not only with the CEPRO, but also with the CERAS created on the other southern lots that had previously been part of the ex-fundo Esperanza. In addition to having recovered usurped Mapuche lands, this emerging coalition had three goals: to radicalize the process of popular power, educate themselves politically, and prepare a response to landowner violence.[101]

This, then, was the challenge that emerged along the coastal region between late 1972 and early 1973: Mapuche territorial restitution; agricultural redistribution; the creation of popular power. Under such conditions it should come as no surprise that the peasants understood the importance of working out a defense plan. The ex-landowners and other powerful local actors had been mobilized since the middle of 1970 and were waiting for the right moment to begin the decisive confrontation. In the coastal region, the right moment came on the morning of 29 August 1973, before the September coup, when helicopters and army troops arrived looking for a guerrilla school.

Reflecting on the moment of confrontation when he and other members of the Ailío committee had taken the fundo Rucalán by surprise and managed to throw the landowner off, don Heriberto Ailío told me, "Taking the fundo at the time was totally illegal, but we said it wasn't illegal. Why? Whose permission had they asked earlier when they'd taken over our lands in the first place? Nobody's. They just arrived and they said, OK, move over that way, this land is ours now. So afterward we also said to them, clear as day: this land is ours. You get out, tomorrow you grab your things because the fundo is ours now. That's the conclusion we reached, clear as day."[102] Beginning at dawn that December morning in 1970, a coalition of Mapuche and non-Mapuche peasants from Cautín province's coastal region, with the help of the MIR and the Popular Unity government, had managed to turn the tables on the area's landowners and their allies. Two years and eight months later, this time on a cold winter's morning and with blood and fire, the landowners and their confederates would get their chance to strike back.

CHAPTER 5

WHEN THE HEARTHS WENT OUT, 1973–1992

It was cold the winter morning of 29 August 1973, when the soldiers, trucks, and helicopters arrived at the CEPRO Jorge Fernández. "It seemed like it was the last day of our lives," a Mapuche woman identified as Margarita Paillao would later tell the MIR publication *Punto Final*. "The *compañeras* dissolved in tears when they heard the screams and moans of their husbands." According to Paillao, who lived next to the ex-landowner's house that had been converted into offices for the production center, three helicopters had arrived at the CEPRO Jorge Fernández, ex-*fundo* Nehuentúe, at approximately 9:00 a.m. About thirty men, both army and air force, descended from the choppers, and later more men arrived in military trucks from Puerto Saavedra. The soldiers broke down the doors of the houses, including her own, which served as the mothers' center and from which she helped run the first aid headquarters also located in the ex-landowner's mansion. As they scattered her possessions they found forty-two hundred *escudos* tucked away in one of her medical books, a tome on the treatment of diarrhea, and they pocketed the money. Then the man in charge read a list of names, and the soldiers arrested the people they found. The *Punto Final* article, based on Paillao's testimony, continued: "Those arrested were taken to the second floor of the ex-landowner's house. The windows of the room they were taken to were open, and from below the peasants could see perfectly what was going on inside." Paillao saw that the prisoners were stripped naked, and then she heard some tremendous blows being delivered, followed by shouts, moans, and crying. After witnessing a series of tortures, which she discussed in detail in the article, Paillao had an attack of nerves and was taken to the hospital in Puerto Saavedra. When she later returned to Jorge Fernández with a doctor, he was not allowed to enter the property. Her companion Orlando Beltrán, president of the CEPRO and one of the original members of the group initiating the takeover the year before, was tied to a helicopter by his waist and flown around dangling in the air in an attempt to force him to confess where the weapons were. Beltrán would subsequently spend three years in jail, endemically ill as a result of torture.[1]

This military operation was carried out two weeks before the 11 September coup, while the country was still under civilian democratic rule. As we will see in more detail below, it was part of a series of raids, called *allanamientos*, implemented by the armed forces between July and September under the umbrella of the arms control law. Despite being nominally under the control of the civilian government, the military began to evidence a worrisome degree of autonomy during these raids. Between the end of August and the beginning of September, the peasants of the coastal agrarian reform sector would feel on their very bodies the growing arrogance and independence of the armed forces.

The next day, 30 August, about three in the morning, a military detachment reached the community of Ailío and entered the house of don Antonio Ailío asking for his son Hugo. Sixteen years old at the time, Hugo was sleeping with his younger brothers René and Antonio. "I had a night table made of boards, I'd made it myself," Hugo remembered, "and on it they found some leftist newspapers, *El Rebelde*, and also, I think, a picture of Che Guevara in uniform." Though he had continued to live at home with his family, Hugo had been traveling around the coastal region, from Puyangue, Trovolhue, and Moncul to Arnoldo Ríos, Nehuentúe, and Puerto Saavedra, distributing the *mirista* newspaper *El Rebelde*. Because he was intelligent and, as don Heriberto Ailío described him, had a good memory and knew how to talk, he had also participated in political education at the various agrarian reform centers. "They grabbed the things they found," Hugo continued,

> I guess you could say they had evidence on me, and they said, you don't know, son, the seriousness of what you're mixed up in. And I was quiet, just hanging my head, like the thief caught red-handed. So we're going to have to go now, we're going to take you to a place where you can make a statement. And my mother starting crying then, she's always been so sensitive, and that's what really hit me hardest, it hurt me to see her that way and I felt guilty. And I thought to myself, well, whatever comes I'll just have to deal

with it. And the sargent said to her, don't worry, ma'am, the boy is just going to make a little statement and then we'll bring him right back.[2]

Things changed quickly once they left his parents' house. About ten meters down the hill, the soldiers told Hugo to run, so he began sprinting down the hill until he got to the fence, when they told him to stop, and he did. "I waited there and they came down fast and a soldier said to me, weren't we telling you to stop, and he hit me on the shoulder with his rifle butt, and I fell to the ground, and would you believe that still today I have problems with that shoulder?" A while later, when they got to the landowner's house at the ex-fundo Nehuentúe, a soldier hit him with a chain that had a lead medallion attached to the end, opening a gash in his head. Then they took him into the house, making him wait in the hall before entering, as they explained, "the torture chamber." Indeed, as Hugo remembers it, the psychological torture involved in waiting was to some extent the most effective way to break someone down. While in the hall and later shut up in a closet he could hear the moans and screams of another prisoner being tortured and imagined what was in store for him. He remembered what he had read about Nazi tortures, "and the tears rolled down my cheeks." When it was finally his turn he was so afraid that, at first, he admitted a few things. Then he tried to stop, denying that he knew people; but at that point they began to pressure him harder, hitting him, applying electricity to his head, the soles of his feet, his mouth, lips, and nose. The moment came when he simply could not stand it any longer. Though the combination of everything finally got to him, the worst was the electricity. "I just started quacking like a duck."[3]

The next morning, 31 August, around eleven o'clock, a delegation of German journalists accompanied by functionaries from the Ministry of Agriculture arrived at the CEPRO Jorge Fernández to tour the facility. The idea was to report on the successes of Chilean agrarian reform. The peasants who received them explained that "they could not cooperate because their center had been militarily occupied for two days, and they had been badly treated by the soldiers. The wife of the CEPRO's president reported that her husband had been arrested and savagely tortured, to the point that they had crunched his testicles." The delegation then continued on to the town of Nehuentúe to find the official in charge of the CEPROS program, returning to the center with him. Upon their return they were detained by army personnel, their vehicles and persons were searched, and they were kept under arrest without explanation for two hours. Around 4:20 p.m. the foreign journalists and one of the officials from the local office of the Agriculture Ministry were set free, while the rest of the personnel from the CEPROS program remained in military custody. "Our comrade Alfonso Somoza," continued the delegation's report, "and the rest of the group were taken to what used to be the landowner's house, where they were interrogated once again and shown the peasant leaders detained there. According to the information provided by *compañero* Somoza, he saw one of the peasants badly beaten and in extremely poor physical condition." The rest of the group was finally released around six in the evening, and as they were traveling along the road toward Carahue, "more or less in front of the *Asentamiento* Arnoldo Ríos, about 9 kilometers outside Carahue, a helicopter flew over them and forced them to stop, pointing its machine gun at them. They were forced out of their vehicles and once again searched. Then the helicopter left them and landed in the Asentamiento Arnoldo Ríos."[4]

The helicopter that landed at the asentamiento was looking specifically for don Heriberto Ailío, who had been identified as a MIR "terrorist" and "ideologue." His sister Elisa remembered that she had never seen a helicopter before, and she was "absolutely terrorized with fear." She continued, "They just came down, we'd never seen anything like it, at least I never had, the soldiers got down with their machine guns ready, pointing at us, looking for Heriberto." She was so afraid, doña Elisa assured me, that she miscarried; she was in the second month of pregnancy.[5] Fear, however, also prompted people to elaborate strategies of mutual protection and self-defense. "The one in charge of the military command," don Heriberto remembered,

asked who was Heriberto Ailío, but no one said anything, neither did I, because I was there, and then I felt sort of a shiver go down my spine at that moment, when they named me. And a Mapuche brother who had done his military service in the Navy, he took charge, and since we had all received some military training, he stood at attention before me and said, you, man, you go find Heriberto Ailío . . . It was a strategy he came up with to help me escape. So I left calmly, and walked calmly for quite a while until, suddenly, I felt the impulse, and began running.

Don Heriberto hid out in the surrounding Mapuche communities, where he had many collaborators and friends, for a number of days. After the coup, however, he lost the contacts he had established to help him leave the country, and, knowing that the military was pressuring his family and others at the asentamiento, he decided to turn himself in. "They were pressuring my family, my wife, my mother, my brothers and sisters," he explained, so "I had to turn myself in to the military. And in addition there were some people who turned against me, they told me that it was my fault that the army and the repression had arrived, though I didn't see it that way, I felt I had been defending their rights, defending their right to enough bread."[6] Doña Eduardina also remembered how people began blaming her brother for the repression. "I think it was because of the fear," she said,

> and also they felt tricked, cheated, as if they had gotten involved in something they shouldn't, like they had made a big mistake. People became hard, they had no mercy, our same *compañeras*, they became hard. One of the ladies, she came forward and said, why are we here surrounded by so many soldiers, afraid? Why doesn't somebody go find Heriberto and bring him here, fettered like a lamb, and turn him in? It was terrible for us when she said that, what could we answer, we just stood quietly.[7]

The struggle to explain the inexplicable, to find someone to blame, was immediate and widespread among the peasants who were the targets of military repression. Some, as don Heriberto and doña Eduardina recalled, blamed the local leaders of the agrarian movement for having gotten them involved in the first place. Others put the blame on outside organizers, especially the members of the MIR, who, as one of the local peasant organizers expressively described it, "turned into cats' claws" in the sense that, after showing themselves in order to mobilize everyone, they disappeared when the repression got bad.[8] But even during the repression itself, there seemed to be an internal debate about the role of the MIR. "One day a group was taken to make a declaration," doña Eduardina later remembered, and when one of the *asentados* commented that "it's the *miristas'* fault that we're in this condition," doña Juana Ríos "came up to him [and] calling him a coward she slapped him, adding 'don't blame those young people. It was all of us. The fault belongs to all of us.'"[9]

Still others tied the violence, repression, and fear to older, more recognizable relations of power. On the nearby ex-fundo Lobería, for example, Juan Segundo Quian Antiman, identified as the president of the CEPRO Lobería, died on 8 September 1973, as a result of the mistreatment he had suffered during the Nehuentúe military operation. "When the soldiers arrived he was working, and they punished him because he was a leader," Pascual Segundo Traipe told the historian Christian Martínez more than twenty years later.

"When I went to see him he was in really bad shape," Traipe remembered, "and he told me, I'm going to die, it's Durán [the previous owner of Lobería] who's going to kill me, it was really Durán who was in charge, the soldiers were [doing his bidding], the whole property was blanketed with soldiers."[10]

This destructive invasion, however local inhabitants struggled to explain it, was a joint operation by personnel from the Third Helicopter Group of the Chilean Air Force (FACH) and the army regiment Tucapel, headquartered in the provincial capital of Temuco. Carried out autonomously without authority from the civilian government, this sweep of the area from Arnoldo Ríos in the west to Moncul and Lobería in the northeast to Nehuentúe and Puerto Saavedra in the southeast was justified as part of the overall campaign to control arms possession among the civilian population. According to Col. Pablo Iturriaga, commander of the Tucapel regiment, it was necessary to carry out the Nehuentúe allanamiento because the MIR had established an arms factory and guerrilla school there.[11] Placed in the context of other similar events that had begun to happen in July and August 1973, however, the emerging pattern puts Iturriaga's claim in a different light.

Before the National Army Command could be persuaded fully to collaborate in the coup plans—something which was impossible before constitutionalist Gen. Carlos Prats was forced to resign as commander in chief and turned out to be difficult even after Gen. Augusto Pinochet assumed the position—the Chilean Air Force and its commander, Gen. Gustavo Leigh, had established de facto links with local army units in various parts of the country, collaborating with them in violent disarmament forays against the civilian population. While technically legitimate under the terms of the recently promulgated arms control law, some of these allanamientos began to look suspiciously like autonomous mini-coups. Such had already been the case at the beginning of August in Punta Arenas, in the southern province of Magallanes, when the local FACH commander had orchestrated a multiple foray into three industrial establishments, using force so excessive that it had led to many injuries and the death of two workers.[12]

As the leftist weekly *Chile Hoy* made clear in its edition of 10–16 August, a full week before the Nehuentúe operation, an extremely worrisome pattern of violence and repression had begun to emerge during the previous month and a half. Although the arms control law had been promulgated nearly a year earlier, on October 21, 1972, it was only after the unsuccessful coup of 29 June 1973, referred to as the *tanketazo*, that the military began to apply it systematically. A "chronology of allanamientos" compiled by the magazine listed twenty-four separate operations carried out between 2 July and 3 August, the day before the allanamientos in Punta Arenas. Though most of them had occurred in or near Santiago or Valparaíso, there were several in the south. While distinct combinations of personnel from various branches of the armed forces took part in these operations, there was a strong presence of the FACH and the Navy, and local army regiments also were involved in nearly half the cases. Indeed, on 1 August Temuco's Tucapel regiment had carried out an allanamiento at the Korach lumber company, an industry under workers' control in the city of Temuco itself. The troops from the Tucapel regiment that took part in the Nehuentúe operation were thus already seasoned in the business of violence and intimidation, and their commander, Col. Pablo Iturriaga, as well as the FACH commander Rigoberto Pacheco, who was in charge of the helicopter group, had "a well-known track record as proponents of a coup within the armed forces."[13]

As had been the case in Magallanes, then, a coalition of army and FACH forces practiced in Nehuentúe all the tactics that would later be used in the post-coup repression. They invaded and destroyed private residences, terrorizing the civilian population. They beat and tortured suspected activists, using the methods that later became well known: hanging people by their feet; applying electricity to their testicles; submerging heads in septic water; forcing people to drink water until they were bloated and then jumping on their stomachs; hanging people from helicopters and then submerging them in the river. And finally, a campaign of disinformation was carried out concerning the motives and methods of the action. So successful was this campaign that, for many years afterward, the simple mention of Nehuentúe would elicit, among important segments of the region's population, images of guerrillas, subversives, and buried weapons.[14]

In the ten days before the September coup, disinformation about Nehuentúe spread quickly through the opposition press. Between 1 and 4 September, local and national newspapers reported the arrest of many "guerrillas" and the discovery of a large arsenal of weapons. On 3 September, the Santiago daily *Las Ultimas Noticias* dusted off a rumor that had circulated through the coastal region at the end of the previous year, that "unknown vessels" had plied the coastal waters between the fishing port of Tirúa and Trovolhue, Nehuentúe, and Puerto Saavedra, carrying "suspicious loads." Five days before the allanamiento Rodolfo Riquelme Montecinos, a Christian Democratic member of the Puerto Saavedra municipal council, had made a public statement reiterating these rumors, "affirming that he had concrete evidence about the existence of a clandestine coastal transport system along Cautín's shoreline, with stopping off points in the aforementioned towns where mysterious cargo was unloaded, presumably full of arms and explosives. He added that this illicit activity was connected to an unaccustomed amount of movement by peasants affiliated with the MCR, from the coastal asentamientos to the locations along this route."[15]

But perhaps the most elaborate disinformation work was done by Santiago's *El Mercurio*. Beginning on 4 September, this most famous opposition daily published a series of unsubstantiated charges, among them that the MIR had used the ex-landowner's house on the ex-fundo Nehuentúe as a bunker, stockpiling thirty-six boxes of explosives, antitank grenades, and bazookas; that all the properties in the region had stopped producing when occupied by the extremists; and that a group of MIR "bandits" with mandarin moustaches had turned Puerto Saavedra into a "far west" frontier town. A front-page spread on Sunday, 9 September, superimposed a grainy photograph of cars, trucks, and soldiers at the ex-fundo Nehuentúe's front gate on a map of Cautín province, with a "you-are-here" circle highlighting Nehuentúe and Puerto Saavedra. Across the top part of the map was splashed in boldfaced black print, "The Liberation of Nehuentúe." The article repeated pretty much the same charges of five days before, with the additional information that the whole operation had been run from Puerto Saavedra's hospital. Also included in the article was an introductory paragraph on Che Guevara's defeat in Bolivia, to which the allanamiento in Nehuentúe was likened.[16]

The coup de grace was given by *El Mercurio* on the very day the military coup took place. An article reported a supposed groundswell of protest throughout the Cautín region concerning a program broadcast on national television that had "gravely offended our armed institutions by lying about the [Nehuentúe] military operation." The reference was to an interview of Margarita Paillao shown on Channel 7's program "Vamos Mujer" in which she had essentially repeated the version of events reported in *Punto Final*. In addition to repeating the already familiar accusations about the arms factory and guerrilla school, the *El Mercurio* article moved into as yet uncharted territory:

Only the explosives found in plastic bags or in bombs already prepared were calculated as enough to blow up a city much larger than Temuco. But in addition to these various kinds of explosives with diverse origins, the military also found firearms, both short and automatic, molotov cocktails, hand grenades, as well as abundant ammunition. The armed forces also confiscated flammable materials whose purpose is to intensify a fire, as well as blowtorches for soddering grenades, extremely powerful radio transmitters, extremist literature, textiles, bandages, and first aid materials.

Another important number of finds from Nehuentúe have not been made public by the armed forces because they would reveal "surprising" origins.[17]

And yet surprisingly few of these charges were supported by available evidence, not even that provided by Iturriaga himself at the press conference he gave on 5 September 1973. There he exhibited the confiscated arms and ammunition, photographs of which were published in the local press. The photographs show little more than a few shotguns, sticks, revolvers, and some Molotov cocktails. Even the most famous weapons, the "anti-tank" bombs also known as *vietnamitas*, which, according to Iturriaga, were capable of blowing up something the size of a city block, turned out to be homemade, in pots and pans; the picture shows about twenty of them. This does not a weapons factory make. In addition, I have found no evidence, direct or indirect, to support the existence of a guerrilla school in the area. In fact, as one of the MIR organizers who had worked in the area pointed out, it would have been foolhardy to train there, since the ex-fundo Nehuentúe was in full view of the local police post![18]

At first, the local testimonies I collected disagreed on whether or not defensive weapons were kept on the asentamientos, CERAS, and CEPROS. When I first discussed the Nehuentúe operation with don Heriberto Ailío, for example, he related the same version of events that he had likely repeated, over and over, during the torture sessions that followed his arrest in September 1973. There were no weapons, he said. They had been doing nothing wrong. The military had made up the whole story and had planted the weapons later exhibited at the Tucapel regiment. The peasants arrested in connection with the Nehuentúe operation had never been successfully charged with any crime, even though most of them were jailed for at least two years. What more proof could anyone want, especially at a time like the mid-1970s when the rules of evidence that governed military tribunals were lax at best? Clearly, in don Heriberto's memory and estimation, the prisoners of Nehuentúe were innocent victims, almost like lambs taken to the slaughter.[19]

Initially, therefore, my forays into other documentation on the incident, particularly in the local and national press, were motivated by my desire to help expose the military's lies and thus validate don Heriberto's version. But my work yielded two conflicting images of Nehuentúe and the local population that offered competing claims to truth. The one provided by the opposition press before the coup is detailed above. In it, the local peasants were seen either as conspiratorial revolutionaries ready to attack all peace-loving citizens in their homes or as innocent dupes in a violent extreme-left conspiracy in which the MIR had turned the Nehuentúe region into its first fortress or bunker. The other version was given by publications that either supported or stood to the left of the Popular Unity government. In addition to the MIR publication *Punto Final*, which on the very day of the coup published the in-depth interview with the Mapuche woman that opened this chapter, progovernment publications like *Puro Chile*, *Clarín*, and *La Nación* published a series of articles blaming the right for fabricating the conspiracy and characterizing as ridiculous any charges that Mapuche peasants, who barely had enough money to buy their daily necessities, could have been stockpiling weapons or conducting military training. In this context, the charges of torture presented by local inhabitants against the military emerge as violations against the bodies of hardworking, upstanding, innocent citizens.[20] These two opposing versions would define the discursive options, both within the military and among its prisoners, for years to come. And yet, given the superior force of the pro-coup forces, it should not surprise us that the military version emerged publicly triumphant after 11 September.

Indeed, by the end of the month, a combination of repression, censorship, and creative disinformation had assured the preeminence of the military's version of events in Nehuentúe. This was further assured by an exhibition organized in the second half of September by Temuco's military high command. Along one block of the Plaza Recabarren, directly in front of the Tucapel regiment, military personnel laid out on tables, for all to see, a collection of rifles, radio transmitters, boxes of dynamite, shotguns, Molotov cocktails, *vietnamitas*, political banners, and other paraphernalia allegedly collected in the allanamientos that had taken place since August. The booty from the Nehuentúe operation took center stage. As reported in the local newspaper, thousands of local citizens paraded by the exhibit on Friday, 28 September, and saw with their own eyes "the impressive destructive power that had been stored in the province, waiting for the right moment to unleash death and destruction." Amidst evocations of the hundreds of innocents who could have been killed by these "subversives"—an imaginary roster of victims that included men, women, children, and the elderly—the newspaper cited the messages written on signs placed at strategic points throughout the exhibit. Next to the table with the rifles and shotguns, for example, was a sign that read, "With this they had planned to eliminate you. Why?" At the end of the exhibit, as a parting shot, were the words, "THIS IS NOT ALL. IT'S NOW UP TO YOU TO FIND THE REST."[21]

Under such conditions, when the military's version of events was transformed into truth through the destruction of people's bodies and lives, it is hardly surprising that survivors like don Heriberto Ailío would hold on tenaciously to the counter-version, the version that held them to be innocent, which, in the broader scheme of things, contained a great deal more truth in any case. The rendition that portrayed those arrested as innocent victims received further support from the human rights movement during the dictatorship as well as from the most widely and publicly circulated versions of the post-1990 discourse developed by the Commission on Truth and Reconciliation, which emphasized the body counts of the victims of military repression.[22] But in the long run, one dimension common to all these stories of innocence and abuse became increasingly troubling to me: by rendering people as the "victims" of repression, the stories tended to remove their individual agency, political legitimacy, and human complexity. I became convinced that representing people as Christlike sacrificial lambs, while comprehensible and perhaps inevitable under the conditions existing in Chile after September 1973, sold short the fact that many of them had been involved in morally defensible, if sometimes shortsighted, efforts to achieve social justice. Was there a way to emphasize and preserve their innocence, while at the same time respecting their political vision and activism?

This was my main concern when I interviewed don Heriberto Ailío again in April 1997. By that point I had found enough evidence in other sources to confirm the existence of some weapons, and at least the informal manufacture of some grenades, in Nehuentúe.[23] When I showed him the newspaper photographs and asked him what he thought, don Heriberto answered,

> Well, the truth is that there were some, but they weren't very many, because that depends on money, and we were poor. There's other weapons that they put into the pile at the end, so they could declare we had a guerrilla school, and that we were making weapons and ammunition, but that wasn't true, it wasn't as much as they put in the newspaper. So these are pure lies. Yes,

we were preparing ourselves, just like they were preparing themselves, we couldn't just be there with our arms crossed, we had to prepare. We knew they were preparing themselves for a coup, and to repress the poor, to repress the people.[24]

Over two decades later, in light of the knowledge now available concerning the military's methods of prevarication and repression, don Heriberto's admission that there had been some self-defense preparations going on helped remove the worst implications of helpless victimization; but equally important, it also highlighted the justice of the peasants' cause.

Torture, Treason, and Desertion, 1973–1978

A little further down on the same page of the local paper that featured the exhibit of arms that Friday in late September 1973, another headline screamed, "I lied because they paid me." In the article, a Mapuche woman whose name was given as Gertrudis Quidel Quidel "spontaneously confessed" she had been paid by members of the deposed leftist government to lie about the events in Nehuentúe. The article went on to explain that Quidel was the real name of the woman who, in the days immediately before the coup, had gone on national television under the alias "Margarita" to "denounce tortures and beatings supposedly carried out by the armed forces" in Nehuentúe. The reader is informed here, by contrast, that Quidel had seen nothing in Nehuentúe because, when the "airplanes" arrived, she had suffered an attack brought on by her pregnancy and had immediately gone to the hospital in Puerto Saavedra. When she returned to the site, a mysterious journalist she identified as "Gloria" Elgueta had taken her to the office of the provincial council and written up, on a typewriter, what she was supposed to say. She was then taken to Temuco, where the intendant had given her money to go to Santiago and tell this story. In the capital city she had met with Allende, who also gave her money. Finally, Quidel claimed, when she returned to the region the same journalist told her that the army was going to kill her for the story she had told, but if she changed it, militants from the MIR would kill her. The MIR militants who had worked in Nehuentúe, according to Quidel, "had been the bosses, and whom could she turn to if they were the ones who gave the orders?" Sometimes, the article continued, Quidel had been forced to use up to three hundred pounds of flour preparing their meals.[25]

This news story appeared the day after the ex-intendant of Cautín and the journalist named by Quidel had been arrested in connection with the case. Ex-Intendant Sergio Fonseca was kept under house arrest, while Fireley Elgueta, a female journalist who had worked for the Ministry of Agriculture in the Temuco region, was arrested in Santiago, tortured, and sent to Temuco to face a military tribunal. Under existing martial law, the charge was extremely serious: insulting the armed forces.

Gertrudis Quidel was Margarita Paillao, who in Santiago in the days immediately before the coup had given testimony about the human rights abuses in Nehuentúe. Fireley Elgueta was named to accompany her to Santiago at a Temuco meeting of government officials from the Ministry of Agriculture, where it had been unanimously decided that the information from Nehuentúe was serious enough to take personally to the capital city. The delegation to Santiago, which included Quidel and Elgueta, had gone to speak to the minister of agriculture first; but given the seriousness of the case, they had subsequently been invited to speak directly to President Salvador Allende. Present at the meeting with Allende, where the delegation had repeated its testimony, was Commander of the Air Force Gen. Gustavo Leigh, shortly thereafter one of the members of the military junta and recognized today as one of the earliest proponents of a coup solution. When Leigh heard testimony about the participation of the Temuco branch of the FACH, he went pale and began furiously taking notes. It was on the day subsequent to his arrival in Temuco, in the second half of September, that arrest orders went out for ex-Intendant Fonseca and Elgueta.[26]

The military version was correct about one thing, however: Margarita Paillao's name really was Gertrudis Quidel Quidel. Ten years earlier, in May 1963, she had been listed under that name in the census of the Mapuche community of Andrés Curiman in Rucahue-Moncul, along with her first husband José Isaías Toro. Nineteen years old at the time, Gertrudis Quidel already had two children and was listed as being in "bad health." The census taker recorded that the family was very poor, that Toro had just begun working on his own, and that the two hectares they possessed were "exhausted, full of brambles; they have no [usable] field." At some point in the late 1960s or early 1970s, Maritza Eltit remembered, doña Gertrudis had come to the Puerto Saavedra hospital to be treated for tuberculosis. By the time of the coup she was twenty-nine or thirty years old and had seven children.[27]

Doña Gertrudis was arrested when she returned from Santiago and tortured at army headquarters in Temuco, where the soldiers threatened the lives of her children in order to force her to change the story she had told.

When Fireley Elgueta was taken to the jail in Temuco, the two women were brought face to face. At that very moment doña Gertrudis was coming back to the jail from military headquarters, where people were taken to be interrogated. Her escorts pulled her along in front of a line of women prisoners, among whom stood Elgueta. At first, in an effort to protect her, doña Gertrudis pretended not to recognize the journalist. But the inconsistencies between the two women's stories ultimately made it clear that doña Gertrudis was lying. Shortly after she admitted knowing Elgueta she was released.[28]

People from Ailío remember that, later, even as she continued to visit Beltrán in jail, doña Gertrudis began dating a policeman. They also say that, one day, via the visitors whom the Nehuentúe prisoners received in jail, came the news that doña Gertrudis had gone out one night with her boyfriend and left Luciano Ernesto, the son she had with Beltrán, alone in the house. While she was out the house caught fire and the child died in the flames. When Beltrán received the news he became gravely ill with depression. After he was released from jail in 1976 with the rest of the Nehuentúe prisoners, he went first to Concepción. At some later point it seems he went to Santiago to live with his first wife and later died there.[29] Doña Gertrudis stayed on in Nehuentúe, working for a family named Garrido who sharecropped for Astorga on part of the forty-five hectares Ailío had lost so many years before. She began a relationship with the son, Ramón Garrido, and they had a daughter. But tragedy pursued her, it seems: first the mother of the Garrido family died, then the little girl; finally Ramón's father died as well. Doña Gertrudis then developed cancer, and, despite Ramón Garrido's best efforts to secure treatment for her, she died in 1979. People said she had been bewitched, since the illness consumed her bones and shrank her down to a fraction of her original size.[30]

In 1997, when I first began talking with people about the time of the repression, there was a lot of anger toward Gertrudis Quidel. She was seen as a traitor, someone without moral fiber or responsibility. Indeed, the story of her relationship with the policeman and the death of her son with Beltrán—symbolically named Luciano Ernesto in honor of a MIR martyr and of Che Guevara—through her negligence served as a touchstone that represented her treachery and selfishness better than any other single image. In this context it is especially significant that don Robustiano, doña Eduardina, and don Heriberto Ailío and Enrique Pérez, all of whom were individually affected by the military repression unleashed in the operation of Nehuentúe, remembered the incident of the burning of Luciano Ernesto. Doña Patricia Valenzuela, on the other hand, who lives in Nehuentúe and still goes to the same Anglican church that both doña Gertrudis and the Ailío Pilquinao siblings used to attend, but who did not suffer personally from the repression, told me she did not remember it.[31] Don Heriberto also considered that Quidel and Beltrán had both been partially to blame for what had happened to them. "Orlando also had to share the guilt," he told me, for

> that woman was recently married, she had her own husband and Orlando had his own wife, he left his wife to follow Margarita [sic] . . . so something was bound to happen. You have to believe in God, I've always said, so if it wasn't according to God's law that he could be with that woman, there wasn't any reason for him to be with her. He left his own wife suffering and, well, one day I talked with him and told him what you did was bad, you left your own wife, a good woman, to follow another woman who was bound to let you down, and that's how it was in the end.[32]

Yet as I conducted more interviews and gained further perspective, I began to understand that doña Gertrudis, too, had been a victim of circumstances, a person who even at the last minute had tried to protect the journalist at the Temuco prison. As many others did, she paid dearly for her belief in a better kind of society; she was among those whose bodies and lives were destroyed in order to ensure the dominance of the military's version of events.

As one of the MIR organizers who spent time in the area put it, people were irrevocably branded by the experience of arrest and torture. This organizer, who requested anonymity, recounted his treatment after being arrested. He experienced two mock executions and numerous beatings, and his testicles were struck with rocks. Another example is don Luis Ernesto Quijón, a rural worker, agrarian reform activist, and health worker who accompanied Arturo Hillerns, supervising physician at the Puerto Saavedra hospital and today one of the disappeared, on his rounds to the Mapuche communities in the zone. Arrested for these activities after the coup, to this day he carries indelible wounds on his body and in his heart. In November 1996, as we sat at a rickety wooden table in his smoke-stained kitchen, cats, chickens, and small children underfoot, he unbuttoned the sleeves of his shirt and pulled them up. Pointing to some purple marks on his wrists, he explained to me that they were the places where electricity had been applied to his body during the torture he suffered after his arrest in September 1973.

Moving his hands along his body, he continued, "I have a fractured sternum, ah. Here I still have a lump from where it was cracked open with the butt of a gun. Broken ribs, there's no point in telling you how many I have, these are all mementos I still have from '73. I think I'll die before I'll be able to get beyond this because it's marked on my being, on my body. This isn't a fairy tale, ah. Now, of course, what do some people say, many want this to go away like a fairy tale. But this is not a fairy tale, because it turns out that it was me who suffered it, not the guy next door."[33]

Ironically, in such a situation of pain, fear, and isolation, being part of a community of political prisoners could become, for some, a source of solace. This was certainly the case for Hugo Ailío, who after having "named names" spent the first year and a half in the minors' section of the Temuco jail with the common prisoners. Then he managed to get transferred to the cell block that held the political prisoners or, as they were called, the prisoners of war. He remembered that they were organized:

> We had daily programs, for example, we did artisanry, we played a lot of soccer, which was good therapy, it helped us relax. Later we organized our own soup kitchen, because the food they gave in jail was bad, completely antisanitary, even worse than feeding the dogs, so we thought about it together, discussed the situation together. There were *compañeros* whose economic situation was better, and when someone visited them they brought good things; but others got nothing. So the ones who had an economic advantage realized that it would be better to organize a soup kitchen so we could all eat together. So we went ahead and did that.

Because of the soup kitchen, however, they were punished. Accused of attempting a prison break, they were sent to solitary confinement, though one of the lieutenants from their block made sure they had mattresses and blankets, and Hugo was even given a sweater. At some point during the night another order came down from above, and all their bedding and warm clothing were taken away. Hugo and his compañero were left in T-shirts, Hugo barefoot, shivering on the cold cement. He remembered that in Cautín in July, during the dead of winter, "we spent the night jogging around, we'd take turns, and exhausted we'd fall on the floor to sleep, but of course then we'd wake up with the cold." To make things worse, Hugo continued, "in the morning the jail's cleanup crew came through and hosed it all down, it was the only way they could clean, because when the prisoners were in solitary they'd often just defecate right there, so the janitors threw water so they could then sweep out all that stuff, and afterward they'd bring these huge pots by and throw us a spoonful of beans full of worms to eat."[34]

This first experience in jail, which for most of the Nehuentúe prisoners lasted about three years, is remembered as involving a combination of suffering, harassment, solidarity, and internal disagreements. Hugo remembered the sense of connection he felt in the political prisoners' cell block, where he was free to read books, organize events, and occasionally listen to guitar music. In contrast to the fear and isolation he experienced earlier, for this teenager there was at least a collective atmosphere, an occasional political discussion, a shared *mate* brew, cigarette, or even chocolate bar late at night. Enrique Pérez painted a less rosy picture. Efforts to organize a soup kitchen or collectively distribute goods that came in through the solidarity movement sometimes met with conflict and inequality among the prisoners. Some, Enrique remembered, did not want to participate in the pooling of goods because they were embarrassed at having nothing to contribute. In other cases there was a lack of confidence between prisoners because everyone feared infiltration by the intelligence service.[35]

Between 1976 and 1977 most of the Nehuentúe prisoners and others who had been with them in the Temuco jail were released. Some of the more recognized militants in the MIR, like Enrique Pérez and Víctor Maturana, were released directly into exile. Those from the Nehuentúe operation, however, were simply let go, nothing ever having been proven against them. Along with several other released prisoners, Hugo Ailío went to Temuco at first and stayed at the charitable organization the Traperos de Emaús, since neither he nor any of his jail mates had money to pay for the bus fare home. "If I'd had money I'd have gone home that very afternoon," Hugo remembered,

> to be with my folks, but we ended up at the *Traperos* for about a week. They welcomed us generously, and we helped them out in their work, which was mainly recycling different materials, and that's how we'd earn the plate of food they'd give us. And it also helped get us oriented and to be safe, to have a refuge, because the agents of the CNI [Intelligence Service] were going around and around, and of course that was the greatest terror we felt, that . . .

[Q: That they could take you back to jail?]

Yes. And in later years they did arrest some of the compañeros again, even after we were free, without any problem, some of us were harassed again, they grabbed Heriberto again, the guys from the CNI, and brought him to Temuco, or maybe it was Imperial. And they made the poor man see stars again! I saved myself because I came here [Concepción], but even here they came around. I ended up safe because I worked only a little while around here, as an apprentice in the furniture shop of the guy who lives across the street, he used to rent a piece of land to my uncle, may he rest in peace, and he had a factory, a furniture workshop and I'd help him, but I had an accident and cut this finger in the machine. After that machines made me nervous and I couldn't keep working here, so I went to work for a lumber company and spent a long time working in the forest.[36]

Some of the other prisoners stayed in Temuco, working in a copper workshop set up by the Traperos in the city. They produced artisanry that was marketed through the Vicaría de la Solidaridad and also overseas. Surveillance continued, however, and when an allanamiento turned up a clandestine printing press, the workshop was closed down.[37]

Although don Heriberto had returned almost immediately to the community, he was arrested again in connection with the work project in Temuco. Released relatively quickly, he went back again to Ailío where, in 1977, agents came for him a third time at his home. He remembered that they kept him at police headquarters in Nehuentúe all afternoon, and about eleven in the evening they loaded him onto a jeep and took off along the road to Carahue. He was in the back, "my hands and feet were tied, and I think it must have been June, in the middle of winter, and the ground was frozen, the roads covered with water. And even though the jeep was tall, still the water splashed in the back, so I traveled being sprayed with water, all wet, and I couldn't move to get out of the way because I was all tied up." They transported him the same way from Carahue to Temuco: "By then I didn't know what had hit me, and they threw me in a dungeon and a common prisoner said to me, sir, he said, you need to cover up better. I was chilled to the bone and all I had was two soaked blankets, so I told him my blankets are wet, and he said pass them over, we'll lay them out here and they'll dry. But it was all in the shade, so how were they going to dry? So instead he sat right up next to me, and together, our bodies side by side, we started to get warm."[38]

The third arrest turned out to be the worst for don Heriberto. As Hugo remembered, they really made him see stars. They tied his hands with a piece of metal so that the electricity would conduct better and placed the wires in his mouth. He truly feared for his life that time because in essence he was disappeared—no one knew where he was. What saved him was the release of the common prisoner who was sharing his cell:

> I said to him, can you do something else for me? And he said what is it, pops? When you get out go to this place in Temuco, to this street, this number, and talk to so and so, and if he's not there, talk to this other guy, and tell them, I said, let them know they have me here and I don't know where they're going to take me.
>
> And so the gentleman goes where I said, at first he couldn't find the people, but the next day, barely past dawn he went back and wouldn't you know that my buddy was an early riser and he's just arriving at the office, and when he opens the door this other guy comes out of nowhere and goes right in after him, and my buddy got scared and raised his hands, thinking maybe he was being held up or something.
>
> But my cellmate says no, no, I have a message for you. And my friend told me later that he put down his hands and asked, what message. Do you know so and so? Yes. Well, they arrested him, and he doesn't know where they're going to take him. So my buddy right away began to search for me, alerted the Human Rights Commission, a commission had already been formed, and alerted the Bishop and they began to look for me, people got organized really quickly to look for me, and they found me.[39]

When don Heriberto was released thanks to pressure from the Human Rights Commission, they threw him by the side of the road near Temuco, in the middle of the night. He was very ill and just managed to drag himself to a clump of bushes before he fell asleep. The next morning, burning with a fever brought on by the combination of the soakings and torture he had suffered, he stumbled to a house where they gave him directions to the bus station. A woman recognized him at the terminal and thought he was drunk because he was staggering as he walked and seemed to be falling asleep. "She said to me, you got drunk. No, I said, it's something else." The bus driver let him get on without paying and advised him to sit in the back. "If they catch you," he told don Heriberto, "I'm not responsible." Despite all the obstacles, don Heriberto finally made it home. His wife, doña Marta Antinao, remembered that "he arrived in really, really bad shape, he almost didn't make it to the house, he was pale, and he was walking like a drunk."[40]

The fear of disappearing and of the physical pain and torture were in some ways worse the second or third time around, and not only because a second or third arrest meant that the person had been identified as especially dangerous or stubborn. It was also worse because of the isolation. Don Heriberto managed to connect with a cellmate who, when released, carried the news to friends who could help. But not everyone was that lucky. "When they put me away for the second time," don Luis Ernesto Quijón remembered, "who did I have to lean on? There was no one, no one. There was no lawyer, right? There was no fancy gentleman with money willing to pay my bail. There wasn't, for example, a general I could hold onto, saying, tell the general to get me out of here. No, not there, not then, not ever. The only support for the prisoner at that moment was God, no one else. And I held onto Him." In fact, don Luis Ernesto had a conversion experience in prison. "Around nine, ten o'clock at night someone spoke to me and told me, you're going to be here for three months and ten days. And would you believe it that, three months and ten days later, I got out?"[41]

Hugo Ailío, too, had a conversion experience that he personally related to his experiences during the Allende years and the subsequent repression, especially to the sense of abandonment and of being used that began to descend on him the more time passed. One weekend while visiting a woman in Concepción with whom he had a long-term relationship and several children, he was walking along a street next to a church:

All of a sudden I'm walking along, by myself, thinking, and I hear the most beautiful music and I stop and look, and of course it was the church, and I just stood there, listening to the beautiful music, and said to myself that I should go in, so I did. I made the decision, crossed the street and went inside, and the brothers and sisters were singing, and the brother greeting people at the door treated me with so much love, how are you, he asked me, and I said fine, and sat down, he found me a seat, and then the sermon began. Afterward the pastor said, all those who have a problem, who are sick, who are suffering in their soul, anyone who is suffering and wants the Lord to lessen their load, I invite you in the name of God to step forward. And I stepped forward. Now I don't know if you'll believe me or not, but I went to the front and kneeled down next to a huge group of people who were already up there, and this is the beautiful part, what I'm going to tell you. I kneeled down, closed my eyes and began to pray, not even knowing exactly what to say, and that's when I had a vision.

First I saw a glowing light, it was a beautiful light with lots of rays that seemed to be made of gold. And then in the middle, a kind of epicenter of the rays, a red book appeared, and I even remember its size, it was 12 centimeters wide and 20 centimeters long, and it had a frame around it made of pure gold, and it was shining, and in the middle were the hammer and sickle. At that point I opened my eyes and was left with this vision, and after I finished praying I got up and went back to my seat.[42]

It would take several years before Hugo understood the meaning of his vision, though he did join the church as a result of his experience. He had remained a dedicated follower of world news, and one evening, when he was ushering in the church, he rushed out immediately after the service to watch a special television report on the Peruvian guerrilla movement Shining Path:

> I came home without even saying good-bye, and a brother who saw me said boy, you're in a real hurry, Brother Ailío. No, I said, it's just that I have something I have to do. And I came home running, and the minute I got here I told my old lady, listen, put on the t.v. because they're showing that Special Report, and she put it on. And they showed everything about how Shining Path operated, what were its principles, its origin, it seemed they were kind of Maoist, something like that. How they acted, what was their form of struggle and warfare, all of that. And at the end they showed an image and there was the book I'd seen in my vision at the Church. It was exactly the same, the same shape, identical, the only thing I didn't see was the inlay along the edge, but I saw the book, in the same position, and that's when I had my answer, years later I had the answer.

As we kept talking, I came to understand that the vision had confirmed Hugo's growing conviction that the cause he had worked and suffered for was no longer worth the trouble. For many people who had been committed to social change in Latin America, the Shining Path guerrilla movement, with its extreme violence and lack of respect for peasants and other lower-class folk, became a symbolic parting of the ways. For Hugo, it was the last straw in a long process of reflection about suffering and abandonment, a process made all the more intense by the fall of the Soviet Union and the defeat of the Sandinistas in Nicaragua.

> Many people gave their lives for a cause they thought was just, and they were willing to die and they did die, fighting as good and generous soldiers, men like Paine himself [one of his cellmates who later perished at Neltume in the MIR's failed attempt in 1981 at creating a guerrilla *foco* in an attempt to topple the dictatorship militarily]. I also learned through different sources

that there were a lot of Chileans who died in Nicaragua fighting against Somoza, maybe a lot of them were tortured, or executed, or they died in the line of duty, in combat, and I really admire these men, these women, they're real heroes.

But then later one finds out that people took advantage of them. And that's a terrible disappointment. When later I got to understand that the Soviet Union, which people called a socialist paradise, was really a heap of garbage, that the dictatorship of the proletariat, quote unquote, had killed so many people, had done awful things just like the Nazis, or like the repressive forces in Chile, or Argentina, or Bolivia, all I wanted to do was grab a mallet and hit myself over the head a hundred times, saying, how could I have been mixed up with such garbage?[43]

This deep regret and sense of abandonment, of having been betrayed, was not limited to people like Hugo who had left the community. When don Heriberto returned after his third arrest, he found that poverty and a sense of isolation and despair had permeated the coastal region. People were afraid of politics, they were angry at being tricked into believing that things really could have changed for the better. It would take time, and a lot of work, before people were willing to trust their neighbors enough to organize again. Even then, as we will see, some wounds were too deep and simply could not heal.

When Push Came to Shove: Fear and Repression on the Coast, 1973–1978

It had begun with the terror of the allanamiento, followed by the coup. Don Heriberto's family had suffered through his periods of hiding, of arrest, sometimes simply not knowing where he was. "They kept looking for him, day and night," his sister doña Eduardina remembered, "that was the terrible thing, such horrible things were happening, with my mother all we could do was pray, we had no other weapons, what could we do against those people who were armed, so we just prayed. There is a God, we knew there was a God, all day we spent praying, praying to the Lord, that nothing happens to him, if they grab my brother please save his life, don't let them kill him Lord, because we knew they were killing, they were killing people."[44] Doña Marta Antinao also remembered the pain and suffering of those days, the isolation as well:

I really suffered a lot, also because I was left alone, I had no one but my mother . . . I was expecting a baby when they grabbed him [don Heriberto], they'd been after him, guarding the house day and night, thank God nothing ever happened to me, I was afraid that they would come in and rough me up, I was pretty large by then, I was close to delivery, I was afraid I'd lose my baby and everything, but they never did anything to me, only asked me where my husband was and they'd tell me that he had to appear because they were looking for him, alive or dead, they had to find him, they said. And they kept watch over the house, the soldiers did, day and night, I couldn't go out anywhere . . .

[*Q: And did you know where don Heri was at the time, had he let you know where he was?*]

Yes, I knew where he was, more or less, but I never told the soldiers, he's in such and such a place, I never said anything. They harassed me a lot but I never told them the truth. Then finally he came and spent the night one time and told me, better that I give myself up, it could be more dangerous on the run, because they could just kill me at any point, so that's when he went to give himself up.

Like her sister-in-law Elisa, doña Marta associated miscarriage, and newborn death as well, with the pain and fear she felt during the years of repression:

That little girl died on me, a pair also, they were born ill and they died, they stayed with me only a few days . . .

[*Q: And do you think that maybe it was because of the times, what you went through during those years?*]

Yes, I think it was.[45]

The sense of personal loss was made worse by the fact that, soon after the allanamiento, fear made people turn against each other, trying to find someone to blame for the horror they were facing. Don Heriberto recalled the disappointment he felt at the time: "Well, that's how it was, sometimes we don't understand, we don't see clearly what poverty is, we don't see that we all deserve to have a piece of bread. So people turned against us, our own people, and actually some even tried to look for me to turn me in, but I didn't show myself, because it wouldn't have been good for them to turn me in. It was only when I knew that my family was being badly repressed that I felt obliged to turn myself in."[46] As a deeply religious person who had earlier conceptualized the struggle for the land as an exodus from oppression similar to the Israelites' Exodus from Egypt, don Heriberto also remembered the repression and subsequent lack of trust in biblical terms, likening himself to a sacrificial lamb. On his last visit to Arnoldo Ríos before he turned himself in, he explained,

> I went by one morning early and told them to be brave. To make decisions, to work hard, to work calmly, that the land was theirs now, and that was why we had fought, in order to get the land, in order to live at peace. And well, if something happened, if I was going to be arrested I alone would be blamed for everything. . . .
>
> So when the soldiers arrived asking for me, the people fingered me for all the things that they had been doing.[47]

It is difficult to exaggerate the depth of the feelings of abandonment, treachery, and anger that descended upon the peasants who had been involved in the Agrarian Reform and the model of the new society promoted by the Popular Unity government. Blaming the organizers at Arnoldo Ríos for the repression, the other asentados tried to take away their rights in the asentamiento. In addition, there was a general feeling that people had not been prepared for what the repression would really mean. "They got him involved in important things," don Luis Ernesto Quijón recalled, referring to one of the two teenagers arrested during the allanamiento, most likely Hugo Ailío, "gave him lots of responsibility, without seeing whether this kid really had the maturity to keep what he'd seen to himself. Once they pressure him, scare him, once he sees the other guy with a uniform and a gun, boy, is it different from what we'd been used to around here."[48] And referring directly to Hugo, don Heriberto remembered that "he got involved in the movement and he wanted to participate, to support us, to help out, he was a young kid, and as a kid he was weak, he ended up turning the rest of us in. He was a very good kid," don Heriberto continued, "that's why he was accepted in the movement, but no one considered whether in the end he'd be weak, and once pressured he'd give away everything he knew, that that's how it was, he affected all of us, he sent us all up the river."[49]

On the other side as well, among the people who had been less committed, there was a feeling of betrayal and abandonment. They had family members in jail; the helicopters kept hovering over houses and fields; soldiers entered peoples' homes; there had to be an explanation. It must be somebody's fault. Or people were afraid. Few had the sense of humor shown by Enrique Antinao, who after his arrest "laughed and said that he felt happy because he'd gotten the chance to ride in a helicopter."[50] For whatever reason, problems between neighbors and complaints to the police continued for several years after the coup—with painful consequences in many cases. "If your animals wandered into the neighbor's field," don Robustiano Ailío remembered, "the neighbor would report you to the police as a Communist or *mirista*, and then the police would come get you and beat you up." Left in charge of all his nieces and nephews upon the imprisonment of his brother, don Robustiano had suffered from endemic health problems ever since a ruptured ulcer had led to generalized infection in 1969. As the most prominent member of don Heriberto's family living in the community, he became the target of ongoing efforts at revenge in the years after the coup, and his health only exacerbated his vulnerability. "They came looking for me one day," he remembered,

> one day that a pig had died. This pig died, and I buried it. At the same time, a neighbor's garden had been damaged by animals belonging to another woman who lived nearby. My neighbor named me as a witness in the case she was bringing against the animals' owner. Now the owner finds out that I've been named a witness, and she goes to the police and tells them she saw me burying weapons.
>
> I remember it really well, I have this little tree, an apple tree, I had planted it that year and in June or August I had trimmed it back really well, and with the cold I had gotten a cough, I really suffer a lot from coughs . . . and they came to get me. They took me to Nehuentúe, they stripped me, leaving me only in my underwear and they gave me a good beating . . .
>
> The police really punished me that time, I thought to myself, this time I really bought it, they're going to leave me for dead, and they would throw me in the water, kick me, step on me.[51]

Doña Eduardina was convinced that these accusations were a form of revenge:

> They thought that it was Heriberto's and Robustiano's fault that their husbands were in jail. One lady, I ended up not even able to look at her, she went [to the police] and told them Robustiano had a typewriter, that he was *mirista* . . .

She'd always been blaming them for her husband being in jail, and that's why they came for my brother, they asked me about the machine, the typewriter, they said you have a typewriter. Well, go ahead and look, go right in, I said, to see if we have a typewriter. All you're going to find is an old sewing machine I have, nothing else. So afterward we didn't talk to her anymore, sometimes we'd meet face to face and then we'd meet her eyes to show her we weren't afraid.[52]

In a situation like this, the sense of abandonment went very deep. If those less committed to the previous government blamed the activists, the local activists tended to blame the political parties and party militants. "Many of them turned into cats' claws," don Luis Ernesto Quijón remembered, "they'd show themselves, and then they'd hide. They didn't stay for the whole show, if you know what I mean." At one point he seemed to be referring specifically to the MIR, but he later included the other political parties on the left while also being careful to distinguish between those militants who practiced what they preached and those who did not:

They didn't face the consequences. When this [the coup and repression] happened, boom, they were off this way and that, they had all the connections, right? They had the means, they had the knowledge, and well, who stayed around to pay for the broken china, Miss?

[Q: Those who were left on the ground.]

We did. The poor peasants, we've paid with hunger, nakedness, malnutrition, and many more things, and on top of that beaten and bruised as we are. Now here I'm in agreement with Enrique [Pérez]. When push came to shove Enrique was there with us, hungry, cold, beaten and bruised, and Enrique's out there now, still working for the cause, and on that point I'm still in agreement with him.[53]

Indeed, in my first interview with him, when we discussed the work he had done with Dr. Hillerns from the Puerto Saavedra hospital, don Luis Ernesto had alternated between remembering Hillerns in an affectionate and nostalgic way, emphasizing how the doctor had always been willing to slog through mud and rain at two in the morning to treat Mapuche patients in remote communities, and expressing a deep sense of abandonment because "Dr. Arturo" had left the region and never come back. He had insisted that Hillerns must have sought asylum in an embassy after the coup, as had, in his estimation, most other leftist militants from outside the communities. After interviewing Hillerns's widow, Maritza Eltit, I learned that they had been transferred back to Temuco at the beginning of 1973 to begin work on a nationwide popular health program. Once I had access to the description of Hillerns's arrest, I understood the origin of don Luis Ernesto's presumption: Hillerns had disappeared in Temuco, after not having been in the coastal region for about six months. The next time I visited don Luis Ernesto, I showed him a xeroxed copy of the Rettig Commission Report's entry on Hillerns's disappearance, which I hope helped him close that chapter of his experience on a different note.[54]

In the coastal region, the lives of political prisoners and victims of torture and their families were forever changed. Though twenty years had passed when my questions challenged people systematically to remember, it quickly became clear that the wounds were nearly as fresh as if it had been yesterday. And yet people struggled doggedly to find explanations for the inexplicable. One theme they returned to, again and again, was the expressions of solidarity they and their families had received, sometimes unexpectedly, sometimes even from strangers. Don Luis Ernesto Quijón was convinced, for example, that he survived because his mother constantly traveled from Puerto Saavedra to Temuco, once a week, twice a month, and demanded to talk to the military intendant. She continued traveling even after she ran out of money because the bus drivers let her travel for free:

> Then she had to travel like an indigent person, going up to the driver and saying, sir, could you please take me to Temuco, because I don't have any money, because people had been left without work, there was nowhere to turn. But why should I take you, the driver would ask. Because I have a son in jail, if she had to say it she would—and well, what I want is that they turn him over to me, dead or alive, if he's dead, well all right, but at least they can return him to me. And if he's alive, well, that would be my greatest happiness.
>
> So I think the bus drivers in those years, the ones who drove the routes from Puerto Saavedra . . . maybe it wasn't only my mother who received this favor. Maybe a lot did. Because I think back and I say to myself, those drivers looked at these women, and they must have thought, well, I'm a worker, too, and if these women are running back and forth, it must be for a worker.[55]

In their attempts to overcome the pain and damage caused by repression, however, people seemed to turn most often to their religion, to their belief in God. Even people who had not been in agreement with the Popular Unity experiment, people like doña Felicia Concha de Ailío, wife of don Antonio and Hugo's mother, called on their faith to protect them when soldiers came to the community. Doña Felicia remembered that the helicopters kept passing over her house, that her husband had been taken to Temuco to make a statement, and that her children had run off somewhere:

> I was alone, I was working in the vegetable garden when suddenly I saw a group [of soldiers] coming up the hill, and when they got to where I was they began asking questions. Are you afraid, they asked me? No, I said, I'm not afraid. I haven't seen anything, so there's no reason for me to be afraid.
>
> So afterward they said to me, ma'am, what [political] party do you belong to? A big, fat sargent was in charge of them, the rest of them were big, too. Look, I said. I went back into my bedroom and picked up my Bible. This is my [political] party, I said, I'm not mixed up in anything. And in addition, I said, I don't like these things. I may be a very simple woman, I told him, I may be poor, but I like to live with a clean conscience.[56]

Political prisoners and their families were perhaps the ones who relied most on their spirituality and their belief in God to get them through. Doña Marta Antinao, for example, told me that her mother had been taken to jail from Rucalán when the asentados were forced to return the fundo to its former owner. When they held her in Imperial, "she never allowed the guards to shut her up, those who were inside, she never kowtowed to them. She would talk with them about her faith in God, she'd explain things to them about God. And they said to her, no, little mama [*mamita*], don't worry, you're going to get out, don't let it upset you, they'd tell her." Doña Marta was also convinced that God helped don Heriberto survive. "With all the punishment he was forced to endure," she explained, "I sometimes think he's alive because of God's mercy, I say he's alive, because God always went with him." She referred to the moment, also recalled by her husband and her sister-in-law, when the military arrived at Arnoldo Ríos during the allanamiento of August 1973, and one of the other asentados, duping the soldiers, had ordered don Heriberto, in effect, to go in search of himself, thus giving him the opportunity to escape: "And I say to myself, maybe if they'd taken him at that point, maybe they would have killed him."[57] Her sister-in-law doña Eduardina, who has a penchant for finding the most profound explanation for the way things are, also found great power in religious faith. Doña

Eduardina believes that her faith was a force she was given to help her resist and to aid her brothers:

> That's why I say that God gets through to you before it's time, maybe outside of time, because maybe God knew what was going to happen and He prepared me, gave me a way to defend myself, to defend myself through God, to defend my brothers' lives, because Jesus was also taken prisoner. [My brother Robustiano] was taken to make a declaration and then he had to sign, and that's how they caught him, and what didn't they do to him, they just kept beating and beating him. And with my mother, we had no other defense but the Bible, so I defended myself biblically, again and again. . . .
>
> I said to the man in charge, look sir, you must believe yourself to be very powerful, but remember that there is a season for everything, a time to die, a time to live, a time for war, a time for peace, that's what the Bible says, I told him. And someday, the Bible says, everything will pass, heaven and earth will end, but the world of God will not end. This thing will pass, too. If heaven and earth will pass someday, how couldn't there be an end to Pinochet's government? It, too, shall pass.
>
> He just kept looking at me. Your brother will get out, ma'am, he said. I want you to let him out right now, I said. You are a bad person instead of a good man. You shouldn't do these things to your fellow human beings. And they did release my brother, they turned him over to me.[58]

Adding to the sense of personal suffering and abuse felt by coastal residents was, between late 1973 and mid-1974, the reversal of the agrarian reform. In contrast to the fundo Esperanza, which, as Luciano Landarretche Maffei remembered it, was returned to the family about a month after the change of government, Rucalán remained in peasant hands almost until the end of the military's restoration program. This despite the fact that, according to the regulations established by the Comités Ejecutivos Agrarios (Executive agrarian committees—special provincial committees created by the dictatorship to resolve the land situation), there could be no alternative to complete restoration in cases of illegal takeovers. Today the Landarretche family explains this apparent anomaly in political terms, blaming Héctor Jensen, Juan Bautista Landarretche's school chum but also a Christian Democrat and CORA functionary even before the coup. As Luciano Landarretche explained it, there were two basic issues involved. The first was that CORA and the State Bank had invested a great deal of money in the asentamiento Arnoldo Ríos and thus had incurred a large agrarian debt. The second issue was that the resentments created by the original occupation and violent reoccupation were still floating close to the surface.[59]

These two ongoing problems intensified the differences of opinion between Landarretche and the postcoup transition team that handled CORA in the first months of the counterreform. This team, called Alessandrist by the economist Patricio Silva, was in charge of the Oficina de Planificación Agrícola (Agricultural planning office, or OPA) between September 1973 and April 1974 and had been putting together a more conservative agrarian reform plan based on small private parcels, even while the Popular Unity government was still in power; it had also helped formulate the agrarian program for Jorge Alessandri, a conservative candidate running in the elections of 1970.[60] The team's combination of deep respect for economic efficiency and a certain preoccupation with the social problem in the countryside, however, came into direct conflict with Juan Bautista Landarretche's deeply held feelings of humiliation and injustice. This confrontation is clearly reflected in the technical report on the Rucalán case that was produced by CORA's agronomists in December 1973.

As they reviewed the situation on the property at the moment of expropriation, the agronomists treated the information Landarretche had provided cautiously. "Under the principal rubric of production on the estate, which was livestock," the officials wrote,

> there was, according to Mr. Landarretche, the following herd of animals: 250 cows, 70 heifers, 200 calves, 14 fine bulls and 60 young bulls. But we estimate that this herd did not live permanently on this property because the pastures were only of medium quality, and that he must have combined it with another property he had nearby in Puerto Saavedra where the dairy was located. He could not carry out the fattening operation on this property because of the quality of pasture and the fact that the drinking water was deep in the ground in this hilly region of broken-up terrain.[61]

At the same time, the CORA officials criticized the production system developed under the previous government's agrarian reform, because "right now the cost is extremely high because there is an excess of workers." And they continued,

> There are 36 workers whose wages, social security contributions, and other benefits yield an extremely high cost of production on an estate whose principal activity should be livestock. If we keep in mind that 1 worker per 4 to

8 HRB is enough, and that this production system is extensive in nature, we calculate that the maximum labor force should be between 10 and 15 workers in order to keep an appropriate balance.[62]

But what truly infuriated Landarretche was the agronomists' conclusion about the "social problem" and the investments on the asentamiento:

There exists for Mr. Landerretche a social problem because of the excess of workers on the property, who in principle he should hire in order to not produce social problems and unemployment, or else it would be necessary to find other employment for the majority of them, who according to Mr. Landerretche are the same people who occupied the estate under pressure from extremists.

There is also the problem of deciding what to do with the infrastructure, the 23 new houses that CORA built.[63]

For Juan Bautista Landarretche, none of the alternatives offered by CORA were acceptable. He did not want his lands back if it meant having to confront the so-called social problem, whether this referred to the asentados or the houses that CORA had built for them. He had never signed on to the expropriation, so when he returned to the farm he wanted it to be empty, not only of people, but also of houses and any other evidence that might remind him of the occupation. His demands made the process of restoration a great deal more complicated. "They also built a tremendous number of houses within the fundo," Luciano explained,

which was one of the reasons for the tremendous debt. The CORA's position at that moment was that, if Father wanted to take over the land, first he had to assume the debt held by CORA and the State Bank and in addition he had to take responsibility for all the houses and for all the people who were living there. In other words they tried to force him to sign labor contracts with every one of those people, which of course Father categorically refused to do, since these were the same people who had taken everything from us; and now he was going to give them jobs? He even said that to Héctor Jensen at one point, he said listen, how can you expect me to hire these people, who stole everything from me, when at any moment I could lose my temper and get into trouble? Please remember that.[64]

What finally changed the situation, according to the Landarretche family, was a trip Juan Bautista made to Santiago at the end of 1973 or beginning of 1974. His brother Manuel Landarretche was a colonel in the Carabineros and arranged an audience for his brother with Gen. César Mendoza, the representative of the police on the military junta and charged, in the junta's initial division of labor, with overseeing the agrarian sector. Doña Violeta Maffei remembered that Manuel Landarretche and Mendoza were

> very, very close friends, so he talked with Mendoza, and then he said to my husband listen, Juan, he's extremely busy but he can give you five minutes and Juan went to talk with Mendoza. So Mendoza said, make up a summary of everything that's happened and send it to me. Juan said all right, nothing ventured, nothing gained, and with my brother-in-law Jorge they wrote up a summary of the occupation and reoccupation and sent it off. After doing that he said to me, my dear, we need to go home because we don't have any more money, we need to leave. We left Santiago on the 8 p.m. train coming this way and when we got here we found the order for the fundo to be returned.[65]

Luciano remembered that the order from Santiago

> was crucial, in the sense that it categorically stated that all the houses that had been built had to be taken down by CORA crews and taken off the property, and that don Juan was to receive the farm in that condition and without assuming any debt the farm had incurred with a third party, in this case with the State Bank, CORFO, or CORA itself. So they told Father here is the property and in the coming days we'll start to take the houses off and that's that, that was the order that came from Santiago.[66]

The interview with Mendoza in Valparaíso thus handed Juan Bautista Landarretche his final political victory over what remained of the agrarian reform process. Jensen visited him twice in the first two days after Landarretche returned to Carahue, the first time to ask what he had been doing in the capital city, the second time when he received a complete update on the situation. "Don Héctor Jensen came back to the house" a second time, Luciano remembered, "and stood there, just looking at Father, and said, 'If Muhammed won't go to the mountain, the mountain must come to Muhammed.' And Father just looks at him and says, 'Héctor, why do you say that?' 'Because at this very moment, Juan, I'm here with a police contingent, and we're going to return your land.'" Luciano Landarretche's interpretation was that Jensen had a "personal vendetta" against his father and that Jensen's attitude, which he exhibited toward other persons as well, ultimately cost him his job. "Said another way," Luciano concluded, "this gentleman was tightening the screw in the opposite direction from the government in power at that time, and not only in Father's case, but in several others."[67]

Was Jensen really trying to tighten the screw to the left instead of the right? It is certainly understandable that affected landowners would have seen it that way. But Jensen, as part of the first transition process after the coup, represented the Alessandrist position within the military regime, modernizing in economic terms but based on the regularization of private property. At the same time, he managed to survive the major policy shift from Alessandrists to the syndicalists (*gremialistas*) that occurred, according to Silva, in April 1974. His ability to survive seemed to be grounded, at the local level, in his enthusiastic reorganization efforts within CORA and his generally modernizing position.[68]

About two months after the coup, Jensen explained his view of the situation in the countryside in a document addressed to Col. Hernán Ramírez Ramírez, Cautín's military intendant. The Allende government's agrarian reform had not been motivated by technical or economic criteria, he explained, but was instead merely political because the regime wished "to obtain total power, and in this way, establish a totalitarian society inspired by Marxism." In this context, "rapid and massive expropriation" was a way to abolish an agrarian system based on "the economic, social and political power distributed among numerous owners of the land." In its place power would be concentrated in the hands of the state, that is, of the political parties making up the Popular Unity coalition. Pursuing this goal, the government bypassed the law or used it "arbitrarily. Landowners were pressured, land occupations were encouraged, all sorts of irregularities were committed, leaving the expropriated [landowners], in this way, almost totally defenseless." Sounding a more autobiographical note, Jensen concluded that this process marginalized "all technical personnel who did not support the Popular Unity and did not support the methods just described." Because the politically active functionaries, those interested in establishing political control over the peasantry, were favored, the result in government offices and agrarian reform units was "an absolute lack of labor discipline and numerous irregularities." It was clearly impossible, under such conditions, for the countryside to remain productive.[69]

When Jensen took over CORA, he reviewed all 220 functionaries for the region, firing 55 whom he considered "categorically activists" and naming "suitable" (*idóneo*) personnel to all the leadership positions. He brought judicial or administrative charges against all personnel who had been involved in "anomalous situations." Still in November 1973, however, Jensen believed that "the most serious problem to be solved lies in the resolution of the expropriations, because we lack clarity on policy. We believe that the creation of the CEA [Comité Ejecutivo Agrario] in the province is an important step, but its success will lie in the application of strictly technical criteria."[70] These "technical criteria," which might also be called market criteria, were what Jensen insisted on applying in the countryside. Even if his insistence got him into trouble with Landarretche, it made him the ideal functionary to help conceptualize and apply a militantly mercantile agrarian counterreform whose keynote would become, in the long run, export production.

Under the headline "Nothing Will Stop the Agrarian Reform Process," Temuco's daily newspaper published an interview with Jensen on 20 January 1974 in which he summarized the logic and process of agrarian policy since 11 September of the previous year. Before the coup, according to Jensen, 409 agricultural properties had been expropriated in Cautín, leading to the creation of 179 asentamientos and 21 cooperatives. After the coup, 270 expropriated landowners presented petitions to have their cases reconsidered. As Jensen explained it, in order for the CEA to reconsider an expropriation, the following documentation had to be collected: "The petition from the expropriated landowner, the technical and legal background to the expropriation, the technical field report prepared by agronomists and technical personnel from the CORA, the estimates [of value] carried out by CORA specialists, and the study carried out by CORA's regional council, composed of the heads of the production and technical departments and the heads of the various zones."[71] A carefully prepared file was then presented at one of the weekly CEA meetings, and, if necessary, the ex-owner could be asked to appear. Once the case was heard by the CEA, CORA's regional office made an appointment with the landowner to discuss any legal problems and to sign the necessary agreements with CORA and the peasants established on the property. Since the file still needed to be approved in Santiago, Jensen emphasized that any agreements up to this point were only provisional. But if everything went as planned, the last step in this long process was the return of the property itself. According to Jensen, the only unproblematic returns occurred in cases in which either CORA had not yet taken over the expropriated property or no asentamiento had been created. The return was much more complicated when an asentamiento existed, when CORA had made investments, when the resident population had made improvements or had crops in the ground.[72]

Compared to this general model, Rucalán was a problematic case. CORA had invested a great deal in it, there was a substantial asentado population, and people were still cultivating their crops in January 1974. Landarretche, moreover, simply refused to recognize the legality of the process: of the original expropriation, of CORA's debt, of the presence of peasants on the property. Thus the solution to the problem of Rucalán came from above, from a member of the military junta.

Even after an agreement had been reached, Landarretche was uncooperative. On 22 July 1974, in the midst of returning the estate, Jensen sent an internal memorandum to the national director of land tenure. "In conversations formalized in Acts of Return signed by myself and the owner," he explained, "it was agreed that the owner would only pay for the transference of 10 houses with the rest paid by the Corporation, canceling any field preparations, which are now documented." Yet despite all of this, Jensen continued, when the moment came to estimate the cost of the transference of the ten houses, Landarretche declared that he was "unable to pay that expense, both because it was so high, and because he was given so little time to do so." Jensen concluded by asking his superior to advise him as to a solution to the conflict.[73] The case of Rucalán was therefore extremely frustrating for Jensen. Perhaps he was referring to it when he commented, in January 1974, "We have cases solved in complete harmony; but we also have problems of lack of understanding, of intransigent positions that cannot be solved immediately. Everyone (landowners and peasants) must remember that we did not create these problems; we received things as they were."[74]

Jensen probably took solace, from his point of view, in the fact that he was returning what he called "legality and technical expertise" to the countryside. For the first time, he said, it would be possible to know how much the asentamientos were producing. He was able to state with pride that 101 cases had been solved: in 56 cases the expropriated properties had been returned in their totality (27 of these due to illegal occupations), in 27 the landowner's reserve had been returned, and in 18 the expropriations were deemed legitimate and thus not returned at all.[75] Total or partial restitution—55 percent and 27 percent, respectively—dominated this first batch of cases, only 18 percent being left as they were under the previous regime. The proportions changed in subsequent months, for by August 1974 Jensen reported that 109 of the total 409 expropriated properties had been returned, 27 percent in all. For Jensen, an agricultural technocrat interested in promulgating a rational, market-oriented agrarian policy, this process and its results must have been quite satisfactory.[76]

Like the military government he enthusiastically supported, Jensen was not interested in reversing the entire agrarian reform process. Through "rational" and "responsible" agrarian policy, he wished to demonstrate instead the total bankruptcy of the previous regime. Nowhere did Jensen demonstrate this more clearly than in the trip he made to the coastal region on 1 February 1974, during which he formally returned to Pablo, Enrique, and Fernando Lüer the three properties that had been expropriated from them. On the fundo San Pablo, property of Pablo Lüer, Jensen first accompanied the landowner on a tour of the property that had been occupied on 14 May 1972. He then spoke to the peasants who had been living there:

> He told them: "You know what the punishment is for people who take, rob, or usurp. We would have been perfectly within our rights to arrive in the company of a police or army detachment and throw you out on the street. However, we've preferred a dialogue and a good-faith agreement, conscious that you, along with us, have the same goal, which is the progress and recovery of our country."
>
> Then he added: "The country's orgy has ended; you were maliciously deceived, but you won't be forced to pay the consequences. No. You must understand that the damage done must now be repaired and to do so both landowners and peons must travel down a new path. Those who worked on the fundo before and the boss wants to keep them on, congratulations. Outsiders must find the way to return to their previous places of work. Those who have nothing, well they must find other activities; of course, once the harvest is in and debts are paid they will have some funds with which to begin the next stage of their lives.[77]

And it is here that we can best understand why a "reasoned," "balanced" approach to the agrarian counterreform—no matter how much individual landowners might protest or criticize it—was a most effective tool for sowing disorganization and despair in the countryside. By blaming people for their fate, by equating asentados who had achieved their status through land takeovers with common thieves and criminals, the military government made great strides in its stated goal of achieving "stability" in the countryside. As was clear in the case of the asentamiento Arnoldo Ríos, finally returned to Landarretche between April and July 1974 after that year's harvest and the removal of all evidence of the asentamiento, the military's policy worked at multiple levels to delegitimize what had gone before.

By creating problems for the landowners, for example, rather than nakedly supporting them, the agrarian officials of the dictatorship gave the impression of "objectivity." By emphasizing notions of economic efficiency, as Jensen did in his public declarations and CORA in its technical report of December 1973,[78] the new regime not only delegitimized the social justice orientation of the Popular Unity agrarian reform, but also called into question the peasant vision of moral economy in which land became, beyond its market value, a resource for sustaining the poor and their families. This combination of supposed objectivity and invalidation of social struggle that transformed participants into criminals also facilitated the creation of divisions and a desire for vengeance among the ex-asentados of Arnoldo Ríos. At the moment of removal, "everybody divided up things," doña Eduardina recalled:

> They were dividing up all the things they'd accumulated and they gave nothing to Marta, not even . . . nothing, not a thing. They divided up animals, they divided up tools, everything, plows, carts, everything was divided up but Marta got absolutely nothing. Marta came home with only the things she'd already had, that they'd already had, nothing else, not even the harvest, nothing.
>
> That's what people did, no one said, let's not do this to Heriberto, he's always been a leader, he's always been on our side, we don't know what will happen to him now, let's give something to his family, nothing. We all had to deal with this, Robustiano, myself, my mother. When the children were growing up, there wasn't even food when Heriberto was in jail, the one who had to take over the responsibility was Robustiano, he worked, he fed all the children. Luckily my mother was good at making [herbal] medicines, she would give us part of the money she received from making the medicines, and that's how we'd go visit Heriberto, otherwise we wouldn't have been able to go see him.[79]

An asentado whose story ended in an especially dramatic way was Francisco Llancao. When Rucalán was occupied he was forty-six years old and had worked as an *inquilino* on the estate for thirteen years. There is evidence that the Landarretches might have favored him somewhat. In the evaluation of the property done at the moment of expropriation, the house Llancao lived in was estimated to be worth ten times as much as that of the other resident *inquilino*, and its size was closer to that of the landowner's house. His daughter doña Lidia del Pilar Llancao remembered that her family did not participate in the takeover but came down from their house to the main part of the fundo fifteen days later, that is, after the state had already intervened the property. During the reoccupation, Llancao did not come home for two days because, according to doña Lidia, he was hiding in a ditch. But by 10 March 1971, when CORA completed the technical report and estimate of value, Francisco Llancao signed the document as spokesperson for the committee of peasants working on the new asentamiento. Even though he joined the asentamiento with some ambivalence, doña Lidia remembered that Llancao paid a high price for his actions: Landarretche never forgave what he saw as treasonous behavior. During the first years of the dictatorship, once the property had been returned and Llancao was working elsewhere, Landarretche called him in to help plant in Puerto Saavedra. On his way back from work, near Carahue, someone pushed him off the tractor he was riding and ran over him. When he got home he was in very bad shape, but when doña Lidia and her mother called Landarretche he insisted that Llancao was only drunk and refused to help them. Llancao died the next day, leaving his family totally destitute; in his daughter's eyes he was a victim of landowner revenge.[80]

Between 1974 and 1978 the only sources of solidarity for people along the coast were the archdiocese office in Temuco and the Traperos de Emaús. One of the founders of the Traperos, originally a railroad worker, became unemployed in 1974 and, together with two teachers, began to visit the jail and help take care of the prisoners' families when they came to visit. A solidarity committee formed with help from the bishop not only worked with the prisoners themselves, but also began to run soup kitchens in Nehuentúe, Tranapuente, and the community of Ailío. Gustavo Marín, a member of the MIR's regional committee in Cautín and in exile in France, raised funds to help run these projects. Starting in 1977 with the organization of a child nutrition project, both the Vicaría de la Solidaridad and the Traperos began visiting the region more consistently. Despite limited resources and few volunteers, the two groups managed, over the next few years, to establish forty soup kitchens specifically for children, serving a total of one thousand youngsters. In a format used by many soup kitchens at the time, the Temuco archdiocese would buy the food and then the families in the communities would provide the labor and cook it collectively. Solidarity workers also gathered donations of clothes, seed, fertilizer, and food for households in the communities. And finally, among the tasks the members of the solidarity committee set for themselves was to keep in close touch with the lawyers who had been named to defend the Nehuentúe prisoners, among them ex-Intendant Sergio Fonseca, Francisco Huenchumilla, Renato Maturana, and Hugo Ormeño.[81]

Reviving the Organization, 1978–1992

When don Heriberto got out of jail for the last time in 1978, the political climate in the IX Region was beginning to change. At a general level, the military government had announced a decision to divide up and privatize Mapuche lands and was in the process of issuing a decree-law that would end all government protection of indigenous property. In August and September 1978, with the support of Monsignor Sergio Contreras, bishop of Temuco, Mapuche leaders from thirty communities in Cholchol, Temuco, and Lautaro publicly announced their opposition to this decree-law, especially to the lack of information about the project in the IX Region. "We have not been consulted about this law the government wants to pass," they wrote in an open letter to the bishop, "and we would like to be informed as to the content of this Indigenous Law so that we can give our opinion. Our future as a race hangs in the balance," they added, and if the law must be changed, they concluded, then the changes should be positive rather than negative, "and should permit us to survive and to preserve our Mapuche culture."[82]

This was the beginning of a broad movement of Mapuche ethnic renewal called the Centros Culturales Mapuches de Chile (Mapuche cultural centers of Chile), which by 1982 had linked fifteen hundred communities from the VIII, IX, and X regions of Chile in a long chain of cultural ceremonies and events to protest the division of Mapuche lands. At first under the protection of the Catholic Church, then as a syndicalist organization of small agriculturalists and artisans (*asociación gremial de pequeños argicultores y artesanos*) that took the Mapuche name Ad-Mapu, this organization helped revive social movements and encouraged the participation of nongovernmental organizations (NGOs) in development projects in the region. Although internal political divisions would begin to plague Ad-Mapu after 1982 with the revitalization of leftist parties in the context of dramatic antidictatorship protests, its ethnic and syndicalist strategy, which had received limited sanction within the military dictatorship, was extended to other areas. With the support of the Temuco archdiocese's Departamento de Acción Social (Department of social action, or DAS) and with additional financial assistance from CIMADE, a French NGO brought into the effort by the ex-*mirista* Marín, a Comité de Pescadores y Agricultores (Committee of fishermen and agriculturalists) was formed in Tranapuente, its core formed of the fifteen families that had been directly affected by military repression.[83]

Between 1979 and 1984, people began to feel some relief. There was still a great deal of fear, one of the early organizers remembered, so that even something as simple as an attempt to revive agriculture by cultivating vegetables and lentils required that one go house to house, drinking mate and explaining the project carefully.[84] Still, doña Eduardina remembered that, when the committee was formed, "when *señora* Catalina, *señora* Angélica began to arrive . . . it was different then." The women in the community, "we began to work in the vegetable garden, the atmosphere changed, it was as if we forgot all the sadness we had lived through, Pinochet's repression, all those things."[85] Bit by bit the organization began to spread to surrounding areas. In February 1979, people organized the first Cultural Week in Nehuentúe, billed as a folkloric and tourist event, but also as a commemoration for four young peasants whose shackled bodies had been found earlier in Puerto Saavedra cove.[86]

By 1984, funding from CIMADE had been pretty well institutionalized through the DAS, and the Centro de Educación y Tecnología (Center for education and technology, or CET) was brought in to collaborate and help systematize the work. The idea was to help reestablish the viability of the households affected by repression in the years after the Nehuentúe prisoners got out of jail. When CET arrived, Angélica Celis remembered, CIMADE's funding had extended pretty much to the whole region. "Our presence was connected to the technological component, to the productive aspect of the project," she explained. "And it was particularly Heriberto Ailío who decided to open the project to the whole community and the region and not leave it only for the fifteen families affected by the repression." Although at first she did not understand where the boundaries between the communities lay, it was clear to her, even in the early period, that the funding was being used to rearticulate broader connections with the Mapuche communities of Pilquinao, Pichingual, and Rucahue as well as with the fishing village of Nehuentúe.[87]

Even in 1984, the work was complicated at first. It was not made easier by the fact that, at the end of that year, the military government saw fit to legalize the privatization and division of Ailío's lands according to the Law of 1979. Despite the fact that Enrique Antinao Ailío, previously an asentado on Arnoldo Ríos, was courageous enough to formally voice a protest during the privatization ceremony and demand the return of the forty-five hectares still missing from the original *título de merced*, the conditions of intimidation under which the division was carried out meant that the community had no real recourse in the matter. In addition, by dividing the land among the present occupants, and disregarding the original kin ties and family tree of the resettled community, the policy of the dictatorship divided families even further. The people who had migrated to Santiago because of economic need, such as Cecilia and Elisa Ailío, younger sisters of don Heriberto, don Robustiano, and doña Eduardina, lost all legal rights to land in their community, a disfranchisement that would continue to affect them over the coming years.[88]

In 1984, moreover, there was still a lot of hunger in the communities. "Our work began with an effort to address the problems of family subsistence at a particularly difficult moment," Angélica Celis explained, "because I remember, for example, visiting a lot of houses, oftentimes at noon, when there was no fire burning in the hearth." In a Mapuche home, where the hearth is usually the center of both social and subsistence activity, this was particularly dramatic evidence of the lack of viability. At this time, food reached the households mainly through the soup kitchens established by the Temuco archdiocese. "The men were attempting to reestablish productive activities," Angélica continued, "but remember that at this point there was no aid from the state, and obviously it was a politically battered area." In 1984, the law still prohibited public meetings, so group activities tended to be channeled through the churches. The CET arrived, then, with a double mission defined by the bishop: to provide help in the area of human rights and to rebuild the viability of local subsistence production.[89]

CET did not initially work in people's houses. "Our first activities occurred in a space the people themselves defined as a communal area," Angélica recalled.

> We began with a community vegetable garden, where together we developed a certain technology which was able to use already existing local resources. People went to work there, and it was fundamentally the women with support from the men. And afterward we'd have a kind of technical workshop, with a certain amount of socially oriented discussion, and we'd always accompany it with a meal, we'd drink *mate*, and eat plenty of bread. We'd serve

a lot of food, since there really wasn't much to do in the houses, since the hearth, the stove, was never on in most of them.[90]

In time, people began to be less afraid, and activities began to multiply and diversify. The CET began to work with individual families in their homes, and although the communitarian vegetable garden stopped being important, the communal area in which it was located remained a collective space used for meetings. The community as a whole began to consider the formulation of a general production plan or, as Angélica remembered, "a plan of exploitation, because some of them still remembered the asentamiento in Rucalán and used it as a reference point." In addition there were sewing and knitting projects for the women, which also served as a space for social interaction. At a certain point, when the confluence of ocean and river currents allowed fish from the sea to range into the Imperial River, the community collaborated with the fishermen from Nehuentúe port in harvesting this additional resource. Ultimately, Angélica explained, "our team mixed a variety of activities, including a group working with the fishermen, a group working with the farmers, another working with the women, and an underlying support network on human rights issues."[91]

Between 1986 and 1987, this expanding work led to the partial reconstruction of the coastal networks of sociability and cooperation that had functioned under the Popular Unity government. The Mapuche communities of Ailío, Pichingual, Pilquinao, and Rucahue, in combination with the coastal communities near Lobería, especially Coi Coi, formed a coalition with the non-Mapuche peasant and fishing communities of Nehuentúe and Pilmaiquenco, near Trovolhue. When the organization received formal recognition in July 1988 as a syndicalist association (*asociación gremial*), with legal address in the community of Ailío, it was registered as the Asociación Gremial Consejo de Desarrollo Pesquero Campesino (Council for fishing and peasant development, or CODEPECA).[92] With the help of several NGOs from Temuco, including the CET, and some foreign foundations, they were able to advance several projects aimed at improving agriculture. "We did quite a bit of technical work in agriculture," don Heriberto remembered, "including funding the purchase of seeds, fertilizers, herbicides, a lot of different things."[93] His brother don Robustiano agreed. "At that point we were able to beat out Pinochet, because he legally recognized us as an organization," he added. With outside assistance, "we struggled to get a flour mill, and then we got electricity, the electricity we got for the flour mill." When the mill broke down, CODEPECA won a court case against the technical expert who had installed it improperly, and with the settlement they bought a harvesting machine, a tractor, and a truck.[94]

Despite these accomplishments, however, by the end of the military dictatorship, and especially in 1989 and 1990, problems began to surface in CODEPECA. For a variety of reasons — including the inconsistency of the technical assistance available, sloppy accounting procedures, and a series of internal conflicts and disagreements — CODEPECA weakened and split by 1990 and 1991. "People began to lose hope," don Heriberto remembered, "and to pull each in their own direction. And in addition, once people saw themselves freer and no longer tangled up with the military, they said, now what do we need the organization for?"[95]

The funding organizations also began to introduce their own problems, Angélica recalled. One of these was that, around the time CODEPECA received legal recognition, the Temuco archdiocese reorganized the funding and advising responsibilities associated with the organization. The Mapuche part of the association — the communities of Rucahue, Pichingual, Pilquinao, Coi Coi, and Ailío — passed under the wing of the Fundación Instituto Indígena (Indigenous institute foundation), while the non-Mapuche part, composed of the fishermen and divers from Nehuentúe and the peasant colonists from Trovolhue, remained under the supervision of the DAS. Whatever the archdiocese's reason for the reorganization, in the end it led to increasing divisions within CODEPECA itself, as the Nehuentúe divers and fishermen pushed for independent unionization, and the funds were no longer evenly distributed among all the members.[96]

This reorganization along ethnic lines also resuscitated a further and extremely complicated tension. As had been the case in earlier organizing efforts, in its first incarnation CODEPECA had followed the model of a multiethnic coalition of rural poor. Here again the role of don Heriberto was crucial. From the moment he opened up the original funding beyond the fifteen families affected by repression, don Heriberto's goal was to reconstitute the kind of territorial and popular solidarity the region had experienced during the Popular Unity government. Angélica insisted that don Heriberto had seen CODEPECA as "a union between peasants and fishermen, between *wigkas* and Mapuches, all brothers, all proletarians, all children of God," very much in line with the vision he had held in his political youth in the MCR, tempered as it had always been by his deep religiosity. The partition of CODEPECA into two branches by the archdiocese, however, and especially the increased power in the Mapuche communities of the Instituto Indígena, at that point more conservative, deepened internal divisions and drove a wedge between Mapuche and non-Mapuche in the association.[97]

The increasing disunity between Mapuche and non-Mapuche communities also brought into the open existing differences within the Mapuche communities. This intensified with the Instituto Indígena's practice of using *fondos rotatorios*, or rotating funds, to help provide credit in the communities. These funds, which over the long run were supposed to become self-sustaining, operated in a rotating fashion through the community, one peasant household receiving credit and within a set period of time having to pay back the original loan amount with an additional percentage, so that it could move on to the next household. As Angélica remembered it, "Some paid on time and some didn't, some distributed more, others less; in some cases the leadership decided to give them longer to pay it off, and people started to get reputations as dependable or undependable."[98]

Specifically in the community of Ailío, which took a leadership role in the organization, tensions between families erupted. The Herrera family, in which the mother was Mapuche with rights in the neighboring community of Pilquinao and the father was *wigka*, became a lightning rod in the conflicts. In the days of the asentamiento Arnoldo Ríos, Juan Herrera had become an asentado even though, Angélica had learned, he had neither participated in the original takeover nor been present during the subsequent reoccupation by the Landarretches. His failure to commit and therefore to expose himself to risks had generated resentment. At that moment he had seven young sons and was unable to get a CORA house before the military coup. When they were removed from the asentamiento in 1974 the Herreras went back to the wife's land in the community of Pilquinao, which just happened to border on don Robustiano's land in Ailío. Over time, the seven Herrrera brothers grew up and remained in the countryside, working in a variety of income-generating occupations—as carpenters, tractor drivers, merchants. The family's ability to accumulate both capital and labor power made them a force to be reckoned with at the local level.[99]

With the development of the new association in the 1980s, tensions between the Herrera and Ailío Pilquinao families increased; sometimes they even came to blows at public meetings or in private confrontations. An added dimension was the Herreras' membership in the charismatic Church of God, whereas doña Eduardina and don Robustiano had reestablished an Anglican congregation which don Heriberto also joined when he got out of jail.

While the Herreras were hardworking and dependable, at one point taking responsibility for building the community center (*sede*) on Ailío's communal plot, they also tended to react harshly when others did not fulfill their responsibilities, criticizing those who were tardy in repaying their loans or who did not provide needed contributions, whether in money or labor, for communal projects. Because the Ailío brothers were more tolerant, wanting to find ways of including people or giving them extra time when needed, frictions continued and deepened.

The daily round of conflicts intensified with the building of a communal piped water system. The Herreras complained that people were not paying their quotas on time, that the water pipes did not arrive on time, and that CODEPECA was to blame. They felt, moreover, that the families that did not contribute either money or labor should not receive water, while the Ailíos attempted to negotiate with these families in order to give them new opportunities to be included. The Herreras forced the issue by beginning to use water from the communal system to irrigate their lands, which of course cut down on the water pressure of the remaining households. Others followed suit, while the workers in charge of the system began to cut off water to the houses that were not paying their monthly dues.[100]

Parallel to the discord within communities, and contributing to it by further dividing CODEPECA into its constituent parts, new tensions began to emerge along the coastal region, especially in Coi Coi and Lobería, with the arrival of Manuel Santander, an agricultural technician working for the CET. Santander came to the area in 1988, recommended as the best student to have graduated from the Escuela Aguila Sur (Southern eagle school) for outstanding Mapuche students, whose director was the historian José Bengoa. Though his employers at CET were unaware of the fact at the time, Santander was assisting in the formation of a new Mapuche organization, many of whose leaders were emerging from the more radical sectors of Ad-Mapu and who, in the process of transition toward democratic rule, were increasingly critical of the concessions being made by both the Mapuche and non-Mapuche left. Condemning participation in the plebiscite of 1988, which set the terms for the transition to democracy, as well as the negotiations many indigenous organizations were engaged in with the presidential candidate Patricio Aylwin, this organization went public in early 1988 at a meeting at the Universidad de la Frontera attended by an impressive group of *machis* and *logkos* from Mapuche communities. Calling itself Aukiñ Wallmapu Ngulam (Consejo de Todas las Tierras, or All-Lands Council), this group formulated an increasingly militant discourse centered on the recuperation of Mapuche political and territorial autonomy. Indeed, when in December 1989 Aylwin signed an agreement in Nueva Imperial with a coalition of Mapuche and other indigenous organizations in which he promised, if elected, to push for an indigenous law to recognize and protect native peoples, the *Consejo* refused to sign on the grounds that it was just one more cooptation of Mapuche autonomy and militancy.[101]

When Santander brought these ideas to Coi Coi and Lobería they resonated strongly in the leaders of those communities, who not only had suffered through the repression after 1973, but were also facing renewed pressure from Domingo Durán, still the owner of the fundo Lobería. Durán had just constructed a retaining wall along the edge of his property to help drain his lands, thereby causing flooding of the few bits of agricultural land Coi Coi still had to its name. Though he maintained cordial relations with don Heriberto Ailío and other leaders in the region, Don Félix Huaiqui, *logko* of Coi Coi, committed himself to the Consejo's vision. Don Félix thus led his community of Coi Coi as one of the outstanding actors in the Consejo's dramatic campaign of land recuperations in 1991 and 1992, a series of illegal takeovers throughout the IX Region that brought international media attention to the Consejo and its leaders. Together with other coastal communities, Coi Coi (re)occupied the fundo Lobería twice between October 1991 and June 1992, and don Félix Huaiqui would be one of the Consejo's 144 activists accused of violating the Internal Security Law.[102]

By 1990–91, then, the Temuco archdiocese's separation of CODEPECA into Mapuche and non-Mapuche sectors had combined with the actions of the Consejo de Todas las Tierras to break the organization down into smaller units. While CODEPECA as a group continued to meet once every two or three months, in Ailío the meetings involved only the communities of Ailío, Pichingual, and Pilquinao. In this smaller setting the conflicts between the Herreras and other families became larger than life, to the point that people could not meet without the discussion degenerating into a shouting match. Given the very real possibility of physical confrontation, it became common for don Heriberto to request the presence of Roberto Molina, a non-Mapuche fisherman from Nehuentúe who had been president of CODEPECA since 1988, as arbiter or buffer. As the younger generation became integrated into CODEPECA, moreover, without having had previous experience in the correct handling of organizational resources and funds, additional problems emerged. Some individuals in fact began to use the organization's money and property for personal purposes. Indeed, by 1991 the situation was sufficiently tense that don Heriberto Ailío, Roberto Molina, and Angélica Celis decided to conduct a small private survey of households in order to understand the problems more fully.[103]

What they found was both dramatic and heartbreaking. In private, people were more willing to speak up about the fear they felt in the presence of the Herreras, a fear connected directly to the terror of physical punishment they had developed under torture. This was heightened, some people said, because the Herreras were considered to "have a short fuse" (*ligeros de genio*). But the most wrenching issue came up in the interviews with the younger generation, those now in their late teens and early twenties, like Martín Ailío, whose mother, doña Marta Antinao, had taken him with her in the bottom of the small rowboat on the way to Rucalán and protected him from bullets with her body during the retaking of the property. These young adults had been small children during the Popular Unity mobilizations and subsequent repression. The problem came up in relation to CODEPECA's intense participation in the plebiscite campaign, when people had passionately canvassed in favor of the "No." Many younger community members mentioned that they had not been in favor of this; in fact, Angélica remembered that they expressed a "collective rejection" of political involvement. For the first time, the young adults in the community publicly declared that they saw nothing positive in becoming politically active. For them, politics elicited memories of a dimly remembered and poorly understood time when they were small, "and the fathers were absent, mothers alone, fields abandoned. There was hunger, the mothers cried constantly, the hearths were out. They did not have good memories about political participation."[104]

So by 1992 the carefully nurtured vision of solidarity and mutual cooperation—put into practice for a short time between 1970 and 1973; gingerly guarded during years of repression, physical punishment, hunger, and terror; stubbornly reconstructed in the protective shadow of the Catholic Church, human rights groups, and NGOs—had once again shattered. The household survey also prompted don Heriberto and don Robustiano, along with don Antonio Ailío's younger son René, to all reach the same conclusion: Times had changed. Organizing was not what it used to be. "Before," don Heriberto mused, "struggle was about taking over a road, writing up a list of demands. Now struggle is about writing grants. And we don't understand grants, we don't understand projects, we don't understand money." Don Heriberto's comments would be strongly prophetic at the beginning of the 1990s, a decade in which indeed most forms of redistributive social policy would revolve around grants, projects, and money. As he discerned the shape of this future, however, don Heriberto Ailío also continued to mourn his past dream, what in Angélica's words had been "a more international socialist dream, where peasants and fishermen, Mapuches and *wigkas*, all the poor, all proletarians could unite around a common goal."[105] Once again, the Mapuche seemed to be wandering in the desert.

CHAPTER 6

SETTLERS ONCE AGAIN, 1992–2001

In February 1997, the community of Ailío took possession of new land south of Temuco, in the foothills of the Andes mountains. Officials from the National Indigenous Development Corporation (CONADI), the institution created by President Patricio Aylwin's government that had sponsored, through its Land and Water Fund, the purchase of the property, attended the formal ceremony. As leader of the community, Don Heriberto Ailío spoke in *mapunzugun*. A video of the ceremony was later shown in Tranapuente, and several members of the audience wept openly.[1] This was not surprising. After all, the new settlement culminated almost ninety years of struggle for land. Finally people had some, and this time it was legal, and no landowner could change his mind and take it away.

It was not long, however, before things got more complicated. In several ways this second settlement turned out to be rather too much like the first. To begin with, the lack of a real commitment on the part of the government quickly became apparent. CONADI had bought the land, but there were no funds to help with the move or the period of adaptation. A year and a half after having moved, moreover, people learned that, on the ground, the boundaries of the property they had purchased marked off only 147 hectares, or 37.5 hectares fewer than the 184.5 recorded on the bill of sale. The legal implications of this were murky, however, because the leaders had signed the contract and accepted the deal without having measured the boundaries first. And the land they did possess turned out to be contaminated due to the overuse of chemical fertilizers. To these structural and legal problems were added more conjunctural issues, such as deep indebtedness as a result of

Map 3. Comparative locations of Nicolás Ailío I and Nicolás Ailío II within the
IX Region. Inset map shows location of region within Chile as a whole. Cartographic
Laboratory, University of Wisconsin, Madison.

the costs of the move, lack of suitable housing for the winter, and difficulties
in adapting to a new environment and microclimate.

For don Heriberto the difficulties of the new situation were especially
frustrating. As a visionary leader of his community, he had been searching his whole adult life for a solution to the grinding poverty suffered by
his *peñis*. In the 1960s, he and his *compañeros* had chosen to follow a class
struggle strategy in a leftist coalition because they had seen in their parents'
tactic of "living in court" the reason for their ongoing penury. Don Heri had

supplemented his class analysis with a biblical perspective that saw in the suffering of the Mapuche people, as in the Exodus of the Jews from Egypt, a prelude to their eventual liberation. If the prosperity of the agrarian reform was too fleeting to constitute a real liberation, the experience of the *asentamiento* Arnoldo Ríos was nonetheless an example of what was possible with help and dedication. The quick arrival of the military coup, however, and the pain, fear, and destitution of the dictatorship marked a return to their wandering in the desert.

With the end of the dictatorship, a new conflict was added to the already familiar challenge of finding a pathway to prosperity: a generation gap. Ironically but understandably, the new generation, which had grown up under military rule, was convinced that leftist politics, the kind their parents had once seen as the solution to their problems, was in fact the source of their poverty. In that context, don Heri and his closest friends and relatives could find in access to new land an answer to the concerns and questions of the new generation. By using the new land and its resources to create work opportunities for younger family members, it would be possible to re-create the prosperity of the agrarian reform years, though now with the security of having really arrived in the land of milk and honey. Once again, they thought, an organized community would, like the phoenix, rise from the ashes.[2]

On the Other Side of the Desert:
The Reconstitution of the Community

A short time after Patricio Aylwin became the first postauthoritarian president, he presented to Congress a proposal to create an Indigenous Law. Inspired by the indigenous movement of 1978–90, Aylwin had promised to pass this law to repay part of the "social debt" the state owed the Chilean people, specifically the obligation to provide reparations to the indigenous peoples of the country. When he presented this bill to the legislature, Alwyin articulated the indigenous question to his more general vision of human rights in postdictatorship Chile—not only as reparation for specific abuses, but also as part of a general moral reconstruction of the basis for humane justice in civil society. Recognizing the obligation of the state to assure the ethnic and cultural reproduction of Chile's minority indigenous populations was a new concept in twentieth-century Chilean political thought. It surprised many people, for the majority of the non-Mapuche population, whether entrepreneurs, politicians, or average citizens, shared the impression that the Mapuche were in the process of disappearing. In part for this reason and in part because the bill had to be debated and voted on in a congress still hobbled by the right and by the rules established during the dictatorship, the law that was finally passed in 1993 was a somewhat dismembered and trimmed down version of the original. This frustrated many of the activists who had worked hard to get a more extensive version passed.[3]

Nevertheless, the community of Ailío found the possibility of reconstituting itself legally as an indigenous community appealing, especially after having been dissolved in 1984 by the military government. In 1991, Enrique Pérez remembered, a committee of landless Mapuche had organized in the area, in keeping with the rules set out by the Comité Especial de Pueblos Indígenas (Special commission of indigenous peoples, or CEPI), and considered the possibility of applying for a government subsidy. In order to do so, however, it was necessary first to reconstitute as an indigenous community under the new statute.[4] Thus on 10 August 1994, using the official form provided by CONADI, an institution itself created by the Indigenous Law of 1993, and in the presence of the municipal secretary of Carahue as official witness, the indigenous community of Nicolás Ailío was formally reconstituted. In the elections held to choose the first leadership team, Víctor Coliman Santibañez was elected president; Aniceto Huenuan Méndez, vice president; René Ailío Concha, secretary; and Heriberto Ailío Pilquinao, councilman. As president, Coliman was given the task of registering the community in the Register of Indigenous Communities being kept by CONADI's national deputy director, which was done on 25 August of the same year.[5]

In 1995, when CONADI's Land Fund issued its first call for applications for subsidies, the community proposed buying a property in Teodoro Schmidt county which, from an ecological point of view, was quite similar to their place of origin and would permit them to continue cultivating potatoes. Gonzalo Leiva had joined CONADI in 1994 to help energize the Land Fund. He told me that when he arrived there were no set procedures and nobody had experience as to how to make the subsidy program work. When the first call for applications went out, he was especially taken with Ailío's application, in part because, having been a member of the MIR's Provincial Committee in Cautín and a local functionary in INDAP in 1971–73, he was familiar with the community's history. But the price of the property they wished to buy was too high, and their application was rejected. Perhaps this was why on 24 February 1996, according to the minutes of the community meeting, President Coliman was replaced for "not having kept up with his responsibilities." Vice President Huenuan became president, and Heriberto Ailío, previously councilman, moved into the position of vice president. René Ailío remained secretary, while Luciano Martínez became the new councilman.[6]

Don Aniceto Huenuan presided over his first formal meeting as president at the end of March; twenty members of the community formally ratified his taking office. Among other matters concerning the administration of community property, the new call for land subsidy proposals was read. Over the following year these same twenty members would form the core of the participating community, and, with only minor modifications, they would donate the money and materials to repair the community garage; make decisions about who could drive the community's vehicle, what it would be used for, and how to get it repaired; and apply for agricultural credit from INDAP.[7]

Three months later, the same leaders presided over a special meeting that brought together, for the first time, the sixteen individuals who had agreed to apply for a new land subsidy. Twelve of the sixteen were part of that core of participating community members. At the meeting it was reported that the application had been sent in, that "so far everything looks good for us," and that the necessary steps were being taken to buy the *fundo* Mañío, located south of Imperial and the object of a takeover during the Popular Unity years. By 10 August, however, people were informed during a regular meeting of the community that the fundo Mañío had not worked out "due to problems with debt, and because the price was too high." The subsidy had been confirmed in any case, and it was just a matter of finding another property. The minutes of the meeting concluded with a statement about the lack of participation by community members who had not applied for the subsidy:

> It is duly recorded at this meeting that the rest of the members of the "Community of N. Ailío" are not participating in meetings, and we resolve to postpone new elections until next Saturday 17 August 1996. This is so that the majority of the community's members can participate in the election. If they are not present at this next meeting, new elections will in any case be held with those who are present.[8]

The results of this meeting were clearly publicized because thirty-two members showed up to vote in the new elections, including both subsidy applicants and nonapplicants. The entire leadership roster chosen was nonetheless composed of subsidy applicants: Heriberto Ailío, president; his brother Robustiano, vice president and treasurer; José Garrido Altamirano, secretary; as well as the director and three other members of the finance committee.[9]

When the community's second application to the Land Fund was approved, it was in many ways a great victory; and it was due to a series of factors. According to Leiva, the number of applications by communities went down dramatically in the second year because many applicants who had been turned down did not reapply. In a pool in which the applications of individual heads of household predominated, the case of Ailío stood out even more. Thanks to the efforts of Heriberto Ailío, moreover, the community's leaders had been able to reestablish their connections from the agrarian reform years, not only with Leiva, who helped them with the application process, but also with Enrique Pérez, ex-*mirista* and fellow prisoner in the Temuco jail with the Nehuentúe group, who had helped form the first landless committee in 1991 and then participated in the process of reconstituting the community. Having the support and solidarity of these old *compañeros*, and enjoying both a more substantial savings base and a larger group of families participating, who insisted that this second time around neither the distance from the original community nor a change in ecological surroundings would make a difference to them, the Ailío applicants were in a much better position to succeed. On 15 November 1996, don Heriberto and don Robustiano Ailío, representing their community, signed a sales contract with Clemente Seguel before a notary public in Temuco on four contiguous properties in the region of Huellanto Alto.[10]

At the same time, success helped bring to the fore new problems that had been accumulating between 1994 and 1996, a combination of the structural difficulties inherent in the indigenous policy of the Aylwin government and some enduring fears and wounds that had their origin in the community's own particular history. Although the Aylwin government had made an effort to consult indigenous leaders in their formulation of policy and had empowered the CEPI to consult with the communities on the content of the Indigenous Law, in the end the regulations adopted for the reconstitution of indigenous communities were grounded in a general model of association as practiced in political parties and trade unions rather than in the traditions and practices of Mapuche politics. Reconstitution based on statutes and leadership slates countered older practices that had emphasized informal consensus and lines of authority based on kinship and inheritance. If one adds to this the effects of repression and of the formal dissolution of the community carried out by the military dictatorship, it is easy to see why

Ailío's families faced a confusing situation when trying to define the new community and its principles of membership.[11]

Pinochet's Land Division Law of 1979, as we have seen, privatized and titled community land to the occupant of the moment rather than taking into consideration the inheritance or kinship rights of any absent descendants of the original settlers. In one stroke, therefore, this law had erased the land rights of community members residing in urban centers and substituted a principle of squatters' rights, no matter who the squatter might be. In the case of Ailío this led, in 1984, to an outsider by the name of Carlos Riquelme Godoy receiving five hectares of land by pretending to be a member of the community. This was one of the two largest plots given out in the whole community. Some people blamed Gilberto Ailío Alonso for letting the stranger in. He was taking care of the land belonging to his cousin Hilda Ailío, and his name appeared on the title of the plot that bordered on Riquelme's. In general those who were not living in the community were left without land and, despite the reestablishment of the right of nonresidents after the democratic transition in 1990, the problem of community membership, of the right to land and the complicity of some in the land division process, continued to cause tensions and resentment.[12]

All of these factors were in the mix when the new leadership submitted the second application to the Land Fund in 1996. From the beginning, when the community had been reconstituted in 1994, membership had been defined, according to the statutes, as those who came to meetings, paid their dues on time, and took part in communal activities. This political, trade union definition lessened the importance of kinship and lineage criteria and thus departed from the traditions of hereditary authority that had been transmitted along the family tree of the original cacique. The problems of migrants who lived in Santiago and other places also stood out, since these individuals could not participate regularly in community activities and thus felt pressure to return or else renounce their possible membership or participation. At the same time, however, political or trade union practices were familiar to the community, not only through their experience in the agrarian reform, but also through the organizations created under the dictatorship, such as CODEPECA. But was it possible to apply these earlier experiences to the new situation created by the Indigenous Law and the formation of CONADI? Which criteria should the community apply in legitimating a land subsidy application that began with the state's recognition of an indigenous right to restitution?

To this must be added the comparisons that some began to make between this new moment and the agrarian reform years. The similarities between the two periods increased with the election of a new leadership, since the Ailío brothers and their allies were well represented on the roster. In addition, some felt that the help of two ex-*miristas*, one of whom was regularly visiting the community and taking an active role in the search for a new property, only resuscitated old fears and misgivings. Some of the people who had not played a part in the initial reconstitution of the community, and even some who had, began to feel uncomfortable about the new project. "A lot of people were afraid," doña Eduardina explained,

> because they thought the same thing would happen again, that they'd be thrown off; many people advised those who were interested in applying, they said don't do it, because the same thing will happen to you, you'll be thrown off violently, the same thing will happen as on Rucalán, they'll take away the land. And we had to say no, that's not true, because now it's a subsidy, like the kind of subsidy they give you to build a house, it's the same thing, they don't take it away, they'll never take it away because it's legal. So then some people began to understand, several people.[13]

According to René Ailío Concha, who had been secretary on the first two leadership teams of the reconstituted community, people also did not dare subscribe to the application because it was too much of a change. Especially in regard to the second application, when the properties identified were further away, many said they could not get used to the new location, that it would snow, that there would be too much frost. Therefore many did not sign up or pay the fees. A clear division began to form between those who were willing to apply for the subsidy and thus play an active part in the community's meetings and those who were not. With the group that was formed in March 1996 it was nonetheless possible to carry the process forward, even though the September minutes recorded that Teodocia Ailío and Juan Garrido "have voluntarily made the decision to not accept the land subsidy." Once it was known that the application had been successful, the situation began to change once again, and more people became interested. Twenty-three people were present at the meeting held on 26 October, when don Heriberto Ailío was designated community representative in negotiations to buy the properties from Seguel. But once the land was purchased, conflicts intensified over how to choose those who would move to the new property and how to organize production once the new settlers had arrived.[14]

When the list of families that might move to the new property was drawn up, it was decided to start from the list of participants in the original re-constitution of the community. But with new land hanging in the balance, suddenly all decisions were questioned, and the definitions involved, at least according to some, became rather murky. A basic problem seemed to be the changing definition of community. According to the Indigenous Law, a community could be constituted with ten adults defined as belonging to the same indigenous ethnic group. The legal definition of who was indige-nous was, moreover, quite broad, and included the children of an indigenous father or mother and the nonindigenous husband or wife who had adopted the practices and beliefs of his or her spouse.[15] Within such ample criteria, the definition of community might go in many different directions; thus, not surprisingly, the process of applying for new land intensified, rather than solved, existing tensions. Those who had struggled from the start to recon-stitute the community questioned why they should include those who had not participated when the going was tough? From the standpoint of those who had not been involved before, how was it possible to strip someone of an ancestral right?

This abstract conflict was made concrete, at the local level, by the case of don Antonio Ailío's family. His sons Antonio and René, despite their active role in reconstituting the community, had not initially been willing to apply for the subsidy. In the end, René, upon learning that two of the original ap-plicants had decided not to go, changed his mind and formally petitioned to be included. When all the parties in the subsidy met in November 1996 to decide how to organize production on the new property, Aniceto Huenuan "asked for the floor and in the presence of those assembled petitioned in the name of René Ailío Concha." According to the minutes of the meeting, how-ever, "after a long discussion of said petition it was decided by a majority of votes to not give him the opportunity to join, since this community mem-ber had already had previous opportunities to become part of the group, and that this earlier refusal, by René Ailío himself, was ample reason to refuse him now."[16]

When his petition was rejected, René began to question more deeply the criteria by which the list of settlers had been finalized, especially the idea that only members of the reconstituted community whose dues were up to date could apply. He thought about his sister Juana, who had not participated in the reconstitution of the community and clearly was not current on her dues, but who lived in the community with all her relatives. She was, moreover, an especially poor woman with several children to support. Thus, her brothers thought, she should have been included even though she was not a formal member of the reconstituted community. In addition, René Ailío reasoned, Juana had a better claim than Cecilia Ailío, youngest sister of Eduardina, Robustiano, and Heriberto, who had worked for years in Santiago to support her children who still lived in the community. It was true she sometimes came to the meetings, René thought, and her brothers paid her dues, so they were current; but she did not live in the community.[17] Interestingly, while René's argument concerning his sister was based on an older criterion of community belonging—that is, on kinship—when he considered the case of Cecilia Ailío, he gave central importance to the issue of physical residence in the community, which had become a criterion of membership only with the Pinochet Land Division decree. So in the end, how and under what criteria would the group be defined?

Similar questions surfaced in the minds of some people when it became clear that part of the group going to Huellanto Alto was not originally from Ailío. This was the case with don José ("Chami") Garrido and his wife, doña Juana Pincheira, who had arrived in the community in 1985. Doña Juana was originally from a Mapuche community near Imperial. In a family with fourteen children and one hectare of land, it is not surprising that the older siblings would migrate early in search of work in order to help the family. Doña Juana, however, had fled from her house when she was nine years old because, she remembered, they were very poor and her parents treated her badly. "I ran away to my brother's house," she recalled,

> because my parents were really old-fashioned, they mistreated me a lot, they'd hit me if I lost a pig, or a sheep. We all had to pay attention and take care of things, they'd hit us if we didn't do something right and before, parents didn't hit you just with the hand nor with a reed, they'd hit you with a big stick, really hard, you know? So they were really mean and I got tired of it so I left. My whole life I'll remember that my father had sold a pair of young bulls and I stole the price of an ox from him. I hadn't even gotten to Santiago when my father had already let his sister know I was coming. I had taken her address with me and so we took a taxi to her street and the driver took us and everything, and we hadn't even gotten out of the car when she'd already taken away the money. So she paid for the taxi and everything and found me a job, and that's how I got to Santiago and afterwards I never wanted to come back.[18]

Doña Juana stayed in Santiago as a domestic worker for a number of years and then worked in Lautaro, Carahue, and other places. She never returned to her community for more than a few days. She managed to go to school for a total of two years along the way while she worked, but after that she was unable to continue studying and thus, she thinks, the only kind of work she could really do was domestic work. She met don Chami in Carahue, in a restaurant where the two of them worked. When they began to live together, she continued working. She took seriously her responsibility to pay for the education of two of her sisters. "Chami and I were living together," she explained,

> but the truth of it was that he only arrived on the weekends when the girls left, because I never wanted to set a bad example for my sisters. They only knew I was living with someone when I became pregnant. I was about five months along when they noticed, and only then did my parents and everyone else know that I had someone. I finished paying for my sisters' education, Dominga finished high school and the other grade school. After that things got tough when my kids started arriving and I had to get an operation for my oldest son, for Yonattan, he had to be operated on his little head, we had to take him to Santiago. So then everything started getting tough for me.[19]

From then on the problems began multiplying. Doña Juana had to quit working during her second pregnancy, and don Chami's wages were delayed at his job. They did not have enough money for food, electricity, water, and rent. "I had a bit of money deposited at the bank," she remembered:

> It wasn't much but it was something. So he convinced me to buy some fishing nets, and that we should just go fishing for a season. And that's how we ended up downriver somewhere, and got stuck, because it was a lot harder to come back, because no matter how bad off we were when we set out, we were worse off down there. So from there I decided to find refuge with my mom, but we lasted a month with her, I think, and afterward they just threw me out because it seems they were spending too much putting up the four of us, my two boys, me and my husband. So they threw me out. I'll always remember it was winter, the river was way up and we left in a boat, we went downriver again toward Ailío. We couldn't even take all our clothes because the boat was so darn small, we left my parents in charge of the rest of our stuff. So we got into the little boat and we left, willing to die, at least if we died we died the four of us together, because we got caught in this big wave,

with a whirlpool going downriver, and we gave ourselves over to God and we arrived in one piece, the only thing is that we were very wet.[20]

They camped out at the spot where they emerged from the river, in the community of Ailío, and "another family gave us permission to build a lean-to under a pear tree. We cut reeds from the river and made a hut, all rustic and everything because we really had nothing, no comforts of home."[21]

The family settled down bit by bit. They marked off an area about thirty meters long by twenty-seven meters wide by the side of the river, and here, doña Juana remembered, she "had [her] house and raised a few chickens, nothing else." It turned out that don Heriberto and doña Marta were their closest neighbors. "The truth is they're like family for us," doña Juana explained.

> If I don't have something they'll have it, if they're lacking something they ask me, we always give each other a hand. And since he belonged already for many years to this Committee they had here, they were organized, they invited us and we began to go to meetings. We were really helpful people, my husband and I, so people in the community liked us. After that we were reconstituted, as a community, and we were legal.[22]

While doña Juana worked in Santiago, don Chami spent his time fishing, taking care of the children, and participating in community affairs. Even though he was not originally Mapuche, once the Indigenous Law gave him the opportunity to do so, don Chami declared himself Mapuche by adopting the beliefs and practices of his wife. Under the new definition of community they were also members of Ailío because they took part in meetings and kept their dues payments up to date. In the second election of officers don Chami was elected secretary and was one of those who most actively pushed for the second application to the Land Fund. When this opportunity presented itself, however, doña Juana was not entirely convinced:

> Since we were already members there, we'd been members for several years, this opportunity came up and my husband signed up, you know. At first I wasn't very excited. When all of this came up my husband told me look, they're going to set up this proposal, we're going to apply for land and since you're Mapuche you can do it. I don't think so, I said. Those proposals take years and years, and we had to pay about 12,000 pesos, he told me, and we could pay in installments. If you want to go ahead, but not me, I said. You go ahead and apply, I told him, if you're interested, because I'm working here

and I can't go to the meetings back there. Besides I was a pretty cynical person in all of this. And he kept talking to me about it, I don't know, and finally I said just pay the whole amount, we'll just resign ourselves to losing the money, and if it works out, great, and if it doesn't work out, great. And he was participating in the meetings, and when I was home I'd participate, too. I never stopped participating when I was home. And then one day he called me on the phone to tell me that our proposal had been accepted. And then a part of me was happy, because my husband had always dreamed of having land, he'd always dreamed of farming.[23]

The welcome don Heriberto's family gave doña Juana and don Chami and the easy integration of don Chami into the community's second elected leadership were due in part to the definition of community that had been used during the Popular Unity years, in the previous process of land recuperation. From this perspective, community was constructed through the historical struggles and concrete practices of its members. In order to accumulate strength during the Popular Unity government, "we marked the stages together, between *wigka* and Mapuche," don Heriberto explained; but with the coup, "in the end we were the guiltiest ones, we were the biggest terrorists." The lesson don Heriberto learned from this experience was that "we the indigenous people had to wage our own struggle"; but without excluding from the community the landless *wigka*, those who were willing to participate.[24] In the case of a *wigka* who was poor, like don José Garrido, the new Indigenous Law also facilitated his integration by giving him a way to define himself as Mapuche by accepting his wife's culture and customs and demonstrating his commitment to his new community.

For the community of Ailío, the new emphasis on ethnic identity in the indigenous politics of the first Concertación government, under President Aylwin, brought new challenges and contradictions. On one side, the existence of CONADI and of a policy of indigenous restitution made it possible, finally, for the community to have access to new land. On the other side, however, the specific form taken by the Indigenous Law complicated the process of reconstitution and redefinition, channeling old resentments and reopening old wounds from the years of repression. Like other Mapuche communities, Ailío had to confront the contradiction between being a community—an entity that since the time of the first Mapuche resettlement had been created on terms and with rules established by the state—and a people, a more global identity that, with the rise of a broader indigenous movement, had taken on a more autonomous and militant meaning denoting solidarity among distinct sectors of the Mapuche throughout the region. Seen from this perspective, the Aylwin regime's policy of community reconstitution and land restitution, even as it deployed a language of ethnic identity, still confronted the so-called indigenous problem mainly as an aspect of the more general problem of rural poverty.

In such a context it was difficult not to remember the lessons learned during the agrarian reform years, the political consequences of the divisions lived within the community. For don Heriberto, the most crucial lessons were still the importance of working in an organized way and of taking risks in order to get results. He recalled that even those who had not agreed with the takeover of Rucalán had been forced, in the end, to rely on those who had in order to get back even part of the original forty-five hectares. "Even though the trial was won we still had to occupy the land by force, a fence running, because the rich guy who was there didn't want to give it up, so we had to fight with him, too," he remembered. And perhaps the greatest irony of all was that, despite the added sacrifice and risk on the part of the people on the *asentamiento*, those who ended up benefiting from the fence running on the forty-five hectares were not those who had taken the risk themselves, and besides, despite the legality of the proceedings, they were unable to hold onto the land after the coup. "Because it turns out that people took advantage of the situation there," don Heriberto concluded,

> people who had never put themselves at risk, never made an effort to regain things that had been lost. So there we ended up feeling injured because that should have been for people who were making an effort, struggling to regain those things, and instead they ended up disorganized, they didn't work in an organized way.[25]

The lesson don Heriberto learned from these earlier experiences, therefore, was that people should benefit from what they achieved through sacrifice and struggle, through risk and effort. When other people were allowed in, the result would undoubtedly be disorganization. Thus don Heriberto disagreed with those who saw the community only as a relationship of kinship or permanent residence. For him, the community was and continued to be an active creation, something that one kept building daily through effort and cooperation. That was why don Chami, being neither originally from Ailío nor Mapuche by birth, could be a valued member through work and commitment, while people who did not participate fully could be sidelined, whatever their origin.

Don Heriberto's work with CODEPECA during the 1980s had also demonstrated his willingness to include all those who wished to participate. Although the archdiocese's original project had been slated for the fourteen families affected by repression, it was don Heriberto who insisted that the aid should reach everyone. Despite this inclusion, however, some continued to think that the leaders were taking advantage by selecting the best charitable donations, whether goods, clothing, or toys. Against such a backdrop it is perhaps not surprising that there was also resentment when some received a land subsidy and others did not. In general, however, the conflicts seemed to revolve around the relationship between participation and birthright in the definition of community. How and when would different concepts apply? When would a definition based on ancestry, on family tree, be most important? When would a definition based on action be dominant, including people who took risks, struggled, and actually put into practice the definition of community? The hardest element to negotiate in all of this was ethnic identity itself, which at least at an abstract level would include people who had struggled as well as those who had not. Was it possible, in some way, to combine ancestry-based and action-based definitions of community and reach some kind of reconciliation?

A Fork in the Road: The Creation of Nicolás Ailío I and II

On December 5, 1996, nine of the people who were moving visited their new property, called Las Vertientes (underground springs). They were accompanied by an agronomist, a veterinarian, a French photographer, the previous owner Clemente Seguel, several representatives of the Centro Simón Bolívar, and me. The idea was to look over the property and figure out how to organize production. When they arrived, Sandra and Cecilia Ailío and several others from the group walked immediately over to the cherry trees along the western boundary of the property. They picked sweet, ripe cherries right off the trees, a symbolic first gesture of ownership. Then don Heriberto, don Chami, and others walked the boundary along the property's northern edge, their silhouettes quickly shrinking in the distance.

I spent a few moments talking with Seguel. He told me his great-grandparents had been Spanish colonists who established themselves in Gorbea. He began with one family farm and started expanding; he later established some businesses in Temuco, including a fabric store and a rental service for agricultural machinery. He would still be the community's neighbor, since he had another property next door. He told me he had sold Las Vertientes because he wanted to increase his investments in the neighboring dairy farm. Enrique Pérez later mentioned that Seguel had sold the property because he was in debt. A business partner had embezzled more that thirty million pesos from him.[26]

When the community took formal possession of the new land in February 1997, doña Juana Pincheira was accompanied by her mother:

> My mother told me, that is, not me but the whole community that was present, that she was giving me to the community of Nicolás Ailío, that she gave me to the community in this way, so that the community would recognize me as their daughter. And that affected me very deeply and I couldn't talk afterward, because she'd never really worried about me before, and right at that moment she was paying attention to me. So it was a mix of pain and emotion, something that for me at that moment had no explanation, the only thing I felt was that I wanted to cry.
>
> Also, I felt like my whole life I'd been abandoned, I'd never had anything, and suddenly I had it all. So at that moment I looked up at the heavens and thanked God for this beautiful opportunity, not only for me, but for all my Mapuche brothers and sisters.
>
> That's what I felt at that moment, and I wasn't able to say it to anyone. In other words I could have said it but I just couldn't talk, because it was like I had something in my throat and the words just couldn't come out, not in Spanish and not in Mapuche. My voice just didn't come out and my mom, at that moment, dictated to me the words that I should say but she seemed very far away to me and I think I was only able to murmur. I don't think I realized it and I was looking around me, all the people were feeling emotional and this only made me want to cry more, the only thing I felt at that moment was the need to cry, nothing more.[27]

Although doña Juana did not say this directly, I suspect that part of her emotion came from the sense of continuity her mother's gesture expressed. Traditionally among Mapuche families and communities, a part of the wedding ceremony entails the parents of the bride giving their daughter away, not only to the husband, but also to the husband's community. By giving doña Juana to the community of Ailío, her mother was recognizing the legitimacy of her new belonging. For doña Juana, this was the first time she felt settled in a place, the first time she felt protected and cared for, that she "had it all." And for everyone this feeling of abundance, of having finally received something for which one has been fighting all one's life, was very strong, at least at the beginning.

When I returned to Huellanto Alto in the middle of March 1997, things were no longer quite so simple. Winter was coming; people had just moved their things; they still had to rebuild their houses. Besides, they were beginning to wonder, how will we make this land produce? Winter was going to be difficult, they all agreed; there was fear in the air. The neighbors had already informed them that dairy production was the most profitable activity in the region, but they were potato farmers. Besides, in Tranapuente they had finished the year in debt because the price of agricultural products had been low, and the move had been very expensive. How were they going to start up the next agricultural year? And the ever-present worry, murmured along the edges of the conversation, was paying the property tax. Lands bought from nonindigenous owners were not considered indigenous land, according to the current interpretation of the Indigenous Law; how would they pay the land tax?[28]

A new committee was organized in Tranapuente in April and May to move forward with a loan from INDAP and plan the new agricultural cycle. People there were upset by a disagreement they'd had with those in Huellanto Alto. Those who relocated had taken the entire wheat harvest with them even though people in Tranapuente thought they had agreed to leave a good part of it to pay for the expenses of the people left behind. People in Tranapuente also resented the fact that those who had left ended up finding sharecroppers who were not members of the community for their old plots. René Ailío, in particular, thought Robustiano Ailío had not lived up to a verbal contract to allow René to sharecrop his lands.[29]

Don Heriberto remembered things differently. He insisted that they had wanted to leave René in charge of the land, but on the day they were leaving for Huellanto Alto no one from the community appeared to say anything to them. Only people from Pichingual showed up to say goodbye, and so Ricardo Mora's daughter was appointed as sharecropper on don Robustiano's lands. Don Heri left his with a first cousin from Pichingual.[30] From the point of view of René and his family, however, to choose Mora's daughter as sharecropper—Mora, a leader of the takeover of Rucalán and an old political ally of don Heriberto—was to give greater importance to previous political alliances than to the desire to maintain solidarity between the two parts of the community.

Perhaps it was inevitable that the move would present a series of conflicts and challenges for the community of Nicolás Ailío. During the application process, as we have seen, the applicants had also been the most important participants in the reconstituted community. Between November 1996 and February 1997, community meetings in Tranapuente were still attended almost exclusively by the people who were planning the move and resettlement. In January 1997, the lack of participation by community members who were staying was recognized as a communication problem for all involved. No one was sure what it would mean, legally speaking, that only a part of the reconstituted community was moving to a new location. What would happen to the lands of the families who were moving? Would these necessarily have to pass into the hands of the community members who were staying? During a discussion of the ongoing commitment that should exist between the two parts of the community, the following was recorded in the minutes:

> The President laments the scarce participation of the rest of the community's members. Until this point it has been impossible to confirm the responsibility of the other people who must really be present at the monthly meetings in order to carry out the obligations that we, the fourteen families that are leaving, share with the rest of the community's members who are being left in charge of the community's belongings. Those present at this assembly agree to call a special meeting with the members who must take responsibility for the community's obligations and of the property belonging to our group, where we will divide up the community's property in the following way:
>
> The community building, the barn and its extension, kitchen, baling machine, threshing machine, disk-based plow, and tools that will soon be enumerated will all stay with the original community. A document will be drawn up to this effect. The TOYOTA truck will go with the 14 families that have the land subsidy.[31]

It was understandable, to a certain extent, that the rest of the community was not motivated to attend the meetings. What role could the members that were staying play in community assemblies that had become spaces to hammer out the details of the move? René Ailío had already demonstrated leadership ability when he was elected secretary of the community, but once his petition to join the subsidy group was denied, his motivation for attending the meetings declined.[32] Finally, as was recorded in the minutes of 8 February 1997, the leaders had to organize a special meeting with the rest of the community at which "people took on responsibility and willingness to work for their community, since it is only a part that is moving; they understood that those who stay will constitute the original community." At that same meeting, encouraged by the leaders who had called it in the first place, the members who were staying elected their own leadership, with René Ailío as president. They accepted the distribution of property as it had been divided at the previous month's meeting and reached the following agreement: "Once both groups from this Community are settled in their respective locations, each one will be autonomous and CONADI will let us know when each group will have its own separate documentation."[33]

Even in February 1997, therefore, when the move was still being planned, the two parts of the community had agreed that, in the future, they would live separate lives. What this separation would mean legally and politically, however, was just beginning to emerge and would not be resolved until the end of that year. Although the resentments incurred during the separation itself probably helped deepen the conflict between the two parts of the original community, part of the problem was simply that they were breaking new ground. If a community, Nicolás Ailío, had applied for a land subsidy, the very success of their proposal, given the physical distance between the original community and the land they purchased, necessarily resulted in a separation into two groups. That being the case, which group then had the right to the community's recognized legal status? There were no precedents to resort to, either in Mapuche custom or in the national legal code, to answer this question.

On December 5, 1997, the executive committees of the indigenous communities Nicolás Ailío I and Nicolás Ailío II met in Tranapuente to concretize and confirm the agreements they had reached in November. The meeting began by reiterating that in Temuco on 4 November the leaderships of both parts of the community of Nicolás Ailío had agreed "to leave the original recognized legal status in Tranapuente with the 14 families staying there." The rest of the families who had moved to Huellanto Alto "renounced this status and began taking the necessary steps in order to obtain a new recognized legal status." On 25 November, in the presence of Gorbea's municipal secretary, the members of the indigenous community Nicolás Ailío II–

Huellanto Alto approved their new statutes and elected their new executive committee, thus receiving formal recognition from CONADI. Two days later in Temuco, in the presence of representatives from CET and the Social Action Department (DAS) of the Temuco archdiocese, both considered advisers to the community, the two executive committees signed an agreement dividing up the property they had owned in common since the days of CODEPECA. At the same time they agreed to work together, and CET and DAS promised to push forward with development projects and administrative reorganization in both communities.[34]

This pact of 1997 marked the end of the community of Ailío's transition out of military rule. Only with the mediation of trusted outsiders did the confusion and legal conflicts between Tranapuente and Huellanto Alto finally get resolved. Part of the issue was, of course, the very particular history of the community, the wounds and resentments accumulated throughout the previous century of poverty, mobilization, and repression. And yet these problems were not exclusive to Nicolás Ailío, for the Mapuche people as a whole had suffered poverty, land scarcity, and discrimination throughout the twentieth century. In that context the experience of the Ailío community is quite typical, even as it demonstrates an outstanding ability to struggle and endure under extremely difficult circumstances. Looking more closely at the lives of people in Nicolás Ailío II, the community don Heriberto wished to see as a rebirth from among the ashes, helps us focus more closely on both its typicality and unusual strength.

Rising from the Ashes: Daily Life in Huellanto Alto

When under the leadership of don Heriberto and don Robustiano Ailío the community was reconstituted and received a land subsidy, the idea had been to re-create the prosperity and productivity of the *asentamiento* Arnoldo Ríos. With this in mind, people began to discuss the production plan for the new land, and initially the model suggested was very similar to the plan used on the asentamiento. In November 1996, when the community meeting had rejected René Ailío's petition to join the subsidy group, the applicants had come together to discuss whether they should work the new land individually or collectively. From the beginning, don Heriberto and the others who had lived on Arnoldo Ríos understood the benefits of a collective agricultural enterprise, but the younger members of the group had not personally lived through such an experience. At this meeting an initial agreement was reached that in part reflected the earlier experience of the older leaders:

> After a broad discussion those present agree unanimously to work collectively as a Community for the period of three years, and at the same time the majority agrees that each family will live on 3 hectares, where each will build its house and use the rest of the plot as best suits its own family group. Also to promote the strengthening of community spirit and solidarity among its members. The 14 participants in the subsidy agree to live on a total of 42 hectares, in a settlement where they will install running water, electricity, build a community building and a soccer field, a *palin* field and a school, and they will identify themselves as an Indigenous Community by installing their "Rehue." [35]

Soon thereafter, at another meeting, it was calculated that each family would have only two hectares. But at a structural level the model was the same as the one used on the cooperative between 1971 and 1973: two hectares of individual usufruct, and the rest in collective production. The difference in this case was the model of the indigenous community, which would construct a palin field and install a *rewe*. [36]

In the following months another profound difference between the present and the agrarian reform era surfaced: the government showed no ongoing commitment to provide credit, technical assistance, or support of any kind. When I returned in August 1998, I learned that people had gone hungry that first winter and that planting had not taken place until September because the fertilizer had been delayed. A drought made things even worse, and the wheat had not done well. After a part of the wheat crop was sold to partially pay off their debt to INDAP, Huellanto Alto's families were still indebted and had little food stored for the winter. In the family garden plots the plants were small and plagued by unfamiliar worms and birds. People were forced to use nitrates, ash, and chemicals. [37] Some began to murmur about the possibility of dividing up all the land into equal individual plots. But then others asked: if people do not have the tools and resources to work a small plot efficiently, what will they do with a larger parcel if the whole property is divided up? [38]

The debate over how best to organize production on the new land became symbolic of broader discussions about the future among the community members in Huellanto Alto. But it was not the only, and perhaps not even the most urgent, difficulty confronted by the newly settled families. The problems of adaptation began more immediately with the extremely different ecological conditions they encountered in this new region in the Andean foothills. The soil and the climate, the infestations that affected the crops — everything was new. People had to face this new situation when their need for food and survival was immediate and acute, and thus any mistake, no matter how small, had an immediate effect on their level of subsistence. In contrast to the coastal region, where the community of Ailío was surrounded by other Mapuche communities to which it was related through longstanding relations of kinship, exchange, and mutual aid, in Huellanto Alto Ailío II was the only Mapuche community. They decided not to participate in the area's Neighborhood Council because "we already have our own organization." As a result, their neighbors called them "racist Indians" who did not want to participate.[39] Not only did they encounter problems of hostility and discrimination, but they were also not accustomed to being so isolated and so removed from the solidarity of their friends and kin.

Another facet of the same problem was the children's situation. Because the area was isolated, it was hard for the children to travel back and forth from school every day. Thus the parents were forced to request weekly room and board at the local school, and the children returned only on Fridays for the weekend. The parents were saddened by the children's absence during the week, missing their laughter and games, and they worried about their sons and daughters living so far from home. The arrival and departure of the school bus were often delayed, and the parents had to wait near the gate at the entrance to the property, frequently in the rain, and then walk the long distance to their houses over poor roads and often in the dark. In addition, their children were the only Mapuche at the nearest school, and some suffered discrimination at the hands of the teacher and the other children. Several had to move to other schools, many attending a boarding school near Villarrica where there were more Mapuche children.

The road that passed by the entrance to the property was a secondary access road that connected the Pan-American Highway to the city of Villarrica. A single public bus made the trip from Villarrica to Temuco in the morning and returned in the afternoon. In addition to the problems this created for the schoolchildren travelling to and from Villarrica on weekends, the adults in the community also found it difficult to attend to health problems or errands that came up. If an emergency need for cash presented itself, it was difficult to travel to a job outside, especially if the person did not want to migrate for a longer period of time.

In the first two and a half years, the community leadership dealt with these problems in the most creative way possible. From the beginning they applied to the municipality of Gorbea for aid in the form of food, construction materials, and tools. During the first winter, when hunger stalked people's homes, disagreements continued between Tranapuente and Huellanto Alto, and problems with adaptation intensified, the community decided to change advisers. They stopped working with Enrique Pérez and requested help once again from CET and DAS, the two organizations that had worked with the community during the time of CODEPECA in the 1980s. They worked to install running water and to build fences to minimize the damage caused by animals wandering from one family plot to the next or into neighboring properties.[40] They talked with the mayor's office about how best to build a road from the entrance gate to people's houses, and how to get access to electricity. They presented petitions to INDAP and CONADI about the lack of credit, boundary problems, and definition of their property rights that remained unresolved within the land subsidy program. With CET's and my help, they applied for larger grants that would have permitted a more systematic exploitation of the entire property—unfortunately, these grants did not materialize.

During the writing of proposals for broader grants it became possible to understand more fully the challenges facing the community. In June 1998, in a proposal submitted to the Kellogg Foundation, the community's leaders presented a fairly complete summary of the problems they were confronting. They emphasized the problems they faced on the property itself:

> The property the community has acquired has an extreme lack of infrastructure, with no fences, warehouses, and barns; its soil is impoverished and has low productivity because of the overexploitation to which it was subjected by the previous owner. The soil is predominantly good for livestock and forestry with only a few areas appropriate for the cultivation of cereal crops. It requires, however, a process of regeneration in order to increase its levels of organic material and, thus, its fertility. The property's existing forest is presently overexploited, and subjected at this very moment to intense pressure from the resident families who can only use its resources right now through the sale of lumber, firewood, and charcoal.[41]

They also discussed the lack of support from national agencies, in the sense that if they wanted credit they needed to work within the production system already organized from the top down:

Even though communities like Nicolás Ailío have the ability to make proposals that can be turned into programs for sustainable development, they have no one at the national level to hear or support these ideas and programs, and on the contrary, the public agricultural extension agencies already work from a "Green Revolution" perspective, offering the communities a previously formulated package that includes technology and credit and cannot be modified by the peasants who receive it.[42]

And finally they noted the problems with reorganizing the labor system from one in which people emphasized individual work on individual plots to one that emphasized collective work on a collective enterprise. In part it was a problem of emphasis. In Tranapuente, the original Ailío community had worked on a series of collective projects, especially those connected with CODEPECA. This was in addition to the venture in which some had participated on the asentamiento Arnoldo Ríos. But in the community itself, people worked mainly on individual private plots, on which families took individual responsibility for decisions that concerned subsistence. If there was a need for money someone could migrate to the city or the nearby landed estates. Decisions concerning work hours, crops, when to sell an animal or graze someone else's calf were all made by individual families. In Huellanto Alto the situation was different. There were no seasonal work opportunities in the region, so any decision to migrate in search of work meant that the individual would be absent from the community for a considerable length of time. Making the property produce was inevitably a collective project, and every member of the community had to contribute to the communal work parties. Taking in a neighbor's livestock on a grazing contract affected the quality of the pasture that belonged to everyone and thus could not remain an individual choice. Even if there were greater opportunities for prosperity in the long run, in the short term people had less flexibility when confronting daily issues of scarcity and lack of resources.[43] It is in this sense that the debate over the organizing of production actually subsumed a whole series of other anxieties and concerns affecting the members of the newly settled community. This emerged clearly from the conversations I had with several members in 1998.

In August 1998 I interviewed for the first time five families in Huellanto Alto. Don Armando Ailío, doña Carmen Huentemilla, don Juan Ailío, and doña Magaly Riquelme de Huenuan all worried that there was no money and that they could not work elsewhere. Don Juan Ailío in particular commented that he was not used to communal work and that, being in Huellanto Alto, he could not find additional paid work nearby. Doña Magaly said she thought the land should be divided up, so that people could do what they wanted with their portion. Doña Marcelina Ailío disagreed. She explained that those who wished to divide up the land had the resources with which to work it, and since she had neither oxen nor tools nor money, it would not benefit her to possess more land individually. In several households people had decided to migrate in search of work. Doña Juana Pincheira, for example, had left once again to work in Santiago; several families had adult children working in Temuco. By the end of December 1997, moreover, the community had given permission to three of its members—Sandra Ailío, Jorge Viguera, and Alejandrino Santibáñez—to work in Tranapuente "in order to solve their economic problems."[44]

All the members of the Huellanto Alto community I interviewed agreed on one thing: they did not want to return permanently to Tranapuente. Doña Magaly missed her family very much, but she was sure she would derive no benefit from going back for good. She wished she had enough money to visit every now and then: the cost of a round-trip bus ticket was five thousand pesos in 1998. Don Luis Huenuan assured me that he didn't miss anyone, and that in Huellanto Alto he had the space to raise animals and knew how to take advantage of the hectares he possessed. Since under the Pinochet land division his brother had been allocated the family plot in Tranapuente, he did not have room to raise even a pig. And doña Carmen Huentemilla, who was especially unhappy because she had been unable to raise chickens and could not work outside the home, told me she had to stay nevertheless "because if we go back there people will laugh at us and say, look at what happened to the famous *asentamiento*."[45]

By the following year, however, don Eduardo Leal and don Robustiano and doña Eduardina Ailío had returned to Tranapuente, dismantling their houses and taking the materials with them. The loss of the three was sad for people in Huellanto Alto, but the departure of don Robustiano and doña Eduardina, brother and sister of don Heriberto, was an especially hard blow. The year before there had already been an inkling of a possible separation. Don Robustiano had suggested to me in conversation that, as a single man raising his nieces and nephews, he felt it might be better to return to his original land. He had come to Huellanto Alto, he insisted, because he thought productivity would be better on a former landed estate. The rich guy had told them everything was great, but it had not turned out that way.

He had realized that he would be better off in Tranapuente, where he under-stood the land better and knew how to work it; his production system there was more complete. He expected to end the sharecropping agreement on his land by November or December, he told me, and go back. He also implied there were family problems and tensions among community members; to prevent a worsening of relations and not cause further disunity, he felt it was better to separate. That way he could remember the good times and still appreciate what they had accomplished. To this was added the fact that doña Eduardina had been quite ill, and, given the problems with access to medical attention in Huellanto Alto, it was better she return to Tranapuente. Doña Eduardina added that her nephew Samuel, whom she was educating, had suffered a great deal in school. He often came home in the rain wet and crying; he wanted to go back to his previous school. Several families had problems with their children in school, she said; the first year had turned out to be a net loss academically.[46]

In part, don Robustiano and doña Eduardina were able to return because a viable economic option awaited them. Given the sacrifices don Robustiano had made in order to support the extended family when don Heriberto was in jail during the repression, all the brothers and sisters had agreed that don Robustiano should keep most of the family land under the *pinochetista* divi-sion. He therefore had five hectares to farm in Tranapuente, something the rest of the settlers did not.[47] And thus don Robustiano and doña Eduardina set off once again to their original community, looking to regain what they had left behind.

But perhaps the largest frustration faced by those in Huellanto Alto was the discovery, during a routine reconnaissance of the property for the pur-poses of a forestry project with the Corporación Nacional Forestal (National Forestry Corporation, or CONAF), that they possessed 37.5 hectares less than they thought they did. The leadership blamed CONADI for its poor techni-cal assistance; some of CONADI's officials, they said, are wolves in sheep's clothing who care only about their salaries. The problem was the Land and Water Department. The community members stood ready to fight for their rights, so that their children would have something to depend on, unlike what had happened in the original community. They knew that it would be difficult to turn the situation around and that it would be a hard fight—but they were in it for the duration, they assured me. And it came as no surprise to anyone that the missing hectares were in the low-lying fertile areas near the stream, the part that was called "Las Giradanas" on the map and was in

Seguel's hands. The fencing in that area, they told me, was obviously newer than the rest. The advisers from CET confirmed the situation and empha- sized that it was a fairly general problem with the properties CONADI was purchasing. In a random sample of twenty such properties, eighteen were found to have measurement errors.[48]

After reading some of CONADI's internal documents, I confirmed that the organization's inefficiency in the case of Ailío was fairly typical. To begin with, there had been problems confirming the veracity of the data presented by land subsidy applicants on their preselection questionnaires, and con- sequently every year subsidies were handed out to people who already had quite a bit of land or had made false claims on their forms. Between 1995 and 1997, for example, 12 percent of successful applicants already owned be- tween 8 and 15 hectares, while 5 percent owned between 15 and 50 hectares. The conclusion reached by the fund's evaluation team was that "a better pre- selection process would have eliminated the 5% with more than 15 hectares and the Selection Committee could have therefore approved subsidies for a larger number of needy families, as is the purpose of this program."[49]

Even more relevant in the case of Ailío was the lack of planning and follow-up the program offered those who had received a subsidy and had attempted to move on to their new land. Fewer than half of the successful applicants had houses on the acquired land and, according to CONADI's in- ternal evaluation, "the rest of the beneficiaries have not been able to settle on their property because they do not have the necessary infrastructure. This is not a problem when the acquired land borders on the original property, but is obviously a different story when the new land is far away."[50] The same report listed, among the beneficiaries' complaints, boundary problems and distance from their original home. The report suggested establishing co- operation agreements with other state institutions in order to improve the administration of the program and provide a more efficient follow-up to the newly subsidized landowners.[51]

It almost seemed as if Ailío had served as a guinea pig, enabling discovery of the more general problems CONADI admitted to in 1998. But it is also interesting to note the differences between Ailío and the rest of the bene- ficiaries. Ailío's settlers moved before houses were built on the purchased property. In a subsidy program in which most beneficiaries were individu- als—according to CONADI's data, of the 169 subsidies given out between 1995 and 1998, only 4 were given to communities—Ailío was the only com- munal subsidy in 1996. And finally, in a context in which the Land Fund itself recognized that the complicated forms and bureaucratic tangles of the application process made it difficult "for the poorest families to participate effectively," the community of Ailío, through the help of advisers and friends from the agrarian reform and CODEPECA periods, was able to be effective.[52]

So deep were the problems encountered by the land subsidy program that in November 1997 CONADI's National Council concluded, as a part of their institutional plan for 1998, that investing money in the program to purchase lands in dispute was a great deal more efficient than a similar investment in land subsidies. It recommended, therefore, an increase in the budget for the former and a decrease in the budget for the latter. To this was added the need to arrange cooperation with other national and international organizations in order to offer help to the communities that had already received lands between 1996 and 1997, help not only to increase production but also to resolve conflicts and legal battles "concerning the ownership, possession, use, administration, or simple tenure of indigenous lands."[53] At the beginning of the new century, however, CONADI's institutional problems only worsened, and, as of this writing, no progress has been made on Nicolás Ailío II's new usurpation problem.

"Don't Dry Out, Beautiful": Huellanto Alto in 2001

In August 2001, I returned to Huellanto Alto with a completed first draft of this book, ready to invite comments and discuss its ideas. I saw many changes and a new optimism I had not seen before. The community had helped build a gravel road that now reached people's houses. They were reccuperating, with help from CET, some traditional crops such as quinoa. People from Huellanto Alto were beginning to travel to regional agricultural fairs. But what most caught my attention was a new creativity among the women. In part my new awareness was due to my deepening friendship with Angélica Celis, who had been working for a number of years with some of the women who had settled in the new community and thus gave me access to an already existing dimension of local life. At the same time, as women were completing the first arduous stage of their resettlement, adaptation and survival, their creativity—in their household gardens, as healers, and in the spiritual realm—was gaining a new space within the community.

Cecilia Ailío, don Heriberto's youngest sister, settled down permanently in Huellanto Alto at the beginning of the new century. Even though her name had been on the original list for the subsidy application, she recog-

Unpacking and rebuilding of the houses after the move to Huellanto Alto, March 1997. Note the laundry drying on the bushes. Author photo.

Doña Marta Antinao stoking the fire that served as her stove during the first weeks in Huellanto Alto. Author photo.

Don Heriberto Ailío discussing strategy amidst half-unpacked personal belongings, shortly after arriving in Huellanto Alto, March 1997. Author photo.

Doña Eduardina Ailío standing in the doorway of her first makeshift dwelling in Huellanto Alto. In her hand is the transcription of our first interview, which she was in the process of reading and commenting upon. A wild copihue flower picked in the nearby forest hangs over the entryway. Author photo.

Doña Juana Pincheira and Sandra Ailío (cleaning the wild berries the women were using for jam) listen to the discussion at the first community meeting in Huellanto Alto in March 1997. Author photo.

Yanet Ailío relaxes on an overturned basket in Huellanto Alto, March 1997. Author photo.

Enrique Pérez participates in the first community discussion in Huellanto Alto in March 1997. Author photo.

Close-up of a red copihue flower hanging on the vine, Huellanto Alto, March 1997. Author photo.

Wild copihue flowers growing in the native forest in Huellanto Alto. Author photo.

Partial view of the entryway to doña Marta's kitchen, Huellanto Alto, March 2003. Part of her garden is reflected in the window. Author photo.

Doña Marcelina Ailío in her garden, March 2003. Author photo.

Doña Cecilia Ailío
in her greenhouse,
March 2003. Author
photo.

Doña Lidia del Pilar
Llancao standing at the
entrance to her green-
house, March 2003.
Author photo.

(*Left to right*) Yanet Ailío, doña Juana Pincheira, and Sandra Ailío, August 2001. "Come and take our picture, señora Florencia," they told me, "now that we're happier and more settled in Huellanto Alto." Author photo.

Doña Marta and her son Martín, arranging the seeds to start their plantings in their greenhouse (which Martín built), Huellanto Alto, August 2001. Author photo.

A view of the Andes mountains, punctuated by three
snow-covered volcanoes, from the community of Nicolás
Ailío II-Huellanto Alto, August 2001. The dramatic
improvements since 1997, including fencing, pasture,
and more finished houses, can be seen clearly from this
vantage point. Author photo.

nized that for a single woman head of household, the situation on the ground had initially been especially difficult. The men had promised to help her get settled, but when the race starts, she explained, "each horse takes care of itself." She had felt isolated and did not have cash to help her older daughter Andrea with her education. So she was left with no option but to leave again in search of work. But she had finally been forced to return or else lose her share of communal production in lumber, vegetables, and other crops. During the CONAF project the community had taken on, a project for the sustainable exploitation of the forest, she had received less lumber because she did not have someone in the community who could work as a representative of her household. She had thus also found it necessary to use part of her lumber to pay for her share of the community work parties that had built the greenhouse and chicken coop and cooperated on the electrification and road projects.[54]

Once she returned to Huellanto Alto, doña Cecilia confronted once again the special problems of a single woman. The problem was no longer a lack of land, she explained, but a lack of money and labor. If she had had money, she could have planted on her own; she was especially interested in planting chestnut trees and transplanting artichokes because they were particularly profitable. Because she lacked money, she was forced to sharecrop with another member of the community, with whom she shared the cost of the chemical fertilizer and of the machinery for planting and harvesting, while he took care of cultivation and she of weeding. She found that animals prospered in her care; she quickly accumulated more than twenty hens and realized she felt less lonely caring for other creatures. She began to work as a healer, basing herself on the knowledge her mother had passed on; but she refused to charge for her services. Finally, she began to organize a Sunday worship service in the Anglican tradition, in which people read the Bible and prayed together. With the participation of four additional families she tried to get a minister to visit from Temuco, but she was not successful: "People are very cold," she explained.[55]

Doña Marcelina Ailío, another single woman in the community, was able to settle in Huellanto Alto only by taking her son Manuel out of school so that he could contribute their household's labor to the community. She still had to sharecrop her own land because her labor and that of her son were not enough. Despite the problems she faced, however, she felt happy because her new situation was much better than what she had faced in Tranapuente. Wife of Pedro Fuentes Pilquinao, one of the leaders of the takeover of Rucalán and an active participant on the asentamiento Arnoldo Ríos, doña Marcelina had arrived at the agrarian reform center a year after the takeover. She recalled the solidarity people had expressed on the asentamiento and felt something similar in Huellanto Alto because there, too, people worked collectively, and she had exchanged food for work with her neighbors. At the same time, she remembered the deep poverty she and her husband had experienced when they returned to the community of Pilquinao after being evicted from Rucalán. Her husband had to fish in order to get something to eat, since they had absolutely nothing. Later her husband had begun drinking, and the situation only worsened. "I've been separated for about seven years," she explained. "I raised all the kids, I was like a mother and a father to them."[56]

Despite the differences in their adaptations, as single women heads of household doña Marcelina and doña Cecilia shared a lack of money and labor power, not only to cultivate the land designated as individual property, but also to contribute to the collective work parties that stood at the center of the communal project in Huellanto Alto. In contrast to families built around a heterosexual couple, they could not participate on an equal footing in the various construction and forestry projects and collective planting efforts. They did not fit comfortably within the model of community organized as an association of households made up of married couples and their children.

At the same time, however, in their household gardens women in general lived an especially creative process of adaptation to the new environment. Having moved from a coastal *Lafkenche* zone to a *Wenteche* region in the Andean foothills, they discovered new plants and new microclimates. At the beginning it was not easy because their knowledge of the coast and its customs was not helpful in the new location. "The first year we settled here I became disillusioned with the land," doña Marta Antinao told Angélica Celis. For doña Cecilia, getting used to the winds and frost was one of the hardest parts. Doña Marcelina also had to learn new subtleties: "There are different types of frost: those that turn white are the hardest, but there's also another light, soft frost that the wind quickly takes away."[57]

Once they began to adapt, the women developed a new enthusiasm. "Now I'm in love with this place," commented doña Marta; she had gotten to know the native trees, species that did not exist on the coast, in part because of the dramatic deforestation that area had suffered. "I like the trees a lot, they are lovely. I feel sad when they cut some down, now that they're clearing. The women don't get involved in forest work." But doña Marta has definitely gotten involved in her garden plot and in the greenhouse her son Martín built for her seedbeds. In the foothills, the greenhouse is especially important in cultivating seedlings for vegetables and other plants because the growing season is a great deal shorter. "The other new thing I've learned is how to use the greenhouse," commented doña Marcelina. "It's a good thing, it's great because you make up your seedbeds and in eight days the lettuce is already out. For someone like me who knows about seedbeds, it's clear how quick the greenhouse is."[58]

The women, who are in charge of the garden plots and the organization of the domestic sphere, make clear the importance of people's spatial, eco-logical, and spiritual adaptation to the new landscape. In order to plan the garden plot effectively, to know when to plant and how to lay out the fur-rows, first it was necessary to identify the course of the sun, direction of the winds, and cycle of the moon. When planning the crops, doña Marcelina explained, "everything needs to be looking toward the sun. I pay close atten-tion to the moon," she continued, "and put the plants in the ground when it's waning." And doña Marta added, "I use the moon as my guide for the seedbeds, I always keep track, I see when it's a half-moon because that's its moment of greatest force, so if you place the seeds in the earth at that point, the plants come up quickly." Doña Cecilia remembered that "it took me a while to understand the winds, but now I know: there's the southerly and the northerly winds, and the *puelche* . . . back there we had the same ones . . . but in the lowland where I grew up the wind didn't whip around this way."

Once they felt adapted, the women were comfortable letting their new knowledge flow through their efforts to cultivate different forms of life. "I don't know if you're born with a green thumb or you develop it," doña Marce-lina commented. "I talk to the plants, carry on a conversation with them, I ask them, so how are you? Full of weeds? And I begin to clean out all the little plants so they won't dry out." The women have a new sensibility with regard to the adaptation and care of their plants, as if they identify more deeply with the adjustment of a new species precisely because of what they have suffered as they try to prosper in a new landscape. Perhaps it was doña Cecilia who explained it most lucidly:

> When I bring an unknown plant into my garden, first I take out the seed, or the flower, I plant it, treat it with affection, I talk to it, start up a conversa-tion, I water it and find a place for it. I place her somewhere that's similar to the place she comes from, I bring her with lots of soil, a lot of her own

soil so that she doesn't travel alone, and I have her new home ready for her. I take care of her for a while, and when I transfer her to her final location I tell her, "don't dry out, beautiful."

To this sensibility is added a pride in knowing how to innovate as well as a joy in sharing new knowledge. "These little pink flowers that I'd never seen before bloomed for me," doña Marcelina remembered. "I gave some of these little flowers to all my friends."[59]

With help from the CET, the community has shared this new knowledge and enthusiasm more broadly across the region, generating new pride for the women of Huellanto Alto. In addition to the regional agricultural fair at Yumbel, to which several of the women traveled to share and trade seeds, most notably the quinoa they had just recovered, they also gave Mapuche recipes to some of Chile's most famous chefs in exchange for these cooks' favorite dishes. This process culminated for Cecilia in November 2001, when, as she explained in an e-mail, "A very happy event is about to happen, I have many emotions inside me, because for the first time, *señora* Florencia, I will dress in Mapuche clothes. This will be a great satisfaction for me, and the memory of my mother will accompany me, because she used to dress so elegantly. I'll send you photographs." The reason for this happy event was a special dinner to be held in Temuco to mark the conclusion of the exchange between the chefs and the Mapuche women who guarded and reproduced the diversity of local agriculture. "I don't think you know," Cecilia continued,

that we've been working as reproducers of seeds with a group of women from different places. From the community of Ailío II, there's four [sic] of us (Marta, Marcelina, Sandra, Cecilia and Carmela). Marcelina, Sandra and I will dress in Mapuche clothes for a special party. We will have a gala dinner at the Terraverde Hotel (Temuco) where the famous Chilean chefs will cook in reciprocity for the recipes and seeds we have shared with them.

We cooked for them before. I made *simita* (which is a kind of cooked bread you boil instead of frying, and add different spices). Marcelina made potato *truto* (which is a kind of potato dough you roll on a stick with spices and then bake). Marta made a seaweed *pebre* [a kind of dressing or chutney], Sandra made quinoa and carrot juice and a quinoa dessert, and Carmela made a quinoa casserole with blue eggs and quinoa *muday* [a Mapuche drink made with cereals and honey and slightly fermented]. Other women prepared other things and we shared all of this with fifteen chefs from different parts of the country.

So now they will cook for us and it will be a gala dinner and for that reason we'll go in our best clothes. Another big accomplishment is that Andrea will go with me since every woman guest can bring someone from her family.[60]

Conclusions

In 1999, I visited doña Eduardina and don Robustiano back in their original house in Tranapuente. Doña Eduardina was still recovering from her illness of the previous year, but this did not stop her from carefully and critically reading the book outline I gave her and correcting several errors. Don Robustiano was a bit frustrated by the interruptions and expenses he had incurred during the move back, even though he understood that it would take at least a year to complete his readaptation. They seemed sad and nostalgic to be separated from the rest of their family, though at other levels their reintegration seemed to be progressing surprisingly well. Samuel was happy to have returned to his old school. René Ailío was working with don Robustiano on his lands, and don Robustiano had already been invited to stand for a leadership position in the community. He had refused. Doña Eduardina commented that she had not been able to reopen the small Anglican chapel she had previously run in the community, especially since the departure of the Huellanto Alto settlers had convinced everyone else to join the Church of God run by don Antonio Ailío's sons. Even don Luis Ernesto Quijón, an old political prisoner who had worked in the Popular Unity agrarian reform and had been a member of a different Pentecostal church, had joined them. For the moment, she explained, she and her brother had returned to their original Anglican church in Nehuentúe. Perhaps later she would build another chapel in a small lean-to closer to her house so that she could have a church within easy walking distance.

The reintegration of don Robustiano and doña Eduardina into the community of Ailío I once again is a reminder of how complicated it is to define community. We have seen how, in Nicolás Ailío, people have historically deployed a series of distinct definitions. The one formulated during the original settlement of the Mapuche on the land granted by the Chilean state emphasized kinship ties with the original settlers and thus permitted migrants to maintain their membership. At the same time, however, it limited available options for struggle against usurpation, leading to extreme and seemingly dead-end poverty. A part of the generation growing up in the 1940s and 1950s found a way out through a definition of community that emphasized class-based collective work and solidarity. Practiced with great enthusiasm during the agrarian reform years and the Popular Unity government, this new approach subsequently led to violence and repression, fear and poverty, under military dictatorship. Pinochetista land division further intensified conflicts between those who had favored the class-based model and those wedded to legalism. In the 1980s, the creation of CODEPECA once again strengthened the concept of community based on collective work, while adding a certain notion of Lafkenche territoriality through the participation of other Mapuche coastal communities.

The contradiction between a definition of community based on kinship and one based on collective labor and solidarity was lived especially intensely in the first years of postauthoritarian rule. Although the Indigenous Law of the Aylwin government was formulated as a response to an indigenous ethnic and cultural revitalization movement, in consultation with indigenous organizations and communities, in the end its model for the reconstitution of indigenous communities did not help reanimate local Mapuche leadership traditions or communal practices. In Ailío, one of the more important functions of the reconstituted community was to present a land subsidy proposal. On the one hand, this made Ailío's proposal especially strong, and as a result it became one of only four communities that received a subsidy during the first three years of the Land Fund program. But on the other hand, this somewhat specialized function for the reconstituted community set the scene for greater confusion, disagreement, and lack of communication between those who moved to Huellanto Alto and those who stayed in Tranapuente.

In the conflict that resulted in the creation of two communities of Nicolás Ailío, one of the most important bones of contention was the legally recognized status that CONADI provided to indigenous communities. This status gave the community legitimacy in its dealings with state institutions, facilitating the bureaucratic procedures necessary to obtain credit, services, and other subsidies. It also furnished a recognizable group identity with which to apply for grants and act collectively in the broader society. Proof of how important such an identity can be in relation to governmental and nongovernmental organizations is the fact that finally the community of Nicolás Ailío II had to obtain its own legally recognized status from CONADI and the Gorbea municipality.

When we understand the importance of this legalized identity, we can also discern more clearly the institutional limits or barriers that have affected the community generally. On one side, we have seen that the community of Nicolás Ailío, and especially the group that applied for the land subsidy, accomplished something quite unusual with the opportunities that were open to Mapuche communities in the immediate postauthoritarian period. At the same time, however, they were forced to work carefully within the parameters set by the government, and as a result they ended up being victimized by the lack of care and follow-up the state evidenced in its relationship to the communities.

All of this leads us to ask, What, in the end, was the result of the Chilean state's efforts, starting in 1993, to reconstitute indigenous identities? At least with regard to CONADI's Land and Water Fund, the 1998 evaluation concluded that "the Program is oriented toward the socioeconomic implications of poverty, without giving priority to cultural aspects." According to interviews the evaluation panel carried out with high-level personnel in CONADI and the Ministerio de Planificación (Ministry of planning, or MIDEPLAN), "The goal of the program is to recuperate between 180,000 and 200,000 hectares of Indigenous Lands that were lost during the military government's agrarian counterreform. In this sense, the goal would be the restitution to indigenous people of the lands lost during the dictatorship." But the evaluation itself concluded that "the program as it stands cannot meet the established goal."[61] Part of the problem was the low level of state financing. It also turned out that the price of land tended to go up when the owners realized they could sell to the government. For both reasons the program ended up meeting a minute proportion of the historic overall demand for territory and resources. At the same time, by spending all its limited funds on the purchase of land, the program had no resources left for surveying the properties, confirming their boundaries, or providing new settlers with credit and follow-up attention.

The experience of the communities of Ailío I and II suggests, in my opinion, that the government's most important goal in relation to Mapuche communities has been neither territorial restitution nor political or cultural reconstitution. Rather, the goal has been to encourage more mainstream forms of socioeconomic and political organization that can help lower the levels of extreme poverty in the countryside and thus stem the tide of rural to urban migration. In Huellanto Alto, the new settlers of Nicolás Ailío II had a similar goal insofar as they wished to gain access to enough land, resources, and work so that the younger generation could stay in the community. If the government's underlying goal was to lessen the pressure on already overburdened social welfare services and labor markets in urban areas, Ailío's leaders envisioned that their dream of leaving something for the next generation would finally come true.

In the end, the families of Ailío I and Ailío II have experienced directly and personally the state's more general lack of commitment to the fate of Mapuche communities. In order to survive, they have to play by the rules the government sets. But the state attempts to dilute all processes of mobilization and confrontation while creating expectations it can at best only partially fulfill. Perhaps the communities no longer live in court. The few who are getting access to new land are doing so through the market rather than an illegal takeover. In Huellanto Alto, creativity blossoms in unexpected ways, especially in efforts to work out a sustainable model of forestry and in the recuperation of new and traditional crops. The road to Tranapuente is now paved and a new bridge spans the Imperial river; there is talk of the high price of land.[62] But despite these changes, both communities are still short a number of hectares, land usurped by landowners who have historically enjoyed impunity in relation to the state. Sadly, governments throughout the twentieth century, while talking up the importance of indigenous rights, consistently sided with the rich and bent to the will of market forces.

CHAPTER 7

CONCLUSION: WHERE THE PAST MEETS

THE FUTURE IN NICOLÁS AILÍO

In Nicolás Ailío, a small community of approximately thirty families that then divided into two, there are many versions of history. These local narratives try to make sense of the world and of peoples' individual and collective experiences. People and families transmit and preserve their experiences through the stories they tell. As a historian who was granted permission to write a history of the community, I was privileged to listen to a number of these stories, bring them home in my suitcase, and try to write them so that they formed a single, coherent narrative. By weaving together peoples' multiple perspectives, this narrative attempts to provide a broader vision of what the collective experience has entailed.

In part I have had the opportunity to work on this history because Nicolás Ailío did not have an official keeper of collective memory who could transmit an authoritative version based in the community itself. Under such conditions, my attempt as an outsider to bring together divergent perspectives cannot hope to yield complete coherence. I also hesitate to assume authority over the history of the community, something that quite frankly does not belong to me. The give and take among stories has also taught me that if I tried to unify them all, I would end up destroying what is unique and specific to each. Even in a single family there are many versions of the past, and some do not fit neatly together. At the same time, however, there are common themes and struggles worthy of being traced and highlighted. My goal as I conclude this history, therefore, is to find a balance between the specifics of the individual case and what each one tells us about reality more generally.

In the Ailío Concha family, doña Felicia Concha fashions an old-style romance that begins with a shy young girl who sees a young man while sitting at the window of the house where she works. It continues through the daily ups and downs of rural poverty and ends in the satisfaction that children and grandchildren provide in old age. Doña Felicia's husband, don Antonio Ailío, tells of the usurpation his parents suffered at the hands of Duhalde, the almost daily struggle for restitution that proves to be in vain, until finally Duhalde is murdered because of his evil works. The victory here is to have survived, to have endured in the face of life's suffering. Doña Felicia has made such a victory possible by caring for the household with tenderness and patience despite the suffering, and her sensibility is nourished by the romantic origins of her marriage, which began because the young Mapuche man from the countryside approached her "in an honorable way."

In the next generation Hugo chronicles poverty and racial discrimination, narrating a life in which everyone lives "like salmon swimming upstream." His personal frustration in school is followed by the treason and abandonment of the left and his exile from the community as a result of the military dictatorship. He ends up finding solidarity and community in an evangelical church, and in the love of a woman who supports him no matter what. The two generations have in common the personal and collective suffering that poverty imposes, especially a poverty articulated with the discrimination and marginalization lived in a Mapuche community; and the personal moral struggles to overcome this suffering that are nurtured in religious faith, the support of a spouse, and women's emphasis on reproducing life. Hugo's younger brothers René and Antonio, who stay in the community, recognize the value of Mapuche and religious communities to their survival by becoming leaders, respectively, in the community of Ailío I and the Church of God. Antonio also explains the death of Duhalde by pointing to the existence of a King who is above all human beings, thus emphasizing the importance of a religious dimension to the narration of history.

In the Ailío Pilquinao family, the same elements—Mapuche peasants' poverty, discrimination, and marginalization; the moral and intellectual compass provided by religion; the role of the woman and the mother in assuring the reproduction of family life—are articulated in a very different way, in general but also by the individuals within the family group. Doña Eduardina's narrative centers around the frustration of opportunity, of her desire for education and the lack of possibilities owing to the family's poverty. In this context Anglican religiosity becomes, for her, a kind of alternative rationality and intellectual work. Her religiosity allows her to assume leadership in her church and to explain the ups and downs of her family's history of suffering. For don Heriberto the central theme is the search for a way out of poverty's humiliation, a search that prompts him to combine the utopian visions of liberation theology and the revolutionary left. A charismatic leader who is always thinking about a collective future, don Heriberto narrates history in relation to that future, toward a goal that combines solidarity, prosperity, and community: in his rendition, a well-organized community can triumph over injustice. Don Robustiano is more cautious, combining an analytical and rational perspective with a desire to protect his family; that attitude emerges clearly from his role as family anchor during the military dictatorship. According to Mario Castro, don Robustiano is also the brother with the most profound Mapuche spirituality; an important lesson he imparts by moving back to Tranapuente from Huellanto Alto is that sometimes, in order to value or preserve what's good in life, one has to know when to move aside.

Elisa and Cecilia, the two youngest sisters, begin migrating to Santiago at a young age. On one side they are able to benefit from the support of their brothers and sisters, who nurture their children and give them a place to grow up. On the other side, they contribute through their labor to the education of the younger generation. Together they all manage to survive the hard times and the challenges of the dictatorship; and together they keep alive, through their stories, the memory of their mother and her charismatic gift for nurturing, healing, and reproducing life. Alongside her husband don Martín Ailío Porma, the community's *logko* in the second generation, doña María Pilquinao is still a powerful presence in the memory and the strategies of survival of the community's third generation.[1]

Doña María's forceful presence also emerges in the chronicle of her daughter-in-law doña Marta Antinao, wife of don Heriberto, who has managed to nurture a family under the most difficult and unpredictable circumstances. Despite the many differences between doña Marta and doña Felicia, I was impressed by the fact that both are able, in quiet and subtle ways, to organize their families' affective ties around their kitchens or hearths. In this sense they both follow the path that Mapuche culture defines for women. Even if doña María is, in this context, a particularly outstanding example because of her strength and charisma, the majority of Nicolás Ailío's women show a similar dedication to family reproduction, the cultivation of garden plots, and the preservation of communal space. In this way, the division of labor between men and women also extends into the spheres of knowledge and memory, for women nurture expertise about plants, seeds, and healing at the same time they preserve family lore from generation to generation.

Other narratives and versions of history coexist in Nicolás Ailío. Among these is doña Juana Pincheira's vision of community, a view of redemption and fulfillment rooted in Mapuche identity and in the solidarity she has experienced as she has formed part of a new collectivity—despite the fact that, almost immediately, she migrates again to work in Santiago! In part because of her personal history, doña Juana does not seem comfortable with the rural life around the hearth, and instead she takes on another role familiar to Mapuche women: the migrant domestic worker who by sending money home helps maintain her family from a distance. In this case it is her husband, don José Garrido, who takes on the daily responsibility of the community and the family, voluntarily assuming a Mapuche identity in order to help build the prosperity of the group he has joined. Ironically, when don "Chami" moved to Huellanto Alto, his non-Mapuche neighbors explained his combative style by referring to the "warriorlike" characteristics allegedly inherent in the Mapuche "race."

What all these versions and narratives of history have in common is the importance of divergent forms of human community and solidarity in the formulation of survival strategies and in the struggle against oppression. At one level, of course, this may seem a rather obvious point: human beings support each other through solidarity. But what is not so obvious is that this solidarity and the disparate forms of community through which it is lived, from the family to the indigenous community, trade union, and church, are in themselves cultural, social, and narrative constructions within which relations of equality and hierarchy coexist. To simultaneously understand both sides of these relations is quite a challenge, but a crucial one. That a woman's labor is exploited within the household, for example, does not negate that her presence as mother, wife, teacher, reproducer of the entire family environment, and even migratory laborer is absolutely central to the family and kinship system around which Mapuche communities help each other and reproduce themselves. That evangelical churches look down on Mapuche religiosity does not negate that their collective moral codes provide comfort, human connectivity, personal satisfaction, and even a certain group structure or discipline that is helpful to many. That some local intellectuals or visionaries tend to make most decisions in indigenous communities does not negate that the community as such also exhibits many forms of egalitarianism and mutual respect among its members.

In submerging myself in these distinct narratives and forms of knowledge that exist within the community of Ailío, my goal has been to meet these different explanations of history on an equal footing. We historians often tend to privilege written over oral sources, official documentation over other forms of evidence. When we do so, we close ourselves off to a whole series of dimensions and perspectives within human history, aspects of the past that resist narration from a position that reproduces the rationality of power. By establishing a narrative connection to these other elements and forms of knowledge, I have attempted to explore the fissures that result in preexisting or better-known versions of history. By not closing these fissures through the use of an omniscient rationalism, I think we can better see them as "time knots" that allow us access to other meanings and ways of explaining human reality, without having to always establish the superiority of "scientific knowledge." As is clear in this book, of course, honoring explanations of reality that are governed by different principles of logic or rationality does not mean one leaves aside either the logic and rationality of analysis more generally, or the need to compare explanations and dialogue among differing truth claims. But it does mean that we need to take seriously the many interpretations of the events and vicissitudes of history, thus questioning our tendency to assume the perspective of those who construct the archive from a position of power.[2]

The effort to take seriously different interpretations has generated in me an intense process of intellectual growth ever since that day in November 1996, when on the eve of my first visit to the community of Ailío I wrote in my field notebook, "I hope our common process of re-membering works out." At that moment I still had a rather flat image of local history and popular heroism. I did not see or comprehend the perspectives, divisions, disagreements, and wounds from the past that infused the worn hills and gently sloping landscape of that coastal community. Neither did I have access to the new conflicts and misunderstandings that would emerge with the move, or know that in Huellanto Alto people would go hungry that first winter. Perhaps it was important that, as a historian of "the popular," I initially be inspired in a heroic version of history, one in which the Mapuche peasants of Nicolás Ailío could still be pure and transparent protagonists.

One of the most profound lessons my collaborators in Nicolás Ailío taught me, however, was precisely that, if I wished to narrate a true and respectful history, I had to see and understand them as the complex and imperfect human beings they really were. At first it was especially difficult for me to recognize, and to put aside, one of my most enduring and lovingly held prejudices: that oppressed or subaltern groups are in reality morally superior, that in some way their lives have not been touched by the power struggles that mark the rest of society. At a certain level I had already partially overcome this prejudice, at least intellectually, in that I understood that racial and gender hierarchies were embedded also within subaltern groups, and thus could see, among Mapuche and non-Mapuche peasants, the internal disparities and conflicts that were both caused by and helped reproduce these hierarchies. In particular it was relatively easy for me to see that, even within a group as oppressed and discriminated against as the Mapuche peasantry, women could still confront an even more difficult situation within their homes. But I was also able to see that, in daily life, solidarity within a couple, family, or community depended, in turn, on the mutual respect, system of authority, and division of labor created by relationships of gender and generation. If women were not public protagonists in the takeover of Rucalán, being relegated instead to a small rowboat on the river, and if they were secondary to the work on the *asentamiento*, nevertheless the pride their fathers, husbands, and brothers felt at being able, for the first time, to support them with dignity and generosity was a central element of political consciousness at that time.

But the hardest thing, then and now, has been to understand and to narrate the complex combination of resentment and resistance, fear and solidarity, hostility and unity, complicity and strength that forms a part of people's experiences. If sometimes the *asentados* on Rucalán drank too much and crashed the tractors (and their women criticized them for it), the asentamiento was still able to produce more on the *fundos* than their previous owners. If after the *allanamiento* of Nehuentúe many wished to blame don Heriberto, and some took revenge during the dictatorship on members of his family, it was still possible to form CODEPECA in the 1980s and revitalize production in the region. If in a sense the process of reconstituting the community in the 1990s was more beneficial to the part of the community that received the land subsidy, one should still not minimize the risk, fear, hunger, and discrimination experienced in Huellanto Alto. Even if today people still feel resentment and hostility toward those who broke under torture, they recognize that all the peasants who participated in the mobilizations of the Popular Unity period faced abandonment and poverty after the military coup. In truth, a narrative that is able to grant room to all of these elements would overwhelm even the most seasoned storyteller.

I would be less than honest if I did not admit that initially I reacted to these many challenges with a combination of depression and paralysis. But one of the advantages of the dialogic method turned out to be that I could not wallow in self-pity when I owed the community an initial report. I also felt somewhat embarrassed that, as the mere narrator of this history, I could feel a stronger depression or paralysis than that shown by the actual protagonists. In the end, I found a path through this dense forest by articulating the relevant aspects of local complexity with processes and tendencies in the broader society, both at the regional and national levels. In doing so, I think I have demonstrated the importance, analytically speaking, of taking seriously different perspectives on and interpretations of history, precisely because local perspectives, and the "time-knots" they open for us, challenge us to rethink larger issues in Chilean history more generally.

One of the most important issues this research helped me clarify is the role of the Chilean state in relation to the Mapuche people. The history of the community of Ailío reveals an unwavering continuity in state policy, from the original settlement initiative between 1890 and 1930 to the most recent policies of CONADI around the issue of indigenous lands. This continuity is reflected most importantly in a Janus-faced policy toward the Mapuche. On one hand, Chilean legislation seems to protect indigenous lands from usurpation and designate the state as mediator between the Mapuche people and the broader society, thus recognizing the primordial right of indigenous people to the resources of their ancestral territory. On the other hand, however, Chilean private property law and state support for entrepreneurial activity pull in exactly the opposite direction. As the history of land tenure in the coastal region makes clear, time and again state policy favored national and foreign colonists as well as entrepreneurs in general over the legitimate rights of the original Mapuche communities.

Starting at the end of the 1920s, state policy moved toward the division of the communities into individual private plots. The first Land Division law, however, had an important precondition attached: before beginning the division process, a Mapuche community must be in possession of the entire land surface specified in the *título de merced*. This opened the door to many communities that, like Ailío, had problems of usurpation, and a significant number of them began division proceedings simply in order to achieve restitution. This alternative use of the law led to its modification, making clear that the ultimate goal of the state had never been restitution, even when it concerned the already reduced Mapuche territories included in the *títulos de merced*.

This early two-faced policy created, as is clear from Ailío's history, expectations about justice and restitution that in reality could never be met. An entire generation in the communities put its strength and hope into a restitution they hoped would emerge from the legitimacy of their original land-grant titles, even when these already represented a massive usurpation of Mapuche resources. But the existing state was the same one that had designed the original policy of conquest and usurpation and the same one that was overseeing a strong expansion of capitalism in the new frontier regions; not surprisingly, it would not give priority to indigenous claims, no matter how just, over the possibilities for profit offered by the market economy. Seen from a local perspective, everything lined up in favor of a state policy that supported Duhalde and his ilk over the needs of the communities.

This two-faced state policy also had a double effect at the local level. On the one hand, Mapuche communities adapted creatively to the conditions of exploitation created by the state, reorganizing their systems of kinship and authority in order to reproduce their identity in a postsettlement context. Where possible they used existing institutions to resist usurpation and seek restitution. In a few cases they scored partial victories, but in general, as in the case of Ailío, the existing institutional order absorbed energies and deflected strategies rather than generating concrete results. In the long run, therefore, state policy not only fractured Mapuche territoriality and identity, but also attacked directly the Mapuche people's capacity to preserve their culture and memory. The result was the second effect of state policy in the communities: intense poverty and an internal debate over how best to confront the future.

As we saw in the chronicles of don Robustiano, don Heriberto, doña Eduardina, and Hugo Ailío, the generation growing up in the postsettlement context suffered a poverty so intense that in many cases they felt compelled to find a new strategy of restitution that did not go through established legal channels. The search for new alternatives was also facilitated by the development of what José Bengoa has called the "hacienda-community complex,"[3] because Mapuche youth, once forced to migrate in search of work, came into contact with non-Mapuche workers and comrades and began to experiment with class struggle. At a more general level, this radical strategy for restitution through an alliance with the broader popular movement had been debated since the 1930s, but it did not reach the communities in a massive way until the decade of agrarian reform.

Ailío's history also suggests that the agrarian reform years, especially the period of the Popular Unity regime (1970–73), were a partial exception to the continuity of state policy. The Popular Unity government attempted to create a popular development model within which the Mapuche could participate in their capacity as poor peasants, while at the same time recognizing their specific history of usurpation and exploitation. The case of Ailío takes on special importance during these years because of the community's participation in one of the earliest takeovers of the Popular Unity government and also because of the landowner's violent reoccupation, which received prominent coverage in the national news media; the court case against the Landarretches for violation of the State Internal Security Law; and the support given the landowner by the Sociedad Nacional de Agricultura. The numerous agrarian reform centers created along the coastal region would re-create, for a short period of time, a Mapuche territoriality under the auspices of a state development model; they would contribute as well to placing this region once more in the national news in early September 1973, with the pre-coup military operation in Nehuentúe. Thus Ailío emerges as an especially symbolic case in which can be combined the richness of detail possible in the study of one community and the representative nature of its participation in the national processes of the time. If the prosperity people enjoyed under the Popular Unity government would live on in the hopes and memories of the asentamiento's participants, so, too, would the hard lesson that even a popular government was unable to permanently change the balance of forces existing in society.

The military dictatorship can be seen, in this context, less as a fundamental rupture of the democratic order than a resumption of a previous status quo. Decree-Law 2568 of 1979, by providing for the subdivision and privatization of Mapuche land, took to its ultimate conclusion a policy of privatization that had been in progress since 1928. But it is also possible to see continuity with previous regimes in the process of agrarian counterreform. As we saw in the case of Ailío, the military government, by fashioning an institutionalized process through which it considered, case by case and only by petition of the previous owner, the legal status of the properties affected by the reform, applied a veneer of legality and normality to the exercise of violence in the name of the market and of private property. When the dictatorship gave priority to market criteria and private investment over the needs of the majority, unfortunately it was possible to find similarities, in Mapuche territory, with the policies of almost all postresettlement governments. Although it may be an especially difficult pill to swallow in a post-dictatorship context, the truth is that the limitations of Chilean democracy more generally are especially clear from a Mapuche perspective.

One of the most effective aspects of the dictatorship's technocratic and legalistic policies was that, to a certain extent, it made the repressed feel responsible for their fate. I heard several people, at one point or another, say that the Popular Unity government had failed because "we weren't able to rise to the occasion, we didn't deserve it." When don Antonio Ailío used the repression as evidence that the land takeover strategy was mistaken, he also incorporated a part of the military government's moralistic and legalistic discourse. It is worthwhile to remember, in this context, the words of Héctor Jensen, one of the architects of the military's agrarian policy, when he returned the San Pablo estate that had once been part of the fundo Esperanza to Pablo Lüer in February 1974: "You know what the punishment is for people who take, rob, or usurp. We would have been perfectly within our rights to arrive in the company of a police or army detachment and throw you out on the street. However, we've preferred a dialogue and a good-faith agreement, conscious that you, along with us, have the same goal, which is the progress and recovery of our country."[4] Interestingly, the Spanish words for "good-faith agreement" are "arreglo a la buena," very similar to don Antonio's words about the legalistic strategy being "por las buenas," or in a good way. And not only those who opposed the takeover of Rucalán ended up supporting their arguments with echoes of the dictatorship's legalistic discourse. Even the political prisoners taken in the Nehuentúe operation, including don Heriberto, used as proof of their innocence the fact that all charges were ultimately dropped.

All of this suggests an extremely complex relationship between local history and consciousness and the actions and policies of the state. On one side, the Chilean state seems to set the rules of the game, in the sense that it establishes the structures, institutions, and political discourses within which people must struggle and exist. But on the other side, the poor and oppressed push at the boundaries of these discourses, structures, and institutions, trying to modify and adapt them to their own requirements for struggle and identity. The result, therefore, is neither the system that those in power originally conceptualized and hoped for, nor the way of life desired by subaltern groups. Starting from the very formation of the resettled Mapuche communities, one can see this double evolution in more detail.

After the military defeat of the Mapuche, the state created economic parameters within which the newly resettled indigenous population would have to build a different life as an integral, if marginalized, part of Chilean society. By reducing the amount of land and other resources controlled by the communities, for example, the state forced the Mapuche to transform themselves from semi-migratory livestock herders into small peasant producers. The size of the original land grants, whose boundaries were defined with the goal of "civilizing" the Mapuche by denying them their extensive livestock economy and transforming them into agriculturalists, generated dramatic impoverishment by the second and third generations. Ironically, because they did not have the necessary expertise to develop intensive agriculture, Mapuche peasants ended up contributing to the degradation of their own land. The final result of this economic vicious circle was that Mapuche small producers were forced to work for others because they did not possess the necessary capital, seed, animals, or tools to cultivate the little land they had left. In this way, the state created a part of the cheap labor supply needed by the capitalist economy.

At the moment of resettlement, the state also reorganized the political and cultural conditions under which Mapuche communities could exist. By redefining Mapuche political units as the resettled communities, the state cut the political-military ties that had permitted alliances within a broader territory. Lines of authority became fragmented and atomized, reconstituted within the model of the "original caciques" of the resettled communities. At the same time, because the state dealt with Mapuche justice and restitution issues through a parallel institutional system centered in the Ministry of Colonization, it was able to segregate the Mapuche politically, supposedly in order to protect them, but in reality to isolate them from the broader discourse of participation and social justice that began to be elaborated in Chilean society between 1938 and 1964. The contemporary Mapuche movement has shown, starting in the late 1970s, that this form of political segregation is most effectively combated through a strategy that revindicates the identity and territory of the Mapuche people as a whole. Rethinking Mapuche politics from the perspective of a broader claim to territory has dramatically highlighted how the Chilean state, by dividing Mapuche territory into small communities under the authority of original caciques often chosen by the local bureaucrats themselves, acted in classic colonial fashion. This was clearly a policy of divide and rule.

What is left out of such a criticism of state policy, however, is that Mapuche peasants managed to adapt and make theirs the postresettlement institutional order, using the legal legitimacy of the land-grant titles to resist subsequent usurpation. They rebuilt broader territorial relationships among communities through kinship and exchange of products, establishing a system of sharecropping different from that practiced by the medium-sized agriculturalists or owners of large estates. Religious and cultural customs, especially *gillatun* and *palin*, also helped maintain broader networks of sociability and reproduce, even if under conditions of poverty, a broader social and cultural world. When they migrated to the city, young people maintained their connection with their families and communities, sending back money and going home to get married or to establish a household. And despite their apparent political segregation, some Mapuche migrants and intellectuals began to make common cause with the popular movement and the emerging leftist parties, in which new discourses of inclusion and social justice were being formulated.

As we saw in the case of Ailío, the 1960s were years of dramatic change and transition. As the first generation of resettled Mapuche began to die out, among them many of the *logkos* and *machis* who had been the cultural and spiritual leaders of their communities, a crisis of traditional authority spread through many localities. In the new climate of agrarian organization and mobilization sponsored by the Christian Democrats, this crisis led in many communities to a political rethinking and tentative acceptance of the option of peasant organization. Once again, as had happened during the original resettlement, the state defined a new option of struggle for the Mapuche through agrarian reform, peasant organizations, and rural cooperatives.

As is clear from the history of the asentamiento Arnoldo Ríos, under these new conditions Mapuche peasants were still able to adapt state-given parameters to their own social, cultural, and family needs. In contrast to many non-Mapuche asentamientos, in Arnoldo Ríos people used networks of kinship and exchange between Mapuche communities in order to distribute more broadly and efficiently the cooperative's resources and income. Even if somewhat clandestinely, a machi was also present on the asentamiento. And through Mapuche sharecropping arrangements, family members from the communities got access to land on the agrarian reform center.

The fear and repression of the dictatorship, along with Decree-Law 2568, created a climate of aggression toward the Mapuche to which people could not easily adapt. An entire generation would be marked by the experience of growing up with no fire in the hearth. But despite it all, with national and international solidarity it was possible, during the 1980s, to create an association under the dictatorship's own syndicalist (*gremialista*) rules in order to reconstitute the relations of territoriality and solidarity that had been destroyed by repression. Even under such extreme conditions, therefore, the communities took advantage of both national and international solidarity and of the military government's own legal statutes to create their own organization.

Finally, with the transition to democratic rule, the community of Ailío was able to use the new Indigenous Law, its statutes for the reorganization of indigenous communities, and the Land Fund established as part of CONADI to reconstitute itself and expand its land base. Once again, it was not possible to act within parameters the community itself established, but rather under the institutional conditions set by the state. As a result, the newly reconstituted community took the organizational form of a more mainstream trade union or political party rather than a Mapuche community, and the new land was acquired through additional suffering, hunger, and boundary conflicts. But today there are two communities of Nicolás Ailío, and they have more land than they did twenty years ago.

In their conversations and discussions within the community, people also combine state-generated categories and discourses with their own notions of solidarity and justice, notions they have been reproducing and modifying across three generations of struggle. In the case of the debate over legality and justice in the context of land restitution, don Antonio's "legal" position was based in the process of original resettlement and in the two-faced policy the Chilean state formulated around the problems of usurpation and restitution developing between 1900 and 1930. With the agrarian reform and then the military dictatorship, don Antonio added threads from the military discourse and from the charismatic morality of the Church of God to his multidimensional phrase *por las buenas*. And don Heriberto's much more radical and critical position, which differentiated so forcefully between legality and justice, was also formulated under the wing of two agrarian reform governments, in the context of the peasant committees and asentamientos created by the Christian Democratic government and additional influences from the more radical *mirista* positions and from liberation theology. In the new era unfolding in the 1990s, with the application for a subsidy through CONADI, we also find a layer of Mapuche ethnic revitalization emerging in don Heriberto's desire to build a *rewe* in Huellanto Alto.

The differences between René and don Heriberto Ailío over how to define community deploy definitions of Mapuche community that the state has formulated at various times in the twentieth century. Is the community a kinship network built around the family of the original cacique (definition created by the resettlement and the land-grant titles)? Is the community constructed through struggle and solidarity among all the poor and oppressed (definition of the left and the agrarian reform)? Is it simply a place of residence like any other (definition of the military dictatorship)? Or is it a trade-union or syndicalist organization under legally defined statutes and bylaws (the Indigenous Law of 1993 and the postauthoritarian governments of the 1990s)? These diverse ways of thinking about community interlock and mix, depending on the moment, specific struggles, and needs.

The dynamic between state and local levels, therefore, does not mean there is a lack of local creativity. On the contrary: time and again, under the most difficult and painful conditions, the community manages to transform and establish ownership over state discourse and practice. Local mixes of practice and discourse are, moreover, extremely creative and eclectic. Just because the state has stopped using the agrarian reform model does not mean that people at the local level abandon the notions and collective organization and labor practices used on the asentamiento. Even if the original Mapuche resettled community no longer exists in many cases, people still care about the notions of legitimacy that were tied to the original cacique's family tree. It is in this context that one must also understand the ongoing discussion, especially in the new community of Huellanto Alto, between a collective model of agricultural production and the alternative of individual plots. On one hand, people remember with affection and nostalgia the prosperity generated by the collective model during the agrarian reform; but on the other, especially among the younger families, people deploy the discourse of prosperity through privatization that the state has used to confront the Mapuche since the beginning of the twentieth century. In this way Mapuche peasants reorder and reconnect the discourses and practices at hand in order to create their own strategies of struggle and survival.

In the community of Ailío, the most dramatic example of such a strategy has to do with the dynamic between a class consciousness and identity and an ethnic consciousness or identity as a people. We have seen how, in contrast to communities in which Mapuche lines of authority and religious practices have been maintained until the present day, in Ailío by the 1960s people were already combining Mapuche beliefs and practices with peasant popular culture. The new peasant organizations created by the Christian Democrats, in combination with the arrival of Protestant religions, had a great deal to do with this development. But in order to understand this process more fully I needed to go further back and trace the evolution of a labor market in the coastal region that involved both Mapuche and non-Mapuche peasants and in which, given the extreme poverty of their community, the men of Ailío participated from early on. Through a combination of daily labor relations and the Protestant churches, especially the Church of God in Rucahue and the Anglican church in Nehuentúe, a broader solidarity and sociability began to emerge that would culminate in the asentamientos and *centros de producción* established on the coast during the agrarian reform.

This regional sociability evolved in two directions. On one side, by creating ties among all the rural poor, it tended to distance indigenous participants from Mapuche identity and practice, emphasizing instead class-based and trade-union organizations. But on the other side, the same regional ties facilitated exchange among Mapuche from different communities and thus helped sustain broader territorial networks. We can see, in this context, the joint participation of the communities of Cullinco, Rucahue, Pichingual, Pilquinao, and Coi Coi in the agrarian reform, and the majority of these communities would also participate in the syndicalist organization of CODEPECA in the 1980s. One of the central figures in this process was don Heriberto Ailío, grandson of the original cacique, active first in the Church of God and then in the Anglican church, and founding member of the MCR. Don Heriberto inherited from his father, Martín, and his grandfather Nicolás a capacity for visionary leadership that always looked for the path to change, to innovation, that would help bring his people to the "promised land." If in the agrarian reform decade this path took a predominantly class-based turn, by the 1990s it was to be found instead in a strategy of cultural renovation and indigenous reconstitution.

What the case of Ailío most clearly demonstrates about Mapuche identity, therefore, is that it is neither unidimensional, nor independent from the state or from power relations in society more generally. Long before the military defeat of the Mapuche in 1883, interactions with the broader society, as well as the political and military actions of colonial and postcolonial Chilean governments, already had affected Mapuche society and culture in important ways. One could argue even that *mestizaje* and the intermingling of European and indigenous strategies, traditions, and lineages have their deepest roots in the period before military defeat. When the Mapuche became directly subordinated to the Chilean state, therefore, they already had long experience in adapting creatively to outside forces.

As the state attempted to reduce and fragment Mapuche resources, resettled communities took state institutions and adapted them, where possible, to their own needs. When the state segregated indigenous demands, first under the Ministry of Foreign Relations and then under the Ministry of Land and Colonization, Mapuche activists in the cities demanded full citizenship and justice. Allowing for differences and disagreements between groups and factions, Mapuche movements shared a desire to preserve indigenous identity and territory while demanding equal treatment from the state. From these adaptations and mobilizations emerged, in the twentieth century, really existing forms of Mapuche identity.

From the beginning, therefore, contemporary Mapuche identity evolved from a mix of state action and the Mapuche's own resistant and creative strategies. When the state attempted to segregate, sometimes strategies of inclusion and class alliance were the best response. If the state attempted to integrate, sometimes the best path was through a militant revindication of Mapuche autonomy. Within these complex, creative negotiations, the relationship between class and indigenous identity was not simple or unidirectional. The same person or community could change from one to the other, at different times, depending on the balance of forces in the region or in the broader society.

To understand the diversity, complexity, and historical flexibility of Mapuche identity and culture, one must start at the local level and listen to the voices and narratives in the communities. This is how one begins a dialogue with different "time-knots" and allows one's own perspectives to expand beyond what is already known or accepted. It is in this sense that I most profoundly disagree with Alejandro Saavedra, who in his recent book reflects on the situation of the Mapuche in contemporary Chilean society. In part this book is a follow-up to an important publication of his of 1971, in which he systematically presented the position of the revolutionary left at the time, insisting that the Mapuche were neither a people nor an ethnic group, but rather a dominated subculture within the class system of Chilean society. As in his previous book, Saavedra develops a structuralist argument based on demographic data and a theoretical framework based on class analysis.

The conclusions reached in the two works are also similar: the Mapuche are a part of Chilean society, and thus they are neither a nation nor an ethnic group, but an "indigenous people," by which he means they are a part of the Chilean people that has also suffered colonial exploitation as Indians.[5]

Despite offering some important perspectives, however, the book remains squarely within categories already familiar in the social sciences and the discourse of scientific objectivity. This, by itself, is not a bad thing, as I have tried to show above by establishing a dialogue among different types of sources and information. The problem is that the exclusive attitude the author has toward "objectivity," toward "a correct analysis of the Mapuche question," makes impossible any sort of conversation among different forms of knowledge and of historical memory. In this context it is not accidental that Mapuche voices, especially those of the communities and their local leaders, simply are not present. It is easier to "attain cross-cultural knowledge, knowledge that is as valid, reliable, and exact as possible . . . for people from any culture" when one does not listen to the voices that could most strongly disagree with one's position. Among other things, this allows Saavedra to ignore the complex cultural, political, and historical creativity with which the Mapuche people have managed to reconstruct themselves, again and again, for more than a century of colonization.[6]

Ailío's history is proof of this complex creativity. When the "traditional" strategy of restitution established during the resettlement was shown to be useless, from the land-grant community's very leadership emerged the alternative of class alliance. When military repression cut short the popular mobilization model, preferentially jailing and torturing Mapuche activists and overturning the agrarian reform, economic and social reconstruction was accomplished through the dictatorship's own syndicalist institutions, even if conjoined with the solidarity of the Catholic Church and of international foundations. When the first postauthoritarian government passed an Indigenous Law setting the conditions for the reconstruction of the communities, Ailío reconstituted itself with the goal of applying for an indigenous land subsidy in order to expand its resources. This mix of identities and strategies has been truly impressive.

And yet throughout, there has been an important continuity when it comes to territory, kinship, and sociability. In the coastal region since the time of resettlement, neighboring communities have maintained relations of cooperation and mutual aid. These remained especially strong, for the community of Ailío, with neighboring communities such as Rucahue, Pichingual, and Pilquinao. Ceremonial relations, including gillatun, palin, and weddings, for a long time helped reproduce this territoriality and human connection. During the agrarian reform years, these relations were maintained, and even deepened and extended, through the asentamientos and centros de producción. CODEPECA involved the same group. Religious connections were also reconstituted in the Protestant churches, even if the result was a further distancing from Mapuche ceremonial and religious practice. When the Aylwin government reopened an indigenous alternative in the 1990s, Ailío stood in the vanguard once again by becoming one of the very few communities that received a land subsidy from CONADI. The formal ceremony in which Ailío took possession of the new land at Huellanto Alto was conducted in Spanish and *mapunzugun*; don Heriberto has kept alive the possibility of playing palin and maybe even reorganizing Mapuche cultural ceremonies in Nicolás Ailío II. At the same time, however, they invited a dance troupe from another community to perform at the formal possession ceremony because none of the people moving to Huellanto Alto knew Mapuche dances any longer. Perhaps the very loss of coastal networks of sociability and identity will contribute, in the long run, to Nicolás Ailío II's search, as the only Mapuche community in Huellanto Alto, for more "traditional" and openly Mapuche forms of reproducing its identity.

Within this densely woven history of Ailío, my nine-year presence seems a single thread that is quickly lost in a broader pattern that no single person can control. I find satisfaction in the fact that I now belong to a larger history I have helped articulate. I am only a small part of a larger group of people who, for the past five decades, have made an impact on this impressive community and in turn have been impacted by it. I am referring to the outsiders who have shown solidarity and accompanied the community of Ailío and its neighbors in their various struggles.

At the end of the 1960s, when Chileans were dreaming of egalitarian social transformation, a young Christian community interested in social justice arrived in Puerto Saavedra. They opened the local hospital, welcoming the Mapuche communities and creating a solidarity network that supported agrarian mobilization for the next several years. This group, together with other mirista students who passed through the coastal area between 1971 and 1972, was the first to develop relatively horizontal relations with the Mapuche communities. Despite all the problems at the time and what happened after the 1973 coup, several of these outsiders nevertheless formed enduring friendships with the community of Ailío. Among them were Enrique

Pérez and Mario Castro and also some individuals who talked with me on condition of anonymity. One of them (whom I have not interviewed) was able, while in exile in France, to channel international solidarity into the formation of CODEPECA. When the dictatorship ended, and especially in the process of applying for the land subsidy, several of these ex-coastal activists returned to "pay old debts." In part because of this, the community of Ailío was successful with its second subsidy application.

In the meantime, during the darkest years of repression another group of friends and advisers arrived in the coastal region through the Temuco archdiocese and the Centro de Educación y Tecnología. They were people with a social conscience whose activism had been forced to adapt to another historical moment in which conditions had changed dramatically. They no longer organized demonstrations or confrontations, but instead worked in small groups that formulated concrete strategies for survival and for the reconstruction of social networks. The style of this second activist generation, therefore, was more subdued and cautious, though not necessarily less committed. The community formed lasting friendships with this group also as well as commitments that are respected and fulfilled, with or without money, with or without roads, with or without punishing winter rains. The CET's activists in particular, Luis and Gustavo Peralta and María Angélica Celis, worked with the community in the 1980s and today are still helping out, especially in Huellanto Alto.

For my part, I first got to know the community when people were working preferentially with Enrique Pérez and continued my work when Ailío's leaders decided to reconstitute their relationship with the CET. Thanks to this change, I was fortunate to meet Luis, Gustavo, and María Angélica. In general what I have been able to understand is that don Heriberto Ailío, as grandson of the original cacique and the leader whose vision is directed most successfully forward and toward the outside, is the one who best builds and reproduces solidarity with friendly outsiders. He and doña Marta are the preferred hosts, although don Robustiano and doña Eduardina also played that role with me and others. I have been told that the parents of the Ailío Pilquinao clan, don Martín Ailío Porma and doña María Pilquinao, were also hospitable and welcoming to strangers; unfortunately I did not arrive in the community in time to meet them.

Reflecting on these distinct moments in the community's relationship with us friendly outsiders, I have been able to see that as a group we share certain characteristics. We believe strongly in solidarity and react with anger to social injustice. But there are also important differences, of style, personality, and points of view, factors that have made some of us better companions at specific moments. This is what I learned when I found out that Huellanto Alto had preferred to renew its advising relationship with the CET and not continue with Enrique Pérez. Once the political work of the subsidy application was over and it was time to develop a production plan on the new property, it made perfect sense to change advisers from a combative activist to a group of agricultural technicians and activists who already knew the community well and had a more circumspect style. In this sense it is important to note that Ailío's leaders, even if they cannot control the conditions of their lives that make outside advisers a necessity, know very well how to steer that advice toward their desired goals.

This ability to innovate and adapt when faced with difficult and uncontrollable conditions is a central theme in the history of the community. As noted earlier, the settlement of Nicolás Ailío in Tranapuente, indeed the name itself, was a result of the dislocations of war. When the Ailíos began to settle and adapt to this coastal landscape, where two great rivers meet at the sea, they were refugees, shaken to the very core of their identity by the violence that had shattered their people. On the basis of solidarity, mutual aid, and new ties with others in their same situation, they began to form part of another *aillarewe* in which they all became family. If Nicolás Ailío I began this way, it should not come as a surprise that Nicolás Ailío II was also started by a group of refugees, this time fleeing military repression, who sought to heal their wounds by rebuilding community and a collective Mapuche prosperity. Perhaps it was Cecilia Ailío who most intensely represented this deep continuity when she remembered that her mother, doña María Pilquinao, had envisioned the new era: "She told me that I would walk a painful road but at the end I would see the light . . . but that would be here with my people and in a new place, not over there on the coast. . . . [W]hen my mother died we weren't even thinking about the land subsidy . . . she was able to see it and let me know."[7] Thus when Cecilia says to her new plants as they adapt in Huellanto Alto, "Don't dry out, beautiful," she is also addressing all of Ailío's human generations who, through solidarity and connecting with others, have managed to endure.

This talent for adaptation and human connection helps us understand how such a demographically small community can have such a large historical presence. To be small but scrappy is an important part of the community's identity. I remember one of my first visits to Huellanto Alto, in

March 1997. People had just made the move. It was still summer, and most families had not even put up a shack to protect themselves from the elements. We were sitting along the edge of some native forest, and the women had put large pots on campfires in order to make jam from the wild fruit they had just collected. Someone had found vines of red copihue growing in the middle of the forest. There was much laughter, and the girls wanted to have their pictures taken with copihues in their hair. Nearby a pack of dogs was roaming around looking for food, and suddenly a puppy decided to confront one of the larger dogs. The two began to fight, and the runt threw itself on the big one, not seeming to know the meaning of retreat. Finally the big dog escaped, handing victory to the runt. Several of us had stopped talking to observe this drama. There was a short silence, and finally one of the men remarked, "Ailío—that's Ailío." Yes, we agreed. And we all laughed, as if recognizing a deep, longstanding historical truth.

ACRONYMS

CET	Centro de Educación y Tecnología
CEPI	Comisión Especial de Pueblos Indígenas
CEPRO	Centro de Producción
CERA	Centro de Reforma Agraria
CODEPECA	Asociación Gremial Consejo de Desarrollo Pesquero Campesino
CONADI	Corporación Nacional de Desarrollo Indígena
CORA	Corporación Nacional de Reforma Agraria
CORFO	Corporación de Fomento a la Producción
DAS	Departamento de Acción Social
INDAP	Instituto de Desarrollo Agropecuario
MCR	Movimiento Campesino Revolucionario
MIR	Movimiento de Izquierda Revolucionaria
UP	Unidad Popular

GLOSSARY

allanamiento: A search operation carried out by the military or police, often of individual homes. The word developed a more generalized usage and meaning with the repression surrounding the Chilean military coup and subsequent dictatorship and began to designate any repressive operation carried out by the armed forces on a target considered subversive.

aillarewe: A territorially based lineage unit that brought together a half dozen or so Mapuche land-grant communities, often connected through marriage, and served as a unit for ritual and broader forms of sociability.

asentamiento: An agrarian reform unit created under the Christian Democratic agrarian reform law. It was constituted as a cooperative of families to be governed by heads of household alongside government representatives. The members of the cooperative were known as *asentados*.

Asociación Gremial Consejo de Desarrollo Pesquero Campesino (Council for Fishing and Peasant Development, or CODEPECA): With its headquarters in the community of Ailío, this "syndicalist" (*gremialista*) association created in 1988 under the laws of the dictatorship grouped together Mapuche communities and non-Mapuche fishermen in a local self-help development organization legally able to receive international aid for several development projects.

boldo: A large, oaklike native tree whose leaves can be used for a variety of medicinal purposes, especially, when steeped in hot water and served as tea, to aid digestion.

cacique: Originally a Carib word for leader or headman, during the colonial period it was generalized to mean any indigenous leader. In the case of the Mapuche it was often used as a synonym for *logko*.

Caja de Colonización Agrícola: A government agency created in 1928 for the purpose of buying up larger agricultural properties and subdividing them into smaller units that could then be bought by smallholders or landless rural inhabitants.

Centro de Educación y Tecnología (CET): An NGO specializing in sustainable agriculture that began working with the community of Nicolás Ailío in 1980.

Centro de Producción (CEPRO): A multi-unit agrarian reform entity administered directly by state representatives. CEPROS were created under the Popular Unity government in regions where a higher level of commercial production was considered possible.

Centro de Reforma Agraria (CERA): Agrarian Reform Center, a unit of agrarian reform created under the Popular Unity government in which women and youth were declared independent members rather than having their participation mediated through husbands or fathers.

Centros Culturales Mapuches: Created in 1979 under the protection and auspices of the Catholic Church, this first Mapuche revitalization organization took as its main goals resisting the Land Division law passed by the dictatorship and sponsoring a chain of ceremonies of cultural rebirth throughout Mapuche territory.

Comisión Especial de Pueblos Indígenas (CEPI): Special Commission of Indigenous Peoples. The first institution created by the Concertación government as a response to the demands of indigenous peoples, it was created by presidential decree on May 17, 1990, at the beginning of the Aylwin government.

Comité Ejecutivo Agrario: Created by the military government at both the provincial and national levels, these executive agrarian committees had as their task to "regularize," according to the new criteria of the dictatorship, the system of land tenure and hear landowner petitions for the reversal of agrarian reform decrees.

compañero: Literally, "companion." Designates a political comrade-in-arms and was introduced into generalized Latin American usage after the Cuban Revolution of 1959.

Concertación: A political coalition that emerged in opposition to the dictatorship during the 1988 plebiscite, it consolidated into an electoral coalition of the center-left, whose candidates have won the presidential elections since 1990.

Consejo de Todas las Tierras: Literally, the All-Lands Council, this Mapuche organization was created in the late 1980s to protest the agreement reached between the Mapuche movement and then-presidential candidate of the opposition coalition, Patricio Aylwin. The Consejo led a militant and dramatic wave of land invasions in 1991 and 1992.

Corporación de Fomento a la Producción (Corporation for the Advancement of Production, or CORFO): A government development corporation founded under the first Popular Front government (1938–42) to help facilitate investment in production and industry by encouraging partnerships between the state and private capital.

Corporación de Reforma Agraria (Agrarian Reform Corporation, or CORA): A government agency designated to administer and promulgate the agrarian reform, it evolved from the earlier Caja de Colonización Agrícola.

Corporación Nacional de Desarrollo Indígena (National Indigenous Development Corporation, or CONADI): An agency created by the 1993 Indigenous Law to oversee the programs and moneys intended for indigenous development programs as well as to mediate for and protect the integrity of indigenous communities.

Departamento de Acción Social (Social Action Department, or DAS): A branch of the Temuco archdiocese of the Catholic Church, it was dedicated to providing social assistance and financial support to poor peasant and Mapuche communities.

Fundación Instituto Indígena: Indigenous Institute Foundation. Another branch of the Temuco archdiocese of the Catholic Church that specialized in providing aid to Mapuche communities.

fundo: A larger agricultural property or estate.

gillatun: One of the most important Mapuche religious and communal ceremonies, in which neighboring communities reestablish reciprocal ties through a ceremony of prayer and reflection that lasts several days. While it can be organized at specific moments to plead with God to resolve specific problems, in general it occurs in a community once every four years and is carried out on a special field which that year is consecrated exclusively for that purpose.

hectárea: Hectare, or unit of land measurement equivalent to 2.471 acres.

hualle: A variety of tree native to the Chilean south, occurring abundantly in the original forests of the Mapuche region.

inquilino: Service tenant or resident laborer on a *fundo* or large estate.

Instituto de Desarrollo Agropecuario (Institute for Agrarian and Livestock Development, or INDAP): Along with the Corporation for Agrarian Reform (Corporación de Reforma Agraria, or CORA), INDAP was an institution created in the 1960s to facilitate the process of agrarian reform and development carried out between 1964 and 1973. In contrast to CORA, which was abolished by the military government after the completion of the agrarian counterreform in 1978,

INDAP today still provides loans to small agricultural producers, though now very much under market criteria. In 1979, the previously existing Indigenous Development Institute (Instituto de Desarrollo Indígena, or IDI) was abolished and its functions integrated into INDAP.

Lafkenche: A subgroup of the Mapuche people who reside near bodies of water and thus incorporate fishing and the harvesting of other water-based resources into their subsistence practices.

logko: In the Mapuche language, *mapunzugun*, the word means "head." Designates the recognized leader of a Mapuche community, who organizes ritual, mediates in a crisis, and handles the community's relations with the outside world.

machi: A shaman or ritual specialist in Mapuche culture. She or he officiates at various forms of religious ritual and stores and transmits knowledge concerning healing, spirituality, and past events. A *machi* is both greatly respected and greatly feared in the community.

mapunzugun: The language of the Mapuche people.

mate: A caffeinated, tealike beverage traditionally drunk on the plains of Argentina and surrounding regions. Although many people in Argentina drink *mate*, in some parts of Chile *mate* consumption is marked as a Mapuche custom.

médica: A healer who uses herbal remedies and other traditional forms of medicine. While she may often use techniques similar to those used by a *machi*, people distinguish the two roles by saying that a *machi* has greater connections to the spirit world, which can be used either for good or for bad.

mirista: Member of the MIR.

Movimiento Campesino Revolucionario (Revolutionary Peasant Movement, or MCR): The peasant front of the MIR, which promulgated land invasions and fence runnings among the Mapuche communities and non-Mapuche peasantry.

Movimiento de Izquierda Revolucionaria (Movement of the Revolutionary Left, or MIR): Revolutionary left party that stood to the left of the Popular Unity coalition, preaching direct action and calling for armed defense of the socialist project. The MIR was particularly active among Mapuche communities in the province of Cautín, especially in the coastal region and in Lautaro county to the north of Temuco.

muday: A traditional drink made from grain, usually wheat, that is used at most Mapuche religious ceremonies. It can be fermented or not fermented.

ngenco: A spirit who controls a particular body of water, of whom one must ask permission to pass through or near that territory.

palin: A sport similar to field hockey, played with sticks and a wooden ball. The competition is usually between communities, each of which brings to the field, in addition to the players, a large delegation of supporters headed by a *machi*. The sport used to be played as part of the training of Mapuche warriors.

peñi: Brother.

Popular Unity (Unidad Popular): A coalition of leftist parties, hegemonized by the Socialist and Communist parties, that brought Salvador Allende to the presidency in 1970.

Radicación: The process of legal settlement onto land-grant communities that the Chilean state sponsored for the Mapuche people. Although the first *radicación* law was passed in 1866, the process itself did not become generalized until after the Mapuche's military defeat in the 1880s.

reducción: The name given by the Chilean government to a Mapuche land-grant community, ironic in its double meaning as "colonial" land title (the same term was used in the Andes by the Spanish crown) and as a "reduction" or "shrinkage" of original territory.

rewe: A carved post resembling a totem that designates a *machi*'s house; also, the carved post representing the community or lineage that is exhibited at a *gillatun*. Sometimes hispanicized as *rehue*.

sopaipillas: A form of fried bread cooked in animal fat that has become traditional throughout rural Chile in particular. When made for a *gillatun*, they are especially large.

Título de merced: A land title given by the Chilean government to each group of settled Mapuche, allegedly a lineage or extended family, designating the names of the participating settlers and the extension and boundaries of the land grant being provided. Each community was then subsequently known by the name of the "original cacique" who received the title from the government, and all descendants of the original settlers had rights to land within the community.

wigka: The word used today in *mapunzugun* to designate non-Mapuches, it originally meant "thief who operates quickly and violently."

NOTES

Chapter 1. *In the Fog before Dawn*

1 The information in this paragraph comes from two sources: Interview with doña Marta Antinao, Community of Ailío-Tranapuente, 18 Jan. 1997, and Corte de Apelaciones de Temuco, Causa Criminal #242—"Intendente Gastón Lobos Barrientos contra Juan Bautista Landarretche Mendoza y otros por Infracción de la Ley de Seguridad Interior del Estado," begun in Temuco, 26 Dec. 1970.

2 The data in this paragraph summarize the essential events on which the majority of the trial witnesses agree: Corte de Apelaciones de Temuco, Causa Criminal #242, op. cit.

3 Corte de Apelaciones de Temuco, Causa Criminal #242: "Declaración de José Segundo Pilquinao," f. 215.

4 *El Mercurio*, 12/20/1970, p. 33; *El Diario Austral*, 12/29/1970, p. 8.

5 For descriptions of twentieth-century Chilean history, see Mariana Aylwin et al., *Chile en el siglo XX* (Santiago: Planeta, 1990); Peter DeShazo, *Urban Workers and Labor Unions in Chile, 1902–1927* (Madison: University of Wisconsin Press, 1983); Thomas Klubock, *Contested Communities: Class, Gender, and Politics in Chile's El Teniente Copper Mine, 1904–1951* (Durham: Duke University Press, 1998); Brian Loveman, *Chile: The Legacy of Hispanic Capitalism* (New York: Oxford University Press, 1979); Brian Loveman and Elizabeth Lira, *Las suaves cenizas del olvido: Vía chilena de reconciliación política, 1814–1932* (Santiago: LOM/DIBAM, 1999) and *Las ardientes cenizas del olvido: Vía chilena de Reconciliación Política, 1932–1994* (Santiago: LOM/DIBAM, 2000); Michael Monteón, *Chile in the Nitrate Era: The Evolution of Economic Dependence, 1880–1930* (Madison: University of Wisconsin Press, 1982); Luis Ortega, ed., *La Guerra Civil de 1891: Cien años hoy* (Santiago: Universidad de Santiago de Chile, 1991); Julio Pinto, *Trabajos y rebeldías en la pampa salitrera: El ciclo del salitre y la reconfiguración de las identidades populares (1850–1900)* (Santiago: Editorial Universidad de Santiago, 1998); Karin A. Rosemblatt, *Gendered Compromises: Political Cultures and the State in Chile, 1920–1950* (Chapel Hill: Univer-

sity of North Carolina Press, 2000); Gabriel Salazar, *Violencia política popular en "las grandes alamedas": Santiago de Chile, 1917–1987* (Santiago: Ediciones Sur, 1990); Luis Vitale et al., *Para recuperar la memoria histórica: Frei, Allende y Pinochet* (Santiago: Ediciones Chile América-CESOC, 1999); Peter Winn, *Weavers of Revolution: The Yarur Workers and Chile's Road to Socialism* (New York: Oxford University Press, 1986). For the exclusion of the rural regions from the Popular Front project, see Brian Loveman, *Struggle in the Countryside: Politics and Rural Labor in Chile, 1919–1973* (Bloomington: Indiana University Press, 1976), pp. 118–24.

6 José Bengoa, *Historia del pueblo Mapuche (Siglo XIX y XX)* (Santiago: Ediciones Sur, 1985), pp. 382–89. Rolf Foerster and Sonia Montecino, in *Organizaciones, Líderes y Contiendas Mapuches (1900–1970)* (Santiago: Centro Estudios de la Mujer, 1988), until now the most complete study of Mapuche organizations in the post-land-grant period, also show that the integrationist attempts by Mapuche organizations in this period had as their goal the protection of Mapuche rights in general, whether with regard to urban or rural sections of that population. For the case of Manuel Maniquilef, see Foerster and Montecino, *Organizaciones, Líderes y Contiendas Mapuches*, pp. 68–74.

7 An example of attempted collaboration between the Mapuche and the trade union left can be found in Martín Painemal Huechual with Rolf Foerster, *Vida de un dirigente Mapuche* (Santiago: Grupo de Investigaciones Agrarias, 1983). A good overview of the Popular Unity (UP) debates on the agrarian reform, and of the UP's position in the more general debates about Chilean agriculture, can be found in Jacques Chonchol, *Sistemas agrarios en América Latina: De la etapa prehispánica a la modernización conservadora* (Santiago, Chile and Mexico City: Fondo de Cultura Económica, 1994), and in María Antonieta Huerta M., *Otro Agro para Chile: La historia de la Reforma Agraria en el proceso social y político* (Santiago: Ediciones Chile América-CESOC, 1989). For the MIR's regional agrarian program for the province of Cautín, see "¡Pan, tierra y socialismo!," *Punto Final*, no. 121, 5 Jan. 1971, pp. 26–32. An important analytical summary of Chilean legislation until 1968 concerning Mapuche lands can be found in Wilson Cantoni, "Legislación indígena e integración del mapuche," Program in the Sociology of Economic Change, University of Wisconsin, in collaboration with the Land Tenure Center, Santiago, Chile, Dec. 1969.

8 Corte de Apelaciones de Temuco, Causa Criminal #242: "Declaración de Ricardo Mora Carrillo," Temuco Regional Hospital, 30 Dec. 1970, f. 140, and 31 Dec. 1970, f. 144; "Declaración de Pedro Fuentes Pilquinao," Carahue, 2 Jan. 1971, f. 217; "Declaración de José Segundo Pilquinao," Carahue, 2 Jan. 1971, f. 215; and "Declaración de Humberto Venegas Riquelme," Carahue, 2 Jan. 1971, ff. 218v–219. One hectare equals almost 2.5 acres.

9 The exact phrase in Spanish is "por las buenas." Interview with don Antonio Ailío, Community of Ailío-Tranapuente, 10 Jan. 1997.

10 Interview with don Heriberto Ailío, Community of Ailío- Tranapuente, 18 Jan. 1997.

11 José Bengoa, *Historia del pueblo Mapuche*, p. 372; Rolf Foerster y Sonia Montecino, *Organizaciones, líderes y contiendas Mapuches*, pp. 73–74, 79, 81.

12 Bengoa, *Historia del pueblo Mapuche*; Pascual Coña, *Testimonio de un cacique mapuche*, dictated to Father Ernesto Willhelm de Moesbach, 5th ed. (Santiago: Pehuén Editores, 1995); Aldo Vidal, "Conferencia sobre historia Mapuche," Catholic University of Temuco, 5 Aug. 1999; José Quidel, "Conferencia sobre historia y cultura Mapuche," Catholic University of Temuco, 6 Aug. 1999; Victor Caniullan, "Conferencia sobre cultura y religiosidad Mapuche," Catholic University of Temuco, 6 Aug. 1999.

13 In the case of a historical work such as this, using aliases for members of the community would have only partially shielded them from being identified, since their real names can be found in any case in the written documents.

14 Interview with don Antonio Ailío, Community of Ailío-Tranapuente, 10 Jan. 1997.

15 Interview with don Heriberto Ailío, Community of Ailío-Tranapuente, 18 Jan. 1997.

16 Interviews with don Antonio Ailío, Comunidad de Ailío-Tranapuente, 10 Jan. 1997; and with don Heriberto Ailío, Community of Ailío-Tranapuente, 18 Jan. 1997, and Temuco, 18 April 1997.

17 This double meaning of the word *partial*, and the importance of this to the work I am doing with the community of Ailío, was emphasized in conversations I had with the graduate students who read an earlier version of this manuscript in my graduate seminar "Native-State Relations in Latin America," which I offered in the fall of 2000. Molly Todd in particular has discussed these meanings with me, not only as they relate to this book, but also in our conversations about Mario Benedetti's poem "Soy un caso perdido (I'm a lost cause)" (in *Cotidianas*, 1978–79). I am grateful to Víctor Maturana, who first recommended the poem to me.

18 When I helped organize the Intendant's Archive in the IX Region, I became especially aware of how noticeably "selective" the documentary collection at the regional level was; everyone commented on how in the last months of the military dictatorship many documents were destroyed. In addition, the judicial documents that arrived at the Asuntos Indígenas Archive after the abolition of the special indigenous courts are very incomplete. I detected similar lacunae when I looked for the documentary collections of certain ministries in Santiago. This is not to blame the archivists, who are very dedicated to preserving documents, but rather to point out that in the very making of politics and history, documentary materials go through a "partial" selection—again in both senses of the word.

19 *Azümchefi: Grafemario único del Idioma Mapuche*, Corporación Nacional de

Desarrollo Indígena and Mapuche Organizations Folilche Aflaia-Ad Mapu-Kellukleayñ pu Zomo (Temuco, 1996).

Chapter 2. And Then, Suddenly, the Land Disappeared

1 Interview with doña Eduardina Ailío, Community of Nicolás Ailío-Tranapuente, 18 Jan. 1997.

2 CONADI, Archivo de Asuntos Indígenas, Título de Merced no. 1112- Community of Nicolás Ailío, 29 Dec. 1906.

3 CONADI, Archivo de Asuntos Indígenas, Título de Merced no. 1112- Community of Nicolás Ailío, 29 Dec. 1906; T.M. 1112- Carpeta Administrativa, Censo de la Comunidad Nicolás Ailío, Ficha no. 5, 31/5/63, Grupo Familiar de Segundo Antinao H. con Rosa Ailío Q.

4 See the family tree for more details. It is based on the following sources: CONADI, Archivo de Asuntos Indígenas, T.M. 1112- Comunidad de Nicolás Ailío: Título de Merced, Lugar Tranapuente, 29 Dec. 1906; Carpeta Administrativa: Expediente de División, Juzgado de Indios de Imperial, iniciado 16 de julio de 1930, which includes a 1930 census of the community of Nicolás Ailío; and Ministerio de Tierras y Colonización, Dirección de Asuntos Indígenas, Censo de la Comunidad de Nicolás Ailío, 30–31 May 1963.

5 On Chilean indigenous legislation, its goals and rationale, see José Aylwin O., "Tierra mapuche: derecho consuetudinario y legislación chilena," in Rodolfo Stavenhagen and Diego Iturralde, eds., *Entre la ley y la costumbre: El derecho consuetudinario indígena en América Latina*, pp. 333–54 (México, D.F. and San José, Costa Rica: Instituto Indigenista Interamericano and Instituto Interamericano de Derechos Humanos, 1990).

6 Conversation with don Heriberto Ailío, Huellanto Alto, 10 Aug. 2001.

7 Ministerio de Relaciones Exteriores, 1902, vol. 1021, "Solicitud del Particular Pedro Cayupi, Cacique de la Araucanía," 26 Sept. 1902, Santiago and Cullinco, Carahue. Ricardo Herrera became one of the most prominent landowners in this area. In 1937 he requested that the Ministerio de Tierras y Colonización (Ministry of land and colonization) hand over three plots auctioned off in the same region. In his petition he identifies himself as "living on the *fundo* Cuyinco in the Department of Imperial." ASXX, MTYC, Providencia no. 8920, vol. 1343, 1937. A further interesting fact about the community of Cullinco is that, as we shall see in chapter 4, in 1970 it bordered on the Fundo Rucalán and some of its members ended up living on and collaborating with the agrarian reform center. The wife of Juan Bautista Landarretche, Violeta Maffei Herrera, is a descendant of the same Herrera family on her mother's side; Rucadiuca, the estate she inherited from her parents, had its origins in these same land deals at the turn of the century, having as one of its boundaries "the *reducción* of Pedro Cayupi." SAG, Archivo Ex-CORA, Expediente no. 972- Fundo Rucalán

y Butalón Rucadiuca, Comuna de Carahue: "Informe de los títulos de dominio sobre el fundo denominado 'RUCADIUCA,'" Temuco, 3 Feb. 1971, p. 152, and "Copia de inscripción: Adjudicación en Partición," pp. 153–54.

8 Within the larger Mapuche identity, there are several subgroups defined by particular relationships to the specific ecosystems they inhabit. Since "che" means people and "mapu" means earth or world, Mapuche is a general category for the whole group. "Lafken" refers to bodies of water; "Lafkenche" thus is people of the water, those who use aquatic resources — fishing and shellfish and seaweed collection — as an important part of their economy.

9 Ministerio de Relaciones Exteriores, 1901, vol. 986, "Sección del Plano de Moncul del ingeniero Hugo Petrogrande," Temuco, 18 Dec. 1901.

10 Christian Martínez Neira, *Comunidades y Territorios Lafkenche, los mapuche de Rucacura al Moncul* (Temuco: Instituto de Estudios Indígenas/Universidad de la Frontera, Serie de Investigación, 1995), pp. 54–79. On the development of commercial agriculture in the region, see Florencia E. Mallon, "Cuando la amnesia se impone con sangre, el abuso se hace costumbre: El pueblo mapuche y el Estado chileno, 1881–1998," in Paul W. Drake and Iván Jaksic, eds., *El modelo chileno: Democracia y desarrollo en los noventa,* pp. 435–64 (Santiago: LOM Ediciones, 1999).

11 Museo Regional de la Araucanía, Intendencia de Cautín, Correspondencia Recibida, 1900–1907, "Oficio del Ministerio de Tierras y Colonización al Intendente de Cautín," Temuco, 8 Oct. 1900.

12 Museo Regional de la Araucanía, Intendencia de Cautín, Correspondencia Recibida, 1900–1907, "Oficio del Ministerio de Tierras y Colonización al Intendente de Cautín," Temuco, 8 Oct. 1900.

13 Museo Regional de la Araucanía, Intendencia de Cautín, Correspondencia Recibida, 1900–1907, "Oficio del Gobernador de Imperial al Subinspector de Tierras y Colonización," Nueva Imperial, 4 Oct. 1900.

14 Museo Regional de la Araucanía, Intendencia de Cautín, Correspondencia Recibida, 1900–1907, "Oficio de José Duhalde, Subdelegado de la 3ª Subdelegación de Imperial, al Gobernador," Puerto Saavedra, 22 Oct. 1900.

15 Museo Regional de la Araucanía, Intendencia de Cautín, Correspondencia Recibida, 1900–1907, "Informe de César A. Plaza F., Teniente de Caballería, al Comandante," Temuco, 29 Oct. 1900.

16 Museo Regional de la Araucanía, Intendencia de Cautín, Correspondencia Recibida, 1900–1907, "Manuel F. Urrutia, Juez de Letras de Imperial, al Intendente de Cautín, transcribiendo documentos relevantes a la causa por lesiones seguida en contra de Luis C. Ubeda y Cesar de la Plaza," Nueva Imperial, 13 Dec. 1900.

17 CONADI, Archivo de Asuntos Indígenas, Título de Merced no. 1254, Comunidad de Paillao Curivil, Güedaquintúe, Departamento de Imperial, 14 Dec. 1907.

18 CONADI, Archivo de Asuntos Indígenas, Título de Merced no. 1112, Comunidad de Nicolás Ailío, Tranapuente, 29 Dec. 1906.

19 Interview with don Antonio Ailío, Community of Ailío-Tranapuente, 10 Jan. 1997.

20 CONADI, Archivo de Asuntos Indígenas, Comunidad de Nicolás Ailío, Carpeta Administrativa, Expediente de Restitución y Usurpación de Terrenos, Andres Torres [sic–Ailío] con Duhalde José, en Tranapuente, Nehuentúe, begun 25 April 1930; f. 1.

21 Ibid., f. 30v.

22 Ibid., f. 46.

23 Ibid.

24 Ibid., 31 July 1939, f. 35.

25 ASXX, MTYC, Decreto no. 2331, vol. 1439, 1938.

26 At a meeting in which I reported on my research to the families from Ailío who had moved to Huellanto Alto, today the community of Nicolás Ailío II, we discussed Duhalde at length. A young man from a Mapuche community located on the Isla Huapi, near Puerto Saavedra, was at the meeting and participated because his grandmother had worked as a domestic servant in the Duhalde household. Field notes, meeting in Gorbea, 20 March 1997.

27 Aníbal Escobar V., *Anuario de la Colonia Francesa en Chile, 1925–1926* (Santiago de Chile, 1926), pp. 402–3.

28 The information in this paragraph has been compiled from the following sources: I. Anabalón y Urzúa, *Chile Agrícola: Tomo Preliminar* (Santiago de Chile: Imprenta, Litografía y Encuadernación Moderna, 1922), p. 414; Aníbal Escobar V., *Francia: La Colonia Francesa en Chile* (Santiago de Chile, 1920), pp. 237–38, 288; Escobar, *Anuario de la Colonia Francesa en Chile, 1927–1928* (Santiago de Chile, 1928), p. 383; Conservador de Bienes Raíces-Nueva Imperial (CBI-NI): 10-1-1896; 28-XI-1896; 29-XII-1896; 24-V-1897; 25-V-1897; 2-XII-1899; 10-IV-1899; 7-IX-1899. For Graciano's birth, see his last will and testament in CBR-NI, 1941, no. 185-Testamento de don Víctor Graciano Duhalde Silva, ff. 152–53v.

29 CBR-NI, 1909, no. 254, ff. 140–41v: "Compra-venta de Duhart Hnos. a Echeverría, Domingo y otros."

30 CONADI, Archivo de Asuntos Indígenas, Comunidad de Andrés Curimán, Título de Merced 1381, 31 July 1908, and Expediente de División: "Declaración de Lorenzo Llancaleo Malil y Miguel Soldado Lincopi," Nueva Imperial, 18 Dec. 1970. Later measurements would detect that, at least in 1971, the community was only three hectares short, rather than thirty, along the boundary with Nehuentúe. Between 1908 and 1970, however, a good number of the community's best lowland hectares, located along the most fertile part of the boundary between the fundo and the community, had been swallowed by the Moncul River as a result of the earthquake of 1960. It is possible, there-

fore, that the amount of land seized in 1908 was much closer to the thirty hectares described in the 1970 declaration. The effects of the 1960 earthquake are
described in Archivo de Asuntos Indígenas, Comunidad de Andrés Curimán,
Carpeta Administrativa, "Informe de los visitadores de la Jefatura Zonal de
Temuco sobre la Encuesta en la reserva de Andrés Curimán," Temuco, 9 Sept.
1963. For Duhart Hnos.'s formalization of ownership over Nehuentúe, see
CBR-NI, 1909, no. 255, ff. 141v-42v: "Compraventa Duhart Hnos. a Marin M.R.
y otros," 28-x-1909.

31 CBR-NI, 1910, nos. 151–53, ff. 79v–82v: Purchases by Duhart Hnos. from various sellers. Although these transactions are registered on 3-VI-1910, the document says they occurred in 1904.

32 CBR-NI, vol. 1910, 29 April 1910; 30 April 1910; Anabalón y Urzúa, *Chile Agrícola*, pp. 418–19.

33 ASXX, MinRREE, vol. 1090, 1903: Oficios nos. 1011 and 1110 from the general inspector of Tierras y Colonización to the minister, providing background
information on the petition by the Empresa Colonizadora del Budi, 10 and
22 Aug. 1903.

34 ASXX, MinRREE, vol. 1090, 1903: "Oficio 1011 del Inspector General de Tierras y Colonización al Ministro," 10 Aug. 1903; vol. 1116, 1904: "Solicitud de
Horacio Mujica, representante de la Empresa Colonizadora del Budi al Ministro de Colonización"; "Solicitud de Eleuterio Domínguez, Gerente de la Empresa Colonizadora del Budi, al Ministro de Colonización"; Decretos, vol. 1125
(1904): Decretos no. 1458 y 1462, 21 June 1904, with attached background information; vol. 1154, 1905: "Oficio 1335 del Inspector General de Tierras y Colonización al Ministro, elevando presentación de Eleuterio Domínguez sobre la
perturbación de la colonia," 10 June 1905; vol. 1154 (1905): "Informe del Intendente de Cautín sobre una queja telegráfica de varios colonos del Budi,"
Temuco, 16 March 1905; vol. 1221 (1906): "Oficio de Eleuterio Domínguez al
Inspector de Tierras y Colonización," 17 March 1906.

35 ASXX, MinRREE, vol. 1297: Decree of the Minister of Relaciones Exteriores
(Foreign Relations), Santiago, 25 Oct. 1907. See also vol. 1154, 1905: "Oficio de
Eleuterio Domínguez al Ministro de Colonización, y bases de arreglo adjun-
tas," Santiago, 9 Oct. 1905.

36 ASXX, MinRREE, vol. 1640: "Copia de la Adjudicación hecha en 22 septiembre
1911 ante el notario Abraham del Río, por Arturo Alessandri en representación de la sucesión de doña Maximiana Lasierra vda. de Domínguez, a Samuel
Larraín Bulnes," Santiago de Chile.

37 ASXX, MinRREE, vol. 1640: "Copia de la Adjudicación," op. cit.

38 CBR-NI, vol. 1912, no. 225: "Adjudicación Domínguez, Eleuterio, Sucesión, a
Duhalde, José," 31 July 1912, ff. 166–68v.

39 CBR-NI, vol. 1919, no. 333, ff. 173v–75: "Compraventa de Sociedad Agrícola de
El Budi a José Duhalde"; Anabalón y Urzúa, *Chile Agrícola*, pp. 418–19.

40 Anabalón, *Chile Agrícola*, pp. 401–14, quotations on pp. 401, 411.

41 The land purchases can be found in CBR-NI: 21-VI-1920; 25-IV-1925; 10-IX-1925; 26-IX-1925; 10-VI-1926; 26-XI-1926; 2-VII-1927; 20-VIII-1927; 14-XII-1927; 23-XII-1927. Some evidence of the catastrophic effects of the world depression in the region can be found in ANH-M, IC: vol. 302: "Oficio de Ramón Millán Hidalgo, dueño de los fundos Pulmahue y El Ensueño, a los Sres. Aproma," Temuco, 21 Nov. 1932; "Carta de Luis Benavente al Intendente de Cautín," Las Hortensias, 14 Nov. 1932; "Oficio de José Lamoliatte al Intendente de Cautín," Santiago, 13 Nov. 1932; "Oficio de G. Schneider al Inspector de Subsistencias," Huilío, 11 Nov. 1932; "Dos Oficios de Amós Benítez, dueño del fundo Temuntuco, al Inspector de Subsistencias," 2 Nov. 1932; "Oficio del Alcalde de Cunco al Intendente de Cautín," 21 Oct. 1932; "Oficio de Alonso Sotomayor, Administrador de Sotomayor, Sánchez y Cia., Ltda, al Intendente de Cautín," Hacienda de Santa María de Quepe, 20 Oct. 1932; "Oficio de Pedro Sotos, dueño del fundo Integral, al Comisario de Subsistencias," Temuco, 22 Oct. 1932; "Oficio de Germán Sandoval, Secretario de la Asociación de Minoristas, Comerciantes y Pequeños Industriales de Ñuble al Comisario de Subsistencias," Chillán, 18 Oct. 1932. For hoof-and-mouth disease and the importation of livestock, see ANH-M, IC, vol. 346: "Informe del Veterinario Regional, Servicio de Ganadería y Policía Sanitaria, al Ministerio de Agricultura e Industria," Temuco, 29 Dec. 1930.

42 The direct quotation from Lucila Duhalde can be found in ASXX, MTYC, Decreto no. 2331: "Sobre expropiación del fundo Tranapuente y creación de una colonia," 30 Sept. 1938: "Solicitud de Lucila Duhalde Pinto al Ministro de Tierras y Colonización, que se agreguen los antecedentes de su caso al expediente de expropiación," 16 Sept. 1938. For the judgment concerning the illegal or temporary nature of any transferences of property, see the report of the attorney representing the Caja de Colonización Agrícola, Santiago, 12 Aug. 1938, SAG, Exp. 6090, Colonia Tranapuente, Puerto Saavedra, IX Region.

43 Indirect evidence for the sale of Nehuentúe sometime between 1930 and 1935 can be found in ASXX, MDN, Subfondo de Marina, vol. 2959, Decreto 1482, 15 Oct. 1936, which renews the concession for two piers owned by Duhalde and Co. on the shore of the Imperial River, one fronting the Fundo Tranapuente and the other fronting the Fundo Esperanza. Among the accompanying documents is a query from the head of the Maritime Concessions Unit, dated 26 Dec. 1935, in which he asks, "Why not request the renewal of a third concession for a pier on the Imperial River, in front of the *fundo* Nelentué [*sic*], that had previously been granted along with the two whose renewal is being requested?" On 24 July 1936, the governor of Imperial District informed the minister that "with regard to the third pier located in front of the *fundo* 'Nehuentué' [*sic*], the concession has been requested by Messrs. Larrulett [*sic*]

Hnos, new owners of that property." For the case of the fundo Tranapuente, see ASXX, MTYC, Decreto no. 2331, vol. 1439, 30 Sept. 1938.

44 The division of Duhalde and Co.'s assets after Biscar's death can be found in CBR-NI, 1940, no. 290, ff. 231v–34v, 2 Oct. 1940. Edelmira Duhalde's sale to Pablo Lüer Metzger is recorded in vol. 1941, no. 182, ff. 147–49, 31 May 1941. Graciano Duhalde's will is registered in 1941, no. 185, ff. 152–53v, 31 May 1941, although he dictated it on 8 Oct. 1940.

45 ANH-M, IC, vol. 494: "Informe de Jorge Besoain Ramírez, Tnte. Cor. de Carabineros y Prefecto, a la Intendencia de Cautín," Temuco/Puerto Saavedra, 28 Dec. 1940. The only written evidence we have of a conflict between Graciano Duhalde and Henríquez can be found in CBR-NI, 1921, no. 322, which records a purchase by José Duhalde of a 105-hectare plot belonging to Henríquez that used to be part of the fundo Puyangue. The purchase was made at auction because of debt.

46 Interview with don Antonio Ailío, Comunidad de Ailío-Tranapuente, 10 Jan. 1997.

47 CBR-NI, 1941, no. 182, ff. 147–49: "Venta de Edelmira Duhalde vda. de Biscar a Fernando Lüer Westermeyer y otros"; no. 181, ff. 145v–47: "Inscripción de Posesión Efectiva de Berta Fagalde Maldonado vda. de Duhalde y otros," 31 May 1941; no. 185, ff. 152–53v: "Inscripción del Testamento de Graciano Duhalde Silva," 31 May 1941; no. 385, ff. 330v–32v: "División de Comunidad, Berta Fagalde Maldonado vda. de Duhalde y otros con Don Fernando Lüer y otros," 22 Dec. 1941; 1942, no. 177, ff. 153v–55v: "Adjudicación de bienes a doña Berta Fagalde Maldonado vda. de Duhalde," 7 May 1942. For the situation in Puerto Saavedra in 1951, see ANH-M, IC, vol. 606: Municipalidad de Puerto Saavedra, "Presupuesto presentado al Intendente de Cautín," 14 Nov. 1951; vol. 607: Dirección General de Impuestos Internos, Tribunal Administrativo Provincial, "Lista de los 10 mayores contribuyentes por comuna," Temuco, Oct. 1951. For the renting of Esperanza Norte to Lüer Hermanos, see ASXX, MTYC, Providencias 1955, vol. 3, no. 979, ff. 12–12v.

48 ASXX, MinRREE, vol. 1116: "Informe del Inspector General de Tierras i Colonización al Ministro, sobre el proyecto de colonización presentado por los sres. Yuri y Latorre," Santiago, 23 May 1904, p. 3.

49 León Erbeta Vaccaro, "Situación jurídica y social de los indios mapuches," Report presented to the Prosecutor of the Honorable Supreme Court; Temuco, 3 Sept. 1955; quotations on p. 121.

50 Interview with don Antonio Ailío, Comunidad de Ailío-Tranapuente, 10 Jan. 1997.

51 Ibid.

52 SAG, Archivo Ex-CORA, Expedientes de Expropriación 965 (Fundo "El Budi"), 4152 (Esperanza Norte), 4438 (San Enrique), and 4345 (San Pablo). For more

details and documentation on these later changes in land tenure in the region, see chapter 4.

53 Meeting with the community of Nicolás Ailío I, Tranapuente, 8 Aug. 2001.

54 ASXX, MTYC, Decreto no. 2331, vol. 1439, 1938: "Proyecto de formación de una Colonia Agrícola en el Fundo 'Tranapuente,'" presented by José Maige A., Service Director and Agronomist, Santiago, 21 Aug. 1938, quotations on pp. 1, 2.

55 Interview with don Antonio Ailío, Comunidad de Ailío-Tranapuente, 10 Jan. 1997; SAG, Exp. 6090, Colonia Tranapuente, Puerto Saavedra, IX Región: Lista de Colonos y Números de Parcela de la Colonia Tranapuente; Mapa de la Colonia Tranapuente (1939).

Chapter 3. A Generation without Shoes

1 Alejandro Saavedra, *La cuestión Mapuche* (Santiago: ICIRA, 1971), pp. 24, 52.

2 CONADI, Archivo de Asuntos Indígenas, T.M. 1112- Nicolás Ailío, Carpeta Administrativa: Ministerio de Tierras y Colonización, Dirección de Asuntos Indígenas, Zonal Temuco, "Censo de la Comunidad de Nicolás Ailío," 30-v-63. In 1968, when the Dirección de Asuntos Indígenas, part of the Ministerio de Tierras y Colonización, produced a series of charts mapping the Mapuche population in Cautín province, they calculated the average size of landholding by departments. In the department of Imperial, where the community of Ailío is located, people held an average of 2.03 hectares per person in communities that, like Ailío, had not been legally subdivided, and 0.97 hectares per person in communities that had been legally subdivided. MTYC, Dirección de Asuntos Indígenas, "Cuadros sinópticos sobre comunidades indígenas en la provincia de Cautín," 1968.

3 Alejandro Palacios Gómez and Patricio Pinto Pérez, "Estudio socio-económico de la agricultura indígena en la provincia de Cautín (Tesis presentada como parte de los requisitios para optar al título de Ingeniero Agrónomo—Mención Economía Agraria)," Santiago de Chile, Universidad de Chile–Department of Economics, 1964, pp. 22–23.

4 CONADI, Archivo de Asuntos Indígenas, Ministerio de Tierras y Colonización, Dirección de Asuntos Indígenas, Zonal Temuco: Carpetas Administrativas: T.M. 1822- Bartolo Queipan, "Censo de la Comunidad de Bartolo Queipan," 4-VIII-1962; T.M. 1381- Andrés Curiman, "Censo de la Comunidad de Andrés Curiman," 30-v-1963; T.M. 1005- Comunidad de Juan de Dios Pilquinao, "Censo de la Comunidad de Juan de Dios Pilquinao," 5-VI-1965. The community of Antonio Pilquinao, T.M. 966, near Nehuentúe, is the one most like Ailío, with 3.6 hectares per family: "Censo de la Comunidad de Antonio Pilquinao," 30-v-1963.

5 CONADI, Archivo de Asuntos Indígenas, Ministerio de Tierras y Colonización, Dirección de Asuntos Indígenas, Zonal Temuco: Carpetas Administrativas,

Censuses for the communities of Andrés Curimán (40%); Juan de Dios Pilquinao (38%); Antonio Pilquinao (48%); Juan Queupan (64%); Pancho Curivil
(36%); Manuel Cayuleo (40%); Luisa Calfur (48%); Pascual Segundo Painemilla (livestock raising community: 29%); Pascual Coña (46%); Paillán Paillao
(44%); Bartolo Queipan (40%).

6 CONADI, Archivo de Asuntos Indígenas, T.M. 1112- Nicolás Ailío, Carpeta Administrativa: Ministerio de Tierras y Colonización, Dirección de Asuntos Indígenas, Zonal Temuco, "Censo de la Comunidad de Nicolás Ailío," 30-v-63,
Ficha #3. As part of a general survey of all Mapuche communities being carried
out by the bureau's Temuco office during the 1960s, in Ailío census takers
Darío Gangas Soto and José Cayupi Navarro interviewed 18 families with a
total of 113 people.

7 Interview with doña Felicia Concha Arias de Ailío, Community of Ailío-
Tranapuente, 10 Jan. 1997.

8 Interview with doña Felicia Concha Arias de Ailío, Community of Ailío-
Tranapuente, 10 Jan. 1997. It is common for people in Chile, whether Mapuche
or not, to differentiate between Mapuches and "Chileans," even though all are
technically citizens of Chile.

9 The Cerro Santa Lucía is a small hill located near the center of Santiago; it has
a park that, over the years, has been a popular place for weekend outings.

10 Interview with doña Felicia Concha, 10 Jan. 1997.

11 Ibid.

12 Interview with don Hugo Ailío Concha, Concepción, 12 Aug. 1999.

13 Ibid. *Yerba mate* is a caffeinated tea drunk widely in several South American
countries, including Argentina, Brazil, Paraguay, and Uruguay. In Chile it is
drunk mainly in the south and mainly in the countryside, and it tends also to
be a marker of Mapuche identity.

14 Interview with Hugo Ailío, Concepción, 12 Aug. 1999.

15 Interview with Marcelina Ailío, by Angélica Celis as part of her M.A. thesis in
applied social sciences, "Conversaciones con el territorio desde la interculturalidad: Las huertas femeninas como espacios de conversación," Universidad de
la Frontera (Temuco), January 2003. Quotations on pp. 220–21. I was also able
to find doña Marcelina's family in the 1963 census done in the community:
"Censo de la Comunidad de Nicolás Ailío," 30-v-63, Ficha # 6, which lists all
the names of the members of her family.

16 Interview with Marcelina Ailío, by Angélica Celis, "Conversaciones con el territorio desde la interculturalidad," quotations on pp. 223–24.

17 Ibid., quotations on pp. 247, 225.

18 My interview with doña Marcelina Ailío, Community of Nicolás Ailío II,
Huellanto Alto, 5 Aug. 1998. Doña Margarita Llancaleo appears in the 1963
community census, Censo de la Comunidad de Ailío, Ficha #8.

19 Interview with Cecilia Ailío, by Angélica Celis, "Conversaciones con el territo-

rio desde la interculturalidad," p. 326. The reference to "paying for her" is to the Mapuche custom of bride price, which is paid by the groom and his family in the form of presents to the bride's family.

20 Conversation with don Heriberto Ailío, Huellanto Alto, 10 Aug. 2001.

21 "Censo de la Comunidad de Nicolás Ailío," 30-v-63, Ficha #2.

22 Interview with Cecilia Ailío, by Angélica Celis, "Conversaciones con el territorio desde la interculturalidad," p. 332.

23 Ibid, pp. 329–30.

24 Interview with doña Eduardina Ailío, Community of Ailío-Tranapuente, 18 Jan. 1997.

25 Interview with doña Eduardina Ailío, 18 Jan. 1997.

26 Field notes, conversation with don Heriberto and doña Eduardina Ailío, Community of Ailío-Huellanto Alto, 21 June 1997.

27 Interview with don Robustiano Ailío, Community of Ailío-Tranapuente, 11 Jan. 1997.

28 Reading and discussion of the book manuscript with the communities of Nicolás Ailío, CET-Sur, Temuco, 2 Aug. 2001; commentary by don Armando Ailío. The Ailío Pilquinao family's account is more complete now than it was then because people remembered additional aspects in the conversations that came out of the book presentation. But the stories about shoes and about the abuses of the non-Mapuche sharecroppers to which don Armando was reacting were the same in the earlier version as they are now.

29 José Bengoa, "Las economías campesinas Mapuches," Documento de Trabajo no. 6, Grupo de Investigaciones Agrarias, Academia de Humanismo Cristiano, Santiago, Chile, October 1981, pp. 4–6, quotations on pp. 5, 6.

30 Intendencia de Cautín, Correspondencia Recibida (Providencias), 1961; Providencia no. 664 del Ministerio de Economía, Fomento y Reconstrucción, 15 May 1961.

31 Ministerio de Agricultura, Corporación de la Reforma Agraria, Departamento Formación de Colonias, Correspondencia Recibida de la Oficial Zonal de Asuntos Indígenas, Temuco, 29 July 1964.

32 Don Oscar Jara suggested this in his interview with me, Community of Nicolás Ailío-Tranapuente, 11 Jan. 1997.

33 CONADI, Archivo de Asuntos Indígenas, T.M. 1381- Comunidad de Andrés Curimán, Rucahue Moncul, Carpeta Administrativa, "Censo de la Comunidad," 4-VI-1963; see especially Fichas #45 (Ignacio Yaupe) and #46 (Lorenzo Traipi Lincopi).

34 CONADI, Archivo de Asuntos Indígenas, T.M. 1822- Comunidad de Bartolo Queipan, Rucatraro-Budi, Carpeta Administrativa, "Censo de la Comunidad," 4-VIII-1962. Among the other affected communities in Puerto Saavedra and near Lake Budi are Luisa Calfur, Ñilquilco, and Pinchinhuala Llancaleo, Pitro-

hue. Archivo de Asuntos Indígenas, Títulos de Merced 649 and 993, respectively.

35 Intendencia de Cautín, Correspondencia Recibida, 1964–1965: "Oficio de Flor Maria Andrade en representación de la comunidad de Pascual Painemilla," Puerto Saavedra, 30 June 1964.

36 Celis, "Conversaciones con el territorio desde la interculturalidad," p. 294.

37 Interview with doña Eduardina Ailío, Community of Ailío-Tranapuente, 18 Jan. 1997.

38 ASXX, MTYC, Providencias, 1955, vol. 3, no. 979: "Solicitud de varios agricultores chilenos sobre la expropiación del fundo 'La Esperanza' y otros," begun in Santiago, November 1953; Providencias, 1956, vol. 17, no. 17319: "Solicitud de la Agrupación Chilena de Colonos de Cautín al Presidente de la República," Temuco, September 1955; vol. 18, no. 6704: "Solicitud de José Manuel Garrido y otros, miembros de un Comité de Pequeños Agricultores, sobre la expropiación del fundo 'El Plumo' en Moncul," begun in Tranapuente, January 1954; vol. 20, no. 7619: "Oficio del Jefe de la Oficina de Tierras y Colonización en Temuco al Jefe del Departamento de Mensura de Tierras en Santiago, adjuntando la nómina de presentaciones de postulantes a colonos en el fundo fiscal Santa Celia," Temuco, 30 April 1956 and "Petición del Comité de colonos y ocupantes de parcelas mal distribuidas de la colonia Santa Celia, sector El Manzano, al Presidente de la República," Carahue, June 1953; vol. 27, no. 10143: "Oficio del Jefe de la Oficina de Tierras y Colonización de Temuco al Jefe del Departmento de Mensura en Santiago, adjuntando las presentaciones de postulantes a colonos en el fundo Matte y Sánchez," Temuco, 21 June 1956; Providencias, 1958, vol. 1, no. 106: "Copia del Decreto que autoriza la venta de hijuelas del fundo fiscal 'Santa Celia' en Carahue, a sus actuales ocupantes," Santiago, 16 Oct. 1953; Min. Agri., 1955: Correspondencia Recibida, Particulares: "Solicitud del Comité de Aspirantes a Colonos del lugar de Machaco al Ministerio de Agricultura," entered the Ministry on 3 Feb. 1955; ANH(M), IC, vol. 498: "Oficio de la 'Colonia José Manuel Balmaceda' al Ministro de Tierras y Colonización pidiendo ayuda del Estado," Temuco, 9 June 1939; vol. 509: "Oficio de varios inquilinos medieros del fundo 'Tranapuente,' de la Caja de Colonización Agrícola, al Intendente de Cautín, solicitando amparo," Temuco, 12 May 1941; vol. 510: "Oficios del Ministerio de Tierras y Colonización denunciando al Intendente actividades de agitadores políticos en el fundo 'Las Ñochas,' zona de Trovolhue," Temuco, 23–24 April 1941; vol. 522: "Informe del Gobernador de Imperial al Intendente sobre la situación de carácter social existente en los fundos 'Pilmayquenco' y 'Trovolhue' de la comuna de Saavedra, departamento de Imperial, y de la solución provisoria dada," Nueva Imperial, 23 June 1942.

39 If one uses last names as a guide—not necessarily always an exact method—of

the eighteen households surveyed in Ailío in 1963, five (28%) were organized around a marriage between a Mapuche and a non-Mapuche partner. Through fieldwork I have been able to confirm the non-Mapuche identity of one of the partners in four of these five cases. "Censo de la Comunidad de Ailío," Fichas # 3, 12, 13, 15, 18. Also important was my interview with don Oscar Jara, Community of Nicolás Ailío-Tranapuente, 11 Jan. 1997. On the subject of substituting soccer for *palin*, Hugo Ailío remembered that one of his uncles was such a good soccer player that the large and medium landowners of the region tried to recruit him for their teams. Interview with Hugo Ailío, Concepción, 12 Aug. 1999. As we saw in chapter 1, don Martín Ailío Porma, heir to the *logko* title first held by his father, don Nicolás Ailío, organized a committee of small agricultural producers in the community with his son Heriberto.

40 Interview with don Heriberto Ailío, Community of Ailío, Tranapuente, 18 Jan. 1997.

41 Saavedra, *La cuestión Mapuche*, op. cit., quotations on pp. 127, 125.

42 Interview with Hugo Ailío, Concepción, 12 Aug. 1999.

43 Interview with doña Marcelina Ailío, Community of Nicolás Ailío II, Huellanto Alto, 5 Aug. 1998. In 1963, of the eighteen households surveyed in Ailío, eleven (approximately 60%) lived according to patrilocal custom. "Censo de la Comunidad de Ailío," op. cit.

44 Interview with Mario Castro, Temuco, 15 April 1997.

45 Interview with Mario Castro, Temuco, 15 April 1997. "Enrique" refers to Enrique Pérez, another member of the MIR who had worked in the coastal region during the Popular Unity government and who, after the transition to democratic rule, went back to the community of Ailío and worked with them for several years.

46 Interview with Mario Castro.

47 Conversation with don Heriberto Ailío, Huellanto Alto, 10 Aug. 2001. Another case in which the non-Mapuche attempted to use Mapuche knowledge, in this case not for a good purpose, was remembered by doña Eduardina Ailío when referring to *machi* Margarita Llancaleo: "During the retaking of Landarretche's property the landowners went to her so that she'd use her secrets in their favor. She did not refuse, and did her work." Email from doña Eduardina Ailío, courtesy of CET-Sur, Temuco, 20 Dec. 2001. For the retaking of the fundo, see chapter 4.

48 Interview with doña Marta Antinao, in Angélica Celis, "Conversaciones con el territorio desde la interculturalidad," pp. 287–88.

49 Ibid., p. 293.

50 Ibid., p. 295.

51 Ibid, p. 296, and interview with Elisa Ailío Pilquinao, Santiago, 13 Aug. 2001.

52 Ximena Bunster, "Adaptation in Mapuche Life: Natural and Directed," Ph.D.

dissertation in anthropology, Columbia University, 1968; Milan Stuchlik, *La Vida en Mediería: Mecanismos de reclutamiento social de los mapuches* (Santiago: SOLES Ediciones, 1999), first published in English as *Life on a Half Shell: Mechanisms of Social Recruitment among the Mapuche* (1976). See also Louis C. Faron, *Hawks of the Sun: Mapuche Morality and its Ritual Attributes* (Pittsburgh: University of Pittsburgh Press, 1964), and *The Mapuche Indians of Chile* (New York: Holt, Rinehart and Winston, 1968), who did his fieldwork in Cholchol as well, though based in a different community from Stuchlik.

53 In addition to Bunster's previously cited Ph.D. dissertation, see Ximena Bunster, "Una Experiencia de Antropología aplicada entre los Araucanos," *Anales de la Universidad de Chile* 122 (1964), pp. 94–128, which compares a water pump program in Maquehue that succeeded because it respected Mapuche beliefs and practices with the CORVI (National Housing Corporation) campaign to build new houses that failed because it did not take into account the cultural functions of the traditional *ruka*'s physical layout, and thus the new buildings were not accepted in most communities.

54 Interview with Jacques Chonchol, Santiago, 4 April 1997.

55 José Bengoa, *Historia del pueblo Mapuche (Siglo XIX y XX)* (Santiago: Ediciones Sur, 1985), pp. 382–89; quotation on p. 385. Rolf Foerster and Sonia Montecino, in *Organizaciones, Líderes y Contiendas Mapuches (1900–1970)* (Santiago: Centro Estudios de la Mujer, 1988), until now the most complete published study on Mapuche political organizations in the postresettlement period, also show that the integrationist strategies followed by Mapuche organizations in this period were meant to protect the rights of the entire Mapuche population, both urban and rural. On don Manuel Manquilef, see Foerster y Montecino, pp. 68–74, and Manquilef's own works, *Comentarios del Pueblo Araucano (La faz social)* (Santiago: Imprenta Cervantes, 1911); *¡Las tierras de Arauco! El último cacique* (Temuco: Imprenta y Encuadernación 'Modernista,' 1915).

56 Bengoa, *Historia del pueblo Mapuche*, pp. 390–403; quotations on pp. 402, 396. For his cemetery project, see AHN (M), Intendencia de Cautín, vol. 340: "Oficio de Manuel Aburto Panguilef, Presidente del Comité Ejecutivo de la Araucanía de Chile al Ministro de Higiene, Santiago," Loncoche, 5 May 1931. The rest of the information in the paragraph comes from the summary of this first period in Aburto Panguilef's life given by Foerster and Montecino (pp. 33–52).

57 Florencia E. Mallon, field notes, Huellanto Alto, Aug. 1998; conversation with don Heriberto Ailío, Huellanto Alto, 10 Aug. 2001.

Chapter 4. A Fleeting Prosperity

1 Corte de Apelaciones de Temuco, Causa Criminal no. 242, "Intendente de Cautín don Gastón Lobos Barrientos contra don Juan Bautista Landarretche y

otros, por Infracción de la Ley de Seguridad Interior del Estado," began 26 Dec. 1970; ff. 130v–31v: "Declaración de Camila Fierro Morales, empleada doméstica," Carahue, 29 Dec. 1970; quotations on f. 131.

2 Corte de Apelaciones de Temuco, Causa Criminal no. 242, ff. 115v–16: "Declaración de doña Violeta Maffei Herrera," Fundo Rucalán, 26 Dec. 1970, quotations on f. 115v.

3 Interview with the Landarretche Maffei family: Doña Violeta Maffei, her daughter Arlin, and her son Luciano Landarretche, Fundo Rucalán, 25 May 1997.

4 Luciano's memories come from the interview with the Landarretche Maffei family, Fundo Rucalán, 25 May 1997. Juan Landarretche's testimony is from Corte de Apelaciones de Temuco, Causa Criminal no. 242, ff. 31–31v: "Declaración de don Juan Bautista Landarretche Mendoza," Temuco, 27 Dec. 1970; quotations on f. 31.

5 Corte de Apelaciones de Temuco, Causa Criminal no. 242, ff. 130v–31v: "Declaración de Camila Fierro Morales," quotations on f. 131; ff. 115v–16: "Declación de doña Violeta Maffei Herrera," quotations on f. 115v; interview with the Landarretche Maffei family, Fundo Rucalán, 25 May 1997. *Mirista* denotes a member of the Movimiento de Izquierda Revolucionaria (Movement of the Revolutionary Left, or MIR), and in this context is synonymous with nonpeasant and non-Mapuche.

6 Interview with don Heriberto Ailío, Community of Ailío-Tranapuente, 18 Jan. 1997.

7 There is some evidence to indicate a search at some point, for in Corte de Apelaciones de Temuco, Causa Criminal no. 242, f. 246, Ricardo Mora Carrillo remembered that they had searched the landowner's house, though he insisted they had taken nothing.

8 Corte de Apelaciones de Temuco, Causa Criminal no. 242, ff. 215–16v: "Declaración de José Segundo Pilquinao Ailío," Carahue, 2 Jan. 1971; quotation on f. 215v.

9 Interview with the Landarretche family, Fundo Rucalán, 25 May 1997.

10 The "Plan Zeta" was the supposed blueprint for an armed socialist takeover that the military allegedly uncovered and used to justify the intensity of the postcoup repression. For a detailed critical discussion of the elaboration of this plan, see Steve J. Stern, *Remembering Pinochet's Chile: On the Eve of London 1998* (Durham: Duke University Press, 2004), chapter 2.

11 Corte de Apelaciones de Temuco, Causa Criminal no. 242, ff. 140–43v: "Declaración de Ricardo Mora Carrillo," Temuco Regional Hospital, 30 Dec. 1970; quotation on ff. 141v–42.

12 Interview with the Landarretche family, Fundo Rucalán, 25 May 1997.

13 Corte de Apelaciones de Temuco, Causa Criminal no. 242, "Declaración de Ricardo Mora Carrillo," ff. 141v–42.

14 Interview with the Landarretche family, Fundo Rucalán, 25 May 1997.

15 Ibid.

16 "Declaración de Ricardo Mora Carrillo," f. 142v.

17 Corte de Apelaciones de Temuco, Causa Criminal no. 242, "Declaración de José Segundo Pilquinao Ailío," ff. 216–16v; quotation on f. 216v.

18 Interview with doña Marta Antinao, Community of Ailío-Tranapuente, 18 Jan. 1997.

19 Interview with Doña Carmen Huentemilla de Ailío, Community of Ailío-Huellanto Alto, 5 Aug. 1998.

20 Corte de Apelaciones de Temuco, Causa Criminal no. 242, ff. 117–18v: "Inspección del Tribunal constituído en el fundo Rucalán, especialmente de las casas patronales del fundo y sus alrededores," Fundo Rucalán, Carahue, 27 Dec. 1970; quotations on f. 117v.

21 *El Diario Austral*, 22 Dec. 1970, p. 1; *La Tercera*, 23 Dec. 1970, p. 16.

22 Corte de Apelaciones de Temuco, Causa Criminal no. 242, f. 11v.

23 Ibid., f. 12v.

24 The declaration by Minister Tohá appeared in *El Mercurio*, 20 Dec. 1970, p. 33. Intendant Lobos's comments are in *La Tercera*, 29 Dec. 1970, p. 2.

25 A good summary of the information about "Aquiles" can be found in Corte de Apelaciones de Temuco, Causa No.242, "Oficio de la Prefectura de Investigaciones de Temuco al Ministro Visitador de la Corte de Apelaciones," ff. 245–51. The searches and interrogations are discussed in the same court case: "Allanamiento de la casa del Dr. Arturo Hillerns," Report by the Prefectura de Investigaciones, Temuco, 27 Dec. 1970, ff. 272–73v; "Declaración de Arturo Hillerns Larrañaga," Temuco, 7 Jan. 1971, ff. 323–25; "Declaraciones de Domingo Raúl Prieto Delgado, Roberto Eduardo Halim Liendo y Elisabeth Maritza Eltit Spielmann," Temuco, 12 Jan. 1971, ff. 371–73v; "Declaraciones de Oscar Nolberto Pregnan Aravena, Director Zonal de los 'Traperos de Emaús' y Aquilino Matamala Altamirano, trapero," Temuco, 13 Jan. 1971.

26 *El Diario Austral*, 28 Dec. 1970, p. 6.

27 Landarretche's perspective is summarized in Corte de Apelaciones de Temuco, Causa Criminal no. 242, "Oficio de la Prefectura de Investigaciones de Temuco al Ministro Visitador de la Corte de Apelaciones," ff. 252–53; the surveillance missions are mentioned on f. 253. Other testimonies about the surveillance can be found on ff. 336–37: "Declaración de Jorge Alberto Landarretche Maffei," 8 Jan. 1971; ff. 339–39v: "Declaración de Pablo Lüer," Temuco, 8 Jan. 1971. We discussed the same subject with Luciano Landarretche during my interview with the Landarretche family, Fundo Rucalán, 25 May 1997.

28 Víctor H. Carmine, Congressman for Cautín, solicited editorial, *El Diario Austral*, 28 Dec. 1970, p. 6.

29 In addition to the already cited articles in *El Diario Austral*, see *El Mercurio*, 23 Dec. 1970, p. 27, for a description of the takeover; and 30 Dec. 1970, where

a photograph of Landarretche being escorted to testify at the Temuco Court of Appeals appears on the front page. On 7 Feb. 1971, pp. 1, 21, 25, *El Mercurio* highlights an interview with Landarretche in a broader article about the dangers of the agrarian reform. In the February 1971 issue of its magazine, *El Campesino*, the Sociedad Nacional Agraria published a long article called "What the Landowners Are Doing" ["*La acción de los agricultores*"], whose second part, subtitled "Face to Face with the Facts" [*frente a los hechos*], contained three photographs (p. 17) of the land takeovers in Cautín, two of which were of the Landarretche case.

30 *El Diario Austral*, 31 Dec. 1970, p. 1, for the article on Tohá and p. 5 on Chonchol.

31 *El Mercurio*, 20 Dec. 1970, p. 33.

32 *El Diario Austral*, 29 Dec. 1970, p. 8.

33 *El Diario Austral*, 3 Jan. 1971, p. 9, includes an impressive list of the tasks the Ministry of Agriculture had set for itself.

34 *El Diario Austral*, 4 Jan. 1971, p. 3. *Mapucista* refers to the Movimiento de Acción Popular Unitaria (MAPU), a political party that formed from a split in the Christian Democratic party over whether or not actively to support the UP. MAPU was made up of Christian Democrats who decided to join the UP coalition. The play on words with *mapuchista*, of course, denotes Chonchol's seemingly Mapuche-friendly agrarian policies.

35 *El Diario Austral*, 8 Jan. 1971, p. 1.

36 Ibid., p. 7.

37 *El Mercurio*, 4 Feb. 1971, p. 1; *El Diario Austral*, 4 Feb. 1971, p. 1.

38 Information about the creation of the Ailío Committee comes from Corte de Apelaciones de Temuco, Causa Criminal no. 242: "Declaración de Ricardo Mora Carrillo," Temuco Regional Hospital, 30 Dec. 1970, f. 140, and 31 Dec. 1970, f. 144, which includes the quotation; "Declaración de Pedro Fuentes Pilquinao," Carahue, 2 Jan. 1971, f. 217; and "Declaración de José Segundo Pilquinao," Carahue, 2 Jan. 1971, f. 215. The quotation from the MCR's manifesto comes from *El Diario Austral*, 31 Dec. 1970, p. 8: "Argumento del abogado defensor Miguel Schweitzer a favor del recurso de amparo presentado a favor de Juan Bautista Landarretche y otros."

39 Corte de Apelaciones de Temuco, Causa Criminal no. 242: "Declaración de Ricardo Mora Carrillo," Temuco Regional Hospital, 30 Dec. 1970, ff. 140–40v; "Declaración de Pedro Fuentes Pilquinao," Carahue, 2 Jan. 1971, f. 217; "Declaración de José Segundo Pilquinao," Carahue, 2 Jan. 1971, f. 215; and "Declaración de Humberto Venegas Riquelme," Carahue, 2 Jan. 1971, ff. 218v–19.

40 Corte de Apelaciones de Temuco, Causa Criminal no. 242: "Declaración de Humberto Venegas Riquelme," f. 219.

41 Corte de Apelaciones de Temuco, Causa Criminal no. 242: "Declaración de José Segundo Pilquinao," f. 215.

42 Corte de Apelaciones de Temuco, Causa Criminal no. 242: "Declaración de Pedro Fuentes Pilquinao," f. 217.

43 Corte de Apelaciones de Temuco, Causa Criminal no. 242: "Declaración de José Segundo Pilquinao," f. 215.

44 Corte de Apelaciones de Temuco, Causa Criminal no. 242: "Declaración de Pedro Fuentes Pilquinao," f. 217.

45 Interview with Elena Rodríguez (name changed at her request), Temuco, 19 Aug. 1999. I also discussed the work being done in Puerto Saavedra in my interviews with two additional people: Maritza Eltit, who was a social worker in Puerto Saavedra during those years, Temuco, 14 Jan. 1997; and Don Luis Ernesto Quijón, who worked as a grassroots health advocate with Dr. Arturo Hillerns, Community of Ailío-Tranapuente, 30 Nov. 1996 and 4 Jan. 1997.

46 E-mail from Doña Eduardina Ailío, commenting on a previous draft of this chapter, courtesy of CET-Sur, Temuco, 20 Dec. 2001.

47 Interview with Elena Rodríguez (name changed at her request), Temuco, 19 Aug. 1999.

48 *El Diario Austral*, 31 Dec. 1970, p. 8: "Argumento del abogado defensor Miguel Schweitzer a favor del recurso de amparo presentado a favor de Juan Bautista Landarretche y otros."

49 Quotations from interview with don Heriberto Ailío, Community of Ailío-Tranapuente, 18 Jan. 1997. In 2001, when I returned with a draft of this book to share with the people in Ailío, I asked don Heriberto if he had been a founding member of the MCR, as was indicated on the document found during the reoccupation of Rucalán. He confirmed that he was. He also gave me the additional information about the other land takeovers that appears in this paragraph. Interview with don Heriberto Ailío, Huellanto Alto, 10 Aug. 2001. The death of Moisés Huentelaf was a dramatic event in the region in 1971. See, for example, "Lucha campesina: un polvorín bajo tierra," *Punto Final*, no. 143 (Nov. 9, 1971), pp. 2–5.

50 Interview with don Antonio Ailío, Community of Ailío-Tranapuente, 10 Jan. 1997.

51 The decree intervening the fundo can be found in Archivo Siglo XX, Fondo Ministerio de Trabajo, Decretos, vol. 38 (1970): Decreto 901, "Ordena Reanudación de Faenas que Indica y Constituye Tribunal Arbitral que Señala," Santiago, 31 Dec. 1970. The expropriation agreement can be found in Servicio Agrícola Ganadero (SAG), Archivo Ex-CORA, Expediente no. 972 Fundo Rucalán y Butalón-Rucadiuca, Comuna de Carahue, Juan B. Landarretche Mendoza, p. 144. The expropriation was announced the following day in *El Mercurio*, p. 1, and in *El Diario Austral*, p. 1. The data on the hiring of personnel is based on my interview with the Landarretche family, Fundo Rucalán, 25 May 1997. The cultivation report is in SAG, Archivo Ex-CORA, Exp. 972, "Informe sobre la ex-

propiación de los predios rústicos denominados 'RUCADIUCA Y BUTALON,'"
Temuco, 3 Feb. 1971, pp. 145–49, quotation on p. 148.

52 SAG, Archivo Ex-CORA, Exp. 972, "Solicitud de Juan Bautista Landarretche Mendoza al Consejo de la CORA, sobre dejar sin efecto la expropriación de sus predios rústicos Rucadiuca y Butalón," Temuco, 30 March 1971, pp. 61–85, quotation on p. 62; and "Acuerdo del Consejo de la CORA," Santiago, 30 March 1972, pp. 52–54, quotations on p. 53. The Spanish categorization for the kind of property was *pequeña propiedad rústica.*

53 Interview with the Landarretche Maffei family, Fundo Rucalán, 25 May 1997.

54 Interview with don Heriberto Ailío, Community of Ailío-Tranapuente, 18 Jan. 1997.

55 SAG, Archivo Ex-CORA, Exp. 972, "Informe Técnico para la solicitud de restitución de los predios 'Rucadiuca' y 'Butalón,'" Temuco, 12 Dec. 1973, pp. 24–27; the information cited here is on pp. 25, 26. I discussed the drainage canals with don Heriberto Ailío in Huellanto Alto, 10 Aug. 2001.

56 According to what I learned during my interview with the Landarretche family (Fundo Rucalán, 25 May 1997), there had been at most three or four resident workers, the majority of whom left as a result of the takeover. Juan Bautista Landarretche, in a declaration to the regional newspaper *El Diario Austral* on 3 Feb. 1974, p. 12, defending his fundo's productivity record before the Agrarian Reform, said he had ten permanent workers on his estate, of whom only two stayed on the property after the takeover. However, in the technical report on Landarretche's request for restitution after the 1973 coup, which in general is favorable to Landarretche, the agronomist who stayed on at the CORA after the coup confirmed that there had been four *inquilino* families. SAG, Archivo Ex-CORA, Exp. 972, "Informe Técnico para la solicitud de restitución," Temuco, 12 Dec. 1973, p. 24.

57 SAG, Archivo Ex-CORA, "Encuesta de los asentados en el Asentamiento ex-Arnoldo Ríos," December 1973, pp. 28–30. To differentiate between Mapuche and non-Mapuche, I relied on a combination of last names and the information as to residence and inheritance contained in the survey.

58 The analyses of the agrarian reform that shed the most light on the *asentamiento* model are Cristóbal Kay, "Chile: An Appraisal of Popular Unity's Agrarian Reform," Institute of Latin American Studies, Occasional Papers #13, University of Scotland, Glasgow, 1974; Peter E. Marchetti, S.J., "Worker Participation and Class Conflict in Worker-Managed Farms: The Rural Question in Chile—1970 to 1973," Ph.D. diss., Yale University, 1975, 2 vols.; and William C. Thiesenheusen, "Agrarian Reform in Chile," Land Tenure Center, University of Wisconsin, Madison, June 1970. Information on how the *asentamientos* worked can also be found in CORA, "El Asentamiento," Departamento de Desarrollo Campesino, Difusión, Santiago, 1967. For the presence of the MIR and the MCR in the coastal region, see below, this chapter.

59 Interview with don Robustiano Ailío, Community of Ailío-Tranapuente, 11 Jan. 1997.

60 Interview with don Heriberto Ailío, Community of Ailío-Tranapuente, 11 Jan. 1997.

61 Interview with Mario Castro, Temuco, 15 April 1997.

62 Ibid.

63 Interview with doña Eduardina Ailío, Community of Ailío-Tranapuente, 18 Jan. 1997.

64 Interview with don Robustiano Ailío, Community of Ailío-Tranapuente, 11 Jan. 1997.

65 Interview with doña Eduardina Ailío, Community of Ailío-Tranapuente, 18 Jan. 1997, which also included the comments by Cecilia Ailío.

66 Interview with don Robustiano Ailío, Community of Ailío-Tranapuente, 11 Jan. 1997.

67 Interview with doña Elisa Ailío, Santiago, 13 Aug. 2001.

68 Interview with Mario Castro, Temuco, 15 April 1997.

69 Interview with doña Eduardina Ailío, Community of Ailío-Tranapuente, 18 Jan. 1997; interview with doña Elisa Ailío, Santiago, 13 Aug. 2001.

70 Interview with Marta Antinao, by Angélica Celis, "Conversaciones con el territorio desde la interculturalidad," p. 300. It is interesting to note that doña Marta's memories of what was good about the *asentamiento* confirm Heidi Tinsman's findings about the model of the nuclear family—and of the model housewife—that the Chilean agrarian reform promoted in the countryside during these years. See *Partners in Conflict: The Politics of Gender, Sexuality, and Labor in the Chilean Agrarian Reform, 1950–1973* (Durham: Duke University Press, 2002).

71 Interview with Mario Castro, Temuco, 15 April 1997.

72 Interview with don Heriberto Ailío, Temuco, 18 April 1997.

73 MIR Regional Secretariat (Cautín), "¡Pan, tierra y socialismo!," *Punto Final*, no. 121, 5 Jan. 1971, p. 30.

74 Interview with Mario Castro, Temuco, 15 April 1997. At the same time, in her comments on a previous draft sent to me by e-mail on 20 Dec. 2001, doña Eduardina Ailío doubted that there really had been a Mapuche marriage ritual in Rucalán, since she did not remember such a ritual being practiced in Tranapuente during her childhood. By contrast, her younger sister Cecilia did remember that their mother "had been paid for," in other words, the Mapuche custom of bride price had been observed.

75 Florencia Mallon, field notes from a seminar held on my research project with members of the community of Ailío, Universidad de la Frontera, Instituto de Estudios Indígenas, Temuco, 24 and 25 June 1997; conversation with don Heriberto, don Robustiano and doña Eduardina Ailío and Mario Castro. In 2001, when discussing this part of the manuscript, don Heriberto remembered that

it was *machi* Pascual from Calof who was on Rucalán. Interview with don Heriberto Ailío, Huellanto Alto, 10 Aug. 2001.

76   Marchetti, "Worker Participation and Class Conflict," vol. 1, pp. 130, 203–4. See also Kay, "Chile: An Appraisal of Popular Unity's Agrarian Reform," op. cit.; Vicepresidencia Ejecutiva de CORA, "Dos Años de Reforma Agraria del Gobierno Popular" (Santiago: Impreso de Relaciones Públicas de la CORA, 1972); and, even though it is a propaganda document in which the opposition maintains that the CERAS were in reality disguised state farms, see also "Polémica organización de nueva área de Reforma Agraria: Los Centros de Reforma Agraria," *El Campesino*, Documentos, January 1972, pp. 8–11. On the problematic role of women in the Chilean agrarian reform more generally, see Tinsman, *Partners in Conflict*. In part, of course, the emphasis on the peasant family enterprise would help reinforce the authority structure of the traditional rural Mapuche family, in which men tended to mediate the relationship with the outside world, especially when it came to political issues.

77   Interview with don Heriberto Ailío, Community of Ailío-Huellanto Alto, 23 March 1997. Doña Eduardina Ailío, in her email to me on 20 Dec. 2001, remembered her Aunt Rosa's trip to Concepción.

78   There might also have been other reasons for women's relative marginalization in the *asentamiento*. In Mapuche culture, despite the important authority women have in their homes, households, garden plots, and hearths, men mediate with the larger society. When it comes to relations with the state, therefore, men tend to take a leadership role. The type of agricultural production that was favored, moreover, which emphasized collective work and minimized family garden production, also marginalized women, leading to what doña Elisa Ailío remembered was the ability to be able to plant only "a few little vegetables." Interview with doña Elisa Ailío, Santiago, 13 Aug. 2001.

79   Interview with don Heriberto Ailío, Temuco, 18 April 1997. Doña Eduardina's comment is from her e-mail to me on 20 Dec. 2001.

80   Interview with don Heriberto Ailío, Temuco, 18 April 1997.

81   "Campesinos echan por tierra las intrigas de un momio latifundista," *Punto Final*, 16 Feb. 1971, p. 26. *Punto Final* had its own political axe to grind and often exaggerated the events in the countryside. The editors probably had a hand in the writing of this declaration, which hardly represents a "transparent" version of peasant discourse. Still, it is interesting to note that over a quarter of a century later don Heriberto Ailío confirmed the details of the version appearing in *Punto Final* and even used some of the same phrases and concepts in our conversations. Interviews with don Heriberto Ailío, Tranapuente, 18 Jan. 1997 and Temuco, 18 April 1997.

82   Interview with the Landarretche family, especially Luciano Landarretche Maffei, Fundo Rucalán, 25 May 1997.

83   Ibid.

84 Ibid.

85 Ibid.

86 Ibid.

87 Ibid. Recall, however, that the neighboring Mapuche community was Cullinco, and that doña Violeta had a direct family connection with Ricardo Herrera, who had been accused of usurping Cullinco's lands at the beginning of the twentieth century. For more details on this case, see chapter 2.

88 Ibid.

89 That he was wealthy in 1951 is recorded in AHN (M), IC, vol. 607, Dirección General de Impuestos Internos, Tribunal Administrativo Provincial, "Lista de los 10 Mayores Contribuyentes por Comuna," Temuco, October 1951. Partial evidence that his financial situation was not good in 1970 is the fact that this is the only year he stopped paying his property taxes on the fundos Rucalán and Butalón. Corte de Apelaciones, Temuco, Causa no. 242, f. 394.

90 INDAP's estimate, for example, found that, of a total of 439 hectares, 75 were sown with Vilmorin 29 wheat (under contract with the State Bank), 20 more with *raps*, 10 in cultivated grasses, and 20 were in preparation for future planting. This added up to 125 hectares out of more than 400, a utilization rate of only 28% (Corte de Apelaciones de Temuco, Causa no. 242, ff. 466–67). Milies, on the other hand, saw only 50 hectares of wheat "in good condition," sown under contract with the State Bank specifically for the production of seed. Beyond that, Milies calculated that only 5—not 20—were in preparation for future planting, and he agreed that 10 hectares were sown with cultivated grasses, with the rest of the property in natural pastures of "passable quality with a lot of daisies (weeds)" (Corte de Apelaciones de Temuco, Causa no. 242, f. 401: "Carta de Mortiz Milies Wortzman, Ingeniero Agrónomo, al Director XI Zona SAG," Temuco, 12 Jan. 1971). Milies's appointment as manager on Rucalán can be found in Archivo Siglo XX, Fondo Ministerio de Trabajo, Decretos, vol. 38 (1970): Decreto 901, "Ordena Reanudación de Faenas que Indica y Constituye Tribunal Arbitral que Señala," Santiago, 31 Dec. 1970. Intendant Gastón Lobos summarizes the report on peasant dwellings in a letter to the special prosecutor at the Court of Appeals on 15 Jan. 1971, where the quotations appear: Corte de Apelaciones de Temuco, Causa no. 242, ff. 421–27. And to complete the picture, I need also to cite Gonzalo Díaz Jaramillo, from the Land Acquisition Division of the CORA, who sent a letter to the special prosecutor at the Court of Appeals on 15 March 1971 in which he defined Rucalán as a property "most apt for use in forestry and livestock" and wrote that "this property is considered badly exploited because it does not meet the minimum conditions of exploitation set out in the Standards of Exploitation for Rustic Properties approved by Supreme Decree No. 218, of the Ministry of Agriculture on May 15, 1968" (Corte de Apelaciones de Temuco, Causa no. 242, ff. 472–73: "Carta de Gonzalo Díaz Jaramillo al Ministro Instructor," Temuco, 15 March 1971).

91 The calculation of the rate of exploitation was made as follows. No observer estimates more than 100 hectares in recognizably improved pastureland; when added to the highest estimate of wheat cultivation, the total surface being cultivated amounts to only 175 hectares — a bare 40% of the lowest size calculation, i.e., 439 hectares. The text of the Regulations for Defining the Conditions of Exploitation for Rustic Properties was reproduced in *El Campesino* (Revista de la Sociedad Nacional de Agricultura), May 1973, pp. 52–61; quotation on p. 54.

92 *El Diario Austral*, 1 Feb. 1974, p. 8. It is also interesting to note that, in July 1971, the Oficina de Planificación y Control (Office of planning and control) of CORA's 11th Zone estimated that Arnoldo Ríos had a carrying capacity of twenty-five families, yet at that moment held forty-two families. Intendencia de Cautín, Informe del Departamento de Control y Planificación, "Síntesis de la Reforma Agraria," Temuco, July 1971.

93 Intendencia de Cautín, Correspondencia Recibida, 1971: "Carta de Pablo Lüer Westermeyer al Intendente de Cautín," Temuco, 18 Feb. 1971. The night patrols are mentioned in Corte de Apelaciones de Temuco, Causa Criminal no. 242, "Oficio de la Prefectura de Investigaciones de Temuco al Ministro Visitador de la Corte de Apelaciones," f. 253; ff. 336–37: "Declaración de Jorge Alberto Landarretche Maffei," 8 Jan. 1971; ff. 339–39v: "Declaración de Pablo Lüer," Temuco, 8 Jan. 1971. I discussed this topic with Luciano Landarretche in the interview with the Landarretche family, Fundo Rucalán, 25 May 1997. The intendant's surveillance order can be found in Intendencia de Cautín, Oficio no. 354: "Intendente de Cautín al Prefecto de Carabineros," Temuco, 25 Feb. 1971.

94 On the Moncul takeover, see Intendencia de Cautín, Correspondencia Recibida, Oficio no. 300: "Capitán de Carabineros Sergio Acevedo Oyarce a la Prefectura de Carabineros de Cautín," Nueva Imperial, 11 March 1971. The rumors about Lobería can be found in Intendencia de Cautín, Oficio no. 409: "Oficio del Intendente Subrogante Renato Maturana Burgos al Prefecto de Carabineros," Temuco, 8 March 1971, and are countered in Oficio no. 539: "Coronel de Carabineros Enrique Gallardo B. al Intendente de Cautín," Temuco, 15 March 1971. Jorge Fernández's death is mentioned in Corte de Apelaciones de Temuco, Causa Criminal no. 242: "Carlos Cerda Medina, Fiscal titular de la I. Corte, solicita reapertura del sumario y la práctica de las diligencias que indica," Temuco, 1 April 1971, f. 477.

95 Intendencia de Cautín, Oficios de Municipalidades, "Gobernador Audito Gavilán Tapia al Intendente Subrogante de Cautín," Nueva Imperial, 18 Oct. 1971.

96 Intendencia de Cautín, Correspondencia Recibida, 1971: Prefectura de Carabineros de Temuco, Oficina de Informaciones, Boletín no. 80: "Auscultación en zona de Puerto Saavedra y Requisición de arma," Temuco, 25 Nov. 1971.

97 Intendencia de Cautín, Correspondencia Recibida, 1972, "Copia del Oficio del

Gobernador de Imperial Audito Gavilán Tapia al Subsecretario del Interior, Santiago, remitiendo Declaración del Campamento 'Jorge Fernández' de Nehuentúe," Imperial, 3 April 1972. I discussed the name of the dead student with Enrique Pérez, Temuco, 1997.

98 The quotation comes from the interview with the Landarretche family, Fundo Rucalán, 25 May 1997. The decree intervening the Fundo San Pablo can be found in Intendencia de Cautín, Oficio no. 801, "Intendente de Cautín a Robinson Alarcón Seguel, Interventor del fundo 'San Pablo,' transcribiendo Decreto sobre reanudación de faenas en el Fundo 'San Pablo,' Comuna de Puerto Saavedra," Temuco, 5 July 1972. This view of the coastal region as enemy territory emerges clearly in September 1973 in the reports on the military's actions in Nehuentúe published in *El Mercurio*, 4 Sept. 1973, pp. 1, 10; 5 Sept. 1973, p. 1; 11 Sept. 1973, p. 21. For an earlier example from the regional press that also concerns the *campamento* Jorge Fernández, see *El Diario Austral*, 18 March 1972, pp. 1–4.

99 SAG, Archivo Ex-CORA, Expediente no. 4152: Hijuela Norte del Fundo Esperanza, p.28: "Informe de posesión actual del predio denominado 'Esperanza Hijuela Norte,'" Temuco, 10 Oct. 1973.

100 On the history of the *consejos comunales* and the relationship between those organized at the grassroots and those by the government, as well as the goals of the left with regard to the grassroots *consejos*, see "Consejos comunales pasan a la acción," *Punto Final*, no. 156, 25 April 1972, pp. 24–26.

101 Interviews with Eduardina Ailío, Tranapuente, 18 Jan. 1997, and Heriberto Ailío, Tranapuente, 18 Jan. 1997, and Temuco, 18 April 1997; Robustiano Ailío, Tranapuente, 11 Jan. 1997; Mario Castro, Temuco, 15 May and 17 June 1997; Maritza Eltit, Temuco, 14 Jan. 1997; Gonzalo Leiva, Temuco, 23 April 1997; Gloria Muñoz (name changed), Santiago, 16 May 1997; Enrique Pérez, Temuco, numerous times throughout 1996–97; Luis Ernesto Quijón, Tranapuente, 30 Nov. 1996, 4 Jan. 1997; Francisco Sepúlveda (name changed), Santiago, 9 May 1997.

102 Interview with don Heriberto Ailío, Community of Ailío-Tranapuente, 18 Jan. 1997.

Chapter 5. When the Hearths Went Out

1 Paillao's testimony is quoted from "El sur bajo régimen militar," *Punto Final*, no. 192, 11 Sept. 1973, pp. 2–3. The paragraph has additional information gleaned from an interview with Paillao (identified here as Paillal) that appeared in the last number of *Chile Hoy*, with her photograph on the cover, on the very day of the coup: II: 65 (7–13 Sept. 1973), pp. 32, 29. I am grateful to Elizabeth Lira for the reference. Orlando Beltrán's signature appears on the public declaration made by the group taking over Nehuentúe: Intendencia de Cautín, Cor-

respondencia Recibida, 1972, "Copia del Oficio del Gobernador de Imperial Audito Gavilán Tapia al Subsecretario del Interior, Santiago, remitiendo Declaración del Campamento 'Jorge Fernández' de Nehuentúe," Imperial, 3 April 1972. I got the later information on Beltrán from one of his prison mates: interview with Enrique Pérez, Temuco, 14 April 1997.

2 Interview with Hugo Ailío, Concepción, 12 Aug. 1999.

3 Ibid.

4 The information about the incident with the journalists comes from Intendencia de Cautín, Correspondencia Recibida, 1973: "Informe de Nepomuceno Paillalef Lefinao, Director Zonal de Agricultura Subrogante, al Intendente de Cautín don Sergio Fonseca Fernández," Temuco, 31 Aug. 1973.

5 Interview with doña Elisa Ailío, Santiago, 13 Aug. 2001.

6 Interview with don Heriberto Ailío, Tranapuente, 18 Jan. 1997. Heriberto Ailío is mentioned specifically in the story published by *El Diario Austral* on 3 Sept. 1973, as being one of the "five terrorist elements" still at large who were ideological leaders of the MIR (p. 1).

7 Interview with doña Eduardina Ailío, Tranapuente, 18 Jan. 1997.

8 Interview with don Luis Ernesto Quijón, Community of Ailío-Tranapuente, 4 Jan. 1997.

9 E-mail from Doña Eduardina Ailío with comments on a previous draft of the book, Temuco, 20 Dec. 2001.

10 Traipe's testimony is recorded in Christian Martínez Neira, *Comunidades y Territorios Lafkenche, los mapuche de Rucacura al Moncul* (Temuco: Instituto de Estudios Indígenas/ Universidad de la Frontera, Serie Investigación, 1995), p. 103, note 173. For the death of Quián, see also *El Diario Austral*, 9 Sept. 1973, p. 11.

11 *El Diario Austral*, Temuco, Monday, 3 Sept. 1973, p. 1; and subsequent press conference given by Iturriaga on Wednesday, 5 Sept.; *El Diario Austral*, Wed. 5 Sept., pp. 1, 2.

12 On Magallanes, see the especially dramatic reports in Carlos Prats González, *Memorias: Testimonio de un soldado* (Santiago: Pehuén Editores, 1985), pp. 453–60, where the material is presented as breaking news while General Prats was still commander-in-chief of the army. Though Prats cites the death of one worker, an article in *Chile Hoy*, no. 61, 10–16 Aug. 1973, p. 7, cites two deaths; I chose to accept the later (and higher) estimate. Prats resigned on 23 Aug. 1973 and was replaced by Pinochet (Prats, *Memorias*, pp. 480–86). Pinochet did not join the coup coalition until the weekend before 11 September. See Sergio Arellano Iturriaga, *Más allá del abismo: Un testimonio y una perspectiva* (Santiago: Editorial Proyección, 1985), pp. 43–48; and José Toribio Merino C., *Bitácora de un almirante: Memorias* (Santiago: Editorial Andrés Bello, 1998), pp. 224–34.

13 "Cronología de Allanamientos," *Chile Hoy*, no. 61, 10–16 Aug. 1973, p. 6. The

quotation about Iturriaga and Pacheco can be found in *Chile Hoy*, no. 65, 7–13 Sept. 1973, p. 32.

14 For the tactics used in the operation, see, in addition to the testimonies and sources cited above, Intendencia de Cautín, Correspondencia Recibida, 1973: "Declaración Pública de los Obreros y Campesinos de Puerto Saavedra y Carahue," Provincia de Cautín, 2 Sept. 1973; and "El sur bajo régimen militar," *Punto Final*, no. 192, 11 Sept. 1973, pp. 2–3.

15 Quotation is from *Las Ultimas Noticias*, 3 Sept. 1973, first and last pages. See also *Las Ultimas Noticias*, 1 Sept. 1973, 4 Sept. 1973; *El Diario Austral*, 3 Sept. 1973, p. 1, 5 Sept., pp. 1, 2. The resonance of this version, confirmed and expanded by the military's narratives of leftist guerrillas and weapons caches summarized in the "Plan Zeta," was still quite obvious in my interview with the Landarretche family on the Fundo Rucalán in 1997. Interview with the Landarretche family, 25 May 1997.

16 *El Mercurio*, 4 Sept. 1973, pp. 1 and 10, 9 Sept. 1973, p. 1.

17 *El Mercurio*, 11 Sept. 1973, p. 21. The reference to "surprising origins" would, at the time, have been understood by most readers as a suggestion that the region had received weapons, ammunition, and other war materials from Cuba.

18 The press conference and photos of the "arsenal" appear in *El Diario Austral*, 5 Sept. 1973, pp. 1 and 2. See also *El Diario Austral*, 3 Sept. 1973, p. 1. For the comment about the location of the fundo in relation to the police post, interview with Francisco Sepúlveda (name changed), Santiago, 9 May 1998.

19 Interview with don Heriberto Ailío, Community of Ailío-Tranapuente, 18 Jan. 1997.

20 *Clarín*, 5 Sept. 1973, p. 4; 6 Sept. 1973, p. 10; *La Nación*, 6 Sept. 1973, p. 32; *Puro Chile*, 5 Sept. 1973, p. 2; 5 Sept. 1973, p. 4; 6 Sept. 1973, p. 9.

21 "El alto poder destructivo que se almacenaba en la provincia, a la espera de una ocasión propicia para desatar la muerte y la destrucción."

"Con ésto pensaban eliminarte, ¿por qué?"

"ESTO NO ES TODO. DE TI DEPENDE AHORA ENCONTRAR EL RESTO."

El Diario Austral, 28 Sept. 1973, p. 7.

22 The three-volume report published by the Comisión de Verdad y Reconciliación takes great care to discuss the political activities of the individual "victims," not as justification for what was done to them, but for the purposes of accuracy. This was not, however, the way in which the findings were publicized most extensively. I am grateful to Steve J. Stern, personal communication, for help in making this distinction.

23 By April 18, 1997, when our interview took place, I already had copies of the 5 Sept. 1973 press conference report in *El Diario Austral* as well as an interview with Mario Castro (15 April 1997) in which he confirmed having seen grenades on Nehuentúe and having even participated in making them, and a con-

versation with Enrique Pérez, Temuco, 14 April 1997. Subsequently I would also have access to a number of additional sources which helped me negotiate a further balance between the two mutually complicit narratives of guerrilla culpability and wide-eyed innocence, including Intendencia de Cautín, Correspondencia Recibida, 1973: "Informe de Nepomuceno Paillalef Lefinao, Director Zonal de Agricultura Subrogante, al Intendente de Cautín don Sergio Fonseca," Temuco, 31 Aug. 1973; "Declaración Pública de los Obreros y Campesinos de Puerto Saavedra y Carahue," Provincia de Cautín, 2 Sept. 1973; Correspondencia Despachada, 1973: "Boletines de Prensa"; interview with Francisco Sepúlveda (named changed), Santiago, 9 May 1997.

24 Interview with don Heriberto Ailío, Temuco, 18 April 1997.

25 "La mapuche de 'Vamos Mujer' en TV-7: 'Mentí porque me pagaron,'" *El Diario Austral*, 28 Sept. 1973, pp. 1, 8.

26 The information provided in these two paragraphs is an amalgam of the following sources: Guillermo Torres Gaona y Virginia Vidal, "La dictadura mató a periodistas, pero no al periodismo," in Ernesto Carmona, ed., *Morir es la noticia: Los periodistas relatan la historia de sus compañeros asesinados y/o desaparecidos*, pp. 245–53 (Santiago: J & C Productores Gráficos Ltda., 1997), reference to Elgueta on p. 253; interview with Sergio Fonseca, Temuco, 19 May 1997; interview with a person close to the *Intendencia* who wished to remain anonymous: Gloria Muñoz (name changed), Santiago, 16 May 1997; Interview with Gonzalo Leiva, Temuco, 26 June 1997. I received e-mail confirmation of the meeting in the Moneda from Ariel Dorfman, Chapel Hill, North Carolina, 25 Feb. 1998.

27 CONADI, Archivo de Asuntos Indígenas, T.M. 1381- Andrés Curiman, Carpeta Administrativa: Ministerio de Tierras y Colonización, Dirección de Asuntos Indígenas, Zonal Temuco, "Censo de la Comunidad de Andrés Curimán," 30 May–4 June 1963, Ficha # 24 (31 May); interview with Maritza Eltit, Temuco, 14 Jan. 1997; Faride Zerán, "Cautín: Un nuevo montaje de derecha," *Chile Hoy*, II: 65, 7–13 Sept. 1973, pp. 32, 29. In a conversation on 14 Aug. 1999, when I queried them directly about what had happened to doña Gertrudis, don Robustiano and doña Eduardina Ailío remembered that her first husband had been from Rucahue and that his name was Isaías Martínez (Community of Ailío-Tranapuente). The census listed above records Quidel's husband as "José Isaías Toro M."

28 Interviews with Gonzalo Leiva, Temuco, 23 June 1997; Gloria Muñoz, Santiago, 16 May 1997. In the interviews I carried out in the IX Region in August 1999, it became clear that Gertrudis was the Mapuche woman's real name. Interviews with don Heriberto Ailío, Huellanto Alto, 10 Aug. 1999; don Robustiano and doña Eduardina Ailío, Tranapuente, 14 Aug. 1999; doña Patricia Valenzuela, Nehuentúe, 20 Aug. 1999. Yet people could not or would not con-

firm her last name, something that only became clear to me from the census materials during the writing process.

29 Interviews with Enrique Pérez, Temuco, 14 April 1997; Gloria Muñoz, Santiago, 15 May 1997; don Heriberto Ailío, Temuco, 18 April 1997, Huellanto Alto, 10 Aug. 1999. In conversations with Enrique Pérez concerning an earlier draft of this chapter, he clarified that Beltrán first went to Concepción when he was released from jail. Temuco, 7 Aug. 2001.

30 Interviews with don Robustiano and doña Eduardina Ailío, Tranapuente, 14 Aug. 1999; doña Patricia Valenzuela, Nehuentúe, 20 Aug. 1999.

31 Interviews with Enrique Pérez, Temuco, 14 April 1997; don Heriberto Ailío, Temuco, 18 April 1997; don Robustiano and doña Eduardina Ailío, Tranapuente, 14 Aug. 1999; doña Patricia Valenzuela, Nehuentúe, 20 Aug. 1999.

32 Interview with don Heriberto Ailío, Temuco, 18 April 1997.

33 Interview with Francisco Sepúlveda (name changed at his request), Santiago, 9 May 1997; interview with don Luis Ernesto Quijón, Community of Ailío-Tranapuente, 30 Nov. 1996.

34 Interview with Francisco Sepúlveda (name changed at his request), Santiago, 9 May 1997; interview with don Luis Ernesto Quijón, Community of Ailío-Tranapuente, 30 Nov. 1996.

35 Ibid; and interviews with Enrique Pérez, 19 and 23 May 1997.

36 Interview with Hugo Ailío, Concepción, 12 Aug. 1999; interview with Enrique Pérez, Temuco, 23–24 May 1997; interview with Víctor Maturana, Temuco, 13 and 16 Jan. 1997.

37 Interview with one of the people who worked with the Traperos, Bernardo Cárdenas (name changed at his request), Temuco, 21 Aug. 1999. The Vicaría de la Solidaridad was a national-level solidarity network set up by the Catholic Church that offered political prisoners and their families services of various kinds.

38 Interview with don Heriberto Ailío, Community of Ailío-Tranapuente, 18 Jan. 1997.

39 Interview with don Heriberto Ailío, Comunidad de Ailío-Tranapuente, 18 Jan. 1997; field notes from conversation with don Heriberto Ailío, Community of Ailío- Huellanto Alto, 10 Aug. 1999.

40 Interviews with don Heriberto Ailío and doña Marta Antinao, Commmunity of Ailío-Tranapuente, 18 Jan. 1997.

41 Interview with don Luis Ernesto Quijón, Community of Ailío-Tranapuente, 4 Jan. 1997.

42 Interview with don Hugo Ailío, Concepción, 12 Aug. 1999

43 Ibid.

44 Interview with doña Eduardina Ailío, Community of Ailío-Tranapuente, 18 Jan. 1997.

45 Interview with doña Marta Antinao, Community of Ailío-Tranapuente, 18 Jan. 1997.

46 Interview with don Heriberto Ailío, Community of Ailío-Tranapuente, 18 Jan. 1997.

47 Interview with don Heriberto Ailío, Community of Ailío-Tranapuente, 18 Jan. 1997.

48 Interview with don Luis Ernesto Quijón, Community of Ailío-Tranapuente, 4 Jan. 1997.

49 Interview with don Heriberto Ailío, Temuco, 18 April 1997.

50 E-mail from doña Eduardina Ailío, Temuco, 20 Dec. 2001.

51 Interview with don Robustiano Ailío, Community of Ailío-Tranapuente, 11 Jan. 1997.

52 Interview with doña Eduardina Ailío, Community of Ailío-Tranapuente, 18 Jan. 1997.

53 Interview with don Luis Ernesto Quijón, Community of Ailío-Tranapuente, 4 Jan. 1997.

54 Interview with Maritza Eltit, who was a social worker in Puerto Saavedra during those years, Temuco, 14 Jan. 1997; and Don Luis Ernesto Quijón, Community of Ailío-Tranapuente, 30 Nov. 1996 and 4 Jan. 1997. For the report on the disappearance of Arturo Hillerns, see Comisión de Verdad y Reconciliación, *Informe de la Comisión Nacional de Verdad y Reconciliación*, Volumen 2, Tomo 3 (Santiago: Ministerio Secretaría General de Gobierno, 1991), p. 192.

55 Interview with don Luis Ernesto Quijón, Community of Ailío-Tranapuente, 30 Nov. 1996. Don Heriberto Ailío also emphasizes the theme of solidarity from strangers—both his cellmate and a bus driver—in his account of his third arrest, reproduced above.

56 Interview with Doña Felicia Concha de Ailío, Community of Ailío-Tranapuente, 10 Jan. 1997.

57 Interview with doña Marta Antinao, Community of Ailío-Tranapuente, 18 Jan. 1997.

58 Interview with doña Eduardina Ailío, Community of Ailío-Tranapuente, 18 Jan. 1997.

59 Interview with the Landarretche family, Fundo Rucalán, 25 May 1997. Luciano Landarretche's recollections about the Fundo Esperanza are confirmed in SAG, Archivo Ex-CORA, Exp. no. 4152- Hijuela Norte del Fundo Esperanza, p. 23: "Resolución del Consejo Ejecutivo Agrario de Cautín," Temuco, 20 Nov. 1973, when it is agreed to give provisional restitution of Esperanza Norte to the Landarretche brothers.

60 Patricio Silva, *Estado, neoliberalismo y política agraria en Chile, 1973–1981* (Amsterdam: CEDLA, 1987), pp. 155–57.

61 SAG, Archivo Ex-CORA, Expediente no. 972- Fundo Rucalán y Butalón- Ruca-

diuca, Comuna de Carahue, Juan B. Landarretche Mendoza, "Informe Técnico," 12 Dec. 1973, pp. 24–27, quotation on p. 24.

62 Ibid., p. 26.

63 Ibid., pp. 26–27.

64 Interview with the Landarretche family, Fundo Rucalán, 25 May 1997.

65 Ibid.

66 Ibid. The Corporación de Fomento a la Producción, or CORFO, was a state development agency created under the first Popular Front government in the late 1930s. Its role was to facilitate investment in development-oriented projects in industry and commercial agriculture by facilitating partnerships between private, state, and foreign capital.

67 Ibid.

68 Jensen's enthusiastic work in support of the military government is clear in the following documents: Intendencia de Cautín, Correspondencia Recibida, "Oficio de Héctor Jensen Valenzuela, Director Zonal de la CORA, al Intendente Militar Hernán Ramírez Ramírez," Temuco, 21 Nov. 1973; "Oficio de Héctor Jensen Valenzuela, Director Zonal de Agricultura, y Mario Herrera Barrera, Jefe Zonal ODEPA XI Zona, al Intendente Militar Hernán Ramírez Ramírez, sobre el Programa de Siembras y Necesidades de Insumos," Temuco, 23 Nov. 1973; and "Oficio de Héctor Jensen Valenzuela, Director Zonal XI Zona, al Intendente Militar Hernán Ramírez Ramírez, adjuntando la información solicitada sobre ubicación, estado y uso de las casas patronales de los predios de la provincia," Temuco, 29 Nov. 1973. Evidence of his capacity to survive is to be found in the fact that, in August 1974, he is director of agrarian services for the zone of Temuco: *El Diario Austral*, 18 Aug. 1974, p. 16.

69 Intendencia de Cautín, Correspondencia Recibida, 1973: "Consideraciones Generales: parte de un resumen general que manda Héctor Jensen Valenzuela al Intendente Militar de Cautín Coronel Hernán Ramírez Ramírez," Temuco, 21 Nov. 1973.

70 Héctor Jensen, "Medidas Adoptadas," in ibid. It is perhaps superfluous to point out that bringing charges, especially judicial, against government personnel brought, in the last months of 1973, at the least intimidation by the military and police and often jail time, physical mistreatment, even torture. The worst consequences would be suffered by members of UP political parties and by those with connections to grassroots organizers.

71 "Nada detendrá el proceso de la Reforma Agraria," *El Diario Austral*, 20 Jan. 1974, p. 12.

72 Ibid.

73 SAG, Archivo Ex-CORA, Expediente no. 972- Fundo Rucalán y Butalón- Rucadiuca, Comuna de Carahue, Juan B. Landarretche Mendoza, "Memorandum interno de Héctor Jensen Valenzuela, Director Zonal, al Director Nacional

Tenencia de la Tierra, comunicando antecedentes fundo Ruca Diuca," Temuco, 22 July 1974, p. 16.

74 "Nada detendrá el proceso de la Reforma Agraria," *El Diario Austral*, 20 Jan. 1974, p. 12.

75 Ibid.

76 Despite the complaints by Landarretche and others, it is interesting to note that the early proportions of restitution are extremely high, especially when compared with the final national-level percentages, which show that total restitution occurred in only 16% of the cases, with an additional 12% in which partial restitution is achieved (28% in all). In the early stages in Cautín, therefore, the reform was maintained in a very limited number of cases, especially when compared with the final national figures, where 52% of the land remained in the reformed sector, though with individual titles and subject to petition by *asentados*, a process which excluded those who had been politically active. See Patricio Silva, "The Military Regime and the Restructuring of Land Tenure," *Latin American Perspectives* 18:1 (Winter 1991), pp. 15–32. Once the dictatorship's "regularization" process ended in Cautín, the overall figures were much closer to the national average, with 27% of the properties undergoing some form of restitution and the remaining 73% still under CORA control, whether to be given out in individual parcels or maintained as state-owned reserves. See *El Diario Austral*, "Tenencia de la tierra en Cautín," 18 Aug. 1974, p. 16.

77 *El Diario Austral*, 1 Feb. 1974, p. 8: "Junta Militar Cumple: La tierra vuelve a poder de sus dueños."

78 SAG, Archivo Ex-CORA, Expediente no. 972- Fundo Rucalán y Butalón- Rucadiuca, Comuna de Carahue, Juan B. Landarretche Mendoza, "Informe Técnico," 12 Dec. 1973, pp. 24–27.

79 Interview with doña Eduardina Ailío, Community of Ailío-Tranapuente, 18 Jan. 1997.

80 Interview with doña Lidia del Pilar Llancao Díaz, Huellanto Alto, 10 Aug. 2001. The information about Llancao on the *asentamiento* comes from SAG, Archivo Ex-CORA, Expediente no. 972, "Informe pericial y tasación de mejoras," Temuco, 10 March 1971, pp. 127–35: the estimate of the value of Llancao's house appears on p. 129, where the house of Juan Contreras, the other resident *inquilino*, is also evaluated. Llancao's signature as spokesperson appears on p. 135. Llancao also appears in the December 1973 census of *asentados* on p. 29.

81 Interviews with Angélica Celis and with Bernardo Cárdenas and Catalina Mansilla (names changed at their request), Temuco, 21 Aug. 1999. After the transition to democratic rule in 1990, Huenchumilla served as a member of Congress elected on the Christian Democratic ticket. In 2003 he became only the second Mapuche cabinet minister in modern Chilean history when President Ricardo Lagos named him to the Secretaría de la Presidencia. Renato Matu-

rana often served as interim intendant during the intendancy of Gastón Lobos Barrientos, who is today disappeared. Hugo Ormeño, today a leading member of Temuco's legal community, previously worked as a legal defender for the Dirección de Asuntos Indígenas during the presidency of Eduardo Frei Montalva.

82 *El Diario Austral*, 8 Sept. 1978, p. 3.

83 For an in-depth look at the evolution of and divisions within Ad-Mapu, see Rosa Isolde Reuque Paillalef, *When a Flower Is Reborn: The Life and Times of a Mapuche Feminist*, ed. and trans. Florencia E. Mallon (Durham: Duke University Press, 2002). As Isolde Reuque points out, *Ad-Mapu* has a very rich set of meanings in *mapunzugun* which, taken together, refer to the variety of values and customs through which people live in balanced relationship with the earth and the world. For the reemergence of an organization in the community of Ailío, I have relied on a conversation with don Heriberto Ailío and don José Garrido, Temuco, 29 Nov. 1996; and interviews with Angélica Celis and Catalina Mansilla (name changed at her request), Temuco, 21 Aug. 1999.

84 Interview with Angélica Celis, Temuco, 21 Aug. 1999.

85 Interview with doña Eduardina Ailío, Community of Ailío-Tranapuente, 18 Jan. 1997.

86 Conversation with don Heriberto Ailío and don José Garrido, Temuco, 29 Nov. 1996.

87 Interview with Angélica Celis, Temuco, 21 Aug. 1999.

88 CONADI, Archivo de Asuntos Indígenas, T.M. 1112- Comunidad de Nicolás Ailío, "División de la Comunidad según la Ley de 1979," Carahue, 19 Dec. 1984. Enrique Antinao appears in SAG, Archivo Ex-CORA, "Encuesta de los asentados en el Asentamiento ex-Arnoldo Ríos," December 1973, p. 28. He is also the person doña Eduardina Ailío mentions as having joked after being arrested that at least he had gotten to ride in a helicopter. I discussed the problem of the land and the "Pinochet Law" with doña Elisa Ailío during our interview in Santiago, 13 Aug. 2001. As we shall see in the next chapter, Cecilia Ailío would continue to struggle with the legacies of the land problem and her desire to return to the community even after she had managed to return to the countryside in 2001.

89 Interview with Angélica Celis, Temuco, 21 Aug. 1999.

90 Ibid.

91 Ibid.

92 Ibid. See also Ministerio de Economía, Fomento y Reconstrucción, Secretaría Regional IX Región; "Oficio de Víctor Hugo Berner S., Secretario Regional Ministerial de Economía IX Región al Sr. Juan Florentino San Martín Espinoza, Presidente Asociación Gremial Consejo de Desarrollo Pesquero Campesino, comunicando la inscripción de la Asociación Gremial que Ud. preside," Temuco, 19 July 1988; CET Archive.

93 Interview with don Heriberto Ailío, Community of Ailío-Tranapuente, 18 Jan. 1997.

94 Interview with don Robustiano Ailío, Community of Ailío-Tranapuente, 11 Jan. 1997.

95 Interview with don Heriberto Ailío, Community of Ailío-Tranapuente, 18 Jan. 1997.

96 Interview with Angélica Celis, Temuco, 21 Aug. 1999.

97 Interview with Angélica Celis, Temuco, 21 Aug. 1999.

98 Ibid.

99 Ibid. The rest of the information about Juan Herrera is in SAG, Archivo Ex-CORA, "Encuesta de los asentados en el Asentamiento ex-Arnoldo Ríos," December 1973, p. 28. Interestingly, Juan René Herrera Leal's signature appears, next to Francisco Llancao's, as treasurer of the peasant committee that accepts the estimate of value of the Fundo Rucalán in March 1971. See SAG, Archivo Ex-CORA, Expediente no. 972, "Informe pericial y tasación de mejoras," Temuco, 10 March 1971, p. 135.

100 Interview with Angélica Celis, Temuco, 21 Aug. 1999.

101 Ibid.; Reuque Paillalef, *When a Flower Is Reborn*, esp. chapters 2 and 3. On the history of the Consejo, see especially José A. Mariman Q, "La organización Mapuche *Aukiñ Wallmapu Ngulam*," Denver, Colorado, April 1995, http://www.xs4all.nl/~rehue/art/jmar2.html.

102 People who know the coastal region in this period disagree as to don Félix Huaiqui's degree of participation in the Consejo de Todas las Tierras. Christian Martínez, who wrote an excellent history of the coastal region (*Comunidades y Territorios Lafkenche*, op.cit.) based on interviews and oral history, pointed out in a conversation we had about an earlier version of this book that don Félix Huaiqui was a founding member of the Consejo. In my interview with Angélica Celis, Temuco, 21 Aug. 1999, Angélica had the impression that Huaiqui had actually been more ambivalent and had allowed himself to be convinced to participate by Manuel Santander. This second position could very well reflect Angélica's strong commitment to the community of Ailío, where people decided not to participate in the Consejo's land invasion campaign. For details on the takeovers and subsequent repression, see Ivan Fredes Guerrero, "Estudia el Gobierno: Ley de Seguridad para 'Tomas' en la IX Región," *El Mercurio*, 20 June 1992, pp. A-1 and A-23. According to the article, "Four Mapuche communities yesterday occupied about 300 hectares of the Fundo Lobería, property of Domingo Durán Neumann, President of the Agricultural Producers' Confederation, as part of the so-called 'recuperation of usurped indigenous lands' being pushed forward by the Mapuche organization Consejo de Todas las Tierras. The fundo belonging to this agrarian leader, located 95 km. southeast of this regional capital [Temuco]—from Carahue toward the coast—was occupied by the communities of Coy-Coy, Pilolcura, Lincoli and Champulli,

but as of 6 p.m. the action had not yet been confirmed by police. The property was also occupied on October 10 of last year by the same people" (p. A-23).
103 Interview with Angélica Celis, Temuco, 21 Aug. 1999.
104 Ibid.
105 Ibid.

Chapter 6. Settlers Once Again

1 Florencia Mallon, field notes of visit to Ailío, Tranapuente, 25 March 1997.
2 Don Heriberto used the phrase "rise from the ashes" in a conversation we had in Huellanto Alto, 5 Aug. 1998. He also emphasized the importance of creating work opportunities for the children within the community as well as educating them about the history of the community as it had really happened.
3 Rosa Isolde Reuque Paillalef, *When a Flower Is Reborn: The Life and Times of a Mapuche Feminist*, edited, translated, and with an introduction by Florencia E. Mallon (Durham: Duke University Press, 2002). Among the aspects that most frustrated activists were the lack of constitutional recognition for indigenous peoples, the lack of approval of ILO Convention 169 on Indigenous Peoples, and — perhaps of special importance for the subsequent experience of the community of Ailío — that the lands bought with money from the Land and Water Fund would not apparently be considered indigenous lands unless they were already considered such before the purchase. See CONADI, *Ley Indígena 19253* (Temuco, 1995), pp. 6–7, 11.
4 Discussion with Enrique Pérez about the first draft of this book, Temuco, 7 Aug. 2001. The CEPI was the governmental organization that, during the transition period, took charge of formulating the indigenous policy of the Aylwin government and writing a draft of the Indigenous Law.
5 CONADI, Subdirección Nacional Temuco, "Acta Constitutiva de la Comunidad Indígena de Nicolás Ailío," Tranapuente, Carahue, 10 Aug. 1994, copy found in the Archive of the Centro de Educación y Tecnología (CET); and Archivo CET, Libro de Actas de la Comunidad Indígena Nicolás Ailío: "Acta Constitutiva de la Comunidad Indigena 'Nicolás Ailio,'" Tranapuente, Carahue, 10 Aug. 1994, pp. 1–3.
6 Interview with Gonzalo Leiva, Temuco, 23 June 1997; Archivo CET, Libro de Actas de la Comunidad de Nicolás Ailío: "Reunión de la 'Comunidad Nicolás Ailío,'" Tranapuente, 24 Feb. 1996, pp. 4–5.
7 Archivo CET, Libro de Actas de la Comunidad de Nicolás Ailío: "Reunión de la 'Comunidad Nicolás Ailío,'" Tranapuente, 23 March 1996, pp. 6–7, and 5 June 1996, pp. 8–8v.
8 Archivo CET, Libro de Actas de la Comunidad de Nicolás Ailío: "Reunión Extraordinaria de la 'Comunidad Nicolás Ailío,'" Tranapuente, 20 July 1996, pp. 9–10, quotation on p. 10; and "Reunión de la 'Comunidad Nicolás Ailío,'"

Tranapuente, 10 Aug. 1996, pp. 11–12, quotation on p. 12. The takeover of the Fundo Mañío Manzanal, in which don Heriberto participated, is mentioned in chapter 4.

9 Archivo del CET, "Certificado otorgado por Víctor Hugo Painemal Arriagada, Subdirector de CONADI, sobre la personalidad jurídica de la comunidad indígena Nicolás Ailío," Temuco, 13 Nov. 1996.

10 Interview with Gonzalo Leiva, Temuco, 23 June 1997; conversations with Enrique Pérez, Temuco, November 1996–April 1997; Archivo CET, Copia Certificada de la Escritura No. 237, Notario Juan Antonio Loyola Opazo, Temuco, Venta de Clemente Seguel Q. a la Comunidad Indígena Nicolás Ailío, 15 November 1996. It is important to emphasize that not everyone in the community received Enrique, still known to them by his old *mirista* alias "El Indio" (the Indian), with the same degree of enthusiasm.

11 On the problems associated with the reorganization of indigenous communities under Law 19253, see Reuque, *When a Flower Is Reborn*; and CONADI, *Ley Indígena*.

12 Interview with Heriberto Ailío and José Garrido, Centro de Estudios Simón Bolívar, Temuco, 29 Nov. 1996; CONADI, Archivo de Asuntos Indígenas, T.M. 1112- Comunidad de Nicolás Ailío, Tranapuente, "División de la Comunidad según la Ley de 1979," Carahue, 19 Dec. 1984. For the text of Decree-Law no. 2,568 of 1979, see Contraloría General de la República, *Recopilación de Decretos Leyes dictados por la Junta de Gobierno Constituída el 11 de Septiembre de 1973, que asumió el mando supremo de la nación*, vol. 74, Decree-Laws vol. 13, from 29 Nov. 1978 to 13 June 1979 (Santiago: Official Edition), pp. 346–60. For details on the actual plots, see Archivo CONADI, Ministerio de Agricultura, INDAP, "Plano de División de la Comunidad Nicolás Ailío," Temuco, 31 March 1983.

13 Interview with doña Eduardina Ailío, Community of Ailío-Tranapuente, 18 Jan. 1997.

14 For René Ailío's opinions I am relying on Florencia Mallon, field notes of visits to Tranapuente, 25 March 1997 and 17 May 1997; and interview with René Ailío, Community of Ailío-Tranapuente, 10 Jan. 1997. The rest of the information in the paragraph comes from Archivo CET, Libro de Actas de la Comunidad de Nicolás Ailío: "Reunión de la Comunidad de Ailío," 28 Sept. 1996, pp. 15–16, quotation on p. 15v; 26 Oct. 1996, pp. 16v–17; and no date (although surely in the first three weeks of November), pp. 17v–18.

15 CONADI, Ley Indígena, pp. 3–4.

16 Florencia Mallon, field notes for visit to Tranapuente, 25 March 1997; Archivo CET, Libro de Actas de la Comunidad de Nicolás Ailío: "Reunión de la Comunidad de Ailío," no date (although surely in the first three weeks of November), pp. 17v–18; quotation on p. 18.

17 Florencia Mallon, field notes from visit to Tranapuente, 25 March 1997.

18 Interview with doña Juana Pincheira, Huellanto Alto, 20 March 1997.

19 Ibid.

20 Ibid.

21 Ibid.

22 Ibid.

23 Ibid.

24 Interview with don Heriberto Ailío, Community of Ailío-Tranapuente, 18 Jan. 1997.

25 Ibid.

26 Florencia Mallon, field notes of visit to Huellanto Alto, 5 Dec. 1996.

27 Interview with doña Juana Pincheira, Huellanto Alto, 20 March 1997.

28 Florencia Mallon, field notes of visits to Huellanto Alto, 15 and 20 March 1997. In subsequent years the uncertainty about indigenous lands diminished because personnel at the Land Fund in CONADI decided to register all lands bought with the fund as indigenous lands, without taking into account their origin.

29 Florencia Mallon, field notes of visits to Tranapuente, 25 March and 17 May 1997. According to doña Eduardina Ailío, who at that moment was living in Huellanto Alto, René had not shown up for a meeting to finalize the sharecropping contract.

30 Conversation with don Heriberto Ailío, Huellanto Alto, 5 Aug. 1998. It is important to emphasize as well that kinship relations have historically connected these two communities. Pilquinao, doña María's last name, has a connection to the community of Pichingual. The Mapuche custom was to marry their daughters to men from nearby communities, thus deepening the ties of kinship and exchange within a region.

31 Archivo CET, Libro de Actas de la Comunidad de Nicolás Ailío: "Reunión de la Comunidad de Ailío," Tranapuente, January 1997, pp. 22–24; quotation on p. 23v.

32 After the formal denial of René's petition there was an additional opportunity, when Luciano Martínez decided to leave the subsidy group, to add someone. Even then, however, the group decided to offer the slot to Alejandro Santibáñez Ailío instead of to René Ailío. Archivo CET, Libro de Actas de la Comunidad de Nicolás Ailío: "Reunión Extraordinaria de la Comunidad de Ailío," Tranapuente, 8 Feb. 1997, p. 25.

33 Archivo CET, Libro de Actas de la Comunidad de Nicolás Ailío: "Reunión Extraordinaria de la Comunidad de Ailío," Tranapuente, 8 Feb. 1997, pp. 24v–26; quotations on p. 25v.

34 Archivo CET, "Carta Compromiso entre las directivas de las comunidades Nicolás Ailío I Tranapuente y Nicolás Ailío II Huellanto Alto," Tranapuente, 5 Dec. 1997.

35 Archivo CET, Libro de Actas de la Comunidad de Nicolás Ailío: "Reunión de

la Comunidad de Ailío," Tranapuente, Nov. 1996, pp. 17v–18; quotation pp. 17v–18.

36 Archivo CET, Libro de Actas de la Comunidad de Nicolás Ailío: "Reunión de la Comunidad de Ailío," Tranapuente, January 1997, pp. 22v–24. The change in the number of individualized hectares is mentioned on pp. 23v–24. When I visited don Heriberto Ailío on August 5, 1998, he talked to me a great deal about Mapuche traditions as they existed in his community when he was growing up. It was at this point that he told me he had been a very good *palin* player. He also commented that he would like to organize an indigenous encounter with communities from other areas.

37 Conversation with Gustavo Peralta, José Garrido, and Heriberto Ailío, Temuco, 3 Aug. 1998; conversation with doña Magaly Riquelme de Huenuan, Huellanto Alto, 5 Aug. 1998.

38 Conversation with Gustavo Peralta, José Garrido, and Heriberto Ailío, Temuco, 3 Aug. 1998.

39 Ibid.

40 In conversation with Gustavo Peralta, José Garrido, and Heriberto Ailío, Temuco, 3 Aug. 1998, don Chami and don Heri discussed the problems created by lack of fencing, emphasizing that Clemente Seguel had killed about seven or eight pigs that had passed over onto his land.

41 "Plan de Desarrollo de la Comunidad Nicolás Ailío, Sector Huellanto Alto, Comuna de Gorbea, IX Región de la Araucanía," proposal for funding presented to the Kellogg Foundation, Temuco, 9 June 1998, p. 2.

42 Ibid., p. 4. In conversation with don Heriberto Ailío and don Chami Garrido in Huellanto Alto, 5 Aug. 1998, they told me about a conflict they'd had with technical personnel from PRODEL, an agricultural agency connected to Gorbea municipality. Because they simply did not accept the advice the agents offered, they were called "problematic" and "liars."

43 A series of discussions recorded in the community's minutes help clarify the complex situation faced by Huellanto Alto's settlers. Archivo CET, Libro de Actas de la Comunidad de Nicolás Ailío: "Reuniones de la Comunidad de Ailío," Huellanto Alto, pp. 26v–46.

44 Archivo CET, Libro de Actas de la Comunidad de Nicolás Ailío, "Reunión de la Comunidad de Nicolás Ailío II-Huellanto Alto," 27 Dec. 1997, pp. 43v–46; quotation on p. 45v. At the same meeting there was a long discussion about livestock, and a list of the animals belonging to each member was drawn up. Interviews with don Armando Ailío and doña Carmen Huentemilla, Huellanto Alto, 5 Aug. 1998; doña Magaly Riquelme Méndez de Huenuan, Huellanto Alto, 5 Aug. 1998; don Luis Huenuan, Huellanto Alto, 5 Aug. 1998; and don Juan Ailío, Huellanto Alto, 5 Aug. 1998. In her comments on the book manuscript two years later, doña Cecilia Ailío also did not agree with dividing up the

land, "because the next generations would once again encounter many problems . . . she feels that they would end up in the same place as in the past, and in her own case she would never even have touched a plot of land if the community option hadn't been available." E-mail from doña Cecilia Ailío, courtesy of Angélica Celis, CET, Temuco, 26 Nov. 2001.

45 Interviews with don Armando Ailío and doña Carmen Huentemilla, Huellanto Alto, 5 Aug. 1998; doña Magaly Riquelme Méndez de Huenuan, Huellanto Alto, 5 Aug. 1998; don Luis Huenuan, Huellanto Alto, 5 Aug. 1998; and don Juan Ailío, Huellanto Alto, 5 Aug. 1998.

46 Interviews with don Robustiano Ailío and doña Eduardina Ailío, Huellanto Alto, 5 Aug. 1998. Samuel is Cecilia's son and has lived with doña Eduardina for most of his life while his mother was working in Santiago.

47 Archivo CONADI, Ministerio de Agricultura, INDAP, "Plano de División de la Comunidad Nicolás Ailío," Temuco, 31 March 1983.

48 Meeting with Bárbara Bustos and Gustavo Peralta, Temuco, 4 Aug. 1998; conversation in Huellanto Alto with don José Garrido and don Heriberto Ailío, 5 Aug. 1998. Bárbara Bustos lived for a few months in Huellanto Alto and Tranapuente as part of her research for her B.A. thesis at the Catholic University in Temuco, a copy of which she generously shared with me.

49 CONADI, Fondo de Tierras y Aguas, Dirección Nacional, "Evaluación y propuestas al Programa Subsidio para la Adquisición de Tierras por Indígenas," Temuco, June 1998, p. 11. I am grateful to Gonzalo Leiva for his help in guiding me through the official documentation of the Land Fund.

50 Ibid., p. 13.

51 Ibid., pp. 13–14, 16–17.

52 Ibid., pp. 30, 13.

53 CONADI, Consejo Nacional, Proyección Institucional, 27 Nov. 1997, pp. 7, 8.

54 Interview with doña Cecilia Ailío, Temuco, 31 July 2001.

55 Ibid.

56 Interview with doña Marcelina Ailío, Huellanto Alto, 5 Aug. 1998, quotation from my interview; interview with Marcelina Ailío, by Angélica Celis, "Conversaciones con el territorio desde la interculturalidad."

57 Angélica Celis, "Conversaciones con el territorio," p. 233.

58 Quotations are from Angélica Celis, "Conversaciones con el territorio," pp. 318, 306, 308 (doña Marta); and p. 230 (doña Marcelina). I also observed doña Marta's work in her greenhouse during my visits in 1999 and 2001.

59 The quotations in the last two paragraphs come from Angélica Celis, "Conversaciones con el territorio," in order of appearance: pp. 246, 245, 307, 342, 245, 336, 344, 231.

60 E-mail from doña Cecilia Ailío, courtesy of Angélica Celis, CET-Sur, Temuco, 26 Nov. 2001.

61 República de Chile, Ministerio de Hacienda, Dirección de Presupuestos, *Informe Final de Evaluación, Programa Fondo de Tierras y Aguas*, August 1998, "Formato B," pp. 1–3.

62 Observations based on my visits to Tranapuente in August 2001 and March 2003.

Chapter 7. Conclusion: Where the Past Meets the Future

1 Angélica Celis notes the same thing about doña María Pilquinao's image as it emerges from the memories of her daughter and daughter-in-law in "Conversaciones con el territorio desde la interculturalidad," pp. 348–51.

2 This reflection owes a great deal to the work of the Indian historian Dipesh Chakrabarty, especially his book *Provincializing Europe: Postcolonial Thought and Historical Difference* (Princeton: Princeton University Press, 2000). The concept of "time-knots" is his and is developed mainly in chapter 4. See also his *Habitations of Modernity: Essays in the Wake of Subaltern Studies* (Chicago and London: University of Chicago Press, 2002). A methodologically similar effort to recover alternative explanations and visions of history is present in Steve J. Stern's concept of "memory knots," developed in his *Remembering Pinochet's Chile: On the Eve of London, 1998* (Durham: Duke University Press, 2004).

3 A fuller discussion of this concept can be found in chapter 3.

4 A more detailed discussion of this case appears in chapter 5.

5 Alejandro Saavedra Peláez, *Los Mapuche en la sociedad chilena actual* (Santiago: LOM Ediciones, 2002). His discussion of the phrase "indigenous people" occurs on p. 252. His 1971 book is *La cuestión Mapuche* (Santiago: ICIRA, 1971), which I discuss in more detail in chapter 3.

6 A very important perspective that emerges from *Los Mapuche en la sociedad chilena actual* is that, between 1966 and 1992, the Mapuche population emigrating from their communities of origin increased from 10.9% to 68.1% of the total, dramatically transforming Mapuche identity and conditions of life more generally. See especially pp. 176–79. Quotations in this paragraph are found on p. 7.

7 Celis, "Conversaciones con el territorio desde la interculturalidad," p. 344.

REFERENCES CITED

ARCHIVAL SOURCES

1. Santiago

Archivo Nacional Histórico (Miraflores) (ANH-M)
    Intendencia de Cautín (IC), 1885–1952
    Ministerio de Relaciones Exteriores (MinRREE), 1882–1900

Archivo Nacional Siglo XX (ASXX)
    Ministerio de Agricultura, 1928–73
    Ministerio de Defensa (selected decrees and correspondence)
    Ministerio del Interior (selected decrees and correspondence)
    Ministerio de Relaciones Exteriores (MinRREE), 1900–20
    Ministerio de Tierras y Colonización (MTYC), 1900–72
    Ministerio de Trabajo (selected decrees and correspondence)
    Notarios de Temuco, 1900–30

Biblioteca Agraria
    El Campesino (Sociedad Nacional de Agricultura), 1968–73

Biblioteca de FLACSO
    Punto Final, 1970–73

Hemeroteca, Biblioteca Nacional
    El Diario Austral (Temuco), 1930–98
    El Mercurio (Santiago), 1973–98
    La Epoca (Santiago), 1997–98
    La Tercera (Santiago), 1973–98
    Selected other newspapers, August–September 1973

Servicio Agrícola Ganadero (SAG)
    Archivo de la Ex-Corporación de Reforma Agraria (Ex-CORA), Expedientes

2. IX Region

Archivo del Centro de Educación y Tecnología (CET)
   Libros de Actas de la Comunidad Indígena Nicolás Ailío, 1994–1997

Corporación Nacional de Desarrollo Indígena (CONADI), Temuco
   Archivo de Asuntos Indígenas
   Fondo de Tierras y Aguas

Conservador de Bienes Raíces-Nueva Imperial (CBI-NI), 1895–1941

Intendencia de Cautín (Temuco), 1930–90
   Correspondencia Despachada y Recibida

Museo Regional de la Araucanía (Temuco)
   Intendencia records for the first decades of the twentieth century
   Imprints, 1890–1940

Corte de Apelaciones de Temuco
   "Causa criminal 242, por Infracción a la Ley de Seguridad Interior del Estado,
      seguida contra Juan Bautista Landarretche y otros," Temuco, December 1970

3. United States

University of Wisconsin, Madison
   Land Tenure Library
      Clippings files, Chile
   Memorial Library, Microfiche Collection
      Chile Hoy, 1973

ORAL SOURCES AND INTERVIEWS

1. Community of Ailío

   Antonio Ailío, 11 Jan. 1997 (Tranapuente)
   Armando Ailío and Carmen Huentemilla, 5 Aug. 1998 (Huellanto Alto)
   Cecilia Ailío, 31 July 2001 (Temuco) and e-mail courtesy of Angélica Celis,
      CET, Temuco, 26 Nov. 2001
   Eduardina Ailío, 18 Jan. 1997 (Tranapuente); 15 March 1997 (Huellanto Alto);
      20 Aug. 1999 (Tranapuente); e-mail courtesy of CET-Sur, Temuco, 20 Dec.
      2001
   Heriberto Ailío, 18 Jan. 1997 (Tranapuente); 20 March 1997 (Huellanto Alto);
      18 April 1997 (Temuco); 5 Aug. 1998 (Huellanto Alto); 10 Aug. 1999
      (Huellanto Alto); 10 Aug. 2001 (Huellanto Alto); and various informal
      conversations, 1998–2003
   Juan Hector Ailío, 5 Aug. 1998 (Huellanto Alto)

Marcelina Ailío, 5 Aug. 1998 (Huellanto Alto)

René Ailío, 10 Jan. 1997 (Tranapuente)

Robustiano Ailío, 11 Jan. 1997 (Tranapuente); 15 March 1997 (Huellanto Alto); 20 Aug. 1999 (Tranapuente)

Marta Antinao, 18 Jan. 1997 (Tranapuente), and various informal conversations, Huellanto Alto, 1998–2003

Felicia Concha de Ailío, 10 Jan. 1997 (Tranapuente)

Luis Huenuan, 5 Aug. 1998 (Huellanto Alto)

Oscar Jara, 10 Jan. 1997 (Tranapuente)

Lidia del Pilar Llancao Díaz, 10 Aug. 2001 (Huellanto Alto)

Juana Pincheira Huinca, 20 March 1997 (Huellanto Alto)

Luis Ernesto Quijón, 30 Nov. 1996, 4 Jan. 1997 (Tranapuente)

Magaly Riquelme de Huenuan, 5 Aug. 1998 (Huellanto Alto)

2. Nehuentúe

Patricia Valenzuela, 20 Aug. 1999

3. Fundo Rucalán

Arlis Landarretche de Huerta, 25 May 1997

Luciano Landarretche Maffei, 25 May 1997

Violeta Maffei vda. de Landarretche, 25 May 1997

4. Temuco

Bárbara Bustos and Gustavo Peralta, 4 Aug. 1998

Bernardo Cárdenas (name changed at his request), 21 Aug. 1999

Mario Castro, 15 May and 17 June 1997

María Angelica Celis, 21 Aug. 1999

Maritza Eltit, 14 Jan. 1997

Sergio Fonseca, 19 May 1997

Gonzalo Leiva, 23 June 1997, 19 Aug. 1999

Catalina Mansilla (name changed at her request), 21 Aug. 1999

Víctor Maturana, 13, 16 Jan., 18, 19 March, 17 April 1997

Gustavo Peralta, José Garrido, and Heriberto Ailío, 3 Aug. 1998

Enrique Pérez, numerous interviews through 1996–97

Elena Rodríguez (name changed at her request), 19 Aug. 1999

5. Santiago

Jacques Chonchol, 4 April 1997

Gloria Muñoz (name changed at her request), 16 May 1997

Francisco Sepúlveda (name changed at his request), 9 May 1997

6. Concepción

Hugo Ailío, 12 Aug. 1999

PUBLIC LECTURES AND OTHER UNPUBLISHED SOURCES

Bengoa, José. "Las economías campesinas Mapuches." Documento de Tra-bajo No. 6, Grupo de Investigaciones Agrarias. Academia de Humanismo Cristiano, Santiago, Chile, October 1981.

Bunster, Ximena. "Adaptation in Mapuche Life: Natural and Directed." Ph.D. diss., Columbia University, 1968.

Caniullan, Victor. "Conferencia sobre cultura y religiosidad Mapuche." Catholic University of Temuco, 6 Aug. 1999.

Cantoni, Wilson. "Legislación indígena e integración del mapuche." Program in the Sociology of Economic Change, University of Wisconsin, in collaboration with the Land Tenure Center, Santiago, Chile, December 1969, mimeo.

Celis, María Angélica. "Conversaciones con el territorio desde la intercultura-lidad: Las huertas femeninas como espacios de conversación." M.A. thesis, Universidad de la Frontera (Temuco), January 2003.

Community of Ailío. "Plan de Desarrollo de la Comunidad Nicolás Ailío, Sector Huellanto Alto, Comuna de Gorbea, IX Región de la Araucanía." Proposal for funding presented to the Kellogg Foundation, Temuco, 9 June 1998.

Corporación de Reforma Agraria. "El Asentamiento." Departamento de Desarrollo Campesino, Difusión, Santiago, 1967.

———, Vicepresidencia Ejecutiva. "Dos Años de Reforma Agraria del Gobierno Popular." Santiago: Impreso de Relaciones Públicas de la CORA, 1972.

Dorfman, Ariel. Email confirming the meeting at La Moneda. Chapel Hill, N.C., 25 Feb. 1998.

Erbeta Vaccaro, León. "Situación jurídica y social de los indios mapuches." Report presented to the Prosecutor of the Honorable Supreme Court, Temuco, 3 Sept. 1955.

Kay, Cristóbal. "Chile: An Appraisal of Popular Unity's Agrarian Reform." Institute of Latin American Studies, Occasional Papers no. 13, University of Scotland, Glasgow, 1974.

Marchetti, S.J., Peter E. "Worker Participation and Class Conflict in Worker-Managed Farms: The Rural Question in Chile—1970 to 1973." Ph.D. diss., Yale University, 1975, 2 vols.

Mariman Q., José A. "La organización Mapuche *Aukiñ Wallmapu Ngulam*." Denver, Colorado, April 1995, http://www.xs4all.nl/~rehue/art/jmar2.html.

Palacios Gómez, Alejandro, and Patricio Pinto Pérez. "Estudio socio-económico de la agricultura indígena en la provincia de Cautín." Tesis presentada como parte de los requisitios para optar al título de Ingeniero Agrónomo—Mención Economía Agraria. Santiago de Chile: Universidad de Chile—Department of Economics, 1964.

Quidel, José. "Conferencia sobre historia y cultura Mapuche." Catholic University of Temuco, 6 Aug. 1999.

República de Chile, Ministerio de Hacienda, Dirección de Presupuestos. *Informe Final de Evaluación, Programa Fondo de Tierras y Aguas,* August 1998.

Thiesenheusen, William C. "Agrarian Reform in Chile." Land Tenure Center, University of Wisconsin, Madison, June 1970.

Vidal, Aldo. "Conferencia sobre historia Mapuche." Catholic University of Temuco, 5 Aug. 1999.

SECONDARY SOURCES

Anabalón y Urzúa, I. *Chile Agrícola: Tomo Preliminar.* Santiago de Chile: Imprenta, Litografía y Encuadernación Moderna, 1922.

Arellano Iturriaga, Sergio. *Más allá del abismo: Un testimonio y una perspectiva.* Santiago: Editorial Proyección, 1985.

Aylwin, José. "Tierra mapuche: derecho consuetudinario y legislación chilena." In Rodolfo Stavenhagen and Diego Iturralde, eds., *Entre la ley y la costumbre: El derecho consuetudinario indígena en América Latina,* pp. 333–54. Mexico City, and San José, Costa Rica: Instituto Indigenista Interamericano and Instituto Interamericano de Derechos Humanos, 1990.

Aylwin, Mariana, et al. *Chile en el siglo xx.* Santiago: Planeta, 1990.

Azümchefi: Grafemario único del Idioma Mapuche. Corporación Nacional de Desarrollo Indígena and Mapuche Organizations Folilche Aflaia-Ad Mapu-Kellukleayñ pu Zomo. Temuco, 1996.

Benedetti, Mario. *Cotidianas.* Mexico City: Siglo xxi Editores, 1979.

Bengoa, José. *Historia del pueblo Mapuche (Siglo xix y xx).* Santiago: Ediciones Sur, 1985.

Bunster, Ximena. "Una Experiencia de Antropología aplicada entre los Araucanos." *Anales de la Universidad de Chile* 122 (1964), pp. 94–128.

Chakrabarty, Dipesh. *Habitations of Modernity: Essays in the Wake of Subaltern Studies.* Chicago and London: University of Chicago Press, 2002.

———. *Provincializing Europe: Postcolonial Thought and Historical Difference.* Princeton: Princeton University Press, 2000.

Chonchol, Jacques. *Sistemas agrarios en América Latina: De la etapa prehispánica a la modernización conservadora.* Santiago, Chile, and Mexico City: Fondo de Cultura Económica, 1994.

Comisión de Verdad y Reconciliación. *Informe de la Comisión Nacional de Verdad y Reconciliación.* Volumen 2, Tomo 3. Santiago: Ministerio Secretaría General de Gobierno, 1991.

Coña, Pascual. *Testimonio de un cacique mapuche.* Dictated to Father Ernesto Willhelm de Moesbach. 5th ed. Santiago: Pehuén Editores, 1995.

Corporación Nacional de Desarrollo Indígena. *Ley Indígena 19253.* Temuco, 1995.

DeShazo, Peter. *Urban Workers and Labor Unions in Chile, 1902–1927.* Madison: University of Wisconsin Press, 1983.

Escobar V., Aníbal. *Anuario de la Colonia Francesa en Chile, 1925–1926.* Santiago de Chile, 1926.

———. *Anuario de la Colonia Francesa en Chile, 1927–1928.* Santiago de Chile, 1928.

———. *Francia: La Colonia Francesa en Chile.* Santiago de Chile, 1920.

Faron, Louis C. *Hawks of the Sun: Mapuche Morality and its Ritual Attributes.* Pittsburgh: University of Pittsburgh Press, 1964.

———. *The Mapuche Indians of Chile.* New York: Holt, Rinehart and Winston, 1968.

Foerster, Rolf, and Sonia Montecino. *Organizaciones, Líderes y Contiendas Mapuches (1900–1970).* Santiago: Centro Estudios de la Mujer, 1988.

Huerta M., María Antonieta. *Otro Agro para Chile: La historia de la Reforma Agraria en el proceso social y político.* Santiago: Ediciones Chile América CESOC, 1989.

Klubock, Thomas. *Contested Communities: Class, Gender, and Politics in Chile's El Teniente Copper Mine, 1904–1951.* Durham: Duke University Press, 1998.

Loveman, Brian. *Chile: The Legacy of Hispanic Capitalism.* New York: Oxford University Press, 1979.

———. *Struggle in the Countryside: Politics and Rural Labor in Chile, 1919–1973.* Bloomington: Indiana University Press, 1976.

Loveman, Brian, and Elizabeth Lira. *Las suaves cenizas del olvido: Vía chilena de reconciliación política, 1814–1932.* Santiago: LOM/DIBAM, 1999.

———. *Las ardientes cenizas del olvido: Vía chilena de Reconciliación Política, 1932–1994.* Santiago: LOM/DIBAM, 2000.

Mallon, Florencia E. "Cuando la amnesia se impone con sangre, el abuso se hace costumbre: El pueblo mapuche y el Estado chileno, 1881–1998." In Paul W. Drake and Iván Jaksic, eds., *El modelo chileno: Democracia y desarrollo en los noventa,* pp. 435–64. Santiago: LOM Ediciones, 1999.

Manquilef, Manuel. *Comentarios del Pueblo Araucano (La faz social).* Santiago: Imprenta Cervantes, 1911.

———. *¡Las tierras de Arauco! El último cacique.* Temuco: Imprenta y Encuadernación "Modernista," 1915.

Martínez Neira, Christian. *Comunidades y Territorios Lafkenche, los mapuche de*

Rucacura al Moncul. Temuco: Instituto de Estudios Indígenas/Universidad de la Frontera, Serie de Investigación, 1995.

Merino C., José Toribio. *Bitácora de un almirante: Memorias.* Santiago: Editorial Andrés Bello, 1998.

Monteón, Michael. *Chile in the Nitrate Era: The Evolution of Economic Dependence, 1880–1930.* Madison: University of Wisconsin Press, 1982.

Ortega, Luis, ed. *La Guerra Civil de 1891: Cien años hoy.* Santiago: Universidad de Santiago de Chile, 1991.

Painemal Huechual, Martín, with Rolf Foerster. *Vida de un dirigente Mapuche.* Santiago: Grupo de Investigaciones Agrarias, 1983.

Pinto, Julio. *Trabajos y rebeldías en la pampa salitrera: El ciclo del salitre y la reconfiguración de las identidades populares (1850–1900).* Santiago: Editorial Universidad de Santiago, 1998.

Prats González, Carlos. *Memorias: Testimonio de un soldado.* Santiago, Chile: Pehuén Editores, 1985.

República de Chile, Contraloría General. *Recopilación de Decretos Leyes dictados por la Junta de Gobierno Constituída el 11 de Septiembre de 1973, que asumió el mando supremo de la nación.* 74 vols. Decree-Laws, vol. 13, from 29 Nov. 1978 to 13 June 1979, Decree-Law No. 2,568 of 1979, pp. 346–60. Santiago: Official Edition.

Reuque Paillalef, Rosa Isolde. *When a Flower is Reborn: The Life and Times of a Mapuche Feminist.* Edited and translated by Florencia E. Mallon. Durham: Duke University Press, 2002.

Rosemblatt, Karin A. *Gendered Compromises: Political Cultures and the State in Chile, 1920–1950.* Chapel Hill: University of North Carolina Press, 2000.

Saavedra Peláez, Alejandro. *La cuestión Mapuche.* Santiago: ICIRA, 1971.

———. *Los Mapuche en la sociedad chilena actual.* Santiago: LOM Ediciones, 2002.

Salazar, Gabriel. *Violencia política popular en "las grandes alamedas": Santiago de Chile, 1917–1987.* Santiago: Ediciones Sur, 1990.

Silva, Patricio. *Estado, neoliberalismo y política agraria en Chile, 1973–1981.* Amsterdam: CEDLA, 1987.

———. "The Military Regime and the Restructuring of Land Tenure." *Latin American Perspectives* 18:1 (Winter 1991), pp. 15–32.

Steenland. Kyle. *Agrarian Reform under Allende.* Albuquerque: University of New Mexico Press, 1977.

Stern, Steve J. *Remembering Pinochet's Chile: On the Eve of London 1998.* Durham: Duke University Press, 2004.

Stuchlik, Milan. *La Vida en Mediería: Mecanismos de reclutamiento social de los mapuches.* Santiago: SOLES Ediciones, 1999. First English edition 1976.

Tinsman, Heidi. *Partners in Conflict: The Politics of Gender, Sexuality, and*

Labor in the Chilean Agrarian Reform, 1950–1973. Durham: Duke University Press, 2002.

Torres Gaona, Guillermo, and Virginia Vidal. "La dictadura mató a periodistas, pero no al periodismo." In Ernesto Carmona, ed., *Morir es la noticia: Los periodistas relatan la historia de sus compañeros asesinados y/o desaparecidos*, pp. 245–53. Santiago: J & C Productores Gráficos Ltda., 1997.

Vitale, Luis, et al. *Para recuperar la memoria histórica: Frei, Allende y Pinochet.* Santiago: Ediciones Chile América-CESOC, 1999.

Winn, Peter. *Weavers of Revolution: The Yarur Workers and Chile's Road to Socialism.* New York: Oxford University Press, 1986.

INDEX

Page references in italics refer to illustrations.

FLORENCIA E. MALLON is professor of Modern Latin American History and Latin American Studies, at the University of Wisconsin, Madison. She is the author of *Peasant and Nation: The Making of Postcolonial Mexico and Peru* (1995) and *The Defense of Community in Peru's Central Highlands: Peasant Struggle and Capitalist Transition, 1860–1940* (1983). She edited and translated *When a Flower Is Reborn: The Life and Times of a Mapuche Feminist*, by Rosa Isolde Reuque Paillalef (Duke, 2002).

Library of Congress Cataloging-in-Publication Data

Mallon, Florencia E., 1951–

Courage tastes of blood : the Mapuche community of Nicolas Ailío and the Chilean state, 1906–2001 / Florencia E. Mallon.

p. cm. — (Radical perspectives)

Includes bibliographical references and index.

ISBN 0-8223-3585-9 (cloth : alk. paper)

ISBN 0-8223-3574-3 (pbk. : alk. paper)

1. Mapuche Indians—Chile—Nicolas Ailío—History. 2. Mapuche Indians—Land tenure—Chile—Nicolas Ailío. 3. Mapuche Indians—Chile—Nicolas Ailío—Government relations. 4. Land grants—Chile—Nicolas Ailío. 5. Land reform—Chile—Nicolas Ailío. 6. Nicolas Ailío (Chile)—History. 7. Nicolas Ailío (Chile)—Politics and government. 8. Nicolas Ailío (Chile)—Social conditions. 9. Chile—Race relations. 10. Chile—Politics and government. I. Title. II. Series.

F3429.M255 2005

983'.0049872—dc22   2005009918